Communications
in Computer and Information Science 2024

Rationale

The CCIS series is devoted to the publication of proceedings of computer science conferences. Its aim is to efficiently disseminate original research results in informatics in printed and electronic form. While the focus is on publication of peer-reviewed full papers presenting mature work, inclusion of reviewed short papers reporting on work in progress is welcome, too. Besides globally relevant meetings with internationally representative program committees guaranteeing a strict peer-reviewing and paper selection process, conferences run by societies or of high regional or national relevance are also considered for publication.

Topics

The topical scope of CCIS spans the entire spectrum of informatics ranging from foundational topics in the theory of computing to information and communications science and technology and a broad variety of interdisciplinary application fields.

Information for Volume Editors and Authors

Publication in CCIS is free of charge. No royalties are paid, however, we offer registered conference participants temporary free access to the online version of the conference proceedings on SpringerLink (http://link.springer.com) by means of an http referrer from the conference website and/or a number of complimentary printed copies, as specified in the official acceptance email of the event.

CCIS proceedings can be published in time for distribution at conferences or as postproceedings, and delivered in the form of printed books and/or electronically as USBs and/or e-content licenses for accessing proceedings at SpringerLink. Furthermore, CCIS proceedings are included in the CCIS electronic book series hosted in the SpringerLink digital library at http://link.springer.com/bookseries/7899. Conferences publishing in CCIS are allowed to use Online Conference Service (OCS) for managing the whole proceedings lifecycle (from submission and reviewing to preparing for publication) free of charge.

Publication process

The language of publication is exclusively English. Authors publishing in CCIS have to sign the Springer CCIS copyright transfer form, however, they are free to use their material published in CCIS for substantially changed, more elaborate subsequent publications elsewhere. For the preparation of the camera-ready papers/files, authors have to strictly adhere to the Springer CCIS Authors' Instructions and are strongly encouraged to use the CCIS LaTeX style files or templates.

Abstracting/Indexing

CCIS is abstracted/indexed in DBLP, Google Scholar, EI-Compendex, Mathematical Reviews, SCImago, Scopus. CCIS volumes are also submitted for the inclusion in ISI Proceedings.

How to start

To start the evaluation of your proposal for inclusion in the CCIS series, please send an e-mail to ccis@springer.com.

Wenxing Hong · Geetha Kanaparan
Editors

Computer Science and Education

Teaching and Curriculum

18th International Conference, ICCSE 2023
Sepang, Malaysia, December 1–7, 2023
Proceedings, Part II

 Springer

Editors
Wenxing Hong ⓘ
Xiamen University
Xiamen, China

Geetha Kanaparan ⓘ
Xiamen University Malaysia
Sepang, Malaysia

ISSN 1865-0929   ISSN 1865-0937 (electronic)
Communications in Computer and Information Science
ISBN 978-981-97-0790-4   ISBN 978-981-97-0791-1 (eBook)
https://doi.org/10.1007/978-981-97-0791-1

Preface

Welcome to the proceedings of the 18th International Conference on Computer Science & Education (ICCSE 2023), held December 1–7, 2023, at Xiamen University Malaysia in Selangor, Malaysia. We proudly present these volumes encompassing both online and in-person presentations.

Since its inception in 2006, ICCSE has served as a premier international forum for sharing and exploring cutting-edge advances in computer science, education, and allied fields like engineering and advanced technologies. It bridges the gap between industry, research, and academia, fostering dynamic information exchange and collaboration.

Under the theme "Empowering development of high-quality education with digitalization", ICCSE 2023 invited and received 305 submissions in total, culminating in 106 high-quality manuscripts accepted for these proceedings. Each underwent a rigorous double-blind peer-review process (three reviews per submission) by an esteemed international panel consisting of organizing and advisory committee members and renowned experts.

The proceedings are organized into three volumes reflecting the diversity of submissions: Computer Science and Technology, Teaching and Curriculum, and Educational Digitalization. These reflect the latest developments in computing technologies and their educational applications. Volume 1 covers topics like data science, machine learning, and large language models, while Volume 2 delves into curriculum reform, online learning, and MOOCs. Finally, Volume 3 explores digital transformation and new digital technology applications.

ICCSE 2023 had a dynamic technical program, brimming with cutting-edge insights from renowned figures and diverse opportunities for engagement. Three captivating keynote speeches kicked off the conference:

- Xu Rongsheng, from the Chinese Academy of Sciences, delved into the intricate interplay between the internet, China, and cybersecurity, sparking thought-provoking discussions.
- Andrew Ware, of the University of South Wales, shed light on the transformative potential of generative AI in education, inspiring new perspectives on learning and teaching.
- Zhou Aoying, from East China Normal University, navigated the complexities of digital transformation and its impact on smart education, offering practical guidance for navigating the evolving landscape.

Beyond the keynotes, a dedicated workshop titled "Digitalization Capability Level Certification" provided participants with valuable tools and frameworks for assessing and enhancing their digital skills. Additionally, two Best Paper sessions and 11 parallel sessions offered platforms for researchers to showcase their groundbreaking work and engage in stimulating dialogue with peers.

This comprehensive program ensured that every author had the opportunity to present their research to a receptive audience, fostering a vibrant exchange of ideas and fostering meaningful collaborations.

In closing, we express heartfelt gratitude to everyone who made ICCSE 2023 possible. Our thanks go to the program chairs for their program expertise, the publication committee for their meticulous review process, and the local organizing committee led by the School of Computing and Data Science at Xiamen University Malaysia. We hope these proceedings inspire further discourse and collaboration in the ever-evolving world of computer science and education.

December 2023   Geetha Kanaparan
                                                                Wenxing Hong

Organization

Honorary Chairs

Jonathan Li	University of Waterloo, Canada
Wang Huiqiong	Xiamen University Malaysia, Malaysia
Li Maoqing	Xiamen University, China

General Chairs

Geetha Kanaparan	Xiamen University Malaysia, Malaysia
Hong Wenxing	Xiamen University, China

Organizing Chairs

Miraz Mahdi Hassan	Xiamen University Malaysia, Malaysia
Hu Jie	Zhejiang University, China
Yang Chenhui	Xiamen University, China

Program Chairs

Li Xin	Louisiana State University, USA
Li Chao	Tsinghua University, China
Wang Qing	Tianjin University, China

Publications Chairs

Weng Yang	Sichuan University, China
Yang Fan	Xiamen University, China

Industry Chairs

Ding Yu   Netease Fuxi AI Lab, China
Cui Binyue   Xiamen Digital Twin Information Technology Co,
                                 China

Regional Chairs

Lang Haoxiang   Ontario Tech University, Canada
Xia Min   Lancaster University, UK.

Program Committees

Adam Saeid Pirasteh   Xiamen University Malaysia, Malaysia
Ben M. Chen   Chinese University of Hong Kong, Hong Kong
                                 SAR, China
Cen Gang   Zhejiang University of Science and Technology,
                                 China
Chen Zhibo   Beijing Forestry University, China
Chen Zhiguo   Henan University, China
Ching-Shoei Chiang   Soochow University, Taiwan
Clarence de Silva   University of British Columbia, Canada
Deng Zhigang   University of Houston, USA
Ding Yu   Netease Fuxi AI Lab, China
Dong Zhicheng   Xizang University, China
Farbod Khoshnoud   California State University, Pomona, USA
Geetha Kanaparan   Xiamen University Malaysia, Malaysia
He Li   Software Guide Magazine, China
He Liang   East China Normal University, China
Hiroki Takada   University of Fukui, Japan
Hiromu Ishio   Fukuyama City University, Japan
Hong Wenxing   Xiamen University, China
Wang Huiqiong   Xiamen University Malaysia, Malaysia
Hu Jie   Zhejiang University, China
Huang Jie   Chinese University of Hong Kong, Hong Kong
                                 SAR, China
Jiang Qingshan   Shenzhen Institutes of Advanced Technology,
                                 CAS, China
Jin Dawei   Zhongnan University of Economics and Law,
                                 China

Jonathan Li	University of Waterloo, Canada
Koliya Pulasinghe	Sri Lanka Institute of Information Technology, Sri Lanka
Lang Haoxiang	Ontario Tech University, Canada
Li Chao	Tsinghua University, China
Li Taoshen	Nanning University, China
Li Teng	University of British Columbia, Canada
Li Xiaohong	Tianjin University, China
Li Xin	Texas A & M University, USA
Li Ying	Beihang University, China
Lin Xianke	Ontario Tech University, Canada
Lin Zongli	University of Virginia, USA
Liu Renren	Xiangtan University, China
Liu Tao	Anhui University of Engineering, China
Liu Tenghong	Zhongnan University of Economics and Law, China
Luo Juan	Hunan University, China
Peng Yonghong	Manchester Metropolitan University, UK
Peter Liu	Carleton University, Canada
Qiang Yan	Taiyuan University of Technology, China
Qiao Baojun	Henan University, China
Sena Seneviratne	University of Sydney, Australia
Shao Haidong	Hunan University, China
Shen Xiajiong	Henan University, China
Tom Worthington	Australian National University, Australia
Wang Chunzhi	Hubei University of Technology, China
Wang Jiangqing	South-Central University for Nationalities, China
Wang Ming	Lishui University, China
Wang Ning	Xiamen Huaxia University, China
Wang Qing	Tianjin University, China
Wang Yang	Southwest Petroleum University, China
Wang Ying	Xiamen University, China
Wang Zidong	Brunel University London, UK
Wei Shikui	Beijing Jiaotong University, China
Wen Lifang	China Machine Press, China
Weng Yang	Sichuan University, China
Wu Xinda	Neusoft Institute Guangdong, China
Xi Bin	Xiamen University, China
Xi Chunyan	Computer Education Press, China
Xia Min	Lancaster University, UK
Xiangjian (Sean) He	University of Technology Sydney, Australia

Xiao Huimin	Henan University of Finance and Economics, China
Xie Lihua	Nanyang Technological University, Singapore
Xu Li	Fujian Normal University, China
Xu Zhoubo	Guilin University of Electronic Technology, China
Xue Jingfeng	Beijing Institute of Technology, China
Yang Li	Hubei Second Normal College, China
Yang Mei	Southwest Petroleum University, China
Yu Yuanlong	Fuzhou University, China
Zeng Nianyin	Xiamen University, China
Zhang Dongdong	Tongji University, China
Zhang Yunfei	ViWiStar Technologies Ltd, Canada
Zhao Huan	Hunan University, China
Zheng Li	Tsinghua University, China
Zhou Qifeng	Xiamen University, China
Zhou Wei	Beijing Jiaotong University, China
Zhu Shunzhi	Xiamen University of Technology, China

Additional Reviewers

Aditya Abeysinghe	University of Sydney, Australia
Ahmad Affandi Supli	Xiamen University Malaysia, Malaysia
Akihiro Sugiura	Gifu University of Medical Science, Japan
Al-Fawareh Hejab Ma'azer Khaled	Xiamen University Malaysia, Malaysia
Cen Yuefeng	Zhejiang University of Science & Technology, China
Chen Lina	Zhejiang Normal University, China
Chen Linshu	Hunan University of Science and Technology, China
Chen Zhen	Tsinghua University, China
Ding Qin	Anhui University of Science & Technology, China
Fumiya Kinoshita	Toyama Prefectural University, Japan
Gou Pingzhang	Northwest Normal University, China
Hironari Sugai	University of Fukui, Japan
Huang Tianyu	Beijing Institute of Technology, China
Jiang Huixian	Fujian Normal University, China
Jin Ying	Nanjing University, China
Kenichiro Kutsuna	Thaksin University, Thailand
Lee Sui Ping	Xiamen University Malaysia, Malaysia
Li Ji	Guangdong University of Foreign Studies, China

Li Sibei	Sichuan University, China
Li Xiaoying	Hunan University, China
Li Yifan	University of Sanya, China
Liu Yiwen	Huaihua University, China
Ma Ji	Xiamen University, China
Mahdi Miraz	Xiamen University Malaysia, Malaysia
Mao Jiali	East China Normal University, China
Mallikarachchi Dilshani Hansika	Xiamen University Malaysia, Malaysia
Mailasan Jayakrishnan	Xiamen University Malaysia, Malaysia
Moubachir Madani Fadoul	Xiamen University Malaysia, Malaysia
Qiu Tianhao	Zhejiang University of Science and Technology, China
Subashini Raghavan	Xiamen University Malaysia, Malaysia
Tian Song	Beijing Institute of Technology, China
Wang Ji	Xiamen University, China
Wang Junlu	Liaoning University, China
Wang Ying	Xiamen University, China
Xiong Yu	Chongqing University of Posts and Telecommunications, China
Yasuyuki Matsuura	Gifu City Women's College, Japan
Yu Niefang	Huaihua University, China
Yuan Haomiao	Nanjing Normal University, China
Yue Kun	Yunnan University, China
Zamratul Asyikin	Xiamen University Malaysia, Malaysia
Zhang Ping	Anhui Polytechnic University, China
Zhang Yupei	Northwestern Polytechnical University, China
Zhong Ping	Central South University, China
Zhou Yujie	Henan University, China

Contents – Part II

Online Learning and MOOCs

Teaching Methods and Approaches

Analyzing Children's Behaviors Based on AI Recognition Approach to Promote Child-Friendly School-to-Home Street Design

Qianxi Zhang[1,2,3] (iD), Gang Wang[4](✉), Yat Ming Loo[2] (iD), Xinkai Wang[1], Xiumin Xia[1], and Xingyu Mu[5]

[1] School of Design, NingboTech University, Ningbo 315100, China
[2] Department of Architecture and Engineering, University of Nottingham Ningbo China, Ningbo 315100, China
[3] The Bartlett Development Planning Unit, University College London, London WC1H 9EZ, UK
[4] School of Computing and Data Engineering, NingboTech University, Ningbo 315100, China
smile588@sina.com
[5] Zhejiang Fashion Institute of Technology, Ningbo 315211, China

Abstract. School-to-home streets are an important part of the public space network of child-friendly cities. The improvement of their child-friendliness needs to be based on the investigation and evaluation of the current usage status. The traditional site investigation methods are limited by manpower and time, lack of efficiency and effectiveness. This paper proposes a new analysis framework for children's street behaviors based on AI recognition methods, including action recognition algorithm, human flow statistic algorithm, and target tracking algorithm. It takes one school-to-home street in the Mingdong community, Ningbo city as a case study. Based on the AI recognition of this street's surveillance videos, the result data verifies the effectiveness of street usage analysis. This is valuable to promote the child-friendly school-to-home street design in the future.

Keywords: Children's environmental behaviors · AI recognition algorithms · Surveillance videos · School-to-home street · Child-friendly design

1 Introduction

The rapid expansion of cities has led to an increasing trend of motorized roads, high-density communities, and isolated schools, with fewer open spaces suitable for walking and less child-friendly street environments [1]. Based on the Convention on the Rights of the Child (1989), the United Nations launched the "Child-Friendly City Initiative" (CFCI) in 1996 [2]. In 2015, it proposed the target of building inclusive, safe, and sustainable cities and communities. How to build a safe, connected, and symbiotic urban walking environment for children has become a hot topic nowadays.

School-to-home streets are important public spaces connecting home and school destinations. They are one of the most frequent places for school-age children's daily activities. However, due to the urban traffic dangers and the rise of the "backseat generation" [3], the routes between school and home are only simple roads connecting two destinations, rather than complex places where children can freely choose, stroll and play. How to transform car-centered children's destinations to walkable children's networks is the research context of this study (see Fig. 1). Based on the environmental behavior theory, the first step is to investigate the current usage status of school-to-home streets, then analyze and diagnose the using problems of street spaces, so as to put forward evidence-based design strategies [4].

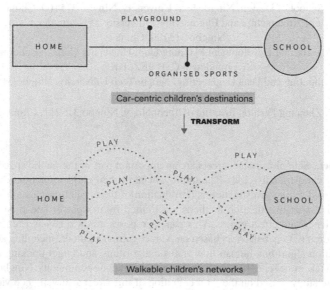

Fig. 1. The concept of child-friendly school-to-home street [1]

As a classic research method to understand the interaction between humans and the environment, behavior observation provides an effective way to study children's environmental behavior psychology. Scholars generally analyze the interaction between children and space from the perspective of behavior types, behavior distribution, behavior trajectory, and behavior frequency [5]. These indicators provide a fundamental analysis framework for our proposed methodology. However, the school-to-home street is not a dedicated play space for children. Children's behaviors are complex and diverse. Their activities are scattered rather than concentrated [6]. Therefore, traditional behavior observation has great limitations in terms of observation time and manpower.

With the rapid development of computer networks and the advent of the artificial intelligence era, a large amount of surveillance video data about urban street spaces is generated [7]. Combined with deep learning technology, it greatly promotes the development of target detection technology, which provides a novel idea for site investigation and analysis methods. However, most of the target detection algorithms are mainly used in urban management, monitoring, warning, and other application scenarios [8]. They are less used in the vitality perception of street public life and site research.

In this context, the paper aims to contribute to the enrichment of existing methodologies by applying artificial intelligence recognition technology. Utilizing surveillance videos from the school-to-home street in Mingdong community, Ningbo City as experimental data, we seek to conduct children's behavior recognition, flow statistics, and behavior trajectory detection to comprehensively evaluate and diagnose the current utilization patterns of the street.

2 Methodology

In order to promote the child-friendly school-to-home street design, this paper focuses on the relationship between children's behaviors and street environment, with the novel AI recognition approach. Taking 5 days' surveillance videos of the targeted street in Mingdong community as the sample data, the artificial intelligence recognition technologies are applied to realize the automatic detection of children's behavior types, flow number, and activity tracks. Then through the open API interface of the Internet platform, the data processed by the AI detection algorithm is processed again. By coupling analysis of children's behaviors and street spaces, children's use preferences and potential needs for street space are obtained.

2.1 Site Location

This study was conducted in Mingdong community, Ningbo City, China. This community occupies 19.56 hectares of land, which was built in year 1996 with around 5500 residents living in it. It's a typical high-density community located in the urban center with a developed traffic network (see Fig. 2). Due to the lack of dedicated play spaces planning in the early 21st century, the streets in the Mingdong community are all traffic-oriented with car parking along the roadsides, which are not child-friendly enough [9].

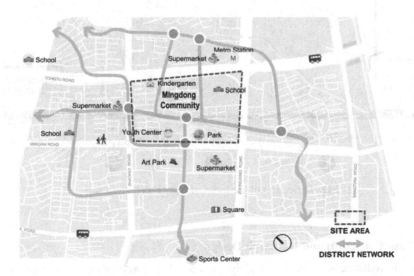

Fig. 2. Site location of Mingdong community

The target area is one street between the community and the adjacent school, which is a main pathway for children to travel from home to school (see Fig. 3). The selected street area is 107 m long, 25 m wide, consisting of a regular sidewalk for pedestrians, a driveway for vehicles and a designed sidewalk with play facilities [10]. The ground floor of the buildings along the west side of the street has some community service facilities, such as committee offices, education institutions, grocery shops, etc. The buildings along the east side of the street are some volunteer services and childcare rooms which are not open to the public yet (see Fig. 4).

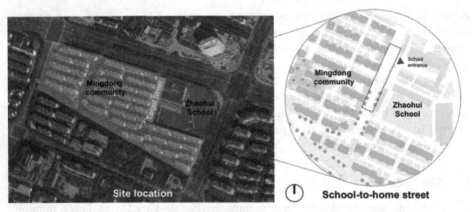

Fig. 3. Site location of Mingdong community

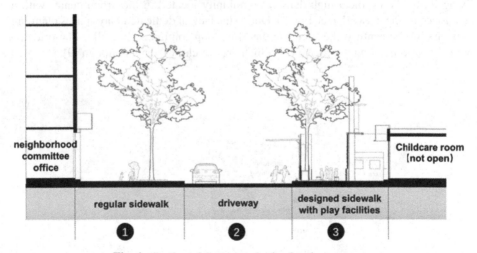

Fig. 4. Section of the targeted school-to-home street

2.2 Data Collection and Research Design

CCTV surveillance systems are widely used as street monitoring tools in public and private areas [11]. This paper obtained 5 days of surveillance videos of the targeted street from the Mingdong community with the approval of research ethics. The selected street is located at the terminus of the community, which is not a main traffic road. Through preliminary investigations, it was found that the period between 16:30 and 17:00 corresponds to the peak hours when school-age children returned home after the school day. Almost no other groups of residents used this street during this time, making it an optimal window to observe and analyze the children's behaviors on the street. Hence, by desensitizing personal privacy in the videos, this paper focuses on detecting children's behaviors in five videos from 16:30–17:00 on March 7 to 12, 2022. The visual threshold range of street surveillance video is shown in Fig. 5.

Fig. 5. Surveillanc photo of the targed school-to-home street

Normally for most of the street surveillance system, there are three major stages involved in AI recognition process which are moving object detection, tracking and classification. Based on it, this paper applies 3 detection algorithms of children's action, flow number and move tracking (see Table 1).

2.3 Application of AI Recognition Methods

Application of the Action Recognition Approach
School-age children are willing to explore and communicate on the way after school. In addition to the general traveling behavior (passing directly alone or in company), they also have the behavior of chasing, sitting, climbing, etc. To intelligently identify these children's behaviors in the targeted street, this paper introduces the action recognition approach into our design. In the action recognition approach, we utilize deep learning network to obtain the heatmap of children's skeleton. Then children's skeleton can estimate children's pose. Through the action recognition approach, three types of children's

Table 1. Research design

Recognition Time	16:30–17:00, 2022.03.07–2022.03.12 (0.5 rush hour after school /day, 5days)		
Weather	1 °C–9 °C, sunny		
Recognition Object	Children in the selected school-to-home street		
Recognition Targets	Children's behavior types	Children's flow statistic	Children's moving tracks
Recognition Approaches	the action recognition approach	the human flow statistic approach	the person tracking approach

skeleton images of walking, sitting and running are obtained, which are used as sample data for in-depth learning to realize the automatic detection and classification of children's behavior.

Application of the Human Flow Statistic Approach

To statistic the number of children in the school-to-home street for a period of time, this paper adopts a YOLO v5-based detection approach. The YOLO v5-based detection approach can predict person detection boxes with scores. So, we can compute each frame from the surveillance camera to the number of boxes. The number of each frame represents the human flow at each time. By counting the human flow in each frame, we can eventually obtain the human flow data for a period of time.

Application of the Person-Tracking Approach

After the person detection is completed by Yolo V5 algorithm, in order to detect the distribution position and moving track of children's behavior, sort algorithm can be introduced to complete the task of target tracking. Firstly, the characteristics of the object are modeled. The formula can be expressed by

$$X = [u, v, s, r, \dot{u}, \dot{v}, \dot{s}]^T \tag{1}$$

where u and v are the horizontal and vertical coordinates of the center point of the detection frame, s and r are the size and length width ratio of the detection frame, $\dot{u}, \dot{v}, \dot{s}$ are parameters of the next frame.

When the feature of the first frame is input, this frame will be as the target to initialize and create a tracker. Each target is marked with a specific number. After the data of the subsequent frame comes in, the tracker will obtain the prediction frame generated by the previous frame through the Kalman filter. Then it can obtain the intersection and union ratio of all prediction boxes of the tracker and the prediction box of YOLO V5 in this frame. Thirdly, we can use the Hungarian algorithm to obtain the maximum matching of the intersection and union ratio and remove the matching pair less than the threshold. Finally, the detection box can be tracked.

3 Results

Through the three AI recognition approaches above, the amount and proportion of children's typical behaviors, the amount of children passing, and the trajectories of children moving on this street are obtained respectively.

3.1 Result of Children's Action Recognition

Based on the action recognition approach, children's behavior poses are recognized as skeleton images (Fig. 6). Three main types of skeleton images of walking, sitting, and running are obtained, which are used as sample data for in-depth learning. Finally, we get the automatic detection data of three behaviors in 5 video clips.

Fig. 6. Children's skeleton images of street behaviors

The results indicate that 251 children are detected, of which 237 are walking (including two types of fast passing and roaming), accounting for 94.4%; 12 are running, accounting for 4.8%; 2 are sitting and resting, only accounting for 0.8%. It shows that the walking behavior type accounted for the highest proportion, the running behavior type is the second, and there is very little sitting behavior. The reason may be there are not many facilities on the street that can attract children to stop and sit down. Children only use this street as a fast-passing area. Unlike adults, railings can also be a supply of sitting. An interesting finding is that the behavior of a child sitting on the fence railing is detected, which reflects that the railing is a kind of potential affordance for children to sit (Table 2).

Table 2. Statistic of children's behavior types

Behavior Types	Amount	Proportion	Skeleton Images sample
Walking	237	94.4%	
Running	12	4.8%	
Sitting	2	0.8%	

3.2   Result of Children's Flow Statistic and Move Tracking

Based on the YOLO V5 and SORT algorithms, a total of 251 children are detected in 5 video clips (Fig. 7). 61 among them are on the west regular sidewalk, accounting for 24.3%; 107 moving trajectories are on the driveway, accounting for 42.6%; 21 moving trajectories are on the east dedicated playable sidewalk; 62 moving trajectories span three areas of streets, accounting for 24.7% (see Fig. 8).

Fig. 7. Detection boxes of children

The data above points out that nearly half of the children choose the middle driveway to walk. The reason may be that although this is a traffic road, there are actually fewer vehicles passing through, and the speed of the vehicle is slower with less danger. Meanwhile, the driveway is wider than the sidewalk, which is more suitable for children traveling together. Surprisingly, the dedicated playable sidewalk attracted the lowest proportion of children to walk. The reason may be that it has to cross the protective fence to enter this area, and the facilities set up along the street block children's sight and cannot attract children to play (Table 3).

Table 3. Statistic of children's move tracking

Street area	Amount	Proportion
1. Regular sidewalk for pedestrians	61	24.3%
2. Driveway for vehicles	107	42.6%
3. Dedicated playable sidewalk for children	21	8.4%
4. Whole areas	62	24.7%
Total Number	251	100%

Fig. 8. Children's moving tracking

4 Conclusion

The analysis results show that the behavioral diversity of children in the target street is insufficient, which is lack of play and physical activities. Even the dedicated sidewalk with play facilities did not meet the expected space performance. The overall results show that the target street is not child-friendly enough and there is necessity for improvement.

In this paper, AI recognition approaches of the action recognition, the human flow statistic and the person tracking are applied to automatically detect children's behaviors in the selected school-to-home street. The recognition result shows the effectiveness of this method in discovering interactions pattern between children and street space. In the field of child-friendly space design, this method is highly novel. In addition, it is also a highly potential approach which could be applied in other scenarios in the residential context, like all-age residents' environmental behavior in square spaces.

The limitation of this study is that the rigor of algorithm data screening is not enough. The amount of video sample is insufficient. In addition, the interpretation of children's behavior lacks objective interviews to verify, which needs to be further deepened in future research.

Funding. This paper is supported by Zhejiang Provincial Philosophy and Social Science Planning Project, grant number 22NDQN291YB; China Scholarship Council, grant number 202208330309; Ningbo Natural Science Foundation under Grant 2023J280, in part by Ningbo Key R&D Program, grant number 202208330309 No.2023Z231; Ningbo Natural Science Foundation, grant number 202003N4307; Research and Creation Project of Zhejiang Provincial Department of Culture and Tourism, grant number 2020KZY003; Zhejiang Soft Science Research Program (Key Project), grant number 2022C25070; Zhejiang Planning Program in Philosophy and Social Sciences (Youth Project), grant number 21NDQN296YB; National-level Student Innovation and Entrepreneurship Training Program Approved Project, grant number 202213022054.

References

1. Where do the children play: designing child-friendly compact cities. https://www.citiesforplay.com/portfoliowhere-do-the-children-play. Accessed 20 June 2023
2. UNICEF. Innocenti Research Centre. Building child friendly cities: A framework for action. UNICEF Innocenti Research Centre (2004)
3. Lambert, A., Vlaar, J., Herrington, S., Brussoni, M.: What is the relationship between the neighbourhood built environment and time spent in outdoor play? A systematic review. Int. J. Environ. Res. Public Health **16**(20), 3840 (2019)
4. Zhang, Q., Wu, S., Wang, X.: Multi-dimensional construction of children's outdoor play space as an old community renewal catalyst. Archit. Cult. **11**, 146–149 (2019)
5. Cox, A., Janet, L., Sarah, L.: Understanding the nature play milieu: using behavior mapping to investigate children's activities in outdoor play spaces. Child. Youth Environ. **28**(2), 232–261 (2018)
6. Li, Z., Chen, W., Li, J.: A study of the relationship between the space surrounding primary schools and students' behaviors off school. Archit. J. **2**, 113–117 (2016). (in Chinese)
7. Wang, G., Zhou, M., Cao, H., Fang, B., Wen, S., Wei, R.: A fast perceptual surveillance video coding (PSVC) based on background model-driven JND estimation. Int. J. Pattern Recognit Artif Intell. **35**(06), 2155006 (2021)
8. Wang, G., Zhou, M., Fang, B., Wen, S.: Surveillance video coding for traffic scene based on vehicle knowledge and shared library by cloud-edge computing in cyber-physical-social systems. Int. J. Pattern Recognit Artif Intell. **35**(06), 2154019 (2021)
9. Zhang, Q., Deng, W., Loo, Y. M., et al.: Environmental affordances: a practical approach for designing child-friendly streets in high-density community. In: Ujikawa, K., Ishiwatari, M., Hullebusch, E.v. (eds.) Asia Conference on Environment and Sustainable Development, pp. 272–282. Springer, Singapore (2022). https://doi.org/10.1007/978-981-19-1704-2_25

10. Zhang, Q., et al.: Towards child-friendly streetscape in migrant workers' communities in China: a social–ecological design framework. Land **12**(10), 1826 (2023). https://doi.org/10.3390/land12101826

11. Wang, G., Li, B., Zhang, Y., et al.: Background modeling and referencing for moving cameras-captured surveillance video coding in HEVC. IEEE Trans. Multimedia **20**(11), 2921–2934 (2018)

A Fast Estimation Network Model Based on Process Compression and an Optimized Parameter Search Algorithm for Q-Learning

Shudong Zhang[✉]

Wuhan FiberHome Information Integration Technologies Co., Ltd., Wuhan, China
zhangsd@fiberhome.com

Abstract. The research content and main work of this paper are as follows: Analyzing the characteristics of the network traffic data set, the key index vacancy rate parameters in the process of cleaning the data set. This paper proposes a fast estimation network model based on process compression and an optimized parameter search algorithm for Q-Learning (QV-QL). The model starts from a predictive model based on deep learning, and on the basis of ensuring the functionality and certain accuracy of the model. Through the compression process and the introduction of mixed-precision calculations, the speed of searching for optimal parameters has been greatly improved.

Keywords: Reinforcement Learning · Network Traffic forecast · Q-Learning

1 Introduction

The bandwidth demand of network traffic appears to be unevenly distributed at the moment. In some enterprises where high strength and stability are required to maintain a high-speed network, excessive network load pressure may be experienced, while in some companies, such high-speed traffic is not needed, resulting in resource waste. It is for this reason that there are great challenges facing us in the current situation. To solve the load capacity limit of network traffic quickly, on-line evaluation of static stability of the network system is a basic requirement for on-line evaluation of static stability. In order to maintain the stable operation of high-demand network operators as well as give full play to the scheduling of network resources, accurate network traffic prediction is an important step towards providing optimal service to high-demand network operators. Additionally, in the field of network traffic data prediction, artificial intelligence based on evolutionary algorithms of deep learning [1] has taken the lead in recent years, aiming to overcome some disadvantages of traditional prediction methods in the field of network traffic data. There is still an increase in applications and development of algorithms and prediction models that are being used in network traffic prediction, but the imbalance between development and planning will lead to an imbalance in resources and an invisible pressure on the field of prediction as a result of the imbalance in resources. Therefore, the specific improvement and optimization still need the continuous exploration and research of relevant experts and scholars to select a better algorithm prediction model that continues to improve and optimize. Despite the fact that these prediction methods are still under development, an imbalance in resources and unseen pressures may result from a lack of balanced planning and development. The refinement and selection of superior algorithmic prediction models require continuous expert exploration.

The main focus of the preprocessing of data used in the development of network traffic prediction models has been on improving the data set as well as handling outliers and null values, but this focus is easily divorced from the reality, which results in a research trend that does not correspond to reality. If it is really applied in the life level, the prediction results are not satisfactory, forming the situation of application limitation. To make data preprocessing more practical, there are new strategies that are being used to make it more practical. When designing a prediction model, the model data indicators tend to be too serious, in order to ensure the integrity of the data, the dimensions of the data and the number of data points are sufficient, leading to too much in cases where the dimensions of the data are not large enough. As an example, combining algorithms with neural networks is often hard to get accurate predictions. Today, a multitude of algorithms have emerged, especially in the current era of artificial intelligence, and these include evolution algorithms that combine evolutionary strategies [4, 5], genetic programming, or algorithms based on physical properties, such as central force optimization (CFO), artificial chemical reaction optimization algorithms (ACROA), and black hole algorithms (BH), have become widely used. Generally, there are a number of algorithms that are used to make animal search decisions such as cuckoo search (CS) [9], Firefly algorithm (FA) [10], Artificial Bee Colony algorithm (ABC) [11], Antlion optimization algorithm (ALO) [12], etc. However, these algorithms are still prone to some deviations and contingencies. Additionally, when it comes to large scale and high latitude data, the data standardization process is difficult and time-consuming. Therefore, it is important to design a system that ensures efficiency and accuracy in prediction, as well as meets the requirements of large volumes of data at high altitudes. It is at this point that the key research content of this paper is focused on network traffic prediction in the context of the problem to be solved.

As part of this interdisciplinary area of research referred to as reinforcement learning [13–15], many aspects of the theory and algorithm have gained great scientific significance during the 1990s, and they have also made significant advances in psychology, intelligence computing, operations research, and control theory over the years. As a result of these achievements, reinforcement learning has greatly expanded in theory. The application of scheduling decisions has proved to be quite successful in artificial intelligence and optimization.

2 Parameter Optimization Algorithm Based on Fast Estimation Network Model and Improved Q-Learning

In traffic prediction, there are a lot of null values and outliers in data due to non-standard operation during data collection, failure of data collection equipment, data system upgrade and other reasons. Poor data quality poses a serious challenge to data preprocessing.

In the data cleaning stage, we can neither blindly remove all the data lines containing null values, nor allow the data lines containing a large number of null values to enter the data enhancement stage or model training stage. In data cleaning process, the non-null rate parameter of valid data is usually used as one of the key indicators to balance data quality.

This parameter determines which rows are retained and moved to the next stage and which are culled from the dataset by controlling the ratio between the number of non-null values contained in the valid data and the total number of values. When the non-null value rate is in the optimal state, data cleaning can improve the overall non-null value rate of the data set while preserving as much data as possible, that is, reducing the number of noisy data in the data set while preserving as much data diversity as possible. Non-null rate index is a percentage, which will not be given automatically. It is generally given by field experts with network engineering and computer background based on experience, and has problems such as difficult to popularize, lack of inter-pretability and non-optimality. At the same time, if the exhaustive strategy is used to search parameters, there are some problems such as high computational complexity and time consuming. In view of these problems, this chapter proposes an optimization search algorithm combining the fast valuation network model and improved Q-Learning, which can automatically complete the task of parameter optimization under the premise of reasonable computational complexity.

Fast valuation network model based on process compression.

Generally null value for data, abnormal value, will adopt the method of data cleaning and enhance the data cleaning operations, the data can improve forecasting precision of the model within a certain scope, but the introduction of these additional operations will increase the burden of the model and the GPU in the process of running too much memory footprint and resource consumption, Valuations so this paper proposes a fast network, shown in the Fig. 3 below you can see the difference, with a quick first look for value network model parameters, through the selection of design of experiment, a new strategy, every five percent for one iteration, omitted to data processing operations of the zero and outliers, ten generations iterative processing directly, when to find the optimal parameters, Then, data cleaning and enhancement processing were carried out,

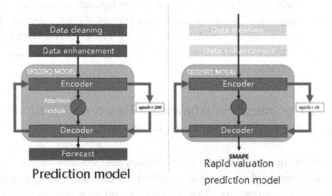

Fig. 1. Comparison of data processing models

so as to omit a lot of useless time. The specific reason why epoch $= 10$ was selected will be analyzed and explained later.

In order to explain why epoch $= 10$ is chosen, the change can be seen from Fig. 2. It can be seen that before epoch $= 10$, the overall loss of baseline has been in a process of rapid decline, that is rapid convergence stage. The increase of epoch at this time has a substantial effect on data processing. However, after epoch $= 10$, the whole convergence stage entered the long tail stage. It can be seen that, although there was still a slight decrease with the increase of epoch, the cost performance ratio at this time was very low. Therefore, considering the cost performance ratio and reality, the epoch $= 10$ with the highest cost performance was selected for the universality of application fields.

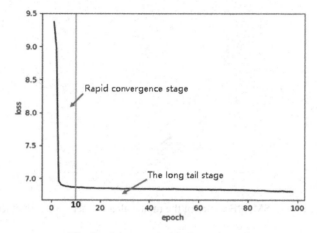

Fig. 2. Cause analysis of epoch $= 10$

After the fast valuation network model is defined, in order to see that there will not be too much difference before and after the network model changes, the reward index in Q-Learning strategy is used to feedback the network and learn the expected value. From the current step to all subsequent steps, the total expectation gets the maximum value(Q value and Value). Action determines the optimal policy for each state in the Q value function. In each state, the Action with the highest Q value is selected. And the network does not depend on the environment model. The current Action is rewarded, add the next step to get the maximum expected value, the current status action reward, plus the maximum expected value of the next status action The learning rate determines the rate of information acquired before the coverage rate of newly acquired sample information. Usually set a small value to ensure the stability of the learning process and the final convergence. Q-Learning requires an initial value Q. By defining a relatively high initial value, the model is encouraged to explore more. This kind of network may have a certain loss in accuracy, but the speed can be greatly improved. It can be seen from Fig. 5 that the overall accuracy is consistent with the change trend of the processed data.

As shown in Fig. 3, the SMAPE value on the ordinate is the symmetric mean absolute percentage error, which is an accuracy measure based on percentage (or relative) error and can be calculated as shown in formula (2). Indicators used to measure the quality of the network model, the lower the SMAPE value is, the better. SMAPE is a correction index for MAPE problems, which can better avoid the problem that the calculation result of MAPE is too large due to the small real value.

$$SMAPE = \frac{100\%}{n} \sum_{t=1}^{n} \frac{|F_t - A_t|}{\frac{(|A_t|+|F_t|)}{2}} \quad (1)$$

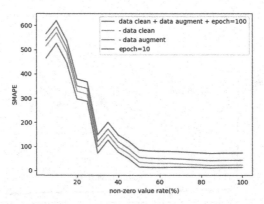

Fig. 3. Comparison of SMAPE values of the rapid valuation network with other treatments

Where At is the true value and Ft is the predicted value.

Can see from Fig. 5, although after data cleaning and data fill of the network is still in the overall effect is the result of the optimal, but fast valuations in network epoch = 10, after the overall trends and processing of network is almost the same, change rule is no discrepancy, and maintained a high level in the accuracy. The iteration of 100 generation to 10 generation is reduced and the speed is greatly improved, so the fast valuation network adopted in this paper has better wide applicability in practicability.

Through the proposed fast valuation network for data storage and transportation experiments, it is obvious that the speed optimization before and after is improved, and the accuracy is not far behind. In order to further demonstrate the feasibility of this fast valuation network, the comparison of actual time saving can be shown in Fig. 4.

It can be seen from experimental Fig. 4 above that data cleaning takes 32 s (using non-null value rate of 93% as standard). Data enhancement time (Laplace algorithm is adopted for convolution kernel length of 5): 64 s to 56 s, because if data cleaning is carried out, the data enhancement speed will be improved after removing part of the data. Among them, the training process (epoch = 100) took 118 s, while the training process (epoch = 10) took 27 s. The speed is significantly improved, which is about six times the speed, which is quite remarkable. So whether the data cleaning process and enhance the filling processing of data in the process of iteration tremendous force and resource consumption, the cost of training time, the consumption of the first three figure is very high, and valuation in the network consume almost negligible, can confirm this fast valuation on the speed of network has the absolute advantage.

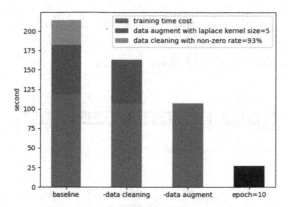

Fig. 4. Comparison of training time for different data processing

2.1 Model Training Process Based on Mixed Accuracy

For circulation data type on the computer, is the most common type of floating-point number, commonly used have double-precision and single-precision floating point, but because of the increasing amount of data now and latitude change big wide, so someone put forward a kind of semi-precision data, double-precision is a 64-bit data, single-precision is 32-bit, semi-precision can reach 16 low storage usage. As the research, the double-precision and single precision are used for calculation, semi-precision is in order to reduce the cost of data transmission and storage, because in many application scenarios, deep learning field, this paper studies the prediction model. For example, with semi-precision data, compared to single-precision can save half of the data transmission cost and resource consumption, In addition, in the field of deep learning, hundreds of millions of parameters are selected for data, so semi-precision transmission is of great significance for research. Figure 7 shows the differences between double-precision, single-precision, and semi-precision floating-point numbers:

float16, a semi-precision floating-point number consists of one sign bit, five exponent bits, and ten mantissa bits.

float32, a single-precision floating-point number consists of one sign bit, eight exponent bits and 23 mantissa bits.

float64, a double - precision floating-point number consists of one sign bit, 11 exponent bits, and 52 mantissa bits.

As you can see three different precision floating point numbers, is divided into three parts, respectively is the sign bit, index and mantissa, the different precision is only the length of the exponent and the mantissa bits is different, so while keeping on the accuracy of the data at the same time, can very good saves space on the space and memory resources consumption, through the study of the compression of data accuracy,

• Double - precision floating - point number:

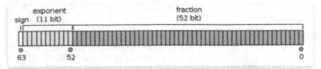

• Float-point number with single precision:

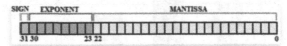

• Semi-precision floating point number:

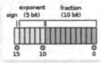

Fig. 5. Feature comparison of three precision data

pre-processing of model algorithms and data can reduce the cost of consumption. The single-pass comparison diagram of the two networks in normal network data processing and fast valuation network can be shown in Fig. 6 below:

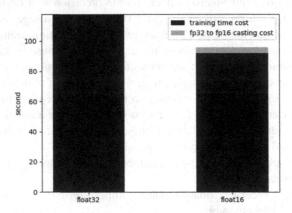

Fig. 6. Comparison of time loss between single precision data and semi-precision data

Can be seen from the comparison above Fig. 6, for data storage and operation process, the data from single precision floating point 32 into half precision 16, get some save time consumption, can probably thirty percent increased performance, further improve the effectiveness of the data preprocessing, illustrates the feasibility of this experiment ideas.

In order to further demonstrate the feasibility of converting from single-precision data to semi-precision data, this paper will verify the comparison between the process of loss value reduction and the effect of amplification in the long-tail stage by high definition comparison in the following two figures. It can be easily seen from the following two figures: The first Fig. 9 shows the comparison of loss values between single-precision data and semi-precision data. The smaller the loss value is, the better. The first figure shows that the overall trend is roughly the same. It can be seen from Fig. 10 that the amplification is about 60 times. It can be seen that although the semi-precision float16 data is not stable in the process of loss decrease, the overall downward trend of loss value is the same as that of float32 single precision data. Therefore, in consideration of the experimental speed, we can use float16 semi-precision data to replace float32 single-precision to realize an optimal data processing.

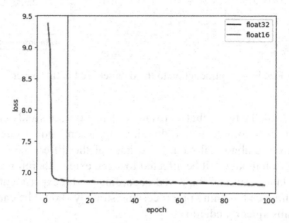

Fig. 7. Comparison of Loss values during training with two kinds of precision

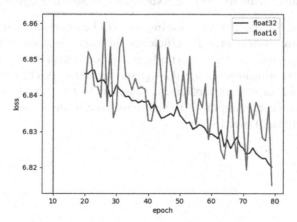

Fig. 8. Comparison of loss values during training with two kinds of accuracy after 60 times magnification

3 Experiment and Result Analysis

3.1 Introduction and Analysis of Data Sets

Because this article research content of the data taken from the records of daily network traffic in and out of an enterprise, is more close to real life, and as a result of the data records have long, data itself exists some days appear more null values, or when business is busy to many outliers, but also there will be a lot of complete data, according to the characteristics of the data, It can be roughly shown as Fig. 11 below:

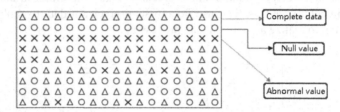

Fig. 9. An introduction to the data set used in this paper

It can be seen from the figure that there are certain null values and outliers in the data. The triangle represents complete data, the circle represents null values, and the cross indicates that there are abnormal values. Because of the difference of these data, the subsequent prediction model will be affected to some extent, therefore, before entering the training, the data should be improved according to the experimental purpose, and the Q-Learning enhanced learning preprocessing strategy should be carried out to pave the way for the subsequent prediction.

3.2 Optimization Parameter Search Experiment Based on Improved Q-Learning

In order to test the difference between the improved Q-Learning and the traditional brute force exhaustive mechanism in search efficiency, this paper carries out an experiment of searching optimization parameters on a traffic prediction system based on deep learning. The basis of the experiment is realized through the improved QV-QL algorithm, in order to better understand the process of parameter search in the experiment, Table 1 shows the operation process of combining the fast valuation network with the improved Q-Learning algorithm in the form of pseudo-code:

Table 1. Quick Valuation Q-Learning algorithm

Algorithm 1: QV-QL (Quick Valuation Q-Learning)

Initialize the reward function r: fast valuation model

Initialize Q(s, a), s: 0.5

Initialize Maximum episode value

Repeat execution (maximum episode detection):

    Repeat execution (knee and elbow detection or reaching the boundary of S):

    Starting from initial S, all actions a_n in the action set are performed simultaneously, observe r_n

    Update Q table with maximum r value:

$$Q(s,a) \leftarrow Q(s,a) + [max(r) + max_{a'}Q(s',a') - Q(s,a)]$$

    End of the cycle

End of the cycle

Knee and elbow test

If the action function a' before is equal to the action function a now:

    Returns (True), interrupts the loop and jumps out of the current episode

Otherwise:

    Return no (False), to continue the current episode iteration

---

The following experimental figure is used to show the search process. First, Fig. 12 shows the SAMPE full solution space obtained by exhaustive method as the baseline. On the basis of the baseline, the improved Q-Learning algorithm proposed in this paper is used to search optimization parameters on the same system, and finally the whole search process is annotated to the baseline manually.

Figure 11 shows the first generation episode of optimization. Starting from the non-null rate of 50%, the left and right actions of the action set are respectively performed. In this experiment, there are two actions, namely left and right search. Search in both directions for a knee and an elbow. After comparing the return values of these two points, namely the SMAPE value, the point of the best return value is taken as the starting point of the next episode, and the current episode ends.

Figure 12 shows the second generation episode of optimization search. Starting from the point of the best return value given by the previous generation episode, search both sides until the non-null rate reaches the boundary and the search ends. Compare the return value of the boundary point with the current best return value and return the better one as the best advantage sought.

Through experiments, it is concluded that the improved Q-Learning comparison and exhaust strategy can save 36 times of calculation of return value, which is of great significance for scenarios with high computational complexity of return function caused by deep learning model.

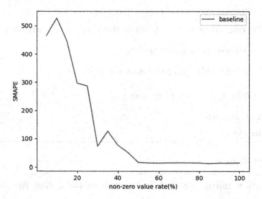

Fig. 10. SMAPE values at different non-null value rates obtained by exhaustive search

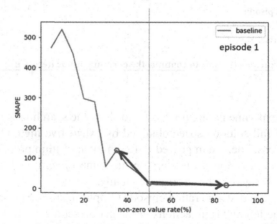

Fig. 11. First generation episode, starting from 50% looking for knee and elbow points

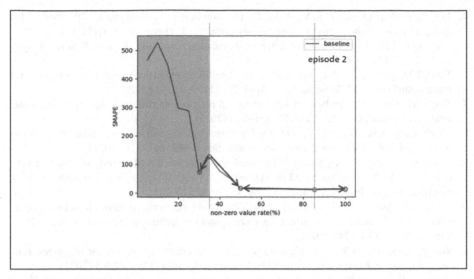

Fig. 12. The second generation episode, starting from the found knee elbow point, search for the next knee elbow point

4 Summary

In this paper, the classic Q-Learning algorithm is introduced in detail and the relevant characteristics are analyzed and summarized, and the good adaptability of the algorithm in the field of traffic prediction is expounded. Then a fast estimation network model based on flow compression is proposed., based on the flow prediction model, a network model that can be used to quickly estimate the return value is constructed by omiting the pre-processing steps of the original model and reducing the training algebra of the prediction model. At the same time, in order to further accelerate the calculation of the return value and reduce the memory consumption of the algorithm, this chapter then proposes a model training process based on mixed precision to accelerate the computational performance of the algorithm by compressing the data tail. It is proved by experiments that the introduction of fast estimation network model based on mixing accuracy has better effect on improving the calculation of return value.

Acknowledgment. This work is funded by the National Natural Science Foundation of China under Grant No. 61772180, the Key R & D plan of Hubei Province (2020BHB004, 2020BAB012).

References

1. Wei, Z.: A summary of research and application of deep learning. Int. Core J. Eng. **5**(9) (2019)
2. Cheng, X.F., Yan, Y.J.: Collaborative path planning for unmanned aerial vehicle based on MAXQ hierarchical reinforcement learning. Res. Inf. Technol. **46**(01), 13–19 (2020)
3. Ma, P.G., Xie, W., Sun, W.J.: A review of reinforcement Learning. Command Control Simul. **40**(06), 68–72 (2018)

4. Jun, S., Kochan, O., Kochan, V., Wang, C.: Development and investigation of the method for compensating thermoelectric inhomogeneity error. Int. J. Thermophys. **37**(1), 1–14 (2016)
5. Ding, Q.F., Yin, X.Y.: A review of differential evolution algorithms. J. Intell. Syst.Intell. Syst. **12**(04), 431–442 (2017)
6. Talal, T.M., Attiya, G., Metwalli, M.R., et al.: Satellite image fusion based on modified central force optimization. Multimedia Tools Appl. **79**, 21129–21154 (2020)
7. Singh, H., Kumar, Y.: Hybrid artificial chemical reaction optimization algorithm for cluster analysis. Procedia Comput. Sci. **167**, 531–540 (2020)
8. Singh, P., Arya, R., Titare, L.S., et al.: Optimal load shedding to avoid risks of voltage collapse using black hole algorithm. J. Inst. Eng. (India) Ser. B **102**, 261–276 (2021)
9. Yingjie, X., Ning, C., Xi, S., et al.: Proposal and experimental case study on building ventilating fan fault diagnosis based on cuckoo search algorithm optimized extreme learning machine. Sustain. Energy Technol. Assess. **45**, 100975 (2021)
10. Vilas, K.J., Asutkar, V.G.: A novel optimal firefly algorithm based gain scheduling proportional integral derivative controller for rotor spinning machine speed control. Int. J. Dyn. Control **9**(4), 1730–1745 (2021)
11. Wang, Y., Szeto, W.Y.: An enhanced artificial bee colony algorithm for the green bike repositioning problem with broken bikes. Transp. Res. Part C **125**, 102895 (2021)
12. Zhang, J.H., Xu, X.H.: A new evolutionary algorithm – ant colony algorithm. Syst. Eng.-Theory Pract. (03), 85–88+110 (1999)
13. Shikang, X., Israel, K., Mani, K.C.: Adaptive workload adjustment for cyber-physical systems using deep reinforcement learning. Sustain. Comput. Inform. Syst. **30**, 100525 (2021)
14. Song, W., Beshley, M., Przystupa, K., et al.: A software deep packet inspection system for network traffic analysis and anomaly detection. Sensors **20**(6), 1637 (2020)
15. Jun, S., Przystupa, K., Beshley, M., Kochan, O., et al.: A cost-efficient software based router and traffic generator for simulation and testing of IP network. Electronics **9**(1), 40 (2019)

Research on Optimization of PTN Based on Bilevel Multi-objective Programming Learning

Song Tian[✉]

Wuhan FiberHome Information Integration Technologies Co., Ltd., Wuhan, China
zhangsd@fiberhome.com

Abstract. The packet transport network (PTN) is becoming increasingly popular in mobile communication as a technology to provide efficient transmission. With the dramatic surge in user numbers, the PTN must be able to carry more. However, the existing PTN has low resource utilization and poor network security, Therefore, optimizing every aspect of the current PTN is essential. For optimizing PTN network, the decision of both carrier users and service product suppliers should be considered. When satisfying the decision of the product supplier, it is necessary to consider a number of evaluation indicators in the PTN, and there may be some correlation between the indicators. Hence, This study introduces a multi-objective optimization approach inspired by the Gray Wolf Algorithm and centered around the optimization of a PTN network. Carrier user is taken as the upper decision maker, and the goal is to pay the supplier with the lowest possible cost. Suppliers play a lower role in decision-making, considering the PTN Optimal performance, mainly including two goals, the first goal is to have the highest evaluation score of the LSPOR, and troubleshoot the label switched path (LSP) anomaly on the network. As a secondary objective, By maximizing chain bandwidth utilization ratio (CBWUR), we can resolve the problem of high committed information rate (CIR) bandwidth usage. Results show that the model allows services to use shorter paths, which improves resource usage and reduces costs for upper-level decision-makers. At the same time, the model can also improve the evaluation scores of LSPOR and CBWUR indicators, which improves the security of the PTN, reduces the cost of additional network resources, and optimizes the performance of the PTN to the greatest extent.

This paper primarily focuses on the following topics:

1. A proposed improvement in the multi-objective gray wolf algorithm involves enhancing the convergence factor through implementation of the sine and cosine functions to address the issue of slow convergence in the original algorithm.
2. Multi-objective optimization can be used to optimize the two primary indicators in the PTN: the active-standby corouting rate for the label switching path and the link committed information rate corresponds to that of the label switching path. In order to solve these multi-objective problems, the wolf algorithm is used, resulting in Pareto optimal solutions. As a result of the user's selection of the most important two indicators, the most suitable solution is then selected.

Keywords: Packet Transport Network · Bilevel Optimization · Multi-objective Gray Wolf Algorithm · Label Switched Path · Committed Information Rate

1 Introduction

In the era of big data, the traditional SDH (synchronous digital hierarchy) and PDH (plesiochronous digital hierarchy) transmission technology is difficult to realize the transmission of large-capacity data services, while the PTN packet transmission technology can effectively send large-capacity data packets. Moreover, for the overall operation and development of mobile network, it is very important to have a secure and stable transmission network. For network practitioners, PTN transmission network planning must be based on geographical characteristics, development patterns and various city sizes. As the basis of the communication network of the three major carriers, the transmission network is the carrying platform of services. Therefore, the theoretical circle and practical network practitioners must consider one aspect – how to construct and plan the transmission network, how to optimize it in the later stage, so as to be more safe and healthy, and to provide guarantee for different business transmission needs and the security of business operation.

As mobile communication networks undergo extensive expansion, a variety of new services, such as augmented reality and IDC (internet data center), are surfacing. During this phase, adaptations are required for the packet transport network (PTN) to accommodate fluctuating levels of service demand. Congestion or obstructions in the PTN resulting from service activities can have a substantial impact on user satisfaction. To meet the low-latency demands of these innovative services, Quality of Service (QoS) measures are enforced in the PTN network to enhance the utilization of PTN resources. However, the current implementation of QoS in PTN networks still encounters resource wastage due to the intricacy of operational networks or inadequately designed network architecture. Consequently, optimizing PTN networks has become a primary focus for relevant researchers.

The evaluation of whether the network structure is optimal typically involves the development of an evaluation system by product suppliers for PTN management. The level of network quality is judged by integrating the evaluation results of major indicators. Therefore, optimizing the network structure necessitates the consideration of multiple indicators, posing a multi-objective optimization problem. Over the past few years, most of the optimization efforts for PTN networks have focused on specific solutions for individual indicators. These studies typically optimize the indicators separately, but in real network data, there are always interdependencies among the indicators. If each objective is optimized independently without considering the potential impact on other indicators, it may result in improvement in one aspect at the cost of a negative effect on another indicator. To address the issue of index optimization, it is necessary to simultaneously optimize all indicators in the PTN network, which requires conducting multi-objective optimization. However, in multi-objective optimization problems (MOP), the presence of multiple conflicting objectives means that enhancing the performance of solo objective may lead to a degradation During another's performance. This makes it challenging to optimize every objectives concurrently. As the dimension of optimization targets increases, the dynamic, nonlinear, and non-differentiable characteristics of various MOPs lead to increasingly complex multi-objective optimization calculations, resulting in a dramatically expanded search space for solutions and making it difficult for researchers to find suitable solutions for diverse MOP applications. Currently, many multi-objective optimization problems are tackled using intelligent optimization algorithms. However, specific analysis is required to identify the most suitable optimization algorithm for the problem to achieve desirable results.

In 2017, Li Jia conducted an analysis of the PTN framework in the Changsha mobile metropolitan area network within Hunan province, establishing an index system rooted in the current network structure and identifying its deficiencies. Subsequently, the network was optimized [2]. In 2018, Zhang Linhao initially scrutinized prospective challenges within the Chengdu metropolitan area network and proposed corresponding enhancement strategies [1]. In 2019, Dingdi formulated enhancement strategies for the Guiyang mobile PTN network based on business requirements at all levels [3]. Nonetheless, the enhancement strategies outlined in these studies are tailored to specific network environments, thereby limiting their general applicability. It was reviewed by Ridwan et al. [4] how MPLS technologies were being utilized across a wide range of industries. A transport layer protection switching integrated circuit (PPSI) designed by Yongwook Ra incorporates multiple protection switches, which ensures network traffic protection on a single or multiple operational paths. Yun Zhanga introduced a reliability-centered algorithm to address cost and reliability concerns, ultimately obtaining an optimal set of operational and backup paths [6, 7]. This kind of literature delves into MPLS-TP techniques and presents a range of protection path strategies. Various QoS indicators, including availability, throughput, and delay, were identified by Yang Guowei in PTN. Suppliers may set varying committed information rates (CIR) for throughput depending on the service type [8]. Based on the requirements of Internet providers, Bo Hui introduced an equitable CIR compensation traffic control method that delivers unique quality of service based on diverse business requirements [9]. Hou Xin offered strategies for implementing QoS within PTN networks, including CIR configuration [10, 11]. Nevertheless, these studies predominantly outline the configuration of the QoS system within PTN without addressing the resolution of issues stemming from improper configurations or high user demand.

1) Above mentioned in the literature of PTN network optimization scheme, optimization is only for a single index, so alone solve the problem of MPLS - TP with considering the QoS configuration, but now the Netcom often is more complex, may also be connected between each index, so for PTN network optimization, all its indicators can be optimized simultaneously, that is, multi-objective optimization.

2) The main content of this topic is to optimize the PTN network, and the main research content is as follows:

3) An Modified multi-objective gray wolf algorithm is proposed. In view of the slow convergence rate in the initial multi-objective gray wolf algorithm, the convergence factor is improved by using the sine and cosine function.

4) Puts forward the way based on multi-objective optimization of PTN network in two indicators: label switching path master for commitment by rate and link information

rate the same way to optimize the bandwidth utilization, using the wolf algorithm to solve multi-objective, end up with a set of pareto optimal solutions, according to the supplier for two indicators of the importance of a set of solution of judgment to select the most appropriate.

2 Multi-objective Optimization of PTN Network

Multi-criteria Optimization Problems (MOPs) involve the simultaneous optimization of multiple objectives. These objectives are often in conflict, wherein improving the performance of one objective can result in the degradation of one or more other objectives. Over the past few decades, numerous approaches have been proposed by researchers to address MOPs. Among these, the primary method is the Multi-criteria Evolutionary Algorithm, which represents a population-based heuristic search approach. It simulates the selection and evolution processes of organisms, and utilizes a strategy of random search to solve MOPs without requiring prior knowledge. Notable multi-criteria optimization algorithms include NSGA-II, which is based on dominance relation, MOEA/D, which is based on decomposition, and the IBEA algorithm, which is based on performance evaluation indicators.

2.1 Model Constraints

Two decision-making entities are involved in optimizing the PTN network: the supplier operators and the users. The operator users are designated as the primary decision-makers, while the suppliers are considered as secondary decision-makers. The process begins by identifying the best decision for the operator users. Subsequently, based on the decision made by the operators, the optimal decision for the product supplier is determined. Finally, as a result of the supplier's decision, operators select a solution aligned with their interests. Product suppliers aim to maximize LSPOR and CBWUR evaluation scores, while operator users aim to minimize fees.

As part of the PTN network, the carrier ensures that each tunnel has a short primary path length in order to minimize costs. When setting the total number of tunnels protected by LSP1:1 to Ntunnels on a PTN network, a tunnel is chosen with its main path NE and board set denoted as [NEP_i1, NEP_i2,..., NEPiLpi], [BoardPi(1,1), BoardPi(2,0), BoardP_i(2,1),..., BoardPi(Lpi,0)]. The set of NEs for alternate paths can be obtained using a similar method. Consequently, relationships are as follows.

(1) As Tunnel i has n corresponding nes, its active or standby path length is n - 1.

$$L_{Pi} = N_{Pi} - 1$$

$$L_{Bi} = N_{Bi} - 1$$

The manufacturer aims to achieve the highest LSPOR and CBWUR assessment scores, seeking to have the maximum amount of data categorized as normal for each metric. In this context, normal data is designated as 1 and anomalous data as 0. The conditions for the anomaly of the LSPOR indicator are as follows:

(2) If the same NE exists in a Tunnel, the conditions are as follows:

$$NE_{Pi}^{m} = NE_{Bi}^{n}$$

$$1 < m < L_{Pi}, 1 < n < L_{Bi}$$

(3) In order for the same board to exist in a tunnel, the following conditions must be met:

$$Board_{Pi}^{(a,c)} = Board_{Bi}^{(b,c)}$$

$$1 \le a \le L_{Pi}, 1 \le b \le L_{Bi}, a = b, c = 0 \text{ or } 1$$

(4) Tunnels must have the same link if they satisfy the following conditions:

$$[NE_{Pi}^{d}, NE_{Pi}^{d+1}...NE_{Pi}^{d+k}] = [NE_{Bi}^{e}, NE_{Bi}^{e+1}...NE_{Bi}^{e+k}]$$

$$1 \le d \le L_{Pi}, 1 \le e \le L_{Bi}, 1 \le k \le \min(L_{Pi}, L_{Bi})$$

(5) LSPOR indicators are scored according to the following criteria:

$$Score_{LSPOR} = 100 \times \sum_{i=0}^{N_{Tunne}} flag_i / N_{Tunnel}$$

$$\forall i \in N_{Tunnel},$$

$$When \nexists NE_{Pi}^{m} = NE_{Bi}^{n}, \nexists Board_{Pi}^{(a,c)} = Board_{Bi}^{(b,c)}, \nexists [NE_{Pi}^{d}, NE_{Pi}^{d+1}...NE_{Pi}^{d+k}]$$

$$= [NE_{Bi}^{e}, NE_{Bi}^{e+1}...NE_{Bi}^{e+k}],$$

$$flag_i = 1,$$

$$When \exists NE_{Pi}^{m} = NE_{Bi}^{n} \text{ or } \exists Board_{Pi}^{(a,c)} = Board_{Bi}^{(b,c)} \text{ or } \exists [NE_{Pi}^{d}, NE_{Pi}^{d+1}...NE_{Pi}^{d+k}]$$

$$= [NE_{Bi}^{e}, NE_{Bi}^{e+1}...NE_{Bi}^{e+k}],$$

$$flag_i = 0,$$

$$P_i, B_i \in Tunnel_i$$

An optical fiber link in a PTN network is represented as [(NE, Board, Port), (NE, Board, Port), Link Speed], which includes the network elements (NE), boards, and ports at both ends of the link, as well as the transmission speed of the link. By linking the Committed Information Rate (CIR) in the L2VPN (Layer 2 Virtual Private Network) flow configuration with all the associated tunnels, the CIR value for each fiber link is derived. The transformation of Link Speed to bandwidth capacity is depicted in Table 1:

Table 1. Mapping between optical fibers and bandwidth capacity

Link Speed	GE	XGE	40G	100GE	155M
Bandwidth capacity	1000	10000	40000	100000	155

CBWUR indicators that are abnormal must meet the following conditions:

(6) The CIR bandwidth usage of an optical fiber is:

$$CBWUR_{Topo_i} = CIR_{Topo_i}/BC_{Topo_i}$$

(7) For CBWUR index, the scoring criteria are as follows:

$$Score_{CBWUR} = 100 \times \sum_{i=0}^{N_{Topo}} flag_i/N_{Topo}$$

When $CBWUR_{Topo_i} \leq 0.8$, $flag_i = 1$,

When $CBWUR_{Topo_i} > 0.8$, $flag_i = 0$,

Overall, the PTN network optimization problem can be modelled using the following multi-objective optimization model:

$$LL: \begin{cases} maxF1 = \max_{Tunnel} Score_{LSPOR} = 100 \times \sum_{i=0}^{N_{Tunne}} flag_i/N_{Tunnel} \\ maxF2 = \max_{Topo} Score_{CBWUR} = 100 \times \sum_{j=0}^{N_{Topo}} flag_j/N_{Topo} \end{cases}$$

Model constraints are as follows:

$$\forall i \in N_{Tunnel},$$

When $\nexists NE_{Pi}^m = NE_{Bi}^n$, $\nexists Board_{Pi}^{(a,c)} = Board_{Bi}^{(b.c)}$, $\nexists [NE_{Pi}^d, NE_{Pi}^{d+1}...NE_{Pi}^{d+k}]$
$$= [NE_{Bi}^e, NE_{Bi}^{e+1}...NE_{Bi}^{e+k}],$$

$$flag_i = 1,$$

When $\exists NE_{Pi}^m = NE_{Bi}^n$ or $\exists Board_{Pi}^{(a,c)} = Board_{Bi}^{(b.c)}$ or $\exists [NE_{Pi}^d, NE_{Pi}^{d+1}...NE_{Pi}^{d+k}]$
$$= [NE_{Bi}^e, NE_{Bi}^{e+1}...NE_{Bi}^{e+k}],$$

$$flag_i = 0,$$

$$P_i, B_i \in Tunnel_i$$

$$\forall j \in N_{Topo},$$

$$\text{When } CBWUR_{Topo_j} \leq 0.8, flag_j = 1,$$

$$\text{When } CBWUR_{Topo_j} > 0.8, flag_j = 0$$

2.2 MOGWO

The gray wolf groups are categorized into four classes: α, β, δ, and ω, and the gray wolf optimization algorithm is rooted in the predatory behavior of gray wolves. In the algorithm, the position of a wolf represents a potential solution to the problem at hand.

During each iteration, the gray wolf optimization algorithm assigns the optimal value of the objective function at three loci to the α, β, and δ wolves. Subsequently, the other individuals adjust their positions based on the positions of these three optimal individuals.

Gray wolf individuals' position is determined by the formula.

$$D_i(t) = |C \cdot X_P(t) - X_i(t)|$$

$$X_i(t+1) = X_i(t) - A \cdot D_i(t)$$

where t symbolizes the current iteration count, $X_p(t)$ represents the location of the prey at iteration t, $X_i(t)$ denotes the location of gray wolf individual I in the t iteration, A and C stand for the coefficients of influence, and the calculation formula is as follows.

$$D_i(t)A = 2a \cdot r_1 - a$$

$$D_i(t)C = 2r_2$$

A linear decrease in a is determined by the following formula when r1 and r2 are both random numbers in the [0,1] interval.

$$D_i(t)a = 2 - 2 \times t/t_{maxiter}$$

The $t_{maxiter}$ represents iterations with the maximum number.

The MOGWO algorithm introduces two distinct elements compared to the GWO algorithm. Initially, a repository is required to access any Pareto optimal solution obtained up to the current iteration count that is not dominated. Leadership selection is also part of the solution repository, which updates solutions and proposes a grid mechanism to enhance them. Gray wolf individuals will be selected according to the revised selection strategy. As part of the repository, exceptional individuals from each generation are retained, specifically non-dominant solutions, and are updated and removed according to specific policies. The MOGWO algorithm employs a roulette method to directly select three exceptional individuals from the repository as α, β, and ω. In the end, A Pareto optimal solution for the optimization problem is represented by the individuals in the external population repository.

A comparison of the performance of the Gray Wolf algorithm with the DE algorithm, PSO algorithm, and gravity search algorithm shows that the Gray Wolf algorithm performs better. Its strengths include its straightforward implementation, simple structure, and minimal parameter requirements. A number of applications have been developed with the GWO algorithm since its inception, including attribute minimization, surface wave analysis, feature selection, and economic load distribution [14].

2.3 PTNMOGWO

Research is currently focused on improving the original multi-objective gray wolf algorithm, since it still has some deficiencies. Wolf optimization algorithms have, however, been criticized for their low accuracy and slow convergence speed, which has prompted researchers to propose a variety of enhanced algorithms. One common improvement approach for multi-objective gray wolves pertains to enhancing population diversity during initialization and addressing the tendency for rapid convergence to local optima. Additionally, attention is given to advancing the speed of global optimal solution search.

For achieving the goal of lowest cost and shortest path, K. Biswas et al. [20] were proposed a new hybrid cellular automata (CA) technology, gray wolf optimization (GWO) and particle swarm optimization (PSO) algorithm to solve this issue of the traditional meta-heuristic algorithm, which only improves the algorithm exploration ability. But it ignores the issue of application development capability. Experimental results also show that the new algorithm works better than other standard methods, such as MOGWO and MOPSO. The proposed optimization method also has minimum spacing measurement and maximum propagation. Qi Yan et al. [21] aiming at the optimization problem of microgrid, MOGWO algorithm was used to solve the problem, and the model was simplified. For the initialization and location update of the gray Wolf are divided into time periods to shorten the computing time. Meanwhile, the nonlinear convergence factor is also established, but the manual setting of the exponential factor in its convergence approach makes it challenging to determine the optimal convergence effect. Amiri S and colleagues [22] proposed the Multi-objective Gray Wolf Optimization (MOGWO) algorithm and non-dominated sorting for addressing the decision objectives related to location selection, product supply, production, distribution, collection, quarantine, recycling, reuse, and disposal during the COVID-19 pandemic. Experimental results indicate that the MOGWO algorithm demonstrates greater reliability in problem-solving and achieves a 25% improvement over NSGA-II in terms of the dispersion of Pareto solutions.

In this paper, the convergence factor is improved

$$a_{traditional} = 2 \times (1 - t/maxiter)$$

$$a_{improved} = \begin{cases} sin(rand()) \times (1 - t/maxiter) & rand() < 0.5 \\ cos(rand()) \times (1 - t/maxiter) & rand() >= 0.5 \end{cases}$$

These consist of maximum number of iterations, which represents the maximum number of iterations; number of current iteration is the number of iterations at the current point; Factors of tradition represents the Convergence factor for linear systems; A random decimal number within the range of 0 to 1 is generated by a mathematical function called rand(). A non-linear concave decline is produced by combining the linear decline with a trigonometric function and the magnitude of the random number. This produces a gradual decline followed by a rapid drop in the number.

For population initialization, this study treats a tunnel as a single individual gray wolf, and does not account for the data correlation between gray wolf individuals in order to optimize the individual gray wolf, aiming to optimize in a solution's optimal direction.

3   Experimental Design and Evaluation

3.1   Experimental Data Set

According to network regulations, three regions in Hubei province of China were chosen for experiments to assess the suitability of the proposed scheme. Region 1 has the most regular network, region 2 also has a regular network, and region 3 has an extremely chaotic network. According to the original data, only some tunnels have mechanisms of 1:1 protection for LSPs, This type of tunnel is the only type of tunnel we consider as the initial population for the experiment. To facilitate network management and optimization, It was decided to store the data in MongoDB. The experimental device was equipped with an Intel(R) Core(TM) i7-8700 CPU @ 3.20 GHz, 16 GB memory, and the Windows 10 64-bit operating system. Using active-standby hops, we can determine how many links are in the active-standby paths in each of the three areas (Table 2).

Table 2. Table of configuring the network

	The total number of Tunnel	Equipped with LSP1 as: 1	Number of network elements	Card number	Port number	Optical fiber number
Area1	15438	6488	2973	26495	94945	4033
Area 2	17267	6677	2435	13724	47671	3577
Area 3	21385	11261	2975	17100	57409	4199

3.2   Experimental Results and Analysis

The PTN multi-objective optimization problem is tackled using the enhanced MOGWO algorithm, conventional MOGWO algorithm, MOPSO algorithm, and NSGAII algorithm in this study, and these algorithms are compared based on various performance indicators. Three primary performance indicators—Epsilon (EP), Hyper-cuboid indicator (HV), and Inverted Generational Distance (IGD) [23]—are chosen for analyzing convergence and distribution settlement. The EP assesses the maximum difference between knowledge sets, with lower values signifying superior algorithm performance. In terms of algorithm performance and convergence, a smaller IGD indicates better performance and better convergence of each reference point. Using the algorithm and the reference points, the HV index represents the volume of the non-dominant solution set in the target space. A larger HV value indicates better algorithm convergence, a more diverse solution set, and enhanced comprehensive performance. With 10 iterations, a mutation operator of 0.3, and a disturbance index of 0.5, the initial population number for testing standard functions such as UF1 and UF8 is set at 100. Table 3, 4 and 5 displays the performance results of the different algorithms.

Table 3. UF1

The evaluation index		algorithm			
		PTNMOGWO	MOGWO	MOPSO	NSGAII
EP	Min	0.132420	0.235409	**0.087060**	0.090084
	Median	0.229681	0.331370	0.174581	**0.143975**
	Max	0.329025	0.420202	0.227263	**0.209745**
IGD	Min	0.122522	0.197619	0.076934	**0.071549**
	Median	0.193988	0.298720	0.144996	**0.109934**
	Max	0.264803	0.365536	0.184091	**0.169617**
HV	Min	0.496013	0.335955	0.584007	**0.596818**
	Median	0.611893	0.414700	0.645996	**0.697046**
	Max	0.681863	0.551439	0.772049	**0.778961**

Table 4. UF8

The evaluation index		algorithm			
		PTNMOGWO	MOGWO	MOPSO	NSGAII
EP	Min	0.103580	1.894131	0.403218	0.959941
	Median	0.294761	2.551003	0.654658	1.430914
	Max	0.598373	3.231418	0.935432	1.696421
IGD	Min	0.072311	2.298665	0.264985	0.862759
	Median	0.134508	3.128341	0.478967	1.701316
	Max	0.414840	3.881885	0.900546	1.969872
HV	Min	0.070812	0.0	0.0	0.0
	Median	0.249725	0.0	0.024253	0.0
	Max	0.374771	0.0	0.153393	0.0

Table 5. PTN Problem

The evaluation index		algorithm			
		PTNMOGWO	MOGWO	MOPSO	NSGAII
EP	Min	**0.0052104**	0.0293335	0.0058917	0.0079682
	Median	**0.0063597**	0.0514568	0.0075437	0.0120854
	Max	**0.0103165**	0.1349445	0.0108211	0.0283012
IGD	Min	0.0056471	0.0165978	0.0063488	**0.0044311**
	Median	0.0061765	0.0263099	0.0067933	**0.0048252**
	Max	0.0067049	**0.0540996**	0.0074419	0.0056595
HV	Min	**0.8290429**	0.7793306	0.8285531	0.8282083
	Median	**0.8292719**	0.8100322	0.8289632	0.8291233
	Max	0.8294074	0.8197893	0.8291818	**0.8294558**

It can be seen from Table 3 that NSGAII has better optimization effect for solving UF1 standard functions with various algorithms. As can be seen from Table 4 in HV index, PTNMOGWO has better optimization effect for solving UF8 standard function with various algorithms. The future research direction can be extended to three-objective optimization; It can be seen from Table 5 that EP index value solved by PTNMOGWO algorithm is optimal for solving PTN problem by all kinds of algorithms, indicating that there is little difference between solution sets solved by PTN multi-objective optimization. In terms of IGD index, PTNMOGWO is not as good as other algorithms in solving PTN problem. The experimental results can be further observed by increasing the number of iterations and optimizing the convergence factor. For HV index, PTNMOGWO optimization results are better than other algorithms.

We directly identify outliers (outliers) in the data through the box diagram. Intuitively judge the discrete distribution of data and understand the state of data distribution. As can be seen from Fig. 1, for HV index, only NSGAII algorithm has a wide solution set distribution among the four algorithms, while the other three algorithms have similar optimization effects. For IGD index, NSGAII algorithm has the widest solution set distribution, and the overall data distribution is in the lowest numerical segment. MOGWO was the least effective. For EP index, NSGAII algorithm has the lowest box line value, which is still better than the other three algorithms, and has no abnormal constant value. As can be seen from Fig. 2, for the three indicators, only PTNMOGWO algorithm has the best effect among the four algorithms, and the solution set distribution is relatively concentrated. As can be seen from Fig. 3, for EP index, PTNMOGWO has the best performance in solving PTN problem, but there are outliers. For other indexes, PTNMOGWO's performance is not as good as NSGAII and MOPSO algorithms.

To sum up, PTNMOGWO algorithm is feasible to solve PTN problem and conforms to the reality of PTN optimization. In reality, there is no significant difference between most schemes for PTN network optimization.

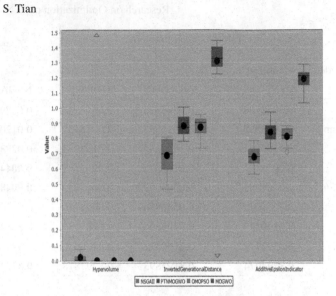

Fig. 1. UF1 box diagram

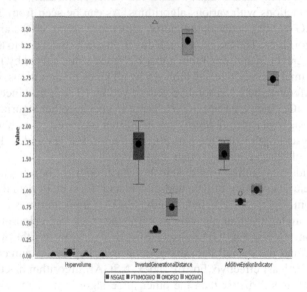

Fig. 2. UF8 box diagram

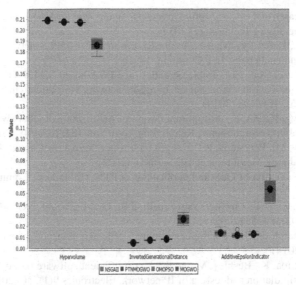

Fig. 3. PTN problem box diagram

4 Summary of This Chapter

This paper firstly presents the PTN technology system, and introduces the packet forwarding mechanism, multi-service bearer, operation and maintenance management mechanism, network protection mode and quality of service mechanism in PTN network based on MPLS-TP technology in detail. Using the PTN indicator system, we introduce two new indicators: LSP same-route rates and link CIR bandwidth usages. We introduce the multi-objective gray wolf algorithm and suggest an appropriate improvement scheme after describing the model and constraint conditions of the multi-objective optimization PTN network. Meanwhile, other common multi-objective optimization algorithms are briefly introduced. Finally, PTNMOGWO, MOGWO, MOPSO and NSGAII algorithms were used to solve the three kinds of problems, including the dual objective standard function UF1, the triple objective standard function UF8 and the PTN Problem proposed in this paper. The corresponding experimental results were obtained and evaluated according to EP, IGD and HV indicators. The feasibility of PTNMOGWO in solving PTN Problem is proved.

Acknowledgment. This work is funded by the National Natural Science Foundation of China under Grant No. 61772180, the Key R & D plan of Hubei Province (2020BHB004, 2020BAB012).

References

1. Li, J.: Optimization of PTN structure and Index System Analysis and Research of Changsha Mobile Metropolitan Area Network. Hunan University (2017)
2. Zhang, L.: Optimization Design and Implementation of Chengdu Metro Transmission Network. University of Electronic Science and Technology of China (2018)

3. Ding, D.: Research on Network Optimization of Guiyang Mobile All-Service Bearer Network. Zhejiang University of Technology (2019)
4. Ridwan, M.A., Radzi, N., Wan, S., et al.: Recent trends in MPLS networks: technologies, applications and challenges. IET Commun. **14**(2), 177–185 (2020)
5. Ra, Y., Bang, J., Ryoo, J.D.: Implementation of FPGA-based MPLS-TP linear protection switching for 4000+ tunnels in packet transport network for optical carrier Ethernet. IET Commun. **13**(5), 481–488 (2019)
6. Zhang, Y., Fang, Z., Xu, Z.: An optimal design of multi-protocol label switching networks achieving reliability requirements. Reliab. Eng. Syst. Saf. **182**, 133–141 (2018)
7. Su, J., Beshley, M., Przystupa, K., et al.: 5G multi-tier radio access network planning based on voronoi diagram. Measurement **192**, 110814 (2022)
8. Yang, G.: Introduction of QoS and application in PTN. China New Commun. **22**(04), 116 (2020)
9. Bai, H., Duan, Z.: A Fair traffic control method for COMPENSATING CIR in DS domain. J. Commun. (03), 84–88 (2002)
10. Hou, X.: Research on QoS deployment strategy of packet transport network. Inf. Technol. (10), 68–72 (2014)
11. Jun, S., Przystupa, K., Beshley, M., et al.: A cost-efficient software based router and traffic generator for simulation and testing of IP network. Electronics **9**(1), 40 (2019)

Practical Teaching Reform of Cybersecurity Courses Incorporating Personalized Recommendations

Yuxiang Chen[1,2], Xiaofan Zhou[1], Linshu Chen[1], Jigang Wen[1], Ce Yang[1],

Shiwen Zhang[1], and Wei Liang[1(✉)]

[1] School of Computer Science and Engineering, Hunan University of Science and Technology, Xiangtan 411201, China
{chenyuxiang,linshuchen,wenjigang,yangce,
shiwenzhang,wliang}@hnust.edu.cn, zhouxiaofan@mail.hnust.edu.cn
[2] School of Information Science and Engineering, Hunan University, Changsha 410082, China

Abstract. In recent years, with the development of cyber security, the national demand for cybersecurity-related professionals is growing, and the practice of cyber security related practices is increasing, which makes it difficult for students to find suitable practices in the massive practice resources, so the practice recommendations method for students emerges. As an emerging technique, Matrix Completion becomes one of the most powerful techniques to predict missing entries of a low-rank matrix from incomplete samples of its entries. Despite its efficiency in discovering and quantifying the interactions between students and practices, Matrix Completion in the recommender scheme suffers from the problems of low rating density and scalability. To conquer the above challenges as well as to provide quick and high-quality recommendations, we propose partition-based Matrix Completion, a novel recommender scheme that concurrently exploits locality-sensitive hash (LSH) and Matrix Completion. Specifically, taking advantage of the good properties of LSHs, our recommender scheme adopts an LSH hash table to reorder students with similar students buffered in close positions. As a result, the original student-practice rating matrix is partitioned into sub-matrices each containing a group of similar students thus having a lower rank. Matrix Completion is then used in the partitioned matrix to more effectively predict the missing ratings of a student for practice. The experimental results show that our recommendation scheme achieves better recommendation results in terms of practicing recommendation compared to other traditional recommendation methods.

Keywords: Cybersecurity · Personalized recommendations · Practice reform

1 Introduction

In recent years, the popularization of network technology, so that more people to use the network, the network brings convenience at the same time, but also lets more people face network security issues. At the same time, each country's network security issues also showed a high incidence trend, security issues have been elevated from the corporate level to the national level. At present, there is a growing demand for network

W. Hong and G. Kanaparan (Eds.): ICCSE 2023, CCIS 2024, pp. 41–54, 2024.
https://doi.org/10.1007/978-981-97-0791-1_4

security-related professionals [1], and many colleges and universities have opened network security courses [2]. The practice of network security-related courses covers a wide range and is comprehensive, and there are problems such as poor pertinence to the practice of courses with different lecture contents, and disconnection between classroom teaching and practical application.

With the rapid development of digital education, many universities have turned to digital transformation one after another and launched many online experiment platforms. These platforms provide convenient and efficient experimental environments, which reduce the environmental constraints for students to do experiments and enable them to practice more network security experiments. Therefore, in the intelligent education system, in the face of a great variety of cybersecurity experiments, how to recommend course practices for students that meet their learning characteristics is an important issue.

Recommender systems are widely used on the Internet due to their great potential. Websites such as Amazon, eBay, Netflix, etc. rely on recommender systems to analyze users' purchasing records and recommend similar goods to attract users, which brings great economic benefits. Currently, researchers have applied the related technology of recommender systems to teaching practice recommendations and carried out preliminary research work. The approaches commonly utilized in recommender systems can be categorized into three types: Collaborative Filtering (CF) [3–6], Content-Based (CB) [7,8], KnowledgeBased (KB) [9,10] and hybrid. Among which, matrix factorization [11–16], a typical model-based collaborative filtering scheme, becomes one of the most powerful methods in recommender systems due to its efficiency in handling huge data sets. However, the plain matrix factorization may not be able to uncover the structure correlations among students and practices well, and the recommendation quality of the matrix factorization method is still not high. With the rapid progress of sparse representation, Matrix Completion [17–23], a remarkable new field, has emerged very recently. Matrix Completion can infer unknown data of a low-rank matrix from the partially observed entries. Despite its potentially big efficiency, applying Matrix Completion to recommendation suffers from the problems of low rating density and scalability. In Matrix Completion, to successfully recover a sparsity matrix, the number of samples should be sufficient and meet some conditions.

To overcome the above challenges, we propose to apply both locality-sensitive hash Function (LSH) and Matrix Completion to provide fast and high-quality recommendations and utilize them in recommending course practices for students that match their learning characteristics. Analyzing students' learning characteristics, interest preferences, learning history, and lab data, similar students are mapped together and a student-practice matrix is created. The original term matrix is divided into sub-matrices and combined with matrix-completion techniques to recommend experimental courses for students that match their learning characteristics and needs. The main contributions of our work are summarized as follows.

- Taking advantage of the property of LSH functions, we adopt an LSH hash table to reorder the student while buffering similar students in the same hash bucket in the table.

- Based on the LSH hash table, we partition the original student-practice matrix into sub-matrices each containing the rating records of similar students in the same bucket of the target students. To further reduce the matrix dimension, zero-rating columns will be removed from the submatrix before reconstructing the submatrix to infer the unknown student-practice ratings and selecting the ones with the highest ratings to recommend to students.

The rest of this paper is organized as follows. We introduce the related work in Sect. 2. We present the overview solution of our recommendation scheme in Sect. 3. The proposed LSH hash table for student management is presented in Sect. 4, and the partition-based Matrix Completion algorithm is presented in Sect. 5. Finally, educational experiment in Sect. 6, and conclude the work in Sect. 7.

2 Related Work

In this section, we summarize the existing research on the advanced techniques of recommendation technology.

As the need for cybersecurity becomes more widespread, a large number of educational programs and curricular practices have been proposed.Lorena [24] et al. conducted a survey of 35 free online courses and found that the web-based lectures were very extensive and the lectures varied in content. So the potential use of recommender systems in cyber security carries on widely.

The main types of recommendation techniques are Collaborative Filtering (CF) [3–6], Content-Based (CB) [7,8] and KnowledgeBased (KB) [9,10], and hybrid. Collaborative filtering is the most commonly used, which is based on the similarity of user behavior, interests and uses the evaluation data of other users or items to make recommendations. However, in the real world, the evaluation data between users and items is usually sparse, and most users have evaluated only a few items. This data sparsity may cause collaborative filtering methods to fail to find a sufficient number of similar users or items, thus affecting the accuracy and reliability of recommendations [25,26].

Recently, several matrix factorization methods [11–16] have been proposed. In the context of the recommendation problem, these methods focus on factorizing the user-item rating matrix into a set of low-rank matrices which are then utilized to make further predictions. The factorized matrices are user-specific matrix and item-specific matrix which include the latent factor vectors to characterize users and items. The motivation behind the matrix factorization model is that there is only a small number of factors that are important. A user's preference is predicted and determined by how each factor applies to that user. Since the matrix decomposition can be predicted by a low-rank user-item rating matrix, to some extent, the data sparsity problem can be alleviated [25,27–29]. However, plain matrix factorization may not be able to uncover the structure correlations among users and items well. The recommendation quality of matrix factorization approaches is still not high and has a lot of room to improve.

To further increase the recommendation quality, in this paper, we propose a Matrix Completion based approach. Different from matrix factorization, Matrix Completion technique models and solves the missing entities prediction problem as a convex optimization problem. When applying matrix factorization [17–22], the latent factor vectors should be firstly identified, while Matrix Completion is more practical solution for inferring missing data as it does not require to derive the latent factor vectors in applications. Our performance results based on extensive experiments demonstrate that our proposed partition-based Matrix Completion can achieve significantly higher performance gain compared with the matrix factorization

As the most related model to this paper, the clustering collaborative filtering model [23, 30] organizes a collection of data samples with similar features or close relationships into a cluster. In [23, 30], clustering is an intermediate process and the clusters formed are applied with collaborative filtering algorithms further. One of the big limitations of the clustering collaborative filtering approaches is the clustering algorithms utilized. For example, in [23, 30], a typical algorithm k-means is applied in the clustering collaborative filtering model to cluster similar users and items. However, k-means runs iteratively which may give high computation cost. Moreover, the performance of k-means is sensitive to the parameter setting, and an inappropriate choice of k may yield poor results. Thus, although k-means may provide good clustering results for fix and stable off-line data set, k-means can hardly perform well in a dynamical environment with on-line operations.

To conquer these challenges, we propose to apply both LSH [31, 32] and Matrix Completion to provide fast and high-quality recommendations. The scheme clusters students with similar preference records together by a simple LSH computation. Based on this, the original large student matrix is divided into small sub-matrices, each containing similar students in only one bucket in the LSH hash table.

3   Solution Overview

The data of many practical applications have inherent correlations. As one example of structure correlation in a recommendation scheme, users with similar tastes (interests) may have similar preferences about items, as shown in Fig. 1. Therefore, the ratings of similar users have higher impacts on each other and can be applied to predicting the unknown ones.

In order to exploit some of these correlations, we propose a scheme to partition the original student-practice matrix into submatrices with each submatrix containing only similar students, and then apply Matrix Completion to the submatrices to predict the students' ratings. This partition will reduce the matrix scale and increase the sampling ratio in the submatrix. Therefore, our scheme can provide quick and high-quality recommendations compared with directly applying Matrix Completion to the original student-practice matrix. Our scheme mainly includes the following two technique components:

- An LSH hash table, which reorders and buffers students based on LSH. The good property of the LSH guarantees that similar students are packed into the same bucket in the LSH hash table.
- A Matrix Completion-based recommender scheme achieves good recommendation performance by utilizing the capability of Matrix Completion to discover and quantify the interactions between students and practices.

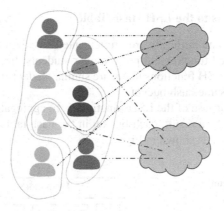

Fig. 1. Hidden structure correlation

In our scheme, student-related operations such as student inserting and mapping, student reordering, and updating are executed based on the LSH hash table. Besides buffering students' records, another important student of the LSH hash table is to facilitate matrix partition, which is the basis of our proposed recommender scheme. For a given set of active students, the scheme's main focus is to predict the appropriate practices of these students through Matrix Completion and recommend the students the practices with the highest potential to attract the students.

4   Student Management Based on LSH Hash Table

In this section, we propose a student reordering algorithm that buffers students in an LSH hash table based on the principle of LSH [31,32]. It utilizes an LSH hash table with an intelligent buffering mechanism to pack together students with similar practice records.

The key idea is to hash the students using several hash functions, and for each function, the probability for the hashed values to fall into the same bucket is much higher for similar students who have close course practices than for students whose course practices arc far apart. To find similar students for the target student to provide the recommendation for, the target student can be first hashed and the similar students buffered in the same bucket can be retrieved. The general characteristics and benefits of our scheme are:

- It reorders and buffers students in a fast and effective way, which ensures data blocks have lower entropy on average.
- It provides a new indexing method for approximate nearest neighbor queries by placing students with similar practice preferences in close-by positions. Without depending on the data size even when the data dimension is high, our scheme eventually helps to speed up recommendations.
- It is simple and easy to implement, and can also be naturally extended to the dynamic setting to support student course practice updating and practice expanding.

4.1   Mapping Students to the LSH Hash Table

The student reordering and buffering are implemented based on the LSH hash table by using several LSH-based functions to pack similar students. In fact, the basic premise of our scheme is to use LSH functions to ensure similar students have a high probability of being hashed to the same hash bucket.

In this paper, the purpose of the LSH functions is to aggregate similar students into the same hash bucket. As a result, each bucket in the hash table eventually contains a chain of similar students, as shown in Fig. 2.

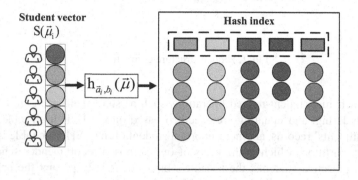

Fig. 2. Student reorder in LSH hash table

Student Vector. Consider our recommendation scheme, which has M students and N practices to be graded. A student-practice matrix $P \in R^{M \times N}$ is applied to store student ratings for completion of practice, where the value $P_{ij}(1 \leq i \leq M, 1 \leq j \leq N)$ denotes student u_i ratings to practice v_j. A student's practice rating can be expressed directly, such as using a range of rating values, or indirectly, using a binary integer to indicate whether the student needs to complete the practice, how well the practice was completed, or whether additional practice is needed. Conventionally, we use $P_{ij} =?$ to denote the case that student u_i is unknown for practice v_j, as shown in Table 1.

In our scenario, we wish to pack together students based on the student practice records. It is a challenge to define a vector that can effectively track student practice records even when the frequency of student ratings is un-uniformly distributed (i.e., some students rate more practices, while others rate fewer practices).

Straightforwardly, we can utilize a vector $z \in R^N$ to denote the student practices record, where N is the number of practices. However, the number of practices is usually very large, which makes the dimension of z very large.

To reduce the dimension, we use a vector $r_i \in R^C$ (where C is the category number) to denote student u_i's practices record, with r_i defined as

$$r_i[j] = \sum_{z \in c_j} P_{iz} \quad 1 \le j \le C, 1 \le i \le M, 1 \le z \le N \tag{1}$$

where P is the original student-practice matrix, c_j is the category index. Obviously, $r_i[j]$ aggregates all ratings of student u_i for practices belonging to the category c_j.

For two students u_1 and u_2 with their vectors $r_1 = \{5, 1, 0\}$ and $r_2 = \{50, 10, 0\}$, the values of the two vectors are obviously very different, and student u_2 may complete and rate more practices while student u_1 complete and rate fewer practices. However, both students have completes in the first and second categories and should be hashed into the same bucket. Therefore, we further propose a normalized vector μ_i to more accurately reflect the student u_i's practice needs based on vector r_i defined in (1) as follows:

$$\mu_i[j] = \alpha \cdot \frac{r_i[j]}{\sum_{j=1}^{C} r_i[j]} \tag{2}$$

where α is a constant. In this paper, we set $\alpha = 100$.

Table 1. Student-practice rating matrix

	SQL Injection	XSS	Password Cracking	Phishing Website Creation
Adam	5	?	2	?
Eric	?	1	?	4
Diana	3	4	?	?
Sally	?	2	?	?

Hash Index Calculation. LSH function families [31,32] exhibit the locality-aware property, which supports similarity aggregation. In this paper, based on the LSH function, similar students with similar practice data are aggregated together with a higher probability.

In the LSH, $c > 1$ and $P_1 > P_2$. In order to increase the gap between P_1 and P_2, our recommendation scheme uses multiple hash functions. Specially, we define LSH hash function $h_{a_i,b_i} : R^C \to Z \; (1 \le i \le n)$ (n is the number of hash functions) to map a student into a single value ("bin"), expressed as:

$$h_{a_i,b_i}(\mu) = \left\lfloor \frac{a_i^T \mu + b_i}{W} \right\rfloor \tag{3}$$

where a_i is a C-dimensional random vector with each component chosen independently from a Gaussian distribution, W is the width of a bin, and b_i is a real number chosen uniformly from the range $[0, W)$.

4.2 Reordering of Students

As time goes on, a student may complete more practices which consequently changes its practice record and results in the need of reordering the student in the LSH hash table. Let $\boldsymbol{\mu}_j(t)$ and $\boldsymbol{\mu}_j(t+1)$ denote the previous and the updated vector of student u_j, the LSH hash table should be updated following two operations below:

- Removing student u_j from the bucket with the position
  $(\sum_{i=1}^{n} h_{a_i,b_i}(\boldsymbol{\mu}_j(t)))\ mod\ T$.
- Rehashing u_j into the bucket with the position
  $(\sum_{i=1}^{n} h_{a_i,b_i}(\boldsymbol{\mu}_j(t+1)))\ mod\ T$.

4.3 Increase of the Number of Practices

Adding new practices may result in an increase in the dimension of the student vector. To avoid instability, a good student management scheme should keep the students buffered at the same location even when the practice number expands. The following theory will show that our student management scheme can achieve this good property even when the number of practices expands to a large value.

Theorem 1. *For student u_j, let $\boldsymbol{\mu}_j \in R^C$ and $\boldsymbol{\mu}_j' \in R^{C'}$ denote the student vectors before practice expanding and after practice expanding, respectively. Let $L = (\sum_{i=1}^{n} h_{a_i,b_i}(\boldsymbol{\mu}_j))\ mod\ T$ and $L' = (\sum_{i=1}^{n} h_{a_i',b_i}(\boldsymbol{\mu}_j'))\ mod\ T$ denote the student positions in the hash table before practice expanding and after practice expanding, then $L = L'$.*

Proof. When the practice number increases from N_1 to N_2, we denote the newly added practices as v_k ($N_1 \le k \le N_2$). Because students buffered in the LSH hash table did not rate the new practices before, the rating values corresponding to these new practices will be zero. That is, for student u_j, $P_{jk} = 0$ ($N_1 \le k \le N_2$).

Depending on whether all the newly added practices belong to the existing C categories, the proof can be divided into two parts.

Part 1, all newly added practices belong to the existing C categories, i.e., $C = C'$. It is easy to see that $\boldsymbol{\mu}_j = \boldsymbol{\mu}_j'$, as the ratings of student u_j on the newly added practices are zero. We have

$$h_{a_i,b_i}(\boldsymbol{\mu}_j) = \left\lfloor \frac{a_i^T \boldsymbol{\mu}_j + b_i}{W} \cdot \right\rfloor = \left\lfloor \frac{a_i^T \boldsymbol{\mu}_j' + b_i}{W} \right\rfloor = h_{a_i,b_i}(\boldsymbol{\mu}_j') \tag{4}$$

Obviously, by summing up all n LSH hash function values, we have

$$(\sum_{i=1}^{n} h_{a_i,b_i}(\boldsymbol{\mu}_j))\ mod\ T = (\sum_{i=1}^{n} h_{a_i,b_i}(\boldsymbol{\mu}_j'))\ mod\ T, \tag{5}$$

Part 2, newly added practices expand the category number from C to C'. According to (2), we have

$$\boldsymbol{\mu}_j'[i] = \begin{cases} \boldsymbol{\mu}_j[i] & 1 \le i \le C \\ 0 & C < i \le C' \end{cases} \tag{6}$$

To handle the category extension, the parameter of LSH hash function $a_i \in R^C$ $(1 \leq i \leq n)$ should be extended by adding $C' - C$ components, resulting in $a_i' \in R^{C'}$ $(1 \leq i \leq n)$. The relationship of a_i and a_i' can be expressed as

$$a_i'[j] = a_i[j] \; 1 \leq j \leq C. \tag{7}$$

Combining (6) and (7), for any hash function i $(1 \leq i \leq n)$, we have

$$h_{a_i,b_i}(\boldsymbol{\mu}_j) = \left\lfloor \frac{a_i^T \boldsymbol{\mu}_j + b_i}{W} \right\rfloor = \left\lfloor \frac{a_i'^T \boldsymbol{\mu}_j' + b_i}{W} \right\rfloor = h_{a_i,b_i}(\boldsymbol{\mu}_j') \tag{8}$$

According to (8), summing up all n LSH hash function values, obviously, we have

$$\left(\textstyle\sum_{i=1}^{n} h_{a_i,b_i}(\boldsymbol{\mu}_j)\right) mod\, T = \left(\textstyle\sum_{i=1}^{n} h_{a_{i'},b_i}(\boldsymbol{\mu}_j')\right) mod\, T \tag{9}$$

The proof is complete.

Therefore, although practice expansion may make the parameter a_i extended to a_i', the table locations for students already stored in the LSH hash table remain the same. Therefore, our proposed recommendation scheme has good scalability and can efficiently handle practice expansion in the recommendation.

5   Partition-Based Matrix Completion

In this section, we introduce the Matrix Completion technique and the specific steps of the partition-based Matrix Completion approach. Based on the student management in Sect. 4, to reduce the complexity of Matrix Completion and increase the recommendation performance, we propose to partition the original large-scale matrix into sub-matrices thus dividing a large Matrix Completion task into small subproblems. The rationale behind this approach is to partition the original student-practice matrix P into sub-matrices such that students with similar ratings thus close relationships are contained in the same submatrix. It allows for a quick and high-quality recommendation because the scale of the submatrix is significantly reduced and the rating density of the submatrix is increased.

5.1   Matrix Completion

Our problem of Matrix Completions in the recommendation scheme is as follows: given a student-practice rating matrix P that represents a known set of M students' ratings to N practices, for a given set of target students, the goal of the completion is to predict missing entries of the matrix, and recommends a list of practices with high predicted ratings to the corresponding group of students for viewing.

The matrix P is generally sparse because the known ratings of students for practices are usually very limited. Moreover, in reality, M and N are very large, which results in high computation costs to recover the rating matrix. The focus of this paper is to reconstruct the matrix for accurate and quick recommendations.

Generally, a student would not like to be recommended a practice that has been already completed. Therefore, the practices with known ratings from a student are not considered for recommendation.

In our study, we use zero as a placeholder to replace the empty entry in the student-practice matrix P to facilitate Matrix Completion.

5.2 Partition-Based Matrix Completion Approach

The complete partition-based Matrix Completion approach is shown in Fig. 3, which comprises the following six steps.

Step 1: Construction of student vectors. When the course is finished, student vectors are generated based on students' learning characteristics, interest preferences, learning history and experimental data.

Step 2: Similar student query. From the LSH hash table, it is very easy to obtain similar students of any target student. That is, for a target student u_i and the corresponding vector $\boldsymbol{\mu}_i$, we can apply the n LSH hash functions to find the corresponding bucket. All the students in the buckets are grouped as similar students.

Step 3: Generating the submatrix by extracting from the original student-practice rating matrix with the rows corresponding to similar students identified in the first step.

Step 4: Pruning columns with zero-rating.

Step 5: Applying the matrix recovery algorithm to the submatrix pruned, denote the reconstructed submatrix as P_s.

Step 6: Recommending the top-k practices to the target student by choosing the k practices that have the highest ratings in P_s.

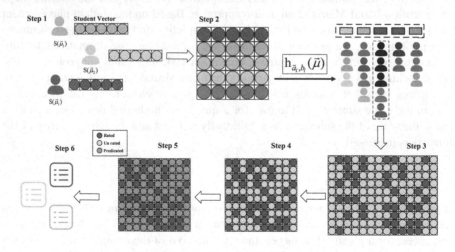

Fig. 3. The detailed partition-based Matrix Completion

One factor that influences the computation complexity of the Matrix Completion is the scale of the matrix. In this paper, the scale of the submatrix depends on W, a parameter that determines the width of a bin in the LSH function. A large W corresponds to a wide bin, which allows more students to be hashed into the same bucket in the LSH hash table. On the other hand, too large a W may make unsimilar students hashed into the same bin. We will show in the experiment section that, in real application scenarios, we can find an appropriate parameter W to facilitate our Matrix Completion approach to achieve high-quality recommendations.

The partition-based Matrix Completion runs on a small cluster of similar students in the same bucket. In our scheme, student sets in different buckets do not overlap. It provides the possibility of parallel and distributed recommendations for large-scale Matrix Completion. Therefore, in such a setup, even very large completion task can be handled efficiently.

6   Experiment and Effect Analysis

In this section, we apply the Matrix Completion method based on partitioning to the practice of cybersecurity courses, describe the content and experimental effect of the experiment, and analyze the effect.

Experiment Description. This educational experiment is for 103 undergraduate students majoring in cyberspace security at Hunan University of Science and Technology. We collected a large number of cybersecurity practices on the Internet and counted the students' completion and grading of these practices. Based on the statistical data, we recommend appropriate new experiments for each student.

Experimental Results and Analysis. We did a satisfaction survey after the students completed the recommended new practice, and the experimental results are shown in Fig. 4. The students' satisfaction with the recommended practice is 74%, which indicates that the recommended practices are appropriate and attractive enough for most of the students. In addition, 21% of the students thought that the scheme could be improved, which could be due to the fact that the accuracy of the recommendation algorithm still needs to be improved or the diversity of the practice content needs to be further improved. This feedback can provide valuable input to improve the practice recommendation scheme. Overall, the majority of students felt that the scheme was effective for them and provided a sufficiently engaging learning experience. This is essential for promoting positive motivation and interest in the subject.

Afterwards, after the students completed the final exam, we compared the performance of the current students with the previous students in the final exam of the cybersecurity course, and the results of the experiment are shown in the Table 2. The experimental results show that the number of current students who participated in the recommended practices and scored more than 80 points in the final exam increased by 14% compared with the previous students. The number of students who scored less than 60 points decreased by 2%. This shows that the scheme facilitates the students to familiarize themselves with the knowledge points of the course and to improve their ability to combine theory and practice so that they can get better grades in the examination.

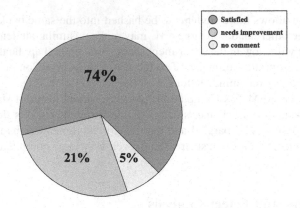

Fig. 4. The results of the experiment

The method recommends suitable practices to students, which improves their practical efficiency and practical operation level. Moreover, using the comprehensive practice score as the assessment standard for the practical part of the grade reflects students' mastery of the knowledge points in a more objective way than the previous standard of practice report. This not only improves the accuracy of the assessment, but also encourages students to actively participate in practical activities and develop their operational skills.

Overall, the application of partition-based matrix complementation scheme in network security course practice has achieved better results. It can provide students with personalized practice recommendations, improve the efficiency of practice and student interest. The assessment method of comprehensive experimental rating scores is used to more accurately assess students' practical ability. However, there is still some room for improvement to further enhance the accuracy of the recommendation algorithm and the diversity of the practice content to better meet students' needs and interests.

Table 2. Session Compare

	100–90	89–80	79–70	69–60	60–0
Current session	9%	58%	27%	4%	2%
Previous session	6%	47%	32%	11%	4%

7 Conclusion

In order to address the problem of recommending course practices for students that match their learning characteristics in the face of a wide variety of cybersecurity experiments in an intelligent educational system. This paper proposes a novel recommender scheme, which incorporates LSH and Matrix Completion to provide quick and high-quality recommendations. Specifically, by exploiting the good property of LSHs, our scheme adopts an LSH hash table to reorder students where similar students will be buffered in close positions. Based on the LSH hash table, the original student-practice rating matrix is partitioned into submatrices with each containing a group of similar students. Matrix Completion is then employed in the partitioned matrix to predict the missing ratings of a student for a practice.

To the best of our knowledge, this is the first work to improve the performance of Matrix Completion for information retrieval from extremely sparse and large-scale datasets without auxiliary data. Compared to the original rating matrix, the submatrix formed with our partition-based approach is significantly smaller and the rating ratio is much larger. Thus the recommender accuracy can be significantly increased while the computation complexity can be significantly reduced.

Acknowledgments. This work was partially supported by the National Natural Science Foundation of China [grant 62202156], the Teaching Reform and Research Project of Hunan University of Science and Technology [grant number 2021-76-9 and 2021-76-26], the Hunan Provincial Teaching Research and Reform Project [grant number HNJG-2022-0786 and HNJG-2022-0792], the Hunan Province Degree and Graduate Teaching Reform and Research Project [grant number 2022JGYB130].

References

1. Knapp, K.J., Maurer, C., Plachkinova, M.: Maintaining a cybersecurity curriculum: professional certifications as valuable guidance. J. Inf. Syst. Educ. **28**(2), 101 (2017)
2. Cabaj, K., Domingos, D., Kotulski, Z., Respício, A.: Cybersecurity education: evolution of the discipline and analysis of master programs. Comput. Secur. **75**, 24–35 (2018)
3. Bobadilla, J., Serradilla, F., Hernando, A., et al.: Collaborative filtering adapted to recommender systems of e-learning. Knowl.-Based Syst. **22**(4), 261–265 (2009)
4. Thorat, P.B., Goudar, R.M., Barve, S.: Survey on collaborative filtering, content-based filtering and hybrid recommendation system. Int. J. Comput. Appl. **110**(4), 31–36 (2015)
5. Wu, L., He, X., Wang, X., Zhang, K., Wang, M.: A survey on accuracy-oriented neural recommendation: From collaborative filtering to information-rich recommendation. IEEE Trans. Knowl. Data Eng. **35**(5), 4425–4445 (2022)
6. Fu, M., Qu, H., Yi, Z., Lu, L., Liu, Y.: A novel deep learning-based collaborative filtering model for recommendation system. IEEE Trans. Cybern. **49**(3), 1084–1096 (2018)
7. Burke, R., Felfernig, A., Göker, M.H.: Recommender systems: an overview. AI Mag. **32**(3), 13–18 (2011)
8. Wang, D., Liang, Y., Xu, D., Feng, X., Guan, R.: A content-based recommender system for computer science publications. Knowl.-Based Syst. **157**, 1–9 (2018)
9. Tarus, J.K., Niu, Z., Mustafa, G.: Knowledge-based recommendation: a review of ontology-based recommender systems for e-learning. Artif. Intell. Rev. **50**, 21–48 (2018)
10. Rosa, R.L., Schwartz, G.M., Ruggiero, W.V., Rodríguez, D.Z.: A knowledge-based recommendation system that includes sentiment analysis and deep learning. IEEE Trans. Industr. Inf. **15**(4), 2124–2135 (2018)
11. Yang, X., Steck, H., Guo, Y., Liu, Y.: On top-k recommendation using social networks. In: Proceedings of the Sixth ACM Conference on Recommender Systems, pp. 67–74 (2012)

12. Wang, X., Pan, W., Xu, C.: HGMF: hierarchical group matrix factorization for collaborative recommendation. In: Proceedings of the 23rd ACM International Conference on Conference on Information and Knowledge Management, pp. 769–778 (2014)
13. Abdi, M.H., Okeyo, G., Mwangi, R.W.: Matrix factorization techniques for context-aware collaborative filtering recommender systems: a survey (2018)
14. Luo, X., Zhou, M., Xia, Y., Zhu, Q.: An efficient non-negative matrix-factorization-based approach to collaborative filtering for recommender systems. IEEE Trans. Industr. Inf. **10**(2), 1273–1284 (2014)
15. Liu, H., et al.: EDMF: efficient deep matrix factorization with review feature learning for industrial recommender system. IEEE Trans. Industr. Inf. **18**(7), 4361–4371 (2021)
16. Yi, B., et al.: Deep matrix factorization with implicit feedback embedding for recommendation system. IEEE Trans. Industr. Inf. **15**(8), 4591–4601 (2019)
17. Jannach, D., Resnick, P., Tuzhilin, A., Zanker, M.: Recommender systems-beyond matrix completion. Commun. ACM **59**(11), 94–102 (2016)
18. Ramlatchan, A., Yang, M., Liu, Q., Li, M., Wang, J., Li, Y.: A survey of matrix completion methods for recommendation systems. Big Data Mining Anal. **1**(4), 308–323 (2018)
19. Chen, X., Lau, N., Jin, R.: Prime: a personalized recommender system for information visualization methods via extended matrix completion. ACM Trans. Interact. Intell. Syst. **11**(1), 1–30 (2021)
20. Quadrana, M., Cremonesi, P., Jannach, D.: Sequence-aware recommender systems. ACM Comput. Surv. (CSUR) **51**(4), 1–36 (2018)
21. Zhang, M., Chen, Y.: Inductive matrix completion based on graph neural networks, arXiv preprint arXiv:1904.12058 (2019)
22. Zhong, K., Song, Z., Jain, P., Dhillon, I.S.: Provable non-linear inductive matrix completion. In: Advances in Neural Information Processing Systems, vol. 32 (2019)
23. Ungar, L.H., Foster, D.P.: Clustering methods for collaborative filtering. In: AAAI Workshop on Recommendation Systems, Menlo Park, CA, vol. 1, pp. 114–129 (1998)
24. González-Manzano, L., de Fuentes, J.M.: Design recommendations for online cybersecurity courses. Comput. Secur. **80**, 238–256 (2019)
25. Natarajan, S., Vairavasundaram, S., Natarajan, S., Gandomi, A.H.: Resolving data sparsity and cold start problem in collaborative filtering recommender system using linked open data. Expert Syst. Appl. **149**, 113248 (2020)
26. Juan, W., Yue-xin, L., Chun-ying, W.: Survey of recommendation based on collaborative filtering. In: Journal of Physics: Conference Series, vol. 1314, p. 012078. IOP Publishing (2019)
27. Mehta, R., Rana, K.: A review on matrix factorization techniques in recommender systems. In: 2017 2nd International Conference on Communication Systems, Computing and IT Applications (CSCITA), pp. 269–274. IEEE (2017)
28. Barathy, R., Chitra, P.: Applying matrix factorization in collaborative filtering recommender systems. In: 2020 6th International Conference on Advanced Computing and Communication Systems (ICACCS), pp. 635–639. IEEE (2020)
29. Guan, X., Li, C.-T., Guan, Y.: Matrix factorization with rating completion: an enhanced SVD model for collaborative filtering recommender systems. IEEE Access **5**, 27668–27678 (2017)
30. Xu, B., Bu, J., Chen, C., Cai, D.: An exploration of improving collaborative recommender systems via user-item subgroups. In: Proceedings of the 21st International Conference on World Wide Web, pp. 21–30 (2012)
31. Chi, X., Yan, C., Wang, H., Rafique, W., Qi, L.: Amplified locality-sensitive hashing-based recommender systems with privacy protection. Concurr. Comput. Pract. Exp. **34**(14), e5681 (2022)
32. Hu, H., et al.: Differentially private locality sensitive hashing based federated recommender system. Concurr. Comput. Pract. Exp. **35**(14), e6233 (2023)

Experiment Teaching Case Design of Computer I/O Channel Virtual Simulation

Dongdong Zhang[1,2]($\boxtimes$), Xinyuan Cheng[1], Zhen Gao[2,3], Guofeng Qin[1,2], Jie Huang[2,3], and Lisheng Wang[1,2]

[1] College of Electronics and Information Engineering, Tongji University, Shanghai, China
ddzhang@tongji.edu.cn
[2] National Computer and Information Technology Experiment Teaching Demonstration Center, Tongji University, Shanghai, China
[3] College of Software Engineering, Tongji University, Shanghai, China

Abstract. The principle of computer composition is an important basic course for undergraduates majoring in computer science, in which the I/O channel control method in the input/output system is mainly applied to mainframes. However, mainframes that support I/O channel design experiments are expensive, complex and costly to operate and maintain, which makes it impossible to carry out hands-on experiments for large-scale students. In this paper, to break the situation that this part of content is mainly taught through textbook in traditional teaching, we design a virtual simulation experiment of computer I/O channel, which is an effective supplement to the practical teaching of computer composition principle. The experimental case has been applied in computer science and technology, information security and software engineering in Tongji University and other colleges and universities, and has been awarded Chinese national first-class course (Virtual Simulation Class). The experimental system has been opened and shared on Chinese national virtual simulation experiment teaching project sharing service platform (www.ilab-x.com). The experiment website is http://www.ilab-x.com/details/2020?id=7256.

Keywords: Computer I/O channel · Virtual simulation · Experiment teaching case · Principles of computer composition

1 Introduction

The Principle of Computer Composition is a core professional basic course for undergraduates majoring in computer science, and plays an important role in many hardware courses. It is a very technical, engineering and practical course. Its teaching requirements are: to master the basic composition of the computer and the basic knowledge of the operation principle, including the computer hardware design principle, debugging and operation and maintenance skills, while

W. Hong and G. Kanaparan (Eds.): ICCSE 2023, CCIS 2024, pp. 55–69, 2024.
https://doi.org/10.1007/978-981-97-0791-1_5

deepening the understanding of the computer's various functional components, as well as the whole computer hardware system composition and operation principle related content.

The course teaching process generally adopts the teaching method combining theory and practice. In order to deepen students' understanding of theoretical knowledge, many computer majors in domestic universities have carried out the construction of virtual simulation experiments. For example, Xi 'an Jiaotong University has established a virtual simulation experiment environment and designed a virtual simulation experiment of the instruction execution process. The experiment deepens students' understanding of instruction execution process and improves students' understanding of the Von Neumann architecture and how it works [2]. National University of Defense Technology proposed a set of customized teaching path of university computer basic virtual simulation experiment construction scheme, which can not only meet the teaching needs of training students' computational thinking, but also provide theoretical and practical reference for further expanding the content and form of virtual simulation experiment [15]. Shandong University has designed and built a highly realistic virtual simulation experiment teaching environment, allowing students to deeply understand the basic design principles of Von Neumann architecture, the structure organization and operation mode of computers [1]. Nanjing University of Science and Technology developed a virtual simulation experiment platform for the principle of computer composition, which consists of five functional components: arithmetic experiment, memory experiment, microprogram controller experiment and interrupt experiment [3]. Inner Mongolia University has researched and established a virtual simulation experiment teaching network platform, which can not only share teaching experiment resources, but also enhance students' practical ability and innovative consciousness [5]. On the basis of the national computer experiment teaching demonstration Center, Shenzhen University established the national network engineering virtual simulation experiment teaching Center, which achieved a breakthrough in the all-round sharing of teaching resources and the social sharing of large-scale experimental instruments and equipments [11].

Other universities use software to carry out virtual simulation experiments. For example, Dalian Maritime University proposed to introduce Proteus software into the experimental teaching of computer composition principles and carry out the virtual-real experimental teaching model based on the experimental box and Proteus virtual simulation technology [12]. Huazhong University of Science and Technology introduced Logisim virtual simulation experiment platform to develop and improve a series of designed experiments and course design, and achieved good results in practical application promotion [6]. South China Normal University proposed a practical teaching mode based on simulation design assistance. The simulation platform Logisim, which focuses on the cultivation of logical design ability, can not only cultivate students' ability of self-learning, problem analysis and solving, and logic design, but also improve the quality and efficiency of engineering verification experiments on experimental boxes [14].

At present, most of the virtual simulation experiments of computer major in China focus on the teaching content such as central processor and memory, and because the I/O channel control mode in the input and output system is mainly applied to the mainframes, the teaching content of this part cannot be practiced by students on the FPGA development board. The mainframe platform system supporting I/O channel is large in scale, complex in structure, expensive in price, limited in resources, complicated in operation and maintenance, and high in operation and maintenance cost, which leads to certain limitations in experimental teaching and open sharing.

To address the above issue, according to mainframe knowledge [4, 7–10, 13], our course team designed a computer I/O channel virtual simulation experiment, in line with the principle of "can be real, not virtual, virtual and real combination", to break the traditional teaching that this part of the content is mainly taught through textbook. The experiment not only effectively supplemented the practical teaching of the principles of computer composition, but also formed a complete practical teaching system for the whole course. The experiment enables students to have a comprehensive and in-depth understanding of the computer from the chip to the composition and working principle of the mainframe, to master the working principle of the computer I/O channel, information processing and control process, to cultivate the ability of students to link the theory to practice, and to lay a solid foundation for the practical process of the subsequent computer system courses.

2 Design of Experiment Case

2.1 The Purpose of the Experiment

This experiment is mainly to help computer major students understand the theoretical knowledge related to the input and output system of computer I/O channel. The low-level basic experiment involves two knowledge points: the structure and composition of I/O channel and the similarities and differences between I/O channel and DMA. The high level design and innovation experiment involves fours knowledge points: Byte Multiplexor Channel, Block Selector Channel, Block Multiplexor Channel, I/O channel design and optimization as shown in Fig. 1.

The Level of Knowledge and Ability that Students Should Achieve After Completing Low-Level Basic Experiments. (1) Can complete the definition and configuration of hardware and software of components at all levels of the I/O channel according to the basic experimental I/O channel architecture; (2) Master the architecture and composition of I/O channel, understand the similarities and differences between I/O channel and DMA; (3) Acquire basic skills in the construction, configuration, and management of mainframe I/O channel subsystems.

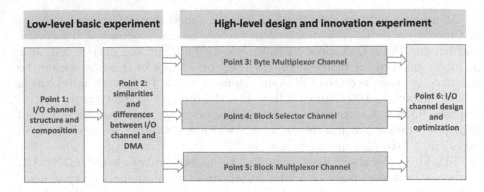

Fig. 1. Knowledge points in the course of computer composition principles corresponding to experiments

The Level of Knowledge and Ability that Students Should Achieve After Completing the Advanced Design Experiment. (1) Master the principle of data exchange mode of Byte Multiplexor Channel, Block Selector Channel and Block Multiplexor Channel; (2) Master the principle of I/O channel design and optimization; (3) Gain the ability to independently design and build I/O channel system according to the given application requirements; (4) Can correct errors and optimize the design according to the design feedback given by the experimental platform.

The Level of Knowledge and Ability that Students Should Achieve After Completing the Advanced Innovation Experiment. (1) Can decompose and solve complex engineering problems by integrating various resources with literature; (2) Have the ability to analyze and conduct overall design of I/O channel system for complex engineering applications; (3) Master the scientific method and cultivate innovative consciousness of designing I/O channel system for complex engineering problems.

2.2   The Content and Task of the Experiment

This experiment requires students to master the composition and working principle of I/O channel, understand the hierarchy and operating mechanism of I/O channel, and realize the virtual simulation design and optimization of I/O channel. The experiment consists of pre-class cognitive experiment, in-class low-order basic experiment and high-order design and innovation experiment, as shown in Fig. 2. The experiment contents and tasks are as follows:

Cognitive Experiments. Learn about mainframe components by reading mainframe equipment documentation. Observe and understand the I/O channel components of mainframe by mouse click, drag and scroll wheel, and understand the position relationship of channel subsystem in computer system.

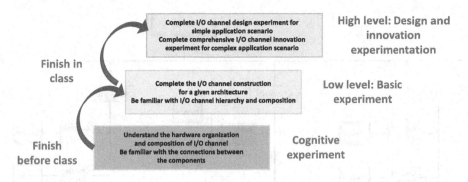

Fig. 2. The hierarchy of experiments

Basic Experiments. According to the basic I/O channel architecture, complete the definition and configuration of the hardware and software of each level component of the I/O channel, master I/O channel architecture and composition, understand the similarities and differences between I/O channel and DMA; Acquire basic skills in building, configuring, and managing a mainframe I/O channel subsystem.

Design and Innovation Experiment. Complete the independent design and construction of I/O channel for small-scale peripheral application scenario, master the principles of Byte Multiplexor Channel, Block Selector Channel, Block Multiplexor Channel, and I/O channel design and optimization; Complete the independent design and construction of I/O channel for large-scale peripheral application scenarios, understand the influence of different settings of channels, switches and control units on the construction of I/O architecture through exploration and trial, and master I/O channel design and analysis methods for complex engineering applications. After the completion of the channel design, the software gives a comprehensive evaluation of the I/O channel reachability and the maximum achievable transfer rate of the peripheral, according to which the I/O channel design can be further optimized by students until the requirement of this application is met.

2.3   The Principle of the Experiment

I/O Channel Architecture and Composition. In a mainframe system, there can be multiple channels. A channel can connect multiple device controllers, and a device controller can manage one or more I/O devices. Channels can provide an independent data and control path between I/O devices and memory, which is the multi-level hierarchical architecture of early mainframe I/O systems, as shown in Fig. 3.

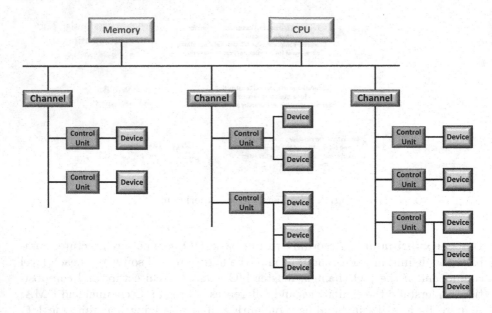

Fig. 3. Architecture of early mainframe I/O systems

In order to accommodate the I/O throughput requirements, most modern mainframe computers use channel switches to extend the connection between channels and control units, through which the control units can be connected to multiple channel subsystems, so that the control units and I/O devices in all subsystems can be shared, as shown in Fig. 4.

Similarities and Differences Between I/O Channels and DMA. Compared with DMA mode, both of them can establish a direct data transmission path between the I/O device and the main memory and improve the parallel processing between the CPU and I/O. DMA directly relies on pure hardware management of input and output, so it is only responsible for data transmission of high-speed devices. The I/O channel can complete the input and output management of peripheral initialization, interrupt, data transmission and so on through channel commands and hardware, so it can be applied to devices of various speeds. A DMA channel can connect to only one device, while a channel can connect to multiple devices.

Byte Multiplexor Channel. Byte Multiplexor Channel is a simple shared channel that mainly serves multiple low-speed or medium-speed peripherals.

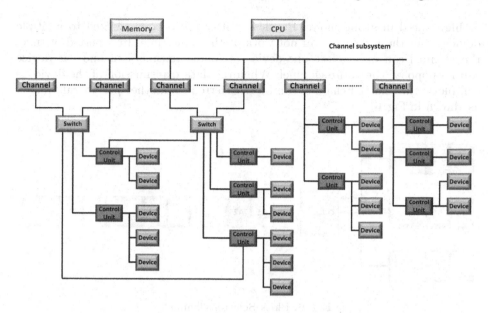

Fig. 4. Modern mainframe I/O system architecture

These devices typically share I/O channel in bytes, and there is a long wait between adjacent transmissions. It serve multiple I/O devices in turn in a way that is interleaved by bytes. Each channel connects to a peripheral, transmits only one byte, and then connects to another device, transmits another byte, as shown in Fig. 5.

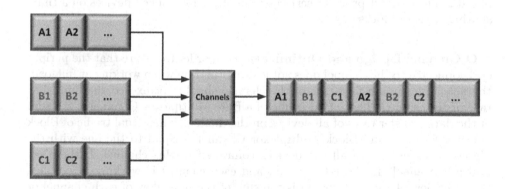

Fig. 5. Byte Multiplexor Channel

Block Selector Channel. Block Selector Channel is mainly used to connect high-speed peripherals, such as disks and tapes, and information is transmitted at high speed in group mode. Physically, it can also be connected to multiple devices, but these devices can not work at the same time. In a period of time, the channel can only select one device for data transmission, and the device can monopolize the entire channel. When the data transmission of the device is complete, the selected channel can be transferred to another peripheral service, as shown in Fig. 6.

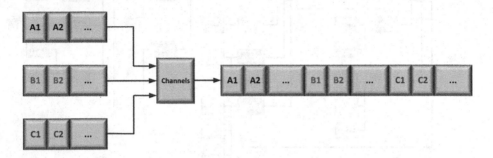

Fig. 6. Block Selector Channel

Block Multiplexor Channel. Block Multiplexor Channel is regarded as a combination of Byte Multiplexor Channel and Block Selector Channel. Like Block Selector Channel, it is also suitable for high-speed devices, but in a different way. It does not transfer all the data of the selected device at once, but re-selects other devices after the exclusive channel transmits a fixed-length block of data. Therefore, it provides services to multiple high-speed devices on a time-sharing basis in blocks of data.

I/O Channel Design and Optimization. In order to ensure that the peripheral connected to the channel does not lose information when working at full load, the actual maximum flow rate of the channel should not exceed the limit flow rate of the channel. The actual traffic of a Byte Multiplexor Channel is the sum of the data transfer rates of all devices on the channel. The actual traffic of Block Selector Channel and Block Multiplexor Channel is equal to the one with the highest transfer rate of all the devices connected to this channel. If there are multiple channels in the I/O system, and each channel is working in parallel, the limit flow of the I/O system is the sum of the limit flow of each channel or subchannel.

2.4   The Process and Requirements of the Experiment

The experiment involves a total of 12 steps, as shown in Fig. 7. Among them, step 1 is a pre-class cognitive experiment, step 2–6 is a low-order experiment during class, step 7–11 is a high-order experiment during class, and step 12 is an online test after class. These steps are described in detail as follows:

Step 1 Observe and understand the I/O channel components of mainframe, and understand the position relationship of channel subsystem.

Step 2 Based on the given I/O channel architecture, configure the processor and understand the meaning of the configuration properties.

Step 3 According to the given I/O channel architecture, select and configure the channel subsystem that meets the requirements.

Step 4 According to the given I/O channel architecture, configure the attributes of the channel switch, set up a reasonable port mapping matrix, and establish the routing path between the channel subsystem and the switch.

Step 5 According to the given I/O channel architecture, select and configure the appropriate control unit, and set up the data path between the control unit and the channel switch through the interconnection between the ports.

Step 6 According to the given I/O channel architecture, various devices were reasonably configured, and the data path between the control unit and device was constructed.

Step 7 According to the requirements of comprehensive design experiment, complete mainframe internal channel construction.

Step 8 According to the requirements of comprehensive design experiment, complete mainframe external channel design and construction.

Step 9 Check the channel reachability. If it does not meet the design experiment requirements, optimize the I/O channel architecture.

Step 10 According to the requirements of innovation design experiment, complete the design and construction of high-load I/O channel system.

Step 11 Check the channel reachability and the maximum achievable transfer rate of the peripheral. If it does not meet the requirements of innovative experiment, it is necessary to optimize the I/O channel architecture.

Step 12 Complete the test questions and submit the experimental results.

3   Teaching Guidance and Evaluation of the Experiment

3.1   Teaching Guidance of the Experiment

This experiment adopts a comprehensive teaching method that combines online and offline, in class and out of class, theory and practice. The experimental teaching process includes three stages: pre-class cognitive experiment, in-class low-order basic experiment, high-order design and innovation experiment, after-class test and experiment report writing, as shown in Fig. 8.

Pre-class Cognitive Experiment Stage (Step 1). Before the experiment, the teacher opens the course platform. Students can understand the experiment purpose, preview the experiment principle and get familiar with the experiment method by browsing the experiment introduction module on the platform. Select the device cognition experiment module, observe various I/O components

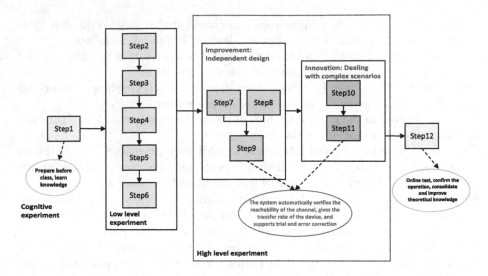

Fig. 7. The step diagram of the experiment

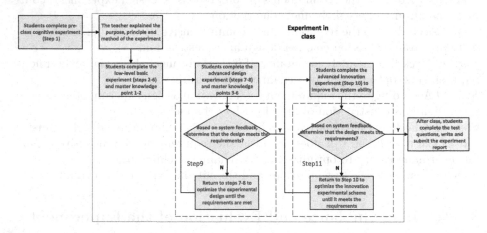

Fig. 8. The teaching process of the experiment

through interactive operations such as mouse click, drag and scroll, get familiar with the location of each component and the position relationship between each other, and establish a perceptual understanding of the I/O channel system.

Experiment Teaching Stage in Class. The experimental teaching stage includes the following processes:

Process 1. The teacher explains the purpose, principle and method of the experiment. Taking IBM mainframe I/O channel system as an example, as shown in Fig. 9, the teacher introduced the I/O channel architecture and composition, the similarities and differences between I/O channel and DMA, Byte Multi-plexor Channel, Block Selector Channel, Block Multiplexor Channel, I/O channel design and optimization principle and other knowledge.

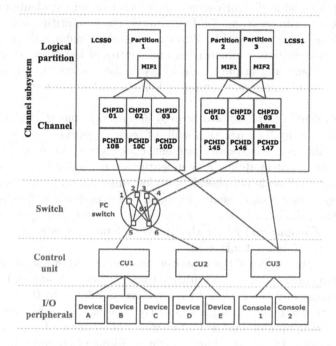

Fig. 9. Multilevel hierarchy of mainframe I/O system

When the teacher explains the experimental method, it is necessary to focus on the principle of classifying and managing different types of I/O devices in multiple channels of the mainframe I/O system, the design elements of I/O channels, the calculation and optimization method of the actual reachable transfer rate of I/O peripherals. In this way, students are encouraged to design I/O channel systems that meet application requirements for I/O peripherals with different speed requirements (including printers, scanners, tapes, disks, consoles, etc.) and improve the utilization rate of I/O channels.

Process 2. Students complete low-level basic experiments (Steps 2–6). Students click on the basic experimental module of I/O channel and complete the experimental steps 2–6 successively according to the multi-level hierarchical structure of the I/O system in Fig. 9. Through the configuration of the attributes of I/O components at various levels, such as CPU, logical channel subsystem, logical partition, channel, switch, control unit and peripheral, realize the construction of logical channel subsystem, channel switch data exchange path, data path between control unit and channel switch, and data path between I/O peripheral and control unit, so as to complete the construction of the entire I/O channel system.

The logic engine of the experimental platform will monitor the students' experimental process according to the constraint rules between different levels, and support trial and error correction, which will help students understand the structure and composition of I/O channels, the similarities and differences between I/O channels and DMA. Through this experimental design, students can master the definition, configuration and control of hardware at all levels of I/O channel system, and acquire basic skills in the construction, configuration and management of large-scale computer I/O channel subsystem.

Process 3. Students complete an advanced design experiment (Steps 7–8). On the basis of mastering the operation skills of basic experiment steps and understanding relevant knowledge points, students click on the I/O channel design and innovation experiment module, independently design and build an I/O channel system serving small-scale peripherals with low, medium and high speed according to the application requirements. Through this experimental design, students can master the principle of data exchange mode of Byte Multiplexor Channel, Block Selector Channel and Block Multiplexor Channel, master the principle of I/O channel design and optimization.

The logic engine system of the experimental platform allows students to freely design hierarchical architecture of multiple channels in the design and innovation experiment stage, and the design does not have to adhere to the fixed process for architecture design and configuration. By clicking, dragging and dropping, students can bring up any level of I/O channel components at any time, add or remove components as needed. Through the windows of component properties, port configuration and path selection, students can adjust the design scheme and make trial and correct error at any time, and instantly optimize the design of the I/O channel architecture.

Process 4. Students examine high-level design experiment based on system feedback (Step 9). After students submit the design experimental scheme, the experimental platform will test the accessibility of channels and automatically light up each accessible channel. Students will check whether the I/O channel architecture meets the design requirements. If it does not meet the design requirements, they will repeat steps 7–8 to optimize the design scheme and verify it again. The system records scores based on channel accessibility and violations of I/O channel hierarchy constraints.

Process 5. Students complete the Advanced Innovation experiment (Step 10). On the basis of understanding the three I/O channel data transmission modes and the principle of I/O channel design optimization, students design and build an I/O channel system serving large-scale I/O peripherals with low, medium and high speed by integrating various resources according to the application requirements of complex scenarios and referring to literature. Students can make trail and correct error in various situations, improve the ability to analyze and solve complex engineering problems, master the scientific method and cultivate innovation consciousness of designing I/O channel system for complex engineering problems.

Process 6. Students examine high-level innovation experiment based on system feedback (Step 11). After students submit the innovative experimental design scheme, the experimental platform will test the accessibility of the channel. Students will check whether the channel path meets the requirements of the question. If it does not meet the requirements, analyze and find out the reasons, repeat step 10, and optimize the I/O channel.

The experiment platform will also give the actual transmission rate of each device in extreme cases, and students will consider whether the design requirements have been met according to the feedback results. If not, the problems existing in each data transmission mode will be analyzed according to the constructed I/O channel, and the application of various data transmission modes will be considered. Then step 10 will be repeated to optimize the I/O channel until the device transmission rate meets the requirements.

After-School Experiment Stage (Step 12). After the end of the experiment in class, students can review the experiment in any environment with Internet and computer, optimize the experiment design, complete the knowledge point assessment test, and write and submit the experiment report.

3.2   The Evaluation of the Experiment

Experimental teaching adopts a five-in-one innovative evaluation system of "process assessment"+"design assessment"+"knowledge assessment"+"student self-assessment"+"teacher evaluation". The logic engine provided by the experiment platform will completely record all the operation steps and processes of all students in the experiment process. The process assessment is made according to the number of students violating the constraint relationship in the I/O channel configuration rules during the experiment process. The design assessment is made according to the accessibility of the student channel design and the reachable rate of the I/O peripheral. Knowledge assessment is evaluated based on the accuracy of the test questions finished by students online. After the completion of the experiment, the students make a self-evaluation of the experiment harvest and experience, and submit it to the platform. The teacher gives a comprehensive evaluation according to the students' assessment results and self-evaluation, and makes a statistical analysis of the time spent by students and the number of mistakes in the experiment process, so as to timely adjust the teaching content.

4   Characteristics of the Experiment

4.1   The Experiment Design Is Highly Simulated and Can Service Multi-level Talent Training

The experiment platform uses 3D technology to reconstruct the physical structure of the IBM Z10 mainframe of Tongji University and accurately model and simulate the mainframe I/O channel system. The experiment accurately reproduces the configuration process of I/O component properties at all levels, such as CPU, logical channel subsystem, logical partition, channel, switch, control unit, and device, and the construction process of logical channel subsystem, channel switch data exchange channel, data path between control unit and channel switch, and data path between I/O peripherals and control unit. Thus, the dynamic reconfigurable experimental environment of the whole I/O channel system is formed.

The experimental design can meet the training needs of all kinds of large-scale computer design and research talents majoring in computer science at different levels in higher vocational colleges, junior colleges, general undergraduate colleges, 985, 211 universities.

4.2   The Experiment Design is Highly Exploratory and Can Stimulate Students' Interest in Learning

The experimental platform enables students to explore the influence of different settings of key components such as channels, switches and control units on the construction of I/O architecture when designing Byte Multiplexor Channel, Block Selector Channel and Block Multiplexor Channel architectures in the design and innovation experiment stage. The platform can give timely feedback on the I/O channel architecture designs submitted by students. Students use the feedback to determine whether they need to continue to optimize the design. The repeated exploration and optimization process will stimulate students' interest in learning, and help students deeply understand the principle, process and optimization method of data exchange of the three I/O channel types.

4.3   The Experiment Design is Flexible Enough to Meet the Demand of Cultivating Students' Innovative Ability

The experimental platform allows students to design dynamically reconfigurable hierarchical architecture of I/O channel system freely in the design and innovation experiment stage, and the design does not have to adhere to the fixed process for architecture design and configuration. By clicking, dragging and dropping, students can bring up any level of I/O channel components at any time, add or remove components as needed. Through the windows of component properties, port configuration and path selection, students can adjust the design scheme at any time, instantly optimize the design of I/O channel architecture, and cultivate students' innovation ability.

5   Conclusion

We propose a teaching scheme based on IBM mainframe to design computer I/O channel virtual simulation experiment, and carry out practical teaching from three levels: equipment cognition experiment, low-order I/O channel basic experiment, and high-order I/O channel design and innovation experiment, so as to meet the training needs of computer professionals in multi-level universities and fill the gap in domestic I/O channel experiment teaching. The experiment platform allows students to design dynamically reconfigurable I/O channel system hierarchy according to the actual engineering application requirements, and the design does not have to be confined to a fixed process. The logic engine independently developed by the platform can monitor the experimental process of students, support trial and error correction, and students can adjust the design scheme according to the feedback of the system, immediately optimize the architecture design of I/O channel, which improves their computer system design and research ability.

References

1. Cai, X., et al.: Design and discussion of instruction execution virtual simulation for von neumann computers. Exp. Technol. Manag. **39**(5), 89–93 (2022)
2. Chen, L., Fang, C., Huang, X.: Case design and exploration of university computer experiment teaching in problem-oriented and virtual simulation mode. Ind. Inf. Educ. **5**, 90–94 (2023)
3. Dai, L., Zhu, H.: Research on the construction of virtual simulation "golden course" - taking the principle of computer composition as an example. Comput. Knowl. Technol. **18**(26), 89–90, 93 (2022)
4. Fremstad, P., et al.: IBM system Z10 enterprise class technical guide (2009)
5. Gao, Y., He, Y.: Construction and practice of computer virtual simulation experiment teaching platform. Softw. Guide **21**(8), 183–187 (2022)
6. Hu, D., Tan, Z., Wu, F.: Research on virtual simulation practice teaching of "principles of computer composition" course. J. Electr. Electron. Teach. **40**(4), 113 116 (2018)
7. IBM Corporation: ESCON and FICON Channel-to-Channel Reference
8. IBM Corporation: Hardware Configuration Definition User's Guide
9. IBM Corporation: Input/Output Configuration Program User's Guide for ICP IOCP
10. International Business Machines Corporation: Mainframe concepts
11. Ming, Z., Cai, M., Zhu, A.: Construction of high-level virtual simulation experiment teaching center with virtual-real combination. Lab. Res. Explor. **36**(11), 146–150, 165 (2017)
12. Sang, G., Liu, Z.: Computer composition principle simulation experiment teaching research. Educ. Mod. **7**(95), 19–22 (2020)
13. White, B., et al.: IBM Z connectivity handbook (2018)
14. Wu, J., Zhong, Q., Zeng, B.: Application of virtual simulation technology in the experimental teaching of computer composition principle. Comput. Educ. **3**, 34–38 (2019)
15. Zhou, H., Jia, N., Zhang, J., Zhou, J., Wu, D., Ning, W.: University computer basic virtual simulation experiment design and practice. Comput. Educ. **3**, 154–158 (2023)

Four-Step: The Whole-Process of Project Practice Teaching and Its Effectiveness Evaluation Based on Apriori

Gang Cen$^{(\boxtimes)}$ (iD), Zeping Yang (iD), Yuefeng Cen (iD), and Shuai Jiang (iD)

Zhejiang University of Science and Technology, Hangzhou, China
gcen@163.com, cyf@zust.edu.cn

Abstract. In order to solve the problem of lack of innovation and practice ability of students in the field of software engineering talent training in China, it has become an important task to train applied talents with innovation consciousness and ability. From the perspective of application-oriented talent training, this work proposes a whole-process project practice teaching model called the *four-step*, and evaluates its effectiveness. The model aims to cultivate application-oriented talents with innovation awareness and ability. It is implemented through such activities as open innovation practice base, student science and technology innovation project and university student discipline competition. Based on the autonomous approach, this model combines the professional curriculum within the teaching plan and the practice teaching of independent planning to meet personalized and free practice teaching needs of students. This paper also presents an evaluation model based on the Apriori algorithm for *four-step*. The evaluation of teaching effectiveness is conducted through seven evaluation indicators, including subject competition practice and outcome promotion. The experimental results show that the *four-step* whole-process project practice teaching mode has significant effectiveness in cultivating innovative applied software engineering talents. This paper provides a new teaching practice model for the training of software engineering professionals in colleges and universities, and verifies its effect on the improvement of innovation ability.

Keywords: project practice · whole-process · Apriori · talent training

1 Introduction

The mismatch between the demand for high quality education and the supply of high quality education resources is a major problem facing the development of software engineering education. Training applied talents with innovative ability and consciousness is an important task of software engineering talents training, which can provide services for the economic development of the whole region. Amidst the context of the "Internet+" era, enhancing the quality of engineering innovation talent development has been a core issue in engineering education.

W. Hong and G. Kanaparan (Eds.): ICCSE 2023, CCIS 2024, pp. 70–86, 2024.
https://doi.org/10.1007/978-981-97-0791-1_6

Numerous scholars have conducted in-depth analyses of talent development in the field of software engineering, focusing on aspects such as the demand for innovative capabilities and the cultivation of innovative awareness. Xiu [1] proposed that in the era of big data, it is necessary to actively reform the teaching model and pay attention to the cultivation of students' practical ability and innovative ability. Tang [2] pointed out that students majoring in software engineering should have strong innovation ability, innovation consciousness and innovation thinking when discussing the basic abilities that students should possess. Tao [3] pointed out that the talent development goals in the field of software engineering are to cultivate applied talents with a solid foundation, practical orientation, and outstanding abilities. According to Zhang and Yang [4], the cultivation of innovative awareness cannot be achieved merely through a 45-min "transmission" in the classroom. It requires the adoption of diverse teaching methods and a progressive approach to foster students' innovative consciousness. On the other hand, Wang, Zhang, and Wu [5] emphasized the orientation towards societal needs and place particular emphasis on developing students' entrepreneurial and technical skills. They highlight that innovation capability and innovative spirit are two important quality evaluation indicators in the process of talent development in software engineering. Compared to traditional curriculum-based learning, the cultivation of extracurricular practical teaching has gradually become a research focus in many applied universities. However, there is a lack of a systematic and comprehensive practical teaching system.

Project-based Learning (PjBL) is a systematic teaching and learning method based on actual projects. It is based on the constructivism theory, emphasizing the transformation and construction of knowledge. In comparison to inquiry-based learning (IBL), which revolves around posing questions, and problem-based learning (PBL), which focuses on problem-solving, PjBL places greater emphasis on students' application of previously acquired knowledge and skills, their practical abilities, and self-management skills. Additionally, PjBL also involves the production of tangible outcomes [6,7]. Indeed, PjBL contributes to the holistic development of students' abilities in various aspects. It is a typical variant of collaborative and inquiry-based learning, characterized by students' active engagement and inductive learning [8]. As a form of practical teaching, PjBL fosters critical thinking and problem-solving skills, interpersonal communication, information and media literacy, collaboration, teamwork and leadership, creativity, and innovative abilities. It is an effective method for cultivating new types of applied talents [9]. Chen and Yang [10], through a meta-analysis, demonstrated that PjBL has a certain impact on students' academic achievement. Factors such as disciplinary domain, school location, educational stage, duration of practice, environmental support, and group size played important roles in this regard. Regarding teamwork in PjBL, Hernández-García [11] utilized the Comprehensive Training Model for Teamwork Competencies (CTMTC) to track and analyze teamwork in PjBL. The study confirmed that students' autonomous communication, coordination, and collaboration abilities are important factors influencing the effectiveness of teaching. Therefore, in the process of PjBL, it is crucial to create a student-centered practical environment, with projects at the core of teaching [12,13]. The establishment of a conducive practical environment and the quality of projects are prerequisites for the smooth implementation of PjBL. Specifically, a well-constructed student-centered practical environment provides students with positive, engaging, and meaningful learning experiences, thereby stimulating their interest and motivation to learn. Additionally, the quality of the projects is also a key element in PjBL. A high-quality project design and implementation offer students challenging, practical, and collaborative learning tasks, encouraging them to apply their acquired knowledge and skills to solve real-world problems while fostering their innovative thinking and problem-solving abilities.

This work proposes a whole-process of project practice teaching model called the *four-step*. It is applied to the process of cultivating applied talents in the field of software engineering and evaluates its effectiveness. Based on constructivist theory and the *Conceive, Design, Implement and Operate*(CDIO) concept, short for conceive, design, implement and operate, this practical teaching model utilizes real-world projects as the vehicles for each stage of practical learning. In the *four-step*, students have the autonomy to choose their practice environment, project content, guiding teachers, and learning partners. Through the four stages of project design, practice, management, and evaluation, students complete the entire PjBL process. Different from the traditional approach where projects are developed within specific courses, the *four-step* emphasizes an independent and project-centered mode of practice. It operates independently of traditional classroom teaching and advocates for the mutual reinforcement of theoretical and practical teaching.

2   The Design of the *four-step*

2.1   The Problems of Applied Universities in China

As a whole-process project practice teaching mode, the *four-step* mainly solves the main problems faced by local application-oriented undergraduate colleges and universities in several aspects of teaching, which is also part of the factors affecting the project teaching quality.

The lack of systematic and professional engineering practice environments has posed challenges in meeting students' diverse, comprehensive, individualized, and optimized development needs. Currently, most PjBL models primarily revolve around courses. However, course instructors often struggle to provide a comprehensive and well-developed practical environment, only meeting partial requirements of the current course. This situation not only hampers students' comprehensive development but also hinders teamwork and affects the effectiveness of the practice. Therefore, there is an urgent need to establish a comprehensive engineering practice environment to fulfill students' need for deep involvement. Such a practice environment should be systematic and professional, allowing students to engage in every stage from planning, design, implementation, to evaluation. Only then can students truly face real-world problems and challenges, solve them through collaboration with peers and mentors, and culti-vate creativity, problem-solving abilities, and a spirit of teamwork.

In many Chinese universities, the practical components of undergradu-ate education, such as open experiments, disciplinary competitions, scientific research projects, papers, and patents, are often conducted independently, lack-ing overall synergy. This poses challenges to the sustainable development of stu-dents' innovative abilities, divergent thinking, problem-solving skills, and team collaboration spirit. To address this issue, there is an urgent need for systematic top-level design to ensure the interconnectedness of these practical components and maximize their comprehensive effects.

Currently, there are several issues in Chinese universities that have resulted in unsatisfactory outcomes in practical teaching. For instance, the practical teach-ing components are excessively passive, and students lack opportunities for active participation and proactive exploration. To address these issues, we need to change the traditional injection education model and turn to experiential prac-tice education to improve the effectiveness of practice teaching. It is essential to ensure that students actively participate in practical projects and receive neces-sary guidance and support. Furthermore, the roles of teachers and mentors need to be transformed from being mere knowledge providers to becoming facilitators and guiders who inspire students' innovative potential and practical abilities.

2.2 The Solution Provided by the *four-step*

Practice Environment Construction. Based on the CDIO engineering edu-cation philosophy, we are committed to construct an engineering practice envi-ronment for whole-process project practice teaching. The CDIO engineering edu-cation philosophy adheres to a constructivist view of knowledge, emphasizing the active cognitive construction of learners and the iterative improvement of arti-facts. This involves learners gradually engaging in the development and applica-tion of products, processes, and project lifecycles. To construct a comprehensive and effective whole-process practice environment, we need to focus on both the hardware and software aspects simultaneously [14,15].

In terms of the physical environment, we need to provide a place suitable for students' independent practice and equip it with necessary instruments, among others. By improving the physical environment, we can ensure that students have the necessary support to successfully complete the entire project and the entire practical process. To achieve this, we plan to establish a comprehensive project practice base and prepare corresponding practice venues and equipment resources. We can also collaborate with external partners such as companies and research institutions to enhance the professionalism of the practice base.

In terms of the non-material environment, we aim to establish a comprehen-sive and well-rounded learning resource repository through Internet technology. This repository will provide design and development systems, application tools, and learning materials necessary for practical activities. Additionally, we form a professional team of instructional mentors and further enhance the development of teaching staff by establishing mentors' studios.

Whole-Process Project Practice Teaching Model. To construct the whole-process project practice teaching model with project as the main line, we have adopted a project-centered teaching approach, dividing the project practice process into four steps: basic project practice, scientific and technological innovation practice, scientific and technological competition practice, and outcome consolidation and promotion practice. This model aims to guide students to gradually participate in project practice activities and enhancing their practical and engineering skills through different stages of practice. Firstly, students familiarize themselves with and experience the whole-process of project practice teaching through participation in foundational innovation practice. Then, they engage in scientific and technological innovation practice by building their own mainline projects, forming teams, and collaborating on development. In the practice bases, students are required to refine their projects and deepen their understanding and application of relevant knowledge and skills. To enhance students' motivation and engagement in *four-step*, they participate in scientific and technological competitions with their mainline projects in the next stage. This step serves to not only evaluate the effectiveness of students' practice but also motivate them to unleash their full potential.

Five-Autonomies. Implementing project practice learning in a manner named *five-autonomies*. In this context, *five-autonomies* means: selecting practice content autonomously, building practice teams autonomously, selecting practice time autonomously, managing the practice base autonomously, and selecting practice mentors autonomously. The establishment of a whole-process project practice base provides more possibilities for students to engage in project practice. In this way, students are able to carry out practical activities in a freer environment. They can choose the right practical content according to their own interests and goals, and form multidisciplinary teams with students from different grades and disciplines to participate in the project practice. During the process of practical teaching, students have greater autonomy, allowing them to manage the practice base and project progress independently, thereby unleashing their creativity and proactiveness. The *five-autonomies* not only empowers students to take a more active role in their own learning but also fosters their teamwork and self-management skills. Students can continuously experience, explore, and innovate during the practice, enhancing their problem-solving abilities and creativity. Moreover, the *five-autonomies* promotes personalized development, enabling individualized learning goals and paths to be achieved.

The structure of the *four-step* is shown in Fig. 1.

2.3 Whole-Process Project Practice Teaching

The *four-step* aims to establish a comprehensive teaching paradigm outside of the traditional university curriculum. It serves as both a supplement and support to the content of the traditional university curriculum, as well as an extension and practical application of professional courses. It plays a complementary role

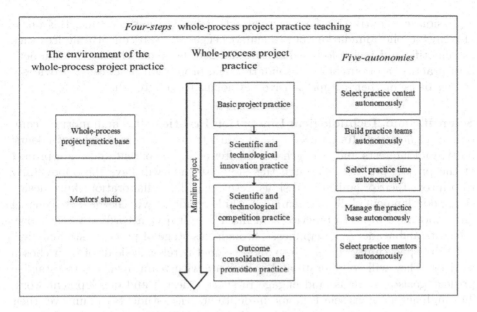

Fig. 1. Structure of the *four-step* whole-process project practice teaching

to a certain extent. In the *four-step*, the whole-process is reflected in the following steps.

Basic Project Practice. It is the first step of the whole-process project practice teaching, aiming to let students explore and experience from the starting point of practice. By visiting the innovation practice base, students can personally experience the atmosphere and resources of the practice environment, and gain insights into advanced tools, equipments, and practical techniques. Additionally, they have the opportunity to interact with existing members of the practice teams, learn about their project achievements and share experiences, which can inspire and motivate them. During this step, students will have the opportunity to form teams and choose relatively simple and fundamental practice projects. These projects aim to help students become familiar with the process and methods of the whole-process project practice, while cultivating their teamwork and problem-solving abilities. Students can choose suitable project topics based on their interests and professional directions. Under the guidance of the instructors, they gradually plan, design, and implement their projects. Through hands-on activities and teamwork during the practice, students will gradually understand and grasp the concepts of active cognitive construction and upward spiral, which are central to the CDIO engineering education philosophy. As the starting point of the whole-process project practice teaching model, basic project practice provides students with a platform for experimentation and exploration. By participating in this foundational practice phase, students can gradually understand the importance and value of project practice, and develop a passion and motivation for practical activities. At the same time, this phase also lays a solid foundation for students to engage in subsequent practices such as scientific and technological innovation, scientific and technological competition practice, and outcome consolidation and promotion practice. It provides a strong basis for their comprehensive development and growth.

Scientific and Technological Innovation Practice. It is an important component of *four-step*. Its purpose is to optimize team structure based on students' individual interests and strengths, and determine the content and main project of the project practice. Through this step, students will have the opportunity to improve their organizational skills, research skills, collaboration skills, design skills, development skills and teamwork skills. Students will choose a challenging and innovative topic to practice as a main line project according to their own interests and academic disciplines. Through this stage of practice, students will have the opportunity to delve into and explore the relevant fields of their chosen project. They will collaborate and coordinate with team members to establish project goals and plans, and engage in specific design and development work. Through autonomous selection and in-depth practice, students can uncover their own potential and creativity, enhance their competitiveness and adaptability in the field of technology.

Scientific and Technological Competition Practice. In this step, students will face higher requirements and challenges. They need to further refine and enhance the outcomes of their previous stage of project practice to meet the evaluation criteria and requirements of scientific and technological competitions. Throughout the process, students need to delve deeper into the knowledge of relevant fields, improve their understanding and grasp of the competition topics, and apply their acquired knowledge and skills to creatively solve problems, demonstrating unique insights and abilities. Scientific and technological competition practice requires students to possess good project management skills. Students need to develop detailed project plans, allocate resources effectively, control project progress, and ensure timely completion of project deliverables. They also need to write comprehensive documents, including project reports, software technical documentation, etc., to showcase the outcomes and value of their projects. Additionally, students are required to clearly express their ideas and achievements through forms such as presentations and exhibitions, enhancing their public speaking skills and communication abilities.

Outcome Consolidation and Promotion Practice. It is the final crucial step of the whole-process project practice teaching model. Students summarize, refine, and transform their previous project practice outcomes to further disseminate and apply the knowledge and experience gained. Outcome consolidation and promotion practice primarily involves presenting and disseminating project practice outcomes through writing papers, filing for intellectual property rights, participating in academic conferences, and other means. Through writing papers, students can systematically summarize and organize the outcomes of their project practice, showcasing the academic and practical abilities they have gained through the practice. The process of applying for intellectual property rights requires students to conduct in-depth technical research and literature review, further deepening their understanding and application of project practice outcomes. It not only protects their innovative achievements but also provides opportunities for students to transform and commercialize their practical outcomes.

2.4   Experiment and Results

Experimental Process. First, we established a whole-process project practice base called Blue Space within the campus. Additionally, we created corresponding renowned teacher studios and provided an environment in relevant professional laboratories to support students' project practice activities. Through the student-developed resource sharing system and project management system in the practice base, we have built a well-equipped software environment, offering students convenient tools and resources. Our experimentation spanned from 2015 to 2022, with over 500 students participating in this endeavor.

The students participating in this experiment started engaging in the *four-step* and practical activities in the Blue Space from their freshman year in university. They conducted project practice following the teaching model of *four-step*. In the second stage, we required students to select and construct their own mainline projects based on their personal interests and professional strengths. They were also required to rebuild and optimize their teams for the new projects. For example, there was a team that focused on the theme of "Tourism Management System" and developed multiple related projects and software systems revolving around this theme. In the third stage, we required students to improve and refine their previous achievements and use them as competition entries to participate in scientific and technological competitions related to their projects. For example, a team developed software systems such as "AI-based Comprehensive Tourism Monitoring and Dispatching System" and "West Lake Impression" as part of the "Tourism Management System" mainline project. These systems were utilized in various interdisciplinary competitions, and the team received honors and awards for their accomplishments. Finally, in the last stage of the project practice, some participating students will write relevant academic papers based on their previous achievements and participate in academic exchanges to summarize and share their experiences and outcomes in the project practice. They also have the opportunity to apply for intellectual property rights for new technologies, products, or methods developed during the project practice, in order to protect and promote their innovative achievements.

Experimental Result. After seven years of experimentation, some students completed the entire whole-process project practice teaching, while others only completed a few steps. Overall, students showed improvement in practical skills and teamwork abilities. In terms of software project development, most students who underwent the *four-step* were able to handle projects independently. They learned key skills such as requirement analysis, system design, coding implementation, and software testing through project practice, enabling them to independently carry out software development work. This laid a solid foundation for their future career development and innovative capabilities. In the second step, students completed a total of 253 projects covering various topics. Through autonomous selection of main projects and in-depth practice, they continuously expanded their knowledge and skills. The completion of these projects not only demonstrated students' professional qualities and innovative abilities but also provided them with valuable practical experience and problem-solving skills. In the third step, students participating in the whole-process project practice teaching received 319 awards in discipline competitions. By applying their project practice outcomes to competitions, they showcased their unique insights and innovative achievements in relevant fields. These honors not only recognized students' individual abilities but also demonstrated the effectiveness and achievements of our comprehensive PjBL model. In the final stage, students published 87 academic papers and applied for 15 invention patents. This showcased their research outcomes and academic contributions in practice and effectively protected and transformed new technologies and methods from project practice.

3   Effectiveness Analysis

For this teaching model, we employed a series of relevant methods for effectiveness analysis to ensure the credibility and accuracy of the research. We utilized quantitative research methods and collected a large amount of student data. By statistically analyzing and assessing students' academic performance, project outcomes, participation in scientific competitions, and publication of papers, we were able to quantitatively evaluate the impact of the *four-step* on students' academic achievements and comprehensive abilities. This approach provided objective data support, enabling us to conduct statistical analysis and comparisons and draw reliable conclusions.

3.1   Association Rule Mining and Apriori Algorithm

Association rule mining was first proposed by Agrawal [16,17], and it is one of the most active research methods in data mining [18]. Association rules were originally used to solve the shopping basket problem to find associations between different kinds of goods in a commodity transaction database. These connections reflect the purchasing habits of customers, which can be used as a basis for scientific shelf design and commodity inventory arrangement.

In association rules, items are used to refer to the things involved, and Itemset is a collection of different items. The sum of all the elements in the item set is the length of the item set, and the item set of length K is called the K-item set. Sample set Y is a subset of item set I. Sample database D contains all samples.

Support and Confidence are two key indicators to evaluate the quality of an association rule. Support is used to indicate how likely a rule is to occur. Confidence is used to indicate how reliable a rule is.

$$A : M \Rightarrow N \tag{1}$$

where $(M \subset I, N \subset I, M \cap N = \emptyset)$ are two sub-item sets of item set I. A is the association rule between M and N.

$$S(A) = \frac{count(M \cup N)}{|D|} \tag{2}$$

$$C(A) = \frac{count(M \cup N)}{count(M)} \tag{3}$$

where S(A) is the support degree of rule A, and C(A) is the confidence degree of rule A. $Count(M \cup N)$ is the number of samples in sample set Y that contain both item sets M and N. count(M) is the number of samples containing item set M in sample set Y. $|D|$ is the number of all samples contained in sample database D.

The minimum support degree of association rules is expressed by S_{min}, and the minimum confidence degree is expressed by C_{min}. If rule A meets both conditions $S(A) \geq S_{min}$ and $C(A) \geq C_{min}$, then association rule A is called strong association rule, which has important guiding significance for guiding practical decisions.

Apriori algorithm is a commonly used data mining algorithm in the field of association rule mining. The algorithm iterates through layer by layer search to obtain candidate sets, and then searches frequent item sets (that is, item sets whose support degree is higher than the minimum support degree) on the basis of which k-1 item sets are used to search K item sets. Apriori algorithm has two important properties:

1. The subset of frequent item set must be frequent. If item set M,N is frequent item set, M and N are frequent item set.
2. The superset of infrequent item sets must be infrequent. If item set M is not frequent item set, M,N and M,O are not frequent item sets either. Where, M, N and O are independent item sets.

3.2   Effectiveness Evaluation Model Based on Apriori Algorithm

In the implementation process of *four-step*, it is very important to test the cultivation effect. For the relationship between the practical teaching of *four-step*, this paper proposes an effectiveness evaluation model that uses Apriori algorithm to evaluate the teaching effect.

The evaluation mode includes seven aspects: Theoretical basis, basic project practice, scientific and technological innovation practice, scientific and technological competition practice, outcome consolidation and promotion practice, technical practice and graduation project. In the theoretical score part, the academic scores of professional courses are selected, and the weight is set according to the credit level to get the score of theoretical scores. The basic project practice includes the results of some basic experimental courses and the practical results obtained by participating in teachers' scientific research projects. In the part of scientific and technological innovation practice, scientific and technological competition practice, outcome consolidation and promotion practice, we set different scores for different levels of project approval, competition award and achievement publication according to the incentive policy of software engineering major of Zhejiang University of Science and Technology (ZUST). In this way, students can objectively evaluate their achievements and contributions in the project practice. The implementation process of the effectiveness evaluation model is shown in Fig. 2.

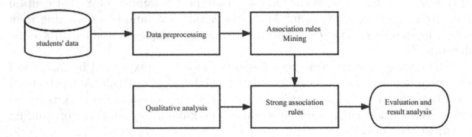

Fig. 2. The basic process of evaluation model

The effectiveness evaluation model comprises two key aspects. Firstly, we established connections between seven phases and students' participation in the *four-step* and utilized the Apriori algorithm to reveal the potential relationships among these phases and the impact of practical teaching on each phase. This helps us gain a deep understanding of the interactions between different phases and evaluate their effects on students. Secondly, based on the degree of influence on the quality of cultivating innovative and applied talents, we assigned different weights to the seven phases. The purpose is to balance the importance of each phase in fostering students' comprehensive abilities and derive the final evaluation scores for students who participated or did not participate in the *four-step*. By establishing the connections between phases and participation and setting weights accordingly, we can comprehensively consider students' performance in each phase and obtain an integrated evaluation score. Such an evaluation model allows us to more accurately assess students' comprehensive abilities and practical level, providing targeted feedback and guidance for their growth. Therefore, the establishment of the effectiveness evaluation model not only helps us reveal the effectiveness of the four steps but also provides a scientific assessment tool for schools to measure the quality of cultivating innovative and applied talents. This is of great significance for teaching improvement and nurturing outstanding talents.

3.3   Evaluation of Model Experiments and Results

This paper uses the data of students majoring in software engineering from 2014 to 2022. We use A-G to represent the links in the seven evaluation modes: Theoretical basis, basic project practice, scientific and technological innovation practice, scientific and technological competition practice, outcome consolidation and promotion practice, technical practice and graduation project. The seven sections are scored on a scale of 1–6.

Before participating in the four-step, students are required to undergo a series of assessments, including evaluating their programming foundation, teamwork ability, and project competition experience. As a result, the proportion of students who participate in the *four-step* is relatively low, accounting for approximately 15% of the total number of students. Consequently, when it comes to setting the test parameters, both the minimum support and the minimum confidence are set at 10% to ensure a reasonable threshold for analysis.

Through data collection, the Apriori algorithm is utilized to mine the data of students participating in the *four-step*. As a result, we have identified 190 items for frequent 1-itemsets, 279 items for frequent 2-itemsets, 125 items for frequent 3-itemsets, 18 items for frequent 4-itemsets, and 2 items for frequent 5-itemsets. After screening, we have obtained 15 association rules with significant reference, which have been sorted in descending order of support. In the association rules, Y represents participation in the *four-step*, F_1 indicates achieving level 1 in the technical internship evaluation, and so on. Table 1 presents the trial results of some students who participated in the *four-step*.

Table 1 indicates that students who participate in the *four-step* have a higher probability of performing well in technical practice, basic project practice, and graduation project, with probabilities exceeding 40% and exhibiting a high level of confidence. Additionally, there is a probability of more than 30% for these students to possess a strong theoretical and practical foundation. Furthermore, the probability of engaging in activities such as paper publication, patent acquisition, or software work publication in the outcome consolidation and promotion practice is close to 30%. Students with a solid foundation in innovation and practice are more likely to excel in technical practice. Moreover, by participating in the *four-step*, students have the opportunity to enhance themselves comprehensively in all aspects of outcome consolidation and promotion practice.

Through the application of the Apriori algorithm, data mining was conducted for students who did not participate in the *four-step*. The results revealed 91 items for frequent 1-itemsets, 244 items for frequent 2-itemsets, 380 items for frequent 3-itemsets, 319 items for frequent 4-itemsets, 133 items for frequent 5-itemsets, and 21 items for frequent 6-itemsets. After applying filtering techniques, 15 association rules with reference significance were obtained and sorted based on descending order of support. In Table 2, N represents not participating

Table 1. Results of participated in the *four-step*

No.	Association rules	Support	Confidence level
1	$F_1 \Rightarrow Y$	50.0%	100%
2	$B_2 \Rightarrow Y$	46.9%	100%
3	$G_3 \Rightarrow Y$	43.8%	100%
4	$A_2 \Rightarrow Y$	34.4%	100%
5	$A_2 \Rightarrow B_2 \Rightarrow Y$	31.3%	100%
6	$E_5 \Rightarrow Y$	28.1%	100%
7	$B_3 \Rightarrow F_1 \Rightarrow Y$	28.1%	100%
8	$Y \Rightarrow D_3$	21.9%	21.9%
9	$F_1 \Rightarrow Y \Rightarrow G_3$	18.8%	37.5%
10	$E_5 \Rightarrow Y \Rightarrow C_5$	18.8%	66.7%
11	$E_5 \Rightarrow Y \Rightarrow B_2$	18.8%	66.7%
12	$E_5 \Rightarrow G_2 \Rightarrow Y$	15.6%	100%
13	$E_5 \Rightarrow F_1 \Rightarrow Y$	15.6%	100%
14	$D_4 \Rightarrow E_5 \Rightarrow Y$	12.5%	100%
15	$E_5 \Rightarrow G_2 \Rightarrow Y \Rightarrow C_5$	12.5%	80%

in the *four-step*, and C_6 denotes an evaluation of grade 6 in the practice section of the science and technology project, and so forth. The table presents the results of some trials where students did not participate in the *four-step*.

From Table 2, it can be observed that among software engineering students who did not participate in the *four-step*, there is a probability of over 40% for those with good theoretical and innovative foundations to exhibit poor performance in the three links of scientific and technological innovation practice, scientific and technological competition practice, and outcome consolidation and promotion practice. Additionally, due to the lack of targeted training in these three core links, the probability of students performing well in technical practice and graduation project is also relatively low. In the outcome consolidation and promotion practice, which reflects students' innovation awareness and abilities, software engineering students who did not participate in the *four-step* also show a lack of outstanding performance.

Based on the practical experience and theoretical methods of the *four-step*, the percentages for the seven links in the overall evaluation score are set as follows: 5%, 10%, 15%, 20%, 30%, 10%, and 10%. Since the improvement of students' abilities through the *four-step* is mainly reflected in the three links of scientific and technological innovation practice, scientific and technological competition practice, outcome consolidation and promotion practice, higher weights are assigned to these three links in the final evaluation stage. The comparison of the overall evaluation scores between students who participated and those who did not participate in the *four-step* is shown in Fig. 3.

Table 2. Results of didn't participate in the *four-step*

No.	Association rules	Support	Confidence level
1	$C_6 \Rightarrow D_6 \Rightarrow E_6 \Rightarrow N \Rightarrow A_2$	50.0%	100%
2	$C_6 \Rightarrow D_6 \Rightarrow E_6 \Rightarrow G_3 \Rightarrow N$	49.1%	100%
3	$B_3 \Rightarrow C_6 \Rightarrow D_6 \Rightarrow E_6 \Rightarrow N$	47.7%	100%
4	$C_6 \Rightarrow D_6 \Rightarrow E_6 \Rightarrow N \Rightarrow B_2$	45.3%	45.3%
5	$A_2 \Rightarrow C_6 \Rightarrow D_6 \Rightarrow E_6 \Rightarrow N \Rightarrow B_2$	41.4%	81.4%
6	$C_6 \Rightarrow D_6 \Rightarrow E_6 \Rightarrow F3 \Rightarrow N$	45.3%	45.3%
7	$C_6 \Rightarrow D_6 \Rightarrow E_6 \Rightarrow G_3 \Rightarrow N \Rightarrow A_2$	21.1%	42.9%
8	$C_6 \Rightarrow D_6 \Rightarrow E_6 \Rightarrow F_3 \Rightarrow N \Rightarrow G_3$	19.6%	69.1%
9	$C_6 \Rightarrow D_6 \Rightarrow E_6 \Rightarrow N \Rightarrow F_1$	18.2%	18.2%
10	$B_2 \Rightarrow C_6 \Rightarrow D_6 \Rightarrow E_6 \Rightarrow G_3 \Rightarrow N \Rightarrow A_2$	17.2%	90.7%
11	$A_2 \Rightarrow C_6 \Rightarrow D_6 \Rightarrow E_6 \Rightarrow G_3 \Rightarrow N \Rightarrow B_2$	17.2%	81.7%
12	$A_2 \Rightarrow C_6 \Rightarrow D_6 \Rightarrow E_6 \Rightarrow G_2 \Rightarrow N \Rightarrow B_2$	14.7%	80.8%
13	$C_6 \Rightarrow D_6 \Rightarrow E_6 \Rightarrow N \Rightarrow G_1$	14.4%	14.4%
14	$B_3 \Rightarrow C_6 \Rightarrow D_6 \Rightarrow E_6 \Rightarrow F_3 \Rightarrow N \Rightarrow A_3$	11.9%	89.5%
15	$B_3 \Rightarrow C_6 \Rightarrow D_6 \Rightarrow E_6 \Rightarrow F_3 \Rightarrow N \Rightarrow G_3$	10.2%	76.3%

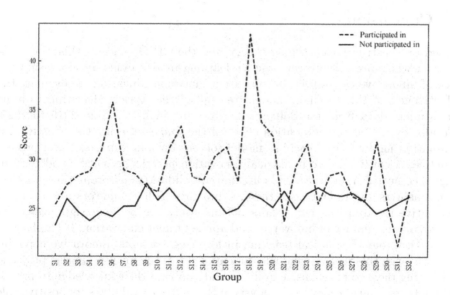

Fig. 3. Comparison of the overall assessment scores of students who participated and did not participate in the *four-step*

We compared the overall evaluation scores of 32 software engineering students who participated in the *four-step* with those who did not participate. The ratio of participants to non-participants was 1:9, meaning that 9 randomly selected non-participating students' average overall evaluation scores were calculated and compared with the participating students. As shown in Fig. 3, the probability of students who participated in the *four-step* obtaining a higher overall score than those who did not participate is greater than 80%. Upon analyzing the original data, it was found that participating students generally scored higher in the outcome consolidation and promotion practice. This, combined with the analysis, confirms that the *four-step* has a certain effect in cultivating innovative and applied talents in software engineering. For students who participate in the *four-step* whole-process project practice teaching and receive low overall evaluation scores, it is necessary to use the test data to identify problem areas and conduct specific analysis based on the actual situation.

By mining and analyzing the data of students who participated and those who did not participate in the *four-step*, we can gain a clear understanding of the differences and connections in the practical teaching aspects between the two groups. The trial results highlight the existing issues in the *four-step*, such as management modes and assessment methods, which need further improvement. It is necessary to address the shortcomings in the teaching model and make targeted improvements. In the future, based on further analysis, research, and improvement of the *four-step*, successful experiences can be extended to related majors and disciplines.

4   Conclusion

Based on constructivist learning theory and the CDIO concept, this work proposes a whole-process project practice learning model aimed at addressing the lack of innovative capabilities in software engineering education. To evaluate the effectiveness of this teaching model, we applied the Apriori algorithm to mine the student data from the Software Engineering in ZUST from 2015 to 2022. We also examined the cultivation effect of the *four-step* using the effectiveness evaluation model. This teaching model focuses on four aspects: Basic project practice, scientific and technological innovation practice, scientific and technological competition practice, and outcome consolidation and promotion practice. These aspects aim to cultivate students' practical skills, teamwork abilities, and innovative capabilities. The results of this study are of great significance for improving the quality of innovative and applied talent cultivation. It emphasizes the critical role of practical teaching in fostering students' innovative capabilities. Through this teaching model, students are actively involved in real projects, enhancing their comprehensive abilities and applying their knowledge to practical contexts. The effectiveness analysis of the *four-step* validates its positive role in software engineering education, providing valuable insights and references for educational reform in universities.

Acknowledgements. This paper was supported by the grants from Zhejiang Xinmiao Talents Program(No. 2023R415026), the Teaching Research and Reform Project of Zhejiang University of Science and Technology: Research and Practice of Multi-campus Collaborative Open Project Practice Form (No. 2023-JG02) and Zhejiang University of Science and Technology Graduate Research Innovation Fund

References

1. Xiu, X.: Analysis on training mode of software engineering innovative talents in big data era. Dig. Commun. World **5**, 235 (2020)
2. Tang, Y., Chen, K., Han, Y.: Exploration of training mode of innovative and entrepreneurial talents in applied undergraduate colleges: a case study of software engineering major in jilin university of agricultural science and technology. Employ. Secur. **13**, 96 (2021)
3. Tao, Y., Shang, C.: The enlightenment of CDIO program to innovation of higher engineering education. J. Higher Educ. **11**, 81 (2006)
4. Zhang, H., Yang, H.: Research on software development talent cultivation model based on blended teaching. Mod. Trade Ind. **43**, 72 (2022)
5. Wang, F., Zhang, B., Wu, X.: Research on the cultivation mode of innovative talents in software engineering majors of applied undergraduate programs. Comput. Educ. **5**, 116 (2018)
6. Oguz-Unver, A., Arabacioglu, S.: A comparison of inquiry-based learning (IBL), problem-based learning (PBL) and project-based learning (PJBL) in science education. Academia J. Educ. Res. **2**, 120–128 (2014)
7. Panasan, M., Nuangchalerm, P.: Learning outcomes of project-based and inquiry-based learning activities. Online Sub. **6**(2), 252–255 (2010)
8. Loyens, S.M.M., Kirschner, P., Paas, F.: Problem-based learning. APA Educ. Psychol. Handb. Appl. Learn. Teach. **3**, 403–425 (2010)
9. Chu, S.K.W., Reynolds, R.B., Tavares, N.J., Notari, M., Lee, Y.C.W.: 21st Century Skills Development Through Inquiry-Based Learning. Springer, Heidelberg (2021). https://doi.org/10.1007/978-981-10-2481-8
10. Chen, C.H., Yang, Y.C.: Revisiting the effects of project-based learning on students' academic achievement: a meta-analysis investigating moderators. Educ. Res. Rev. **26**, 71–81 (2019)
11. Hernández-García, Á., Acquila-Natale, E., Chaparro-Peláez, J., Conde, M.Á.: Predicting teamwork group assessment using log data-based learning analytics. Comput. Hum. Behav. **89**, 373–384 (2018)
12. Conde, M.A., Colomo-Palacios, R., García-Peñalvo, F.J., Larrucea, X.: Teamwork assessment in the educational web of data: a learning analytics approach towards iso 10018. Telemat. Inf. **35**(3), 551–563 (2018). https://doi.org/10.1016/j.tele.2017.02.001. sI: EduWebofData
13. Fidalgo-Blanco, Á., Sein-Echaluce, M.L., García-Peñalvo, F.J., Ángel Conde, M.: Using learning analytics to improve teamwork assessment. Comput. Human Behav. **47**, 149–156 (2015)
14. Cen, G., Lin, X., Fang, Y.: Exploring the reform of engineering applied talents cultivation model: An example of "four steps" talents cultivation model of Zhejiang university of science and technology. J. Zhejiang Univ. Sci. Technol. **28**, 136 (2016)
15. Cen, G., Lin, X., Mo, Y.: Exploration and practice of open-ended practical teaching innovation by 'four steps' - using application-oriented talent cultivation mode of German for reference. J. Zhejiang Univ. Sci. Technol. **27**, 371–375 (2015)

16. Wu, X., Mo, Z.: Frequent item set mining optimization method based on aproiri algorithm. Comput. Syst. Appl. **23**, 124 (2014)
17. Agrawal, R., Imieliński, T., Swami, A.: Mining association rules between sets of items in large databases. In: Proceedings of the 1993 ACM SIGMOD international conference on Management of Data, pp. 207–216 (1993)
18. Jiang, N., Feng, X., Wang, D.: Analysis of medication pattern of professor Feng Xinghua in the treatment of ankylosing spondylitis. Appl. Comput. Syst. **23**(6), 124 (2014)

Research and Practice on the Reform of Undergraduate Personalized Talent Training in the School of Computer and Information Science

Ping Zhang[✉], Lili Fan, Jiashu Dai, and Tao Liu

School of Computer and Information Science, Anhui Polytechnic University, Wuhu, China
{pingzhang,liutao}@ahpu.edu.cn

Abstract. With the construction of new engineering, the development of engineering education has put forward new requirements and challenges for talent training. Since 2017, a personalized talent training model based on the characteristics of disciplines and specialties has beed explored through the innovation and entrepreneurship education. In order to deepen the achievements of the reform, "8+8" whole process education, classified culture, "Five Entries" and all-staff and all-round education have been applied on the reform of undergraduate personalized talent training, which complete the main construction tasks of training program, training mode, growth path and student-centered concept.

Keywords: New engineering · Engineering education · "Five Entries" ·
Personalized Talent Training · Student-centered

1 Introduction

In order to implement the educational policy and the fundamental task of cultivating morality and talents, the school of computer and information science of Anhui Polytechnic University has carried out innovative activities based on student associations since its establishment. With the construction of new engineering disciplines[1], the development of engineering education has put forward new requirements and challenges for innovation and entrepreneurship education. Since 2017, the project team has been exploring innovative and entrepreneurial talent cultivation models based on disciplinary and professional characteristics through the "Five Entries" approach. These approaches have deepen the reform of innovation and entrepreneurship education in secondary colleges and universities, constructed the "12345" innovation and entrepreneurship education work system, and cultivated a group of composite new engineering professionals with innovation and entrepreneurship capabilities.

According to the notice "Implementation Measures of Anhui Polytechnic University of Engineering on Deepening the Comprehensive Reform of Three Comprehensive Education and Improving the Effectiveness of Education Practice", and in combination with the "three comprehensive and six specialized"[2] education work plan of the college, an "8+8" education system has been established, with the goal of building first-class majors[3]. This system includes pre-training from the summer before entering the school, fully utilizing 8 holidays to improve the level of system application development, innovation spirit, and labor literacy, strengthening the knowledge accumulation and ability to solve complex engineering problems over 8 semesters.

According to the educational requirements of the "Implementation Plan for the Three Full and Six Specialized Courses of Anhui Engineering University" and the spirit of "Implementation Plan for Deepening the Reform of Undergraduate Personalized Talent Training" of Anhui Polytechnic University, the college offers top-notch experimental classes to lay a solid professional foundation for students' academic development and assist in the development of their scientific research and innovation abilities. Introduce enterprises to schools, establish Chery Milk vetch classes and industrial internet enterprise classes, promote the integration of industry and education in collaborative education, continuously facilitate communication and cooperation with the government and industry enterprises, and stimulate potential motivation for students to serve society, employment and entrepreneurship. Offering data science and big data minor courses to cultivate interdisciplinary and interdisciplinary interdisciplinary talents.

With the support of the school's personalized talent cultivation[5] policy, the college implements the principle of "Simultaneous Development of Five Educations and Five advancements". In addition to increasing the number of courses, building online and offline course resources, increasing course openness, and providing guarantees for building a curriculum system that meets the requirements of the credit system, rich and colorful activities for the "six majors" has been carried out. Activities such as scientific research education, entrepreneurship and innovation lecture halls, innovation training camps, industry and enterprise expert series reports, employment and postgraduate entrance examination teacher-student exchange meetings, and exchange of experiences between senior and senior students are organized. Based on teaching cases of science education integration and industry education integration, the colledge promotes the construction of a personalized talent training system[6] that is "more interdisciplinary, professional, and integrated" through competitions to promote learning and encourage entrepreneurship (Fig. 1).

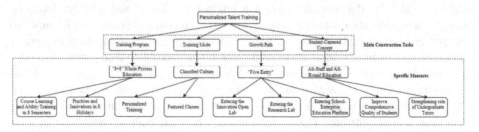

Fig. 1. Architecture of Personalized Talent Training System.

2 Construction Objectives and Concepts

According to the needs of social and industrial development, student-centered concept should be strengthened, which means teaching students according to their aptitude, and provide personalized training[7]. A multi-level, multi-type, and multi-path talent training mechanism should be constructed to accelerate the construction of high-level under-graduate education, and cultivate socialist builders and successors with comprehensive moral, intellectual, physical, aesthetic, and labor development. Adhering to the princi-ples of educating people for the country, following the laws of educational development and student growth, and meeting the needs of social and industrial development, it is necessary to strengthen student-centered education, individualized training, and build a multi-level, multi-type, and multi-path talent cultivation mechanism. Accelerating the construction of high-level undergraduate education is indispensable to cultivate socialist builders and successors with comprehensive moral, intellectual, physical, aesthetic, and labor development.

Through the reform of the credit system, the "Three Plans" (Compound Talent Plan, Top Talent Plan, and Excellent Talent Plan) should be implemented to highlight the broad caliber, solid foundation, strong ability, and personalization, which constructs a "one student, one policy" talent training plan. Utilizing the school's cross integration platform, innovation and entrepreneurship education center, discipline research room, and modern industry college to expand personalized growth space, cultivate indepen-dent learning ability, and enhance students' comprehensive literacy. Actively promote the construction of a personalized talent training system that is more interdisciplinary, professional, and integrated, and effectively cultivate high-quality applied talents with a solid foundation, broad knowledge range, innovative spirit, and practical ability for comprehensive development of morality, intelligence, physical fitness, aesthetics, and labor (Fig. 2).

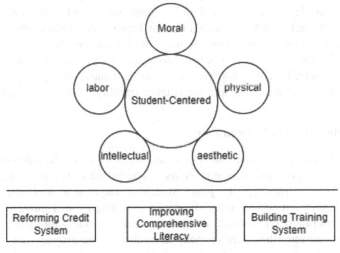

Fig. 2. Objectives and Concepts.

3 Main Construction Tasks

3.1 Personalizing Talent Training Program

It is important to strengthen the top-level design of training programs. Adhering to the simultaneous development of five educations, and increasing credits for cross elective courses and professional training directions, the students are cultivated with interdisciplinary and interdisciplinary knowledge. During the 8-semester teaching process, the objectives of each course are carefully implemented to strengthen students' ability to solve complex engineering problems. By assigning different tasks for 8 holidays to enhance students' self-learning ability, innovation ability, practical ability, and lifelong learning ability, strong support is provided for personalized training. Through Strengthening guidance on the purpose and motivation of students' participation in the second classroom, achieving linkage between the first and second classrooms, and expanding personalized growth space, high-quality applied talents are cultivated with comprehensive development of morality, intelligence, physical fitness, aesthetics, and labor.

3.2 Optimizing Talent Training Mode

We encourage students to join enterprise customized classes, top-notch experimental classes, minor majors and micro majors for different modes of learning according to their personal development direction, and further refine the classified training[8]. By Opening top-notch experimental classes, which are driven by research projects, and focusing on the postgraduate entrance examination and research projects, the students' basic research ability has been improved in computer science. We set up enterprise customized classes and joint training with enterprises, including summer project practice, visiting enterprises, teaching by enterprise tutors and other activities. Students who have spare efforts to choose secondary majors such as minor majors and micro majors are guided, so that students can broaden their horizons and expand their ideas, effectively integrate professional knowledge, technology and application fields, reflect the educational characteristics of "more cross cutting, more professional and more integrated", and achieve the college's "trained people" to accurately connect with the "people in need" of the society. Figure 3 displays the numbers of the teaching projects in recent five years, which concentrate on optimizing talent training mode of the students.

3.3 Improving Student Growth Path

"Five Entries" should be carried out simultaneously to promote the cultivation of personalized talents[9]. Through college students' participation in teams, projects, events, laboratories, and enterprises, each junior student is required to first enter the team, study in the innovation and open activity room according to their interests, and carry out research and practice in projects and events, so as to guide senior students to enter enterprises or continue their further study according to the professional rules, so as to realize personalized training. By Strengthening students' personalized innovation

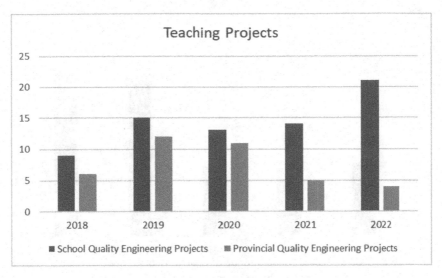

Fig. 3. Teaching Project Number.

and entrepreneurship education, strengthening practical training in personalized training, integrating with industry, the students are cultivated with innovative spirit, strong problem-solving ability, and good collaboration ability.

3.4 Establishing Student-Centered Consciousness

With students as the center[10], we will build a full-time education team of teachers, counselors, teaching managers, undergraduate tutors, supervisors and other staff, and a linkage management mechanism for the construction of study style. Adhere to the working principle of "combining education guidance, standardized management and quality education", and promote the scientific, systematic, institutionalized and standardized activities in the second classroom. Carry out scientific research and education report, mass entrepreneurship and innovation lecture, innovation training camp, series of reports of enterprise experts, teacher-student exchange meeting for employment and postgraduate entrance examination, experience exchange between seniors and sisters, production and labor during holidays, volunteer service, idea leading activities, literary and sports activities, and help in difficulties to achieve all-round education. Figure 4. Demonstrates the number of the teachers who receive teaching training outside the university every year to meet the requirements of improving the abilities of the students.

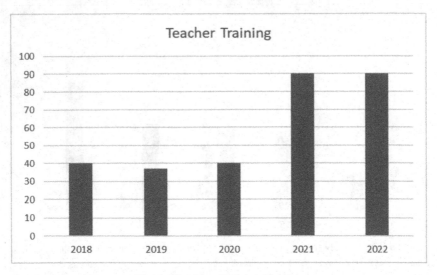

Fig. 4. Teaching Training Number.

4 Specific Measures

4.1 "8+8" Whole Process Education

Course Learning and Ability Training of 8 Semesters: With the goal of building a first-class major[11], taking the professional certification of engineering education as the starting point, and taking the talent training objectives and graduation requirements as the guidance, we should strengthen the ability training, set up the training system and curriculum, reform teaching methods, and carry out project-based or case-based teaching, and cultivate students' ability to solve complex engineering problems. By optimizing the course objectives, updating the course content, constantly expand students' vision and comprehensive quality, the course assessment is strictly implement to set the proposition according to the syllabus, and eliminate the problem of "water drainage" when teachers set the proposition and score. According to the detailed rules for the implementation of the curriculum team and the person in charge of the curriculum team in the school of computer and information technology (Provisional), we should strengthen the construction of grassroots teaching organizations, integrate curriculum resources and teachers, promote curriculum construction and teaching research, deepen the reform of curriculum system and teaching content, and improve the quality of talent cultivation. The teaching quality evaluation mechanism is improved to analyze the learning situation every semester, evaluate the achievement of students' graduation requirements and continue to improve. Guided by social needs, deeply integrate the local economy, reasonably set up practical teaching links, optimize experimental training, course design, cognition practice, production practice, comprehensive practice of professional direction, graduation design (Thesis) and other teaching contents, and improve students' ability to solve complex engineering problems.

Practices and Innovations in 8 Holidays: According to the "pre-school summer vacation and post school summer vacation", students of different grades and different needs are assigned different tasks, and a series of activities are carried out after the start of school to consolidate and apply the learning results. In October of the first semester of Freshmen's enrollment, they submitted their works to participate in the "College of computer and information Freshmen's digital literacy foundation competition". Sophomores participated in the undergraduate programming competition of the school of computer and information technology. Junior and senior non postgraduate students submit innovative practice reports at the beginning of school, and the college organizes awards. Senior students who take the postgraduate entrance examination submit review plans or weekly notes for the postgraduate entrance examination, or participate in the core courses of computer science organized by the college.

Labor practice is increased and winter vacation learning content is enriched. The winter vacation tasks include: first, preparing for the competition or the works of College Students' innovation and entrepreneurship projects. The second is the cultivation of labor habits and quality. In learning the general construction course – "labor education", we provide rich resources, add all students to the course according to the class, and assign a supervisor for each class to urge students to work. Third, the sophomores and juniors preview the professional core courses in advance to cultivate their self-learning ability according to the different courses or practical tasks arranged for different grades; The comprehensive training and graduation design (Thesis) of the second semester of freshman and senior will be mentioned to the beginning of the winter vacation, and the winter vacation will be used to cultivate their practical ability.

4.2 Classified Culture

Personalized Training: Adhering to the five education simultaneously, the top-level design of the training program is strengthened. Through moral education, the "four histories" education is integrated into the "curriculum ideological and political education", which improves physical education, aesthetic education and labor education, and cultivate high-quality application-oriented talents with strong professional foundation, strong engineering ability, sufficient innovation consciousness and comprehensive development of morality, intelligence, physique, art and labor. All majors increase the credits of interdisciplinary elective courses to promote the integration of interdisciplinary knowledge. Some majors are trained in two professional directions. Majors provide more elective courses and set up training program courses in advance. Provide students with more choices, choose courses, teachers, class time and learning process independently, allow students to take elective courses across majors, grades, colleges and schools, and formulate personalized training plans. Let students with spare capacity have more autonomy and choice in learning, and cultivate students' awareness of autonomous learning. During the winter vacation, the work arrangement meeting of individualized training students' course selection guidance was held, and undergraduate tutors were organized to guide students to develop personal learning plans and guide course selection. At the same time, the college strengthens the construction of cross platform courses and provides high-quality computer courses for the school.

Featured Classes: Starting from grade 2022, an experimental class of computer science and technology top-notch class will be set up, which will be driven by research projects[12], take the postgraduate entrance examination and research projects as the starting point, improve students' basic research ability in computer science, encourage students to join the scientific research team, carry out preliminary research work in the team mentor project, create a strong learning atmosphere, create opportunities for collaborative training in teaching and scientific research, strengthen students' innovative literacy training, and lay a solid foundation for students' academic development, Integrate high-quality resources inside and outside the University, participate in academic exchanges, and help students develop their scientific research ability and innovation ability.

Facing the needs of local industries, according to the four professional characteristics of our college, and in combination with Wuhu's "Milk Vetch Talent Plan" and "action plan for accelerating the cultivation of industrial Internet talents", we set up enterprise customized classes - Milk Vetch (Chery) class and Milk Vetch (Industrial Internet) class. Give full play to professional advantages, integrate enterprise resources, carry out corporate culture publicity, work flow visit, practice teaching co construction and employment of industry professors, jointly cultivate undergraduates, and realize the "trained people" of the University accurately connect with the "people in need" of the society.

Students who have spare capacity are guided to choose secondary majors such as minor majors and micro majors, especially the study of courses in economics and management, humanities, law, and art, so as to further broaden students' horizons and broaden their thinking, and organically integrate technologies such as big data, cloud computing, artificial intelligence, Internet of things, software development, information security, and blockchain with other disciplines to make up for the lack of knowledge in the application field. Our college plans to set up a minor major of "data science and big data technology" to help the school cultivate personalized talents.

4.3 "Five Entries"

Entering the Laboratory and the Competition: The innovation and Entrepreneurship Education Center of the college has 8 innovation and open activity rooms in different directions, including computer, network and software applications, Internet of things, smart cars, programming, robots, big data and artificial intelligence, MCU and embedded. Each activity room carries out a series of activities such as "Laboratory Open Day", "innovation practice training camp", "innovation literacy training camp", organizes students to participate in a variety of competitions, and provides support for students to enter laboratories and competitions. Organize student teams to participate in all kinds of discipline competitions at all levels step by step in accordance with the guiding principle of "start, advance and transformation", form a discipline competition pattern of "one room and multiple competitions", and cultivate students' innovation ability and entrepreneurial awareness. Guide freshmen to enter the innovation and development activity room as soon as possible, and all students from grade 2021 will join the activity room according to their own interests. Figure 5 shows the number the school-organized competitions, the number of the participated competitions and the number the awards of category A competitions, which fulfills the requirement of entering the laboratory and the competition.

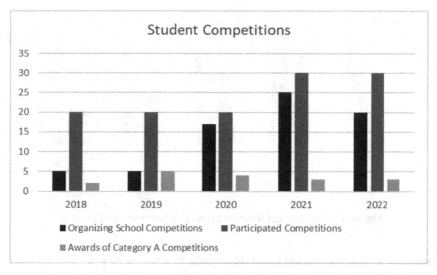

Fig. 5. Student Competitions

Entering the Team and the Project: The college has set up 9 research rooms in different directions, including machine learning and intelligent robots, pervasive computing and security, multimodal big data processing and analysis, trusted computing and system structure, pattern recognition and application, computer vision and intelligent perception control, data mining and knowledge engineering, intelligent software engineering, imaging technology and interactive systems, to encourage students to enter scientific research teams and research projects, and cultivate students' research ability. Taking the top-notch experimental class as a pilot, we will build a scientific research education system, cultivate students' pragmatic scientific research attitude, abide by academic ethics, carry out innovative activities, give full play to the function of scientific research education, and deepen the integration of science and education. Figure 6 gives the number of college student innovation and entrepreneurship program in recent five years to fulfill the needs of entering the team and the project.

Entering Enterprises: Build school enterprise collaborative education platforms such as industrial internet modern industry college, characteristic demonstration software college, big data and intelligent industry college, school level provincial school enterprise cooperation practice education base, implement the integration of industry and education, and provide guarantee for students' entering enterprises. Lead students into enterprises in the practice teaching link, and help students understand the latest application of professional and technical knowledge in enterprises; In the production practice link, industry experts are invited to the school to carry out practical project training to help students master the ability of practical application of technology. Reform the

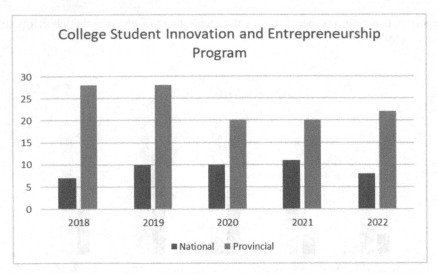

Fig. 6. College Student Innovation and Entrepreneurship Program

comprehensive practice course in the professional direction of 10 weeks a year, with the Industrial College as the carrier, cooperate with multiple enterprises, and set up multiple training modules. The content of each module comes from enterprise cases. The enterprise engineer is also the instructor. Students can choose different modules to participate in practice according to their interests, break the professional boundary, realize the cross integration within the college, realize the docking of industrial needs, and support the cultivation of personalized talents.

4.4   All-Staff and All-Round Education

All-Round Education: We adhere to the working principle of "Combining Education Guidance, Standardized Management and Quality Education", and promote the scientific, systematic, institutionalized and standardized activities in the second classroom. We carry out activities such as scientific research and education, mass entrepreneurship and innovation lecture, innovation training camp, series of reports of industry and enterprise experts, teacher-student exchange meeting for employment and postgraduate entrance examination, experience exchange between seniors and sisters, and help students grow and become talents. The training class of "Qing Ma project" is carried out, including the theme League Day of the Youth League branch, the theme party day, the theme class meeting of the class, various symposiums and reports on ideological growth, voluntary blood donation activities, the Qingming Festival memorial ceremony for heroes and martyrs, etc., which strengthen students' ideological guidance during school. Students are organized and guided to participate in activities such as the challenge cup red project, holiday ideological and political education, Youth Red Dream building trip, three trips to the countryside in summer, and volunteer service of the Youth League, so that students can be influenced, increase knowledge, cultivate sentiment, enhance party spirit cultivation, and cultivate students' sense of historical mission and social responsibility in social practice. We carry out rich and colorful recreational and sports activities, create an atmosphere for everyone to participate in sports, guide students to develop good physical exercise habits, establish college students' Art Troupe and art group, enrich students' cultural and spiritual life, cultivate noble sentiment, promote aesthetic education, and improve students' ability to feel and appreciate beauty. Students are guided to be "upright", "learning", "diligent", "happy", "strong" and "harmonious".

All-Staff Education: The detailed rules for the implementation of students' classroom attendance management in the school of computer and information technology (Trial) is a linkage management mechanism for the construction of a learning style that integrates teachers, counselors, teaching managers, student secretaries, etc., to ensure that the school maintains normal education and teaching order, corrects students' learning atmosphere, helps students develop good learning habits, and improves their education level. Undergraduate tutors interpret the training plan according to the implementation rules of undergraduate tutorial system in the school of computer and information technology (Revised), help students understand their majors, guide students to establish correct professional ideas and values, guide students to make academic plans according to professional needs and personal interests, and guide students to choose courses, directions and minor majors. According to the measures for undergraduate tutors in the school of computer and information to help students with academic difficulties (Trial), help students with academic difficulties out of the predicament, improve their learning enthusiasm, adjust their learning methods, and correct their learning attitude. Use spare time to guide and urge students to carry out labor practice, experience the importance of hard work, honest work and creative work in practice, develop labor habits, and cultivate labor quality and craftsman spirit. Guide students to be "upright", "learn", "diligent" and "harmonious".

5 Quality Assurance System

Organization Guarantee: The college has set up a working group headed by the president and the secretary of the college Party committee to implement the requirements of the "three complete and six specialized" education. Combined with the college's "three complete and six specialized" education program, the college leads and coordinates the implementation of undergraduate personalized talent training and handles various problems in the work. The deputy dean of teaching is responsible for the planning, organization and coordination of teaching related matters in the training process, and the deputy secretary of the party committee is responsible for the planning, organization and coordination of the second classroom and student management.

Teacher Guarantee: According to the school policy and the "School of Computer and Information Technology Innovation and Entrepreneurship Tutor Management Rules(Trial) " to increase the number of industry professors, tutors, distinguished professors, innovation and entrepreneurship tutors, it is promoted to share high-level talents between the school and the local government, and integrate industry and education. Activities are carried out to improve teachers' teaching ability and cultivate young teachers, support teachers to go to enterprises and institutions for temporary training, and improve teachers' engineering practice ability.

Quality Guarantee: Aiming at different learning processes, a tracking and evaluation mechanism based on students' learning process performance is established, which improves the rationality evaluation of talent training quality and the evaluation of goal achievement. Three approaches are providers, including giving full play to the role of teaching supervision, learning supervision, management supervision, reforming supervision and construction supervision, and building a standardized, systematic and perfect quality assurance system.

Service Guarantee: Taking the students as the center, all-round services are provided to actively meet the social needs, which adheres to the whole staff education and the whole process education. The construction of Party and league organizations and the contingent of counselors is strengthen, which gives full play to the role of students in self-education, self-management, self-service and self-supervision.

System Guarantee: The guiding idea of "managing people by system and managing affairs by process" is established, which adheres to the combination of goal orientation and problem orientation. The weak links in the system construction are carefully sort out under the guidance of "three grasps". Taking the "three complete and six specialized" education work as the starting point, we "fill in gaps, strengths and weaknesses" on the basis of existing systems, and revise or formulate rules and regulations.

Resource Guarantee: The number of courses is enriched and curriculum resources are built. By increasing the number of courses including the opening of courses, the construction of a curriculum system is provided to meet the requirements of the credit system. According to the detailed rules for the implementation of the curriculum team and the person in charge system of the curriculum team in the school of computer and information technology (Trial), curriculum resources are constructed, including online and offline resources such as syllabus, textbooks, experimental guidance, teaching plan, MOOC or spooc platform.

Acknowledgment. This research is partially supported by the project of Virtual Teaching and Research Department of Computer Science and Technology in Anhui Local Universities(2021xnjys003), Institute of Industrial Internet Modern Industry (2022xdcyxy01), and Project of the National Association of Computer Education in Colleges and Universities (CERACU2022R10).

References

1. Lin, J.: Curriculum system reform and curriculum construction of new engineering majors. Res. High. Eng. Educ. **180**(180), 1–13, 24 (2020)
2. Yang, X.: "Three comprehensive education" in higher education: theoretical implications, practical problems and practical paths. High. Educ. China **18**, 4–8 (2018)
3. Zhou, G.: Academic breakthrough in the construction of "double first-class"——on the integrated construction of university disciplines, majors and courses. Educ. Res. **37**(05), 72–76 (2016)

4. Lin, J.: How to understand and solve complex engineering problems——based on the definition and requirements of the Washington Accord. High. Eng. Educ. Res. (05), 17–26+38 (2016)
5. Yu, X., Zhang, H., Jing, Z.: Research on individualized talent training mode and teaching method. Chin. Univ. Teach. **02**, 34–36 (2009)
6. Liu, X.: The concept and path of cultivating applied talents. China High. Educ. Res. **10**, 6–10 (2018)
7. Wang, X.: Research on the personalized talent training mode of first-class universities. Central China Normal University (2014)
8. Xi, H.: Innovation and development drive the in-depth cooperation between schools and enterprises: from "title class" to "enterprise trainee." China Sci. Technol. Ind. **01**, 62–63 (2017)
9. The "Five Entries and Three Modernizations" school summarizes and promotes the reform experience of the innovative talent training model. https://www.ahpu.edu.cn/2022/0523/c3a 174274/page.htm
10. Gao, Y.: Discussion on the idea of "student-centered" top-notch innovative talent training model. Beijing Educ. (High. Educ.) **11**, 33–34 (2023)
11. Wu, Y.: First-class undergraduates, first-class majors, first-class talents. Chin. J. Univ. Teach. (11), 4–12+17 (2017)
12. Zhu, J.: Project-based learning research on practical competence in technology and engineering. Hangzhou Normal University (2022)

Curriculum Reform

Curriculum Framework for Integration of Intelligent Computing and Academic Majors

Hong Zhao, Peipei Gao(✉) (iD), and Lipei Song

Nankai University, Tianjin 300071, China
watersky@nankai.edu.cn

Abstract. This paper studies and explores the construction method of the integrated curriculum system under the concept of "five integrations", in which intelligent computing technology helps professional ability improvement. At the same time, the course "Intelligent Computing Fundamentals", which is located at the underlying logic of the integrated curriculum framework, is constructed, and a teaching path that uses CPBL and P-MASE to achieve "five integrations" and course objectives is proposed.

Keywords: intelligent computing · integrated curriculum · digital literacy · CPBL · P-MASE

1 Introduction

At present, with the rapid development of modern information technologies, such as artificial intelligence, big data, block chain, genetic engineering, virtual technology and 5G technology, university departments are increasingly introducing these new technologies into their courses and this has become the core driving force for universities to optimize the structure of courses, promote the development of the quality of discipline construction and the formation of a high-level talent training system. For example, the innovation of the "new liberal arts" being promoted widely in China lies predominantly in the new fields in liberal arts that emerge from the integration of new science and technology and liberal arts, and in the renewal of traditional liberal arts in majors, courses and personnel training modes [1].

Currently, the curriculum/curriculum system with distinctive interdisciplinary characteristics has yet to be implemented. The current integration courses, although aiming to improve students' digital literacy, are facing challenges mainly on: 1) The teachers of the new technologies do not understand the fundamental principles of the subject area, while the teachers from the traditional subjects are not sensitive to new technologies and are reluctant to touch new technologies and new trends; 2) The current state of the integration courses is a rigid combination of new technology and professional subject courses rather than organic integration, and few answers have been given to the fundamental question on how to improve students' professional capability by using new technologies, so these courses are out of touch with the actual problems in the professional field.

This paper studies and explores the construction method of the curriculum system for the integration of professional subject courses and new technologies such as intelligent computing. For the integration courses, we investigate questions including "What should students know and be able to do?", "How should students study?", and "How should students be evaluated?". The concept of "five integrations" of curriculum construction is put forward, and the framework of integrated courses of deep integration of new technology with specialty is constructed. The teaching practice of the course "Fundamentals of Intelligent Computing", which is designed following the underlying logic of this curriculum framework, has been carried out in universities, and the expected results have been achieved.

2   "Five Integrations" of Integration Course

The construction of the current integration curriculum should not only be a combination or fusion of knowledge from different disciplines, but should also reflect more integration based on the characteristics and needs of the curriculum. In the construction of the integrated curriculum, we follow the curriculum construction concept of "five integrations".

2.1   Organic Integration of Subject Content - Content Integration

The most important thing about a fusion course is to first select topics or general questions that are meaningful to learners, and then integrate the content of related disciplines to find common themes, and then let learners learn. Therefore, the teaching content is to organically integrate new technologies into the solution of professional problems with the rise of new professional needs, so that students can master new methods to solve professional problems by means of intelligent computing.

2.2   The Organic Integration of Teachers in Various Disciplines - The Integration of Teachers

The characteristics of integrated courses require teachers from different professional backgrounds and teachers from the industry to jointly teach students from different majors, not only to pass on the basic professional knowledge of the discipline to students, but also to give full play to the scientific research expertise of teachers from different disciplines to solve professional problems. In the process of mutual aid learning, students are effectively trained in scientific research, and students gradually have a certain interdisciplinary way of thinking and scientific research literacy in the process of mutual learning.

2.3   The Organic Integration of Teaching and Learning Subjects - The Integration of Teachers and Students

The fusion course also needs to organically integrate the two main subjects in the teaching process, teachers and students. A university of the top 20 in China started a new round of teaching reform under the concept of "teacher-student community" in 2019. Based on the vector characteristics of the educational subjects of the teacher-student community, the equal rights characteristics of educational subjects, the interaction between subjects and within subjects, and the universality of the space-time view of education, the reform emphasized the community role of teacher-teacher, teacher-student, and student-student interaction in talent training in the teaching process [2].

2.4   The Organic Integration of Teaching and Scientific Research - The Integration of Teaching and Scientific Research

The course introduces the general methods of problem solving in scientific research and the new technological achievements produced by scientific research into teaching, so as to realize the organic integration of teaching and scientific research. Under the guidance of teachers, students choose topics within their ability from the nature, the society and the daily life to conduct research in combination with academic learning, from which they can acquire professional knowledge, master research skills, and be able to actively discover, analyze and effectively solve practical problems.

2.5   The Organic Integration of Universities and the Industry - Integration Inside and Outside the University

Keeping up with the current industry needs and development trends, encouraging and guiding students to deeply understand the industry's needs of the digital literacy of the talents, and aiming to enable them to apply what they have learned instead of working behind closed doors. In terms of case sources, colleges and enterprises jointly produce teaching resources through graduates, enterprise interviews, etc., supplement real industrial data analysis cases, and invite enterprises from the industry to enter the classroom.

3   Constructions of the Curriculum Framework for Integration of Intelligent Computing and Professional Areas

Starting from the integration of intelligent computing and professional subjects, and following the "five integration" curriculum construction concept, this paper investigates in-depth on areas including teaching content, teaching methods, teaching teams, etc., and formed integrated curriculum framework of professional digital literacy kind that is featured as being supported by multiple integrated courses and containing practical training courses as comprehensive ability training. Figure 1 is a schematic diagram of the intelligent computing integrated curriculum framework.

The framework consists of three levels. The bottom layer is general foundation course for all students of the major with new technologies such as data processing and AI as the main content, which is named "Intelligent Computing Foundation". The middle layer is to deeply integrate new technologies into traditional professional courses. In the course, new technologies and new methods will be used to innovatively deal with traditional professional problems. By improving the goals and content of the original

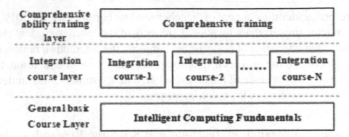

Fig. 1. The Framework of The Integration of Intelligent Computing and Different Majors

courses, the integration of intelligent computing and professional courses will be formed, including a number of new professional compulsory and elective courses. The top layer is the comprehensive ability training layer, which enables students to use what they have learned to solve real problems from the industry and improve their comprehensive ability to apply intelligent computing to solve practical problems.

4   Teaching Practice of "Intelligent Computing Fundamentals" Course

Based on the above curriculum framework, in the spring semester of 2022, a general basic course "Intelligent Computing Fundamentals", which is located at the bottom of the integrated curriculum framework, will be built and opened in a university of the top 20 in China, opening to all first-year undergraduates in business administration and economics.

4.1   Goals of the Course

The training on new technologies, for any department, is not to cultivate professional intelligent computing talents, but to improve the core capabilities of non-computer majored students: to have basic data processing capabilities and gradually improve their digital literacy, and to acquire the awareness and ability to solve professional or daily-life problems independently or cooperatively using intelligent computing. Therefore, as the basic course of general education, the role of "intelligent computing fundamentals" in different majors is to provide new ways of thinking, new expressions, and new problem-solving paths and methods for professional problems.

4.2   Effective Teaching Paths Adopted by the Course

The key to making the course more challenging is to promote deep learning. Through learning activities based on metacognitive strategies, deep learning emphasizes the integration of knowledge, proactiveness, and cooperative research, and the structuring and deep processing of knowledge. The goal is to develop higher-order thinking and problem-solving skills, to promote well-rounded development in active and meaningful learning [3].

In order to achieve the teaching goals, the course practice adopts the CPBL (Challenging Project-Based Learning) challenge project-based learning model proposed in this paper and the research teaching model P-MASE. The core of CPBL is firstly that challenging problems are not given by teachers, but are discovered by students themselves and discussed with their tutors; secondly, students follow the PBL model, in which students explore and solve problems through teamwork in accordance with scientific research methods [4]. The P-MASE model includes five progressive links, namely introduction of problems (Problem), finding methods (Method), scientific analysis (Analysis), effective solution (Solution), and effect evaluation (Evaluation) [5]. The process of research-based teaching begins with the introduction of professional problems, during which it goes through the teaching and learning process of finding suitable inquiry methods, conducting scientific and meticulous analysis, solving problems in a timely and effective manner, and evaluating the final inquiry effect. The interconnected links fully embody the characteristics of research-based teaching, such as advanced goals and step-by-step implementation.

5 Validity Analysis

The number of students enrolled in the "Intelligent Computing Fundamentals" course is 500. One month and two months after the start of the course, a questionnaire survey was conducted on the students who chose the course. The majors of the surveyed students were mainly include business administration (about 70%), economics (about 15%) and other (about 15%) majors. 378 valid questionnaires were recovered for the first time, accounting for 75.6% of the total number of students enrolled in courses, and 403 valid questionnaires were recovered for the second time, accounting for 80.6% of the total number of students enrolled in courses. The questionnaire is divided into four parts, which are: 1. Basic personal information, 2. Judgment on the development status and trend of intelligent computing, 3. Course experience of "Intelligent Computing Fundamentals", and 4. Intelligent computing ability survey. Parts 2–4 of the questionnaire include a total of 17 scale questions, 2 Single-choice questions, and 2 multiple-choice questions.

5.1 Validation of the Questionnaire

The reliability and validity of the 17 scale questions in the two questionnaires were tested and the results are shown in Table 1, 2, 3 and 4.

Table 1. Reliability Analysis of the First Questionnaire

Sample Size	Question Number	Cronbach.α Coefficient
378	17	0.841

It can be seen from Table 1 that the overall Cronbach.α coefficient of the first questionnaire is 0.841, >0.8, so the reliability is within the acceptable range and the results of the first questionnaire are credible.

Table 2. Validity Analysis of the First Questionnaire

KMO and Bartlett Test	
KMO	0.870
Bartlett's Test of Sphericity	3036.267
df	136.000
P value	0.00

The factor analysis was carried out on the first questionnaire. It can be seen from Table 2 that the KMO value is 0.870, >0.5, indicating that the questionnaire data is suitable for factor analysis; the approximate chi-square of the Bartlett sphericity test is 3036.267, the degree of freedom is 136, and the P value of the test result is 0.00 and <0.05, so the questionnaire is statistically valid.

Table 3. Reliability Analysis of the Second Questionnaire

Sample Size	Question Number	Cronbach.α Coefficient
403	17	0.923

It can be seen from Table 3 that the overall Cronbach.α coefficient of the second questionnaire is 0.923, >0.9. The reliability of the scale is good and the results of the second questionnaire are credible.

Table 4. Validity Analysis of the Second Questionnaire

KMO and Bartlett Test	
KMO	0.906
Bartlett's Test of Sphericity	4363.122
df	136.000
P value	0.00

Factor analysis was performed on the second questionnaire. It can be seen from Table 2 that the KMO value is 0.9.6, >0.9, indicating that the questionnaire data is suitable for factor analysis; the approximate chi-square of the Bartlett sphericity test is 4363.122, the degree of freedom is 136, and the P value of the test result is 0.00 and <0.05, so the questionnaire is statistically valid.

5.2 Effectiveness Analysis

Comparing the results of the two questionnaires, it is proved that the students have improved in different degrees in terms of intelligent computing knowledge and ability.

For example, The average score of students' mastery of classification and clustering problems in intelligent computing increased from 1.97 points to 3.37 points (out of 5 points), an increase of 71%. The degree of mastery of the knowledge in this type of question is scored according to 1–5 points. The distribution ratio of the number of people who scored each question in the two surveys is shown in Fig. 2.

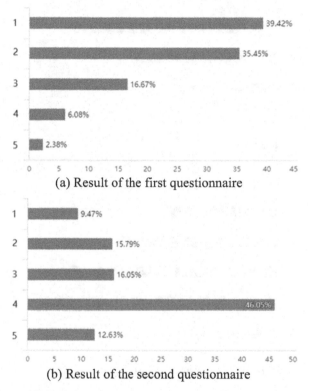

(a) Result of the first questionnaire

(b) Result of the second questionnaire

Fig. 2. Comparison of Students' Mastery of Intelligent Computing Classification and Clustering in the Two Questionnaires

The average score of students' understanding of artificial neural networks in intelligent computing increased from 1.76 points to 2.93 points (out of 5 points), an increase of 66.48%. The degree of understanding this type of question is scored on a scale of 1–5, and the distribution ratio of the number of people scoring in the two surveys is shown in Fig. 3.

The proportion of students who can train intelligent computing artificial neural networks to solve problems has increased from 12.96% to 90%. The questionnaire uses multiple-choice questions to investigate the students' use of intelligent computing methods to solve problems in this subject. The intelligent computing frameworks that can be selected include Tensorflow, Caffe, Keras, Theano, Paddlepaddle and others. In the first questionnaire, 87.04% of the students said that they had never used any intelligent computing method to solve problems in this subject, and this proportion was reduced to 10% in the second questionnaire. A comparison of the results of the two questionnaires for this question is shown in Fig. 4.

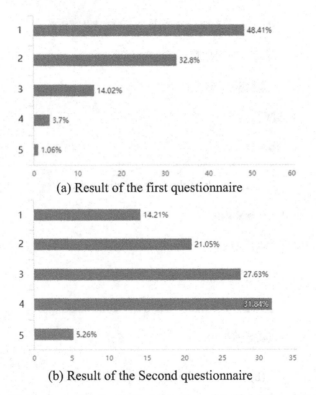

(a) Result of the first questionnaire

(b) Result of the Second questionnaire

Fig. 3. Comparison of Students' Understanding of Artificial Neural Network

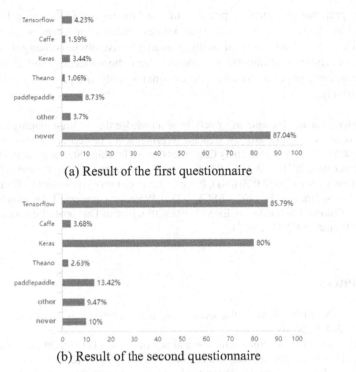

(a) Result of the first questionnaire

(b) Result of the second questionnaire

Fig. 4. Comparison of Students' Use of Intelligent Computing Methods to Solve Problems in Two Questionnaires

6   Conclusion

The construction of integrated curriculum is a powerful tool to promote the improvement of professional ability. The integration courses related to new technologies such as big data and AI are not isolated courses, but need to be deeply and organically integrated with the majors. Based on the concept of "five fusions", this paper constructs a three-level fusion curriculum framework with deep organic integration of computational intelligence and professional knowledge. This framework not only focuses on the integration of interdisciplinary content, but also the integration between teachers of different majors and between teachers and students, the integration of teaching and scientific research, and the integration of universities and the industry. The use of CPBL and P-MASE teaching paths not only organically integrates teaching and research, but also organically integrates teaching content from different majors, interdisciplinary teachers and classmates, as well as universities and the industry into the entire teaching, promoting the implementation the "five integration" concept.

The preliminary teaching practice of the "Intelligent Computing Fundamentals" course has shown that the course stimulates students' awareness of problems and enhances students' autonomy in learning. Students have obvious changes in thinking and innovation, show great interest, and initially have the awareness and ability to actively use intelligent computing to solve professional or daily-life problems independently or cooperatively.

Acknowledgement. The authors gratefully acknowledge the research funding from the following programs: New liberal arts research and reform practice project of the Ministry of Education (2021020001), Project of University Computer Course Teaching Steering Committee of the Ministry of Education(2020-JZW-CT-A02), Educational Research Planning Project of China Association of Higher Education (23SZH041), Project of Association of Fundamental Computing Education in Chinese Universities (2023-AFCEC-335), Project of Computer Education Research Association of Chinese Universities (CERACU2023R01), Nankai University Education and Teaching Steering Project (NKJG2023050).

References

1. Fan, L.: "New Liberal Arts": the needs of the times and the focus of construction. Chin. Univ. Teach. **5**, 4–8 (2020)
2. Yu, H., Li, C., Liu, Y.: Reconstruction and practice of teacher-student community in colleges and universities in the new era. China Univ. Teach. **12**, 82–87 (2021)
3. Zhou, X., Tang, C., Feng, H.: Theoretical analysis and implementation strategies of the "high-order, innovative, and challenge level" in first-class courses. J. Chengdu Normal Univ. **6**, 13–20 (2020)
4. Zhao, H., Guo, Y.: The reform of general computer courses in colleges and universities for comprehensive ability training. China Univ. Teach. No. 6 (2021)
5. Zhang, W., Yan, T., Zhang, Y.: Research-based teaching and quality education based on the P-MASE model. In: Quality Education: Making the Future Better - Proceedings of the 2020 High-level Forum on University Quality Education, pp. 158–165. Higher Education Press, Beijing (2020)

The Practice of Artificial Intelligence Education for Non-computer Science Majors in Universities

Feng Yin[✉], Xiaoqiang Liu, Ming Du, Hui Song, Bo Xu, and Zhenni Feng

School of Computer Science and Technology, Donghua University, Shanghai, China
{wh_yf,liuxq,duming,songhui,xubo,fzn}@dhu.edu.cn

Abstract. Due to the extensive impact of AI technology on various disciplines, universal AI education has become an urgent demand, while the liberal education in AI is still in its infancy, plagued by multiple problems such as unclear training standards, no systematic teaching system, lack of practical environment and experimental cases, and lack of teachers. This paper introduces the teaching mode and method of AI liberal education course cooperated with Baidu, Inc. in all-round, which guides and improves students' application innovation ability of applying AI technology to cross disciplines.

Keywords: Artificial Intelligence · Liberal course · School-enterprise cooperation · Teaching reform

1 Introduction

Artificial intelligence (AI) technologies are changing nearly every area of our lives, transportation, healthcare, education, security, and so on. As one of the fastest-growing domains of computer science, AI is making a powerful impact on modern science and technology. The new generation of AI is developing rapidly under the joint drive of new theories and technologies such as mobile Internet, big data, supercomputing, sensor networks, and brain science. AI is expected to bring a revolution in the near future.

From a global perspective, several countries have made national strategies on AI. It has become a consensus to seize the high ground of AI and make talent training a strategic priority. The United States issued the executive order, titled "Maintaining American Leadership in Artificial Intelligence" [1]. The order proposed to expand opportunities for all Americans to gain the skills needed to participate in an AI-ready workforce. The AI-ready workforce includes people with a broad spectrum of capabilities, from those who are novices in technology but capable of using AI-based tools to those experts who create the next innovations at the cutting edge of AI [2]. According to the UK's National Artificial Intelligence Strategy, "ten-year plan to make Britain a global AI superpower", to continuously develop, attract and train the best people to build and use AI is at the core of maintaining the UK's world-leading position [3]. The program shift the UK from a rich but siloed and discipline-focused national AI landscape to an inclusive, interconnected, collaborative, and interdisciplinary research and innovation ecosystem.

Japan plans to train 250,000 artificial intelligence personnel each year and become the world's top artificial intelligence talent country.

China has released several national strategies since 2013, including "Made in China 2025", "New Generation of Artificial Intelligence Development Plan", "Action Plan for Artificial Intelligence Innovation in Higher Education", etc. The strategic plans have identified the urgent problems of AI talent training in China, focusing on the education concept of interdisciplinary, science and education integration, school-enterprise cooperation, and collaborative education, further proposing the development idea of building an integrated AI talent ecosystem of government, enterprises, universities and scientific research institutes [4].

2 Reconstructing AI Liberal Courses

In order to help more students to get access to artificial intelligence, we developed AI liberal course for students majored in non-computer science. The teaching team composed of Donghua University, Baidu University Cooperation Department carries out the project of artificial intelligence liberal course.

The project carries out industry-university cooperation in the construction of course objectives, teaching contents, teaching resources, experimental environment, and teaching cases to form an original curriculum system and teaching program. It will give students a taste of various technical topics in AI, enable them to take the first step toward solving real-world problems with AI, and promise them a future-proofing career.

2.1 Course Goals

Although non-computer majors and IT professionals have different roles in society, they are the source of AI applications in various fields. Based on Baidu's artificial intelligence talent training standards, we formulate general artificial intelligence course goals to provide guidance and constraints for course construction [5].

Knowledge. The concepts at the foundation of modern artificial intelligence; development history and trend; master the basic principles and implementation technologies of commonly used artificial intelligence algorithms; understand artificial intelligence application scenarios and engineering design principles of intelligent systems.

Ability. Ability to use programming language and AI support package, as well as use visual modeling tools to build common AI models; be able to integrate AI open services; be able to discover and analyze domain problem requirements, and participate in the design of AI solutions.

Value. To understand national artificial intelligence strategy, and form a sense of responsibility and mission to build an innovative science and technology country; to recognize the frontiers and challenges of artificial intelligence technology, cultivate intelligent thinking and the spirit of interdisciplinary innovation and exploration; to understand the limitations of artificial intelligence methods, and establish engineering ethics and intelligence safety consciousness.

2.2 Teaching Content

Artificial intelligence is a cross-integration discipline involving computer science, mathematics, cybernetics, information theory, psychology, and other fields. Its knowledge has a certain degree of theoretical dispersion. Many algorithms need mathematical education background to learn, and the application fields are diverse. For example, undergraduates of computer science are usually required to finish 4–6 series of courses, including basic theory of artificial intelligence, computer vision and pattern recognition, data analysis and machine learning, natural language processing, etc.

The liberal course has limited teaching hours, so it is difficult to select and build the content. While it should also be high-level, innovative, and challenging. However, only by leading students to stand at the forefront of IT technology and breaking the mystery of technology, can it stimulate students' curiosity and provide innovative applications in various disciplines with information technology support.

Starting from the training goals, sorting out the professional curriculum system, popular science materials, and products and services of leading companies, and fully considering the knowledge base and acceptance ability of students, the course content is set into 4 modules:

History of AI. By introducing the ups and downs of artificial intelligence, students will understand the changes of various schools of algorithms, the success and failure experience and lessons of typical applications, and the supportive environment of a new round of artificial intelligence technology and its impact on human social activities.

AI Principles. By introducing classic intelligent system principles from neural networks to expert systems to exhaustive searching, students will explore various tricks and approaches, for example, a tic-tac-toe game that uses a neural network to mimic the human player's strategy. Students will try to teach the game to play tic-tac-toe, and see how it learns to mimic wrong moves as well as right moves.

Machine Learning Algorithms. The course will introduce basic principles, implementation, and applications of machine learning algorithms and deep learning algorithms, including linear regression, logistic regression, decision trees, classification, ensemble learning, clustering, and k-means, etc. Students will acquire skills in application modeling, algorithm implementation, performance, analysis, and result interpretation. For example, students will be asked to complete a puzzle using several triangles to experience the application of genetic algorithms.

AI Application Practice. The course will introduce innovative thinking, AI application micro-lesson resource, product development concepts and vivid AI application practice cases in the industry. It will use the Baidu AI platform as an example to introduce the open services of AI and the calling method of the API interface, so as to expand the application ideas of AI for students.

The AI liberal education explores the fundamental concepts and algorithms of the modern artificial intelligence and dives into the ideas that give rise to technologies. The course uses Python language as the development tool, third-party algorithm libraries, and Baidu AI development interface as the support environment. The course takes the scikit-learn library and keras library as the common AI processing methods, and calls the

AI service interface of Baidu AI open platform to quickly implement the application field practice. Through the practice projects, students get access to the theory behind graph search algorithms, classification, optimization, and other topics in artificial intelligence and machine learning as they incorporate them into their own major programs. Table 1 shows the course modules and the corresponding course practices.

Table 1. General AI course content

Course content	Course practice
History of AI	AI services experiences: AI conversation, intelligent writing, python multidimensional data processing
AI principles	Animal identification, tic-tac-toc analysis, knowledge graph, puzzle, optimal value of function
Machine learning	Advertising forecast, house price forecast, cancer classification, telecom customer clustering, iris clustering
AI application	API service call: face recognition, voice recognition. Text recognition, natural language processing, Chinese character retrieval

2.3 Teaching Platform

A suitable deep learning platform is not only friendly to beginners and has a relatively low learning threshold, but also enables students to seamlessly connect with industry application problems and propose complete solutions. Choosing the right platform for learning can do more with less.

Domestic mainstream deep learning platforms include Baidu PaddlePaddle, Alibaba MNN, Tencent TNN, Huawei MindSpore, Xiaomi MACE, Didi DELTA and so on. Among them, Baidu PaddlePaddle is China's first open-source, technology-leading, and fully functional industrial-grade deep learning platform. It not only provides a framework for deep learning training and inference but also provides a basic model library, end-to-end development kit, and rich tool components in one, making it the leading domestic deep learning open source platform.

The course teaching platform is carried out on Baidu AI studio, which is an AI learning and practical training community for AI learners. The community provides support for teaching videos, quizzes, discussions, and practical assignment submission and review, which can assist in both online and offline teaching. To expand the course teaching that can keep the course novel and active, the AI studio community integrates an ever-increasing number of AI courses, plenty of deep learning sample projects, and classical datasets from various fields and other teaching resources [6].

2.4 Course Resources

The focus of each part of the course is different, so the training and assessment of AI knowledge, ability, and quality should be reflected in different ways. The comprehensive online resources strengthen the learning process support and assist in the integration of online and offline teaching.

Instructional Videos. A total of 700 min of intensive instructional videos have been recorded to explain the principles and key points of knowledge, or to assist learning with animations and videos.

Teaching Cases. All chapters are equipped with demonstration and practical cases to support students in case reproduction, imitation, design, and implementation.

Support Resources. Each chapter has lecture notes, objective test questions, experimental questions, discussion questions, etc., forming a full range of auxiliary teaching support.

Expanding Resources. Micro-lecture videos and application cases from the AI studio platform are introduced in the corresponding chapters, which are closely integrated with cutting-edge applications and can effectively expand course teaching.

3 Building Full-Course Online Resources

The total teaching and experiment hours of the course are 48 h, and students from 10 majors of science, engineering and art classes take the course. Due to a large amount of content but limited credit hours and students' weak foundation in mathematics and programming, effective teaching methods must be explored in order to achieve teaching effectiveness and reach teaching objectives.

3.1 Use Multimedia to Enhance Theoretical Explanation

Artificial intelligence technology is wide-ranging, and many techniques reflect the unique and innovative thinking of scientists. Many artificial intelligence algorithms are derived from computational questions, mathematical thinking, and bionics, etc. The explanation of knowledge is supplemented by rich multimedia materials, which not only deepen the visual understanding of knowledge but also make the exploration process of artificial intelligence full of scientific spirit and humanitarian sentiment. Some AI algorithms are abstract and difficult for students to understand, but through the demonstration teaching of multimedia materials, we can show the students the principle of algorithms, inspire them to experience the processing process visually, and help them understand and master the core of algorithms. For this purpose, a lot of relevant materials, courseware, and videos are collected and produced.

3.2 Integration of Multiple Platforms for Practice

The goal of liberal education is to make students understand technology for solving practical problems in their own areas, therefore application practice is an indispensable training link. The course introduces several practical tools from Baidu better supporting the students' education background, so that the course can be developed in all aspects from theoretical teaching, applied practice to creative design, which solves the problems of experimental environment for large scale teaching [7].

AI Studio. A trinity of open data, open source algorithms, and free computing power in the cloud, providing an efficient learning and development environment for courses, and helping developers learn and communicate.

Paddlepaddle Open Framework. Formed a set of teaching programs and supporting platforms and practices for deep learning practice teaching, supporting deep learning algorithm applications.

EasyDL. Zero-threshold AI development for developers, one-stop support for intelligent annotation, model training, service deployment, and other functions, and support for rapid visual modeling.

AI Open Services. Driven by product development, a series of special applications for multiple data types and various industry sectors have been formed to support students to experience and integrate AI services.

With the support of these multi-level practical environments, demonstrative, verifying and developing type of experiments are designed for thinking, modeling, and practical developing skills according to the needs of liberal education with a close integration from shallow to deep, theory and practice.

3.3 Theme-Based Seminars to Expand Capabilities

Although artificial intelligence has become an industry, it is inextricably linked with its application areas. The course introduces data sets as well as cases from AI studio, various solutions in developing AI services, and a series of micro-lessons on innovative thinking and AI applications to expand students' horizons, combines cases with seminars and debates, and develops awareness of applied solutions and innovative approaches. During the semester, cases such as smart scales, transmission tower bird's nest recognition, wearing a mask, workpiece inventory, intelligent recommendation of recipes, and selection of winner prediction are discussed. The discussion is around the following questions: What is the nature of a problem? Is it a specific problem? How to get the dataset? How to solve it with AI methods? How difficult is it to solve the problem?

4 Team Project-Based Course Practice

This is a project-based course. In order to stimulate students' awareness and interest in the application of artificial intelligence, and to further discover and understand the intelligent needs of businesses in various fields, the course provides practical sessions. The class is divided into teams of 2 to 3 students each. This appropriate team size does make it easier to determine the exact contribution of each team member. Each team is free to choose their own specific project. Students learn through the process from an ambiguous problem description to a running solution through the entire process of designing and developing and implementing an AI application. The project tasks included the following:

Table 2. Project topic sample

Topic	Major
Carbon Alloy Microstructure Identification	Mechanical Engineering
Fiber Microscopic Image Classification	Textiles
Diagnosis based on patient's respiratory audio spectrum	Communication
Interior Decoration Style Identification	Industrial Design
Fungal Classification	Chemical Engineering
Ethnic Clothing Classification	Clothing Design
Online Invigilator Wisdom Eye	Business Administration

Selecting Topic. To excavate the application requirements in professional fields or in learning and life, and determine the topics. To encourage students to discover and design innovative topics through brainstorming. Table 2 shows that the project topics are closely related to the students' majors.

Collecting Data. To obtain and label the data sets. To encourage students to collect and organize their own data sets related to subject areas or social life in conjunction with the proposed task requirements, such as data from professional areas, experimental data, web crawling, etc. If it is a self-built dataset, the project will have extra creative bonus points.

AI Solutions. To propose specific regression analysis, classification tasks, or clustering task goals. To encourage students to search for cutting-edge research and application papers, perform algorithm reproduction and application integration, etc.

Building Models and Performing Training. To use at least 1 of the following implementation options.

Programming Modeling. To select one or more appropriate machine learning methods to build models, implement predictions, and evaluate and compare the performance of different data models.

EasyDL Custom Model. To use EasyDL for model training and publish as API; to write Python program to call API for model prediction application.

Summarize. To write a brief group paper and make a presentation. Students, when displaying their projects at the end of the semester, take pride in their accomplishments. Students responded: "Taking the course of artificial intelligence technology and application, we had a deeper understanding of what AI is and how to use AI technologies through the available platforms and resources. At the same time, we have also mastered one more programming language. By using these and a well-built platform, we can easily use AI to realize our various ideas, which will give us a great help in our professional studies."

5 Conclusion

The course instructors participate in enterprise curriculum training and seminars and discuss with enterprise experts. The course integrates enterprise teaching, practice environment case resources, and closely collaborates with industry-education integration. The university and enterprises collaborate to combine research project experience and enterprise education resources to condense teaching content, design and organize teaching cases, and enhance the teaching ability of the faculty team.

The course has been piloted from a small class to large scale teaching, and has been made a mandatory course for innovation classes in all disciplines. It expands the field of basic computer teaching, empowers students with cutting-edge information technology, and provides support in the field of artificial intelligence. At the same time, students are encouraged to participate in AI training camps and various competitions. These open computer competitions provide a space for students to freely expand from creative topic selection, program design to technology implementation, which provide a challenge platform for potential students.

References

1. American leadership in AI. https://www.federalregister.gov/documents/2019/02/14/2019-02544/maintaining-american-leadership-in-artificial-intelligence. Accessed 25 Aug 2023
2. American Artificial Intelligence Initiative. https://trumpwhitehouse.archives.gov/wp-content/uploads/2020/02/American-AI-Initiative-One-Year-Annual-Report.pdf. Accessed 20 Aug 2023
3. National AI Strategy. https://www.gov.uk/government/publications/national-ai-strategy. Accessed 20 July 2023
4. Li, Y., Li, S.H., Wang, L.G.: The integration development of artificial intelligence and education. In: 16th International Conference on Computer Science & Education (ICCSE), pp. 994–997. IEEE, Lancaster (2021)
5. Wang, W., He, H.Y., Li, P., Zhang, L.: Research on the disciplinary evolution of deep learning and the educational revelation. In: 14th International Conference on Computer Science & Education (ICCSE), pp. 655–660. IEEE, Toronto (2019)
6. Xu, P.F., Pu, L.Y., Zhao, H., Zhang, X.J.: A study of the problems faced by non-computer/AI majors offering AI courses. Comput. Educ. **322**(10), 33–36 (2021)
7. AI Studio of Baidu. https://aistudio.baidu.com/. Accessed 20 Aug 2023

Exploration and Practice of Big Data Major Construction in Local Universities from the Perspective of New Engineering

Ouyang Yong[✉], Shan Lin, and Hong Li

School of Computer Science, Hubei University of Technology, Wuhan, China
oyywuhan@163.com

Abstract. This paper analyzes the current situation and problems of data science and big data technology talents training in local universities. According to the requirements of new engineering on big data major construction, combined with the new engineering construction practice of Big data major in Hubei University of Technology. This paper systematically discusses the construction path of big data major in local universities from the perspective of new engineering from the aspects of training goal formulation, curriculum system construction, talent training mode innovation, deepening of industry-university cooperation mechanism and improvement of continuous improvement mechanism. In order to provide ideas and reference for the construction of big data specialty and talent training in other local universities.

Keywords: Major in Data Science and Big Data Technology · Specialty construction · The new engineering

1 Introduction

In September 2015, China issued the Platform for Action on Promoting Big Data development. The big data strategy has been officially promoted as a national strategy. In order to meet the talent demand of the national strategic development of emerging industries, the Ministry of Education has approved about 680 colleges and universities to establish the major of "Data science and Big Data Technology" (big data for short) since 2016. And the growth spurt. Among them, local universities account for the majority, reflecting the urgent universal demand for big data professionals for industrial economic development.

At present, the construction of big data major has entered a stage of rapid development. But the talent training model is not mature. The vast majority of colleges and universities this major has not yet three graduates. Colleges and universities generally lack understanding of big data [1, 2]. From the perspective of traditional engineering education, most people simply consider it as the interdisciplinary expansion of statistics and computer science and technology. In the formulation of talent training programs for big data majors, the major of computer science and technology or statistics should be the main subject. And the subject attributes should be retained. Talent training should be carried out through simple course expansion. In addition, from the perspective of big data professional talent training mode, many colleges and universities present unclear talent training objectives. The training of engineering talents be scientific. Practice focuses on dogmatic technical training. Lack of more complete and systematic engineering practical education. Engineering literacy is not high and innovation ability is insufficient. And lack of integration of industry and education, engineering education and the actual needs of the industry and enterprises out of line. Complex engineering capacity is obviously inadequate.

From the perspective of new engineering, the major of big data is not subject oriented, but a new major that meets the development needs of emerging industries. It is a multidisciplinary integration with data science as the core, computer science and statistics as the support, and traditional disciplines as the application field [3–6]. As a local university, Hubei University of Technology attaches great importance to the new engineering construction of big data major. After the new major was approved by the Ministry of Education in 2017, pilot classes were established that year. Actively explore the new engineering development model to adapt to the law of big data professional talent development. Based on the actual situation of big data major in local universities and the construction experience of new engineering of big data major in Hubei University of Technology, this paper explores the construction path and countermeasures of big data major in local universities from the perspective of new engineering.

2 New Engineering Requirements for Big Data Major Construction

To active response to the new round of technological revolution and industrial revolution, to speed up the training emerging field of engineering science and technology talents, upgrade the traditional engineering major, layout the future strategy and field personnel training actively, so as to adapt to new technologies, new industries and new forms and new mode of development of new economic forms, the Ministry of Education officially launched in 2017, new engineering construction planning [7]. The state encourages the construction of new disciplines such as "big data, cloud computing, Internet of Things, artificial intelligence and virtual reality". Integration of traditional specialty and new discipline, with new technology, new industry to promote economic development.

Under such demands, as an emerging big data major, we should pursue higher construction standards, take coping with changes and shaping the future as the concept, and take inheritance and innovation, crossover and integration, coordination and sharing as the main approaches. Cultivate diversified, innovative and outstanding engineering talents.

To provide intellectual support for the economic development of new industries. Therefore, the construction of big data major in local universities should be oriented to serve the sustainable development of local industry. Design professional content from the perspective of big data technology application and development. Construct the curriculum teaching system based on the law of students' ability development. Innovate teaching methods from the new generation of students' interests. Cultivate talents from the application ability and accomplishment of complex big data engineering.

3 Exploring the Construction Path of Big Data Major from the Perspective of New Engineering

The big data major of local universities in the new engineering field must first change its educational concept. We should adhere to the principle of moral cultivation, strengthen the construction of grassroots organizations, deepen industry-university cooperation, establish a complete education system, and innovate new modes of personnel training.

3.1 Precise Positioning, Standardized Development of Training Objectives

The establishment of training objectives for big data majors requires extensive research and listening to the opinions of enterprises, graduates and employers, professional teachers and experts. Through multiple rounds of communication and rationality evaluation, it is constantly revised and improved until the professional target positioning and target connotation is finally determined. Professional objective positioning needs to clarify the basic ability and quality of professional talents, service orientation and talent positioning. The connotation of professional objective needs to determine the vocational ability that graduates should have. Expected career and professional achievements five years after graduation.

As a local university, the orientation of the training target of big data major should be consistent with the orientation of the university's development. Integrating the traditional advantages of the university, serving the development needs of finance, industry, agriculture, transportation and other local industries, condenses the major characteristics of big data, defines the core competence and accomplishment of graduates, and expects their career achievements in big data application analysis, big data system development and other positions.

3.2 Construct a Competence-Oriented Curriculum System

Big data is a professional data, especially the big data as the research object, in order to obtain knowledge and wisdom from the data as the main purpose, in mathematics, statistics, computer science, visualization and professional knowledge as the theoretical basis, with data acquisition, preprocessing, data management and data calculation, etc. as the research content of a discipline professional [2]. The major of Big Data mainly trains big data application analysts and big data system engineers. Big data application analysts focus on data processing and model analysis. Big data system engineers focus on big data system architecture design, platform development, testing and management. Based on the development requirements of core competence of big data major, goal-guided, break the disciplinary barriers, reconstruct the knowledge system of big data, and build a competence-oriented curriculum system of multi-discipline integration. Specifically, the first step is to build a theoretical curriculum system based on the big data knowledge system. The courses include mathematics and Statistics, computer Science and technology, data processing and systems, model analysis and Presentation, industrial applications in the field of big data, and big data management and ethics. Refer to the theoretical curriculum system and Table 1.

The second step is to systematically plan the training system of practical ability according to the growth rules of big data talents. From basic practical ability, engineering practical ability, innovation ability to big data complex engineering practical ability, reasonable professional practice and comprehensive engineering practice teaching links are set up. As well as innovation and entrepreneurship courses and practices, as shown in Fig. 1. So as to form a complete curriculum system oriented by ability.

Table 1. Theoretical course system of big data major

Curriculum group	Course name
Mathematical/Statistical theory	Advanced Mathematics, Linear Algebra, Probability theory, Probability and Mathematical Statistics, Applied Statistics, etc.
Computer Science and Technology	Basic programming, data structure and algorithm, principle of computer composition, operating system, computer network, software engineering, information system development technology, etc.
Data processing and systems	Parallel computing, distributed system, Hadoop/Spark development, Database principle, Cloud computing and Big data platform, distributed database principle, data collection and preprocessing, Python, Big data security technology, etc.
Model analysis and presentation	Machine learning, deep learning, optimization modeling, pattern recognition, machine vision, natural language processing, knowledge representation/reasoning, data visualization technology, data warehouse and data mining technology, etc.
Industry application	Business intelligence, intelligent finance, public security big data, intelligent transportation, industrial big data architecture and application, etc.
Big data management and ethics	Big data management and innovation, big data governance and policy, engineering ethics, etc.

3.3 Deepen Industry-University Cooperation, Build and Improve Practical Teaching Guarantee System

Deep exploration of new engineering cooperation, cooperative education and various incentive mechanisms. Build a big data engineering cooperation practice platform, resource platform and teaching team for high-quality innovative application talents of new engineering. To ensure the practice teaching system. Based on the training goal of the hierarchical practical ability of big data engineering, it innovates the incentive mechanism of industry-university cooperation and collaborative education of new engineering, and actively creates platforms for innovation and entrepreneurship, school-enterprise cooperation and inter-school alliance. Build a perfect big data course teaching resource platform, big data engineering training teaching resource platform and big data application scientific research innovation resource platform. For students engaged in scientific research, innovation and entrepreneurship practice, school-enterprise cooperation and development and other innovative practical ability training to provide sufficient conditions. The combination of "teachers under the enterprise" and the introduction of professional and technical personnel in the enterprise. Build a high-quality double-qualified teacher team to support the cultivation of students' innovative and practical ability.

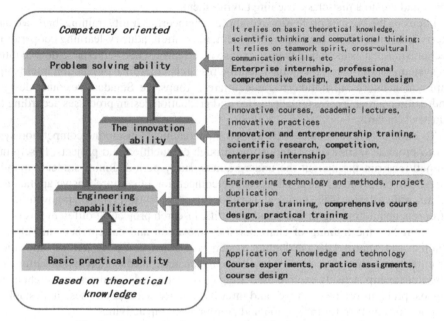

Fig. 1. Capacity development chart of big data professionals

3.4 Innovate the Talent Training Model

In order to adapt to the requirements of educational innovation in the Internet era, big data majors must explore and establish a perfect education system, strengthen course group and course construction, constantly enrich teaching resources, and introduce information and intelligent means to reform the teaching mode of theory courses. Through various innovative mechanisms such as discipline competition, innovation and entrepreneurship practice and industry-university collaboration, the cultivation of practical ability is strengthened to form a good ecology of big data professional talent cultivation. Some good measures are as follows:

To build a "three-in-one education" system, to create a practical platform for ideological and political education, and to deeply integrate ideological and political theory, professional training and social practice.

With the reform of engineering education as the starting point, implement the "output-oriented" curriculum teaching mode and the evaluation mechanism based on curriculum objectives.

Strengthen the special curriculum group and curriculum reform, strengthen the construction of teaching resources platform and teaching materials, and innovate teaching methods and means, especially technical practice courses. We should be good at using the resource platform for teaching, get rid of the dilemma of less practical class hours, integrate the extracurricular practice of small homework, experiment and comprehensive large homework, systematically train the technology and application ability of class hours, and create a first-class teaching environment.

Focus on the big data professional complex engineering ability training, build a characteristic level of ability development system, innovation industry-learning cooperation mechanism, such as the industry project case recurrence, school-enterprise double tutorial system, school-enterprise joint scientific research, enterprise production internship, employment internship, holiday training, interest groups, etc. Standardize course design, production practice, professional practice and graduation design processes according to industry standards.

To build a "whole-course + diversified + hierarchical" discipline competition system to promote learning and innovation through competition and projects. Discipline competitions run throughout the undergraduate study period. Junior students mainly compete in professional basic subjects. The competition of comprehensive application and innovative design is the main category for senior students, relying on innovation and entrepreneurship training projects and scientific research projects at different levels.

Strengthen the training of characteristic innovation and entrepreneurship ability, establish and improve the curriculum system and management system of innovation and entrepreneurship education. We will strengthen general education in innovation and entrepreneurship, actively explore the setting up of cutting-edge courses, comprehensive courses, problem-oriented courses and interdisciplinary seminar courses, and establish a support mechanism for innovation and entrepreneurship activities.

3.5 Improve the Continuous Improvement Mechanism

The major of Big Data should establish quality standards for all teaching links, including the revision of training programs, curriculum objectives and quality evaluation standards. The development plan is based on a planned extensive survey of graduate quality, and based on feedback, the development objectives, professional specifications and curriculum are revised. Reached for a main course set up for target of the combination of quantitative and qualitative evaluation methods, explore the formation of large data professional core ability evaluation mechanism, to gradually build perfect teaching evaluation system and supervision mechanism, and improve the mechanism of continuous improvement, teaching, evaluation and improvement of closed loop iterative control (as shown in Fig. 2), effectively promote the teaching quality of ascension. In addition to the conventional course assessment, on the one hand, the big data application ability level test mechanism corresponding to the stage-level goals is implemented to comprehensively check the achievement of the practical ability course goals; On the other hand, according to the feedback of enterprises and the ability tracking of graduates, the development status of vocational ability of graduates will be continuously monitored. According to the results of monitoring and evaluation, the cause can be traced and continuous improvement can be made.

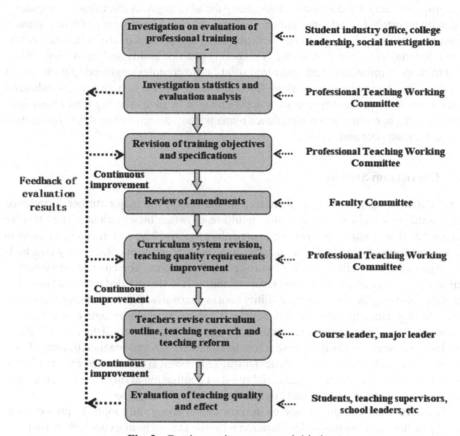

Fig. 2. Continuous improvement initiatives

4 Construction Practice of Big Data Major from the Perspective of New Engineering

The computer science and technology major and the software engineering major of the School of Computer Science of Hubei University of Technology have successively passed the China Engineering Education Certification in 2019 and 2020, and have been successively approved as national first-class professional construction sites. The talent training model based on engineering education has gradually matured. Since its establishment in 2017, the big data major has fully absorbed the engineering education reform experience of these two majors, and actively explored and practiced the new engineering talent training model.

4.1 Specialty Orientation and Training Objectives

Based in Hubei, this major serves the needs of industrial development in Hubei, combined with the school's application-oriented undergraduate education orientation, based on computer science and statistics, integrating the advantageous disciplines of engineering, with industrial big data application as a breakthrough, focusing on multi-disciplinary cross-integration, training good Humanistic quality and professional ethics, solid professional theoretical knowledge, strong engineering practice ability and innovation ability, able to propose innovative and optimized solutions to complex engineering problems of industrial big data, with teamwork ability and international vision, in various Industrial enterprises are high-quality applied talents engaged in industrial big data technology development, operation and maintenance management, design and analysis, integration and testing, support and service.

4.2 Curriculum System

After determining the training objectives of the major, the major further formulated 12 graduation standards that students should reach when they graduate. Then reverse design based on competence-oriented curriculum system. The system also conforms to the national quality standards for undergraduate programs and supplementary standards for engineering education certification for computer majors. The curriculum system of this major plans courses of different levels of ability. It is also divided into basic practical ability course, engineering practical ability course, innovative practical ability course and industrial big data application ability course. Basic practical ability courses refer to professional and technical theoretical courses, which are basically consistent with Table 1. Engineering practical ability course refers to course design and practice training. Innovative practical ability courses include innovative theoretical courses and extracurricular innovative practical activities. Industrial big data application ability courses are mainly industrial application courses and comprehensive practical courses.

The curriculum design is based on the curriculum group and adopts the project case-based practice teaching mode. The duration is two weeks, including comprehensive practice of program design, software system development course, big data system development course and comprehensive practice of big data analysis. Extracurricular innovation practice activities have clear form requirements, such as discipline competition, innovation and entrepreneurship projects, enterprise practice, teachers' scientific research activities, etc. Also clearly defined innovation practice achievement category and credit evaluation standard. Industrial Big data application ability courses mainly include characteristic industry application courses, production practice, professional comprehensive design and graduation design. Featured industry application courses include green industry courses of clean production, low-carbon economy, sustainable development and circular economy, business intelligence methods and applications, industrial big data architecture and application, and industrial big data analysis practice.

In order to better develop practical teaching, Hubei University of Technology implements the system of four semesters a year. In addition to the traditional spring and fall semesters, there are four weeks in summer and two weeks in winter. Specialized social practice and professional practice. The lower grades are mainly social practice. The upper grades are mainly professional practice. Including practice, competition preparation, scientific research, innovation and entrepreneurship activities and other forms, students can choose.

4.3 Comprehensive Professional Reform Measures

The program continues to deepen the reform of engineering education. Always adhere to the "student-centered" teaching philosophy. Continue to carry out comprehensive professional reform and practice. Some results have been achieved. The main initiatives are:

Carry Out the "Output-Oriented" Course Teaching Mode. There are three "supports" that must be identified before any course begins. The competency objectives of the course (to be measurable) should reasonably support the graduation requirements of the program. The course teaching link, teaching content and teaching method should support the training goal of the course effectively. Curriculum assessment methods and evaluation standards should be able to support the achievement of curriculum ability objective evaluation. These three "supports" have logical dependence, which can ensure that teaching activities are carried out based on curriculum competence objectives.

Focus on the Cultivation of Core Competence and Build a Good Curriculum Teaching System Relying on the Platform of Industry-School Cooperation. This major has firstly established the Xipuyang Everbright Data practice teaching platform, the Pocket cloud Big Data Experiment Treasure practice platform of Chinese Academy of Sciences, and the data Cool customer practice platform. It has built a perfect professional curriculum and practical teaching platform. Secondly, the Ministry of Education dawning Big Data Application Innovation Center and Inspur Big Data Supercomputing Center have been built, which have established a good innovation practice platform. Finally, the College of Big Data Industry of Hubei University of Technology, the Industrial Big Data Engineering Center of Hubei Small and Medium-sized Enterprises and the Innovation and entrepreneurship base of Hubei University of Technology students will be established. Construct the diversified practice ability training mechanism.

Platform Teaching Reform the Teaching Mode of the Course. Relying on industry-university cooperation, this major has built a perfect course resource platform. Covering all professional theoretical courses, strengthening course group coordination and reforming course teaching mode. On the one hand, integrate online and offline teaching of courses to break the time and space constraints of the real world. Effective organization of faculty, students, curriculum and resources. It has realized the integration of experiment, extracurricular homework and extracurricular comprehensive homework practice ability training, and the systematization of curriculum group practice ability training. In addition, the platform course teaching adopts the pass-through design. Students "learn by doing", learning experience is good. System rapid automatic evaluation. Teachers can greatly reduce the workload of correcting, timely assessment of students' learning status. Teachers can timely adjust the teaching organization and design, convenient to do personalized guidance.

Pay Attention to the Coordinated Development of Ability and Accomplishment, and Build a Good Education Environment. This professional focus on professional core ability training at the same time, through actively creating "green on the light of" volunteer corps social practice platform, fully implementing course education, definitely require specialized courses focus on communication and communication, teamwork, active learning, the cultivation of professional ethics and engineering ethics, formed the perfect socialist core values and the professional education ecology.

The Characteristic Innovation Ability Training Mechanism Has Been Established. There are 5 credits for innovation and entrepreneurship in this major. Students can achieve innovative results by participating in discipline competitions, innovation and entrepreneurship practices, teachers' scientific research, and enterprise internships. Such as competition awards, patents, soft books, papers, entrepreneurship and so on. Credit will be assessed according to the type and level of achievement. The university has a college students innovation and entrepreneurship base. It has set up innovative courses, created a professional team of teachers, regular training and exchange mechanism, and established a sound innovation and entrepreneurship system.

4.4 Teaching Evaluation and Management

The major has established a perfect teaching evaluation system and continuous improvement mechanism. Besides the supervision of teaching operation, teachers' evaluation, class attendance evaluation and course quality evaluation, the teaching evaluation mechanism has been added. On the one hand, let students self-evaluate the achievement of the learning effect of the course objectives. On the other hand, social industry evaluation is introduced. Junior students are required to take part in THE CSP certification of CCF, while senior students are required to have their professional ability assessed by partner companies during the internship. Thus, a complete evaluation system has been formed, which combines quantitative and qualitative courses of this major and the evaluation of the university and the industry.

The major has clear teaching quality standards, responsibility subjects and guarantee systems in all teaching links. All evaluation results have a clear mechanism to ensure the continuous improvement of professional teaching.

5   Conclusion

This paper explores the establishment of a new engineering development paradigm for big data major in local universities by shifting from subject-oriented to industry-demand-oriented, from specialty segmentation to crossover integration, from adaptation to service to support and guidance. By clarifying the ability system of big data professionals and constructing the curriculum system according to engineering logic, a new mode of cultivating complex engineering ability is explored. Establish and improve the continuous improvement mechanism of engineering personnel training quality. And promote the improvement of professional construction level.

Through five years of exploration and practice, our school has achieved good results in the construction of new engineering major of big data. According to the employment and enrollment situation survey of 2020 and 2021, the employment rate of 2020 graduates is 100%, and the enrollment rate of postgraduate entrance examination is 33%, and the degree of professional relevance of the job is 95%. Graduates' satisfaction with their Alma mater reached 98%. The average salary for new graduates is 6,500 yuan. In addition, AI and Big Data Innovation Alliance of Universities ranked data science and Big data technology-related majors of 482 universities nationwide in 2019, and this major ranked 89th. In 2021, this major was approved as the first-class professional construction point in Hubei Province. At present, we are actively applying for the national first-class professional construction point.

Acknowledgment. This work was supported in part by the funds for the Hubei Province Teaching and Research Project under Grant 2018316.

References

1. He, W., Liu, G.: Exploration and research on core curriculum construction of data science and big data technology. Educ. Rev. **0**(11), 31–35 (2017)
2. Gui, J., Zhang, Z., Guo, K.: Exploration and Practice on the Construction of new majors in universities under the background of new engineering: a Case study of data science and Big data Technology. Comput. Educ. **7**, 5 (2018)
3. Wang, Y., Zhang, M., You, G.: Shaanxi Educ. High. Educ. Edn. (2), 2 (2020)
4. Cui, X., Zhang, M., Zhang, L., Bian, S., Guo, Q.: Research and construction of training courses for application-oriented big data talents under the background of new engineering. Exp. Technol. Manage. **38**(294), 02 218–223 (2021)
5. Luo, E., Huang, J., Duan, H.: Research on training system of data science and Big data Technology under the background of Engineering Education specialty certification. Comput. Inf. Technol. **29**(4), 79–8191 (201)
6. Chen, J., Gao, L., Ma, L.: Exploration and practice of curriculum system construction of data science and big data technology major in local undergraduate universities under the background of new engineering. Educ. Progr. **12**(3), 5 (202
7. Wu, A., Yang, Q., Hao, J.: Innovation and reform of higher education with the construction of "new engineering." Res. High. Eng. Educ. **1**, 1–7 (2019)

Exploration and Analysis of the Training Path for of "Mass Entrepreneurship and Innovation" Talents in Law

Yuzhuo Zou[1] and Jiepin Chen[2(✉)]

[1] Law School, Institute of Law and Economic Development, Guangdong University of Finance and Economics, Guangzhou, China
[2] Law School, Guangdong University of Finance and Economics, Guangzhou, China
chenjiepin@qq.com

Abstract. The basic point of the dimension of legal system is the institutional factor that restricts the teaching methods of law, and it is also the institutional basis that determines us to adopt specific teaching methods. The idea of taking knowledge as the clue in traditional law teaching does not help to cultivate law students' ability of "entrepreneurship and innovation" and character building. We should rely on judicial big data and take the "task-driven" teaching mode as the main line to create a "entrepreneurship and innovation" talent training path for law students.

Keywords: Xi Jinping Thought on the Rule of Law · Entrepreneurship · Innovation · Task-driven

1 Question Raised

Xi Jinping Thought on the Rule of Law represents the latest achievement in adapting Marxist theories on the rule of law to the Chinese context. It is the theoretical basis and guiding ideology for overall law-based governance, building China under the rule of law and promoting a strong country under the rule of law. Its core views include the "eleven insistences", in which it is emphasized that "building a rule of law team with both political integrity and ability" is an important guarantee. It reflects that under the background that overall law-based governance has been raised to the height of national strategy, it must be supported by diversified, multi-level legal talents with innovation and entrepreneurship ability and character. China's talent team for the rule of law includes legislative, judicial and law enforcement personnel, legal service personnel, legal experts and overseas-related legal personnel who engaged in law related work and rule of law in various fields. Universities that cultivate law students are the main places for exporting talents

This paper is part of the phase-in results of the Guangdong Philosophy and Social Science Planning Project "Trial Management Reform and Response under the Perspective of Digital Governance: A Study Based on the Practice in Guangdong" (GD23XFX06) in the year of 2023.

to the rule of law team. Therefore, in order to respond to the needs of the long-term plan for the training of legal talents and the construction of legal team in the new era so that to innovate the training mechanism of legal talents, we should cultivate their critical and innovative legal thinking after teaching the legal professional knowledge of law students. And to cultivate a reserve of legal talents who are familiar with the system of socialist rule of law with Chinese characteristics and with the ideological character of both morality and law, so asto provide strong talent reserve guarantee for accelerating the construction of a socialist country ruled by law [1].

Innovation and entrepreneurship education has always been a dominant topic in pedagogy, that is, through innovation education and entrepreneurship education, integrate with professional knowledge and practical skills, which is pay more attention to the cultivation of students' innovation consciousness and entrepreneurship concept, so as to stimulate college students' innovation and entrepreneurship education. In the field of legal education, the theoretical competition between legal realism and legal formalism induces legal education to wander between idealism and realism. On the one hand, legal norms have extensive coverage, which requires legal education to take all kinds of legal concepts and legal propositions as the logical premise of legal interpretation, so as to carry out formal logic reasoning to ensure the effectiveness and legitimacy of interpretation [2]. On the other hand, the rule of law is far from a simple "rule of rules", but a complex social system engineering. In view of the fact that social phenomena cannot limit their environment and conditions, the realization of the rule of law is inseparable from value judgment and policy considerations [3]. Like other humanities, law and other humanities cannot effectively verify their conclusions under the same conditions as natural disciplines. Which means that the true meaning of legal education is not only to instill as much legal information and cultivate students' general professional practical ability, but also to cultivate students' critical and innovative legal thinking, which must not be satisfied with the full-trained-skill-only and fixed-thinking of professionals, but should be based on broader and solid humanistic theory and science [4].

This paper attempts to take Xi Jinping Thought on the Rule of Law as the theoretical support, relying on judicial big data, to put forward the curriculum concept focusing on improving legal innovation and entrepreneurship skills. By collecting and extracting judicial big data such as China judicial document network, using sand table simulation, promote the "task-driven" teaching mode, to explore the curriculum construction of cultivating law students' "entrepreneurship and innovation" ability and character shaping, and finally to create a "entrepreneurship and innovation" demonstration curriculum for law students in Colleges and universities.

2   Limitations of Existing Legal Education in China

Now the level of legal education in China is complex and diverse, and the starting at a lower level, which is closely related to the historical mission of legal education in the past [5]. Due to the lack of reasonable theoretical and ideological guidance with Chinese characteristics, legal education tends to be informal, low-end and even utilitarian. For a long time, we have no clear understanding of what kind of legal talents to cultivate, but generally organize teaching resources to cultivate law students based on the cultivation of judicial talents (judges, prosecutors and lawyers) [6]. However, the diversity, multi-level and innovation of legal talents that required by the construction of a country ruled by law are far from enough to rely solely on the construction of the judicial field. The fields of legislation, administrative law enforcement, legal experts and foreign-related legal talents all need the excellent law students cultivated by colleges and universities to join the practice. For the cultivation of diversified and innovative legal talents, the combination of professional education with "entrepreneurship and innovation" education for law students is one of the innovative and feasible teaching methods during undergraduate or graduate education stage.

However, innovation and entrepreneurship education is no longer a new institutional concept in the construction of legal education in China. But the supply of relevant education systems in China still stays at the level of institutional oath, and there is no more substantive breakthrough. Under the existing teaching background, the so-called clinic education, moot court and case teaching have been promoted and adopted, but the atmosphere of traditional conceptualist jurisprudence and doctrinal jurisprudence is still quite strong. The positioning of the existing system is unclear, which makes it difficult to effectively play the due function of innovation and entrepreneurship education. Moreover, the existing innovation and entrepreneurship system is difficult to effectively connect with the existing law student education system and their coordination is poor. In short, there are the following problems in the "entrepreneurship and innovation" education of law students in Colleges and universities in China:

2.1 Non-isotropy: The Existing Curriculum System Is Set at Will

As an ideological system, law is only one of the many possible structures of reality. It is not only about the pure rationality of what is justice, but also about how to realize the practical rationality of justice. The duality of legal education determines that we should not care for this and lose that in teaching. We should not only pay attention to imparting legal knowledge through case study, but also pay attention to examining and refining the logical structure and practical skills of handling cases through clinical legal education. However, in the actual law education, the existing curriculum system arrangement in China, which is only limited to ensuring the integrity of curriculum teaching, does not play its due function, and there are many deficiencies in the realization of other functions. Moreover, the response of the current subject system to the cultivation of law students' problem-solving ability is also relatively negative. Throughout the design of China's law curriculum system, it is obvious that there is a non-isotropic situation of "more norms and less innovation". Firstly, some undergraduate colleges are more inclined to theoretical teaching, so that practical education is slightly weaker than theoretical teaching. Secondly, even though some colleges and universities have made great efforts to carry out "entrepreneurship and innovation" education, they still mostly integrate technical education into the innovation and entrepreneurship education system, that is, the "entrepreneurship and innovation" education courses and professional courses are placed in one category, resulting in the shrinkage of the scope of teaching content, and the lack of close connection between "entrepreneurship and innovation" courses and relevant professional courses, also the whole curriculum arrangement focusing too much on the cultivation of College Students' entrepreneurial ability and ignoring the cultivation of innovative ability [7]. Thirdly, most colleges and universities fail to incorporate the "entrepreneurship and innovation" curriculum into the discipline content evaluation, scientific development and talent training system of colleges and universities, leading to the arrangement of innovation and entrepreneurship education curriculum is too casual, which can not clarify the teaching purpose and can not respond to the current situation of the development of the times.

2.2   Ability Worries: Lack of Comprehensive Ability of Teaching Teachers

Influenced by the teaching concept of traditional doctrinal jurisprudence, most colleges and universities still carry out training education with reference to the examination oriented standards. Although some practical factors will be added in the usual class, such as discussing practical cases, social hot spots and other issues in a group way to enhance students' perceptual understanding, they fail to reflect the more prominent innovative paradigm and meet the requirements for the training of practical operation ability. On the one hand, the traditional teaching methods lead college students to still insist on taking classroom notes in the learning process, and memorize all the knowledge points in the textbook before the exam, which fail to cultivate the ability of College Students' autonomous learning, and lack the ability of self-analysis of specific problems. On the other hand, teachers themselves are not experts in legal practice. In view of their limited scope and subject in legal practice activities, they can not teach students the knowledge of legal practice activities, and all legal operation skills can only be realized through students' own practical activities. In addition, in China's current education and teaching system, colleges and universities lack due awareness of the importance of innovation and entrepreneurship education, resulting in the failure to implement various policies and training funds related to their professional teachers.

2.3   Mechanism Dislocation: Lack of Existing Teaching Quality Evaluation Mechanism

With the rapid development of the Internet, the world has entered the information age. Colleges and universities are also carrying out educational information reform and applying the information management system to the daily teaching management (such as educational administration information system, student evaluation system, etc.). There is no doubt that most colleges and universities have a set of teaching evaluation methods for teachers' teaching. The commonly used method is that students grade teachers, that is, manage teachers' teaching through students' evaluation. The school uses this set of evaluation methods to guide and standardize teachers' teaching, so as to ensure the quality of teaching. However, teaching evaluation is a better method, but it is by no means the best method. In fact, external regulation can not have the best method. For one thing, this evaluation is easy to be manipulated when the number of students is small, resulting in a great reduction in objectivity [8]. For another, most colleges and universities have not even established the evaluation mechanism of the practical teaching quality of "entrepreneurship and innovation" education, nor the mechanism of standardizing the assessment contents and giving professional credits. Some schools indirectly judge students' learning progress and validity through incomplete fragmented data such as class average score and pass rate, which is difficult to achieve real fairness and justice due to limitations and fragmentation of data collection. Thirdly, it is difficult to index and detail the indicators of teaching quality assessment, which leads to a greater subjective arbitrariness of assessment and the evaluation index system needs to be improved.

2.4 Function Overload: The Existing "Mass Entrepreneurship and Innovation" Platform Is Difficult to Effectively Connect with the Existing Education Mode

Any new institutional arrangement requires a corresponding process of group learning and social absorption, the length of which depends on the extent to which the idea of the education system fits into the established legal tradition and the extent to which the new institutional arrangement rubs off on the traditional legal framework. The rejection of "innovation and entrepreneurship" by traditional legal education is not only in the level of education resources supply, but also in the difficulty of coordination between education system and other related education modes. At present, most local universities have built multi-level practice teaching bases and legal clinics, but these platforms are mostly used to cultivate students' cognitive ability and basic operation ability in practice teaching, which is difficult to adapt to the needs of "innovation and entrepreneurship" education [9]. The realization of the goal of innovation and entrepreneurship education in law requires further building a simulation platform, or even a real-world platform, emphasizing the empirical nature of legal application, thus guaranteeing the strength of law students in legal skills development.

2.5 Diminishing Effect: The "Entrepreneurship and Innovation" Education Is Clearly Profit-Oriented

At present, "innovation and entrepreneurship" education is still in its initial stage in China, and the over-optimistic attitude towards this topic directly leads to the reduction of the bidirectional effect on the subject and the target. As for the main body of "innovation and entrepreneurship" education, some colleges and universities simply define "innovation and entrepreneurship" education as employment guidance for college students, which directly leads to the alienation of "innovation and entrepreneurship" education at the teaching level, not to mention its integration into the cultivation system of legal talents. As far as the target audience of "innovation and entrepreneurship" education is concerned, the existing utilitarian value orientation of law students binds their vision and takes for granted that innovation and entrepreneurship education can create better material wealth, ignoring the role of innovation and entrepreneurship education on the comprehensive quality and character building of individuals [10]. In other words, the idea of education only stays at the business level, and the comprehensive training and improvement cannot be carried out from student themselves, which leads to the diminishing effect of "innovation and entrepreneurship" education.

It can be seen that the established institutional arrangement will form a more closed field, forming a potential exclusion to the new legislation. Because of this, the field will form its own boundary based on its own logic and necessity, and the determination of this boundary comes from the confrontation of forces inside and outside the field, and the interaction of different systems to define the boundaries of the field [11]. Therefore, there is no a priori answer to the boundary of the field, but the final determination of the place where the action of the field stops under the game and confrontation of many parties. Returning to the educational arrangement of "innovation and entrepreneurship", whether it is the regulation of conflict of interest, the cultivation of students' innovation and entrepreneurship ability, or even the vocational training and guarantee of teachers, when these existing relevant provisions are integrated into the existing legal education field, they will form a conflict with other existing institutional arrangements. In the field of education, the exclusion of this field will reduce the demand of the "innovation and entrepreneurship" system. Therefore, with the rapid development of information technology, the idea of law teaching, which is centered on the teaching of law-making, will be fundamentally changed. The design of law courses should be based on the current data-driven trend, update the concept of traditional legal education, make full use of the advantages of the era of big data and the advantages of digital resources in Colleges and universities, change passivity into initiative, teaching into practice, single classroom teaching into multiple superposition, and professional unification into professional diversification.

3   Optimization and Countermeasures for Cultivating "Innovative and Entrepreneurial" Talents of Law Students Under Xi Jinping's Thought on Rule of Law

The cultivation of legal talents in China's legal education has experienced changes from the science of law, legal system to rule of law, and now the overall trend is towards professional legal education. At first, the concept of "legal talents" was put forward in the Fourth Plenary Session of the 18th CPC Central

Committee, and in the speech of General Secretary Xi Jinping during his inspection at the China University of Political Science and Law in 2017, who mentioned that it should shift from academic legal education to professional legal education required by the rule of law in China. Because the cultivation of talents is closely related to the background and stage of social development, as well as society's demand for talents, Xi Jinping's thought on the rule of law is to put forward and specify the direction and goal of cultivating what kind of rule of law talents China needs nowadays in the context of the times. The ways and methods of law education are extensive and profound, and there is no completely unified and perfect only correct method. Therefore, we should follow the direction indicated by Xi Jinping's thought on rule of law, combine the characteristics of universities and teaching resources to teach law students according to their abilities, and explore and practice various educational innovations [12].

However, how to use big data resources to improve the effectiveness and efficiency of teaching has become the key point of teaching reform. Whether law schools can combine judicial big data and innovation and entrepreneurship projects to cultivate students' big data thinking and the ability to use judicial big data for "entrepreneurship and innovation". This paper intends to design a "three-step" countermeasure for the optimization of "double-creative" teaching for law students with the "task-driven" teaching mode as the main line and judicial big data as the technical support. The so-called "task-driven" teaching refers to the division of course content into several project tasks, which are clearly issued before the lecture, and students are integrated into the corresponding situations by completing the corresponding tasks, in order to enhance students' independent learning ability and desire for knowledge and exploration, as well as the spirit of mutual collaboration [13].

3.1   Step1: The Creation of Contextual Modules

In terms of course design, the first consideration should be to set up a scenario module. The so—called scenario module refers to setting up a virtual simulation case module, choosing current hot issues in law or realistic cases closely related to cutting—edge theories, with problem-oriented focus, and letting students face a realistic situation that needs to be solved. For example, the first trial task of the mock court, the task of the lawyer writing the indictment, etc. The scenario—based modules provide the internal driving force for the "entrepreneurship and innovation" education. There are several basic tasks to be completed during this phase:

1. Firstly, to design teaching programs that focus on the development of knowledge in specialized areas, and to integrate professional knowledge and skills to achieve linkages and integration between them [14]. A professionally strong "entrepreneurship and innovation" curriculum that includes not only general education courses, but also specialized courses [15]. By appropriately increasing the number of online open courses, combining the characteristics and

difficulties of disciplines and specialties, comprehensively sorting out existing educational resources, deeply exploring special educational resources and extraterritorial open class resources, coordinating the allocation of class time between skills training, adjusting curriculum, legal service programs and sandbox simulations.

2. Secondly, coordinate various database resources, such as case database and judgment document database, and use Wolters Kluwer, the magic weapon of Peking University, ICOURT and other legal retrieval databases to ensure the authority and professionalism of all cases during the project. As far as the development stage of rule of law is concerned, the use of judicial big data is conducive to the realization of student learning as the center and the strengthening of teacher-student interaction. The introduction of big data and artificial intelligence into the scientific research and professional teaching of universities is inevitable for social development. The practical teaching of law schools should also pay full attention to and make use of judicial big data and artificial intelligence technology, and incorporate judicial big data mining and artificial intelligence application into the personnel training plan to meet the development needs of the times.

3. Thirdly, the effectiveness of research in feeding teaching. In order to enrich the teaching connotation, teachers need to be encouraged to introduce scientific research results into teaching and integrate scientific research thinking and spirit into the classroom. It is suggested that courses with close integration of specialties or involving interdisciplinary aspects of law can be used as a base point, and the teaching department is encouraged to work as a team to discuss the curriculum and create a brand of the department's curriculum. The classroom teaching should be based on real cases, adopting the paradigm of questioning, discussion, and simulated feedback, allowing students to gain their own factual and legal understanding and judgment through interactive communication, and changing the traditional teaching method of "chalk-and-talk".

4. Fourthly, to build a team of "innovation and entrepreneurship" teachers. We adopt a bidirectional selection method, give full play to the professional refinement of the teachers on campus, explore the externalization of the innovation and entrepreneurship practice ability of the teachers outside the university, establish a collaborative education mechanism between universities and enterprises, research institutes and regions, etc., so as to build a professional team of teachers who understand innovation and entrepreneurship. Through high-quality mentor resources, students can have a deeper understanding of legal practice and practical institutions, guide them to establish the logic of survival and entrepreneurship, and improve the effectiveness and participation of "innovation and entrepreneurship".

3.2 Step 2: Define the Project Tasks

The core of higher education is to cultivate innovative talents. Innovation is contained in personality. At first, it is manifested in strong interest in knowledge, keen critical consciousness, good at putting forward innovative ideas, and completing entrepreneurial projects with innovative and entrepreneurial practice as the carrier. By identifying specific project tasks, students gradually cultivate their critical and rational thinking skills, emphasize their individual passion for knowledge and place it in a broader perspective, apply the theoretical knowledge they have learned to practice, and form their own knowledge structure, which helps to continuously enhance their innovation ability.

In the second stage of shaping, the change from classroom teaching to multiple forms of overlapping teaching can be realized by means of courtroom practical sandbox simulation. Previous law teaching reforms tried to simulate legal practice work through role-playing and classroom simulation, striving to enable students to experience the atmosphere of legal practice work in the school learning process. The reform should not only take advantage of simulation, but also realize the hands-on nature of school students' experience through cooperation with practice departments or enterprises. Through the parallel training of dual-track system, the simulation based on deep understanding of knowledge points will be changed to a practical sandbox simulation of court trial oriented by market demand, and students will really learn how to be innovative and entrepreneurial in the legal consulting market by keenly grasping the opportunities of legal consulting market.

In addition, traction should be developed for cooperation with enterprises. While focusing on direct teaching of school students by word and example, universities should also collaborate with social resources to provide a good practice environment for college students to realize their innovative and entrepreneurial ideas. Attempts can be made to set up relevant platforms or mechanisms for direct communication between universities and governments and enterprises in order to achieve the sharing and win-win situation of various resources such as educational policies, information from all parties and funds and talents. For example, with the collaborative training between our university and the Internet Court, we make full use of the data platform of the court and the digital resources of the university library and the relevant resources of the university experimental center to analyze and process the judicial big data, forming a dual track of teaching content with the mastery of legal skills as the core and project planning oriented to the legal service market demand outside the classroom. By establishing a collaborative cultivation mechanism, we organically combine law classroom teaching with legal service practice, establish an innovative entrepreneurship course with exemplary on-campus experience, and realize the improvement of law students' innovative and entrepreneurial ability.

3.3   Step 3: Collaborative and Self-directed Learning

In the third stage, we emphasize the construction of "Internet+" and take advantage of the research model of big data. Each technology has a different space, with the market as the training goal and practical skills as the training target, focusing on the development of students' legal skills. The activity design part aims to test the completion of project tasks, through which students consolidate what they have learned and familiarize themselves with the skills they have acquired. The teacher can test whether the students are able to apply what they have learned to their practical work by integrating the roles and performance of the project team members in the project tasks with the corresponding evaluation methods and a comprehensive rating for each project member. Therefore, it is necessary to focus on designing the visualization route of project completion, pay attention to the visualization presentation after the specialized argumentation, convey the principle of law and the wisdom of innovation and entrepreneurship in an intuitive and easy visualization way, and strive to create a new power point of innovation and entrepreneurship for law students. This part can learn from the training model of "IRAAC" in American law, i.e. Issue, Rule, Analysis, Application and Conclusion [16,17], and integrate the training objectives of the existing courses on data retrieval, legal service visualization, writing ability and legal negotiation skills. The program integrates the objectives of the existing courses on data retrieval, legal service visualization, writing skills and legal negotiation skills, and adopts the method of case analysis based on judicial big data to train the innovation and entrepreneurship ability of law students in the information age, so that the education of law theory and practice can be seamlessly connected with the innovation and entrepreneurship of students.

What needs to be warned is that in the field of education which lacks experience, the foreign education system transplanted through compulsory institutional change does not fully take into account the existing educational environment in China, and the system transplanted out of the local context falls into the dilemma of "orange in the south and hedge thorn in the north". Moreover, due to the short-sightedness of the system transplantation, some of the education concepts and strategies cannot be carried through, lacking the momentum of sustainable development, resulting in the phenomenon of "chaos when doing, rigidity when managing" in the process of implementation, making it difficult to respond to the real demand of legal education and realize effective supply. Take civil procedure law as an example, the course can be divided into nine modules based on project tasks, and each module is divided into several project tasks, which can be increased or decreased accordingly by each faculty according to their own course implementation plan. Students are divided into 5-6 project teams and work in groups to complete the project tasks. The following is an example of the avoidance system in Chap. 5 of the basic system of civil procedure law.

Table 1. Project task design for Avoidance System

Module example: Avoidance System	
Scenario Assignments	Task 1: master the subjects and reasons of avoidance; Task 2: avoidance procedure
Teaching Contents	1. The concept and value of avoidance; 2. The applicable subject of avoidance; 3. Reasons and procedures for avoidance
Teaching Requirements	1. Be familiar with various laws and regulations on the reasons for avoidance; 2. Understand the relationship between avoidance system and procedural justice
Event Design	Activity 1: simulate the civil trial collegial panel activity; Activity 2: set the reasons for avoidance, and judge whether it should be avoided and how to avoid it
Visualization Display Route	1. Software, methods and core vocabulary of legal retrieval; 2. Systematization of appraisal legal evaluation method; 3. Accuracy and artistic of visualization results
Appraisal/ Evaluation Rules	1. Attendance; 2. Attitude evaluation; 3. Role evaluation; 4. Completion and completeness of legal retrieval; 5. Realization degree of visualization results

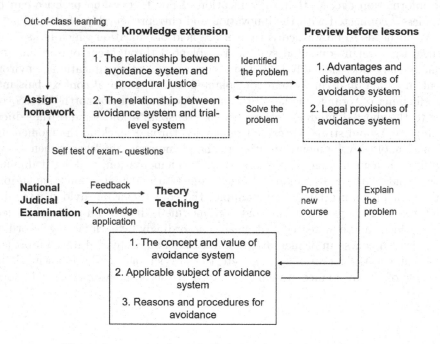

Fig. 1. Instructional program design for avoidance system

4   Conclusion

Based on the scientific nature of law, no matter how much confusion and bewilderment there was and is, we should insist that the highest level of legal excellence cultivation is not simple knowledge impartation, nor utilitarian quality enhancement, but constant character building [18]. As the latest achievement of socialist theory of rule of law with Chinese characteristics, Xi Jinping's thought on rule of law is rich in connotation and complete in system, which provides ideological guidance and theoretical guidance for promoting the reform of legal education and cultivating high quality rule of law talents. Cultivating law students with the ability and character of "dual innovation" is undoubtedly the best response to the urgent need of enriching the outstanding rule of law talents (Fig. 1 and Table 1).

As a long-term strategic plan of the law school, we need to teach not only legal principles and logic, but also cultivate students' ability to analyze cases by applying Xi Jinping's rule of law thinking under the theme of "Xi Jinping's Thought on Rule of Law". We should also build a "project-driven" innovation and entrepreneurship education model with the effect of big data platform to further verify the reliability and operability of theoretical knowledge, cultivate a large number of legal practice talents, and strengthen the understanding of theoretical research and practical supporting experience.

References

1. Decision of the CPC central committee on several major issues concerning comprehensively promoting the rule of law. Technical report (2014)
2. Zhang, W.: Methodology of legal research and education (2017)
3. Bin, W.: The theory and practice of case teaching-an examination centered on American legal education. J. Linyi Univ. **35**(02), 17–22 (2013)
4. Chengguang, W.: The purpose of legal education-and the status, role and relationship of case teaching mode and practical law teaching mode in legal education. Law Soc. Dev. **06**, 33–44 (2002)
5. Wang, D., Miao, H.: The inspiration of American legal education to China's legal education reform. Educ. Explor. (07), 154–155 (2013)
6. Xu, X., Huang, J., Pan, J., Han, D., Shen, S.: Chinese legal education in the forty years of reform and opening up. China Law Rev. (03), 2–27 (2018)
7. Zhao, X.: The construction and improvement of innovative entrepreneurial talent cultivation model in colleges and universities. Educ. Teach. Forum (19), 188–189 (2018)
8. Zhang, W.: Methodology of Legal Research and Education, page 235. Law Press (2017)
9. Yin, S., Tan, Z.: On the construction of practical teaching system of innovation and entrepreneurship education in local colleges and universities of law. Theoret. Observ. (09), 129–131 (2018)
10. Ye, W.: Strategies for integrating innovation and entrepreneurship education into the talent cultivation system of colleges and universities. China Univ. Technol. (06), 92–94 (2018)

11. Quansheng, L.: A brief analysis of Bourdieu's field theory. J. Yantai Univ. (Philos. Soc. Sci. Edn.) (02), 146–150 (2002)
12. Fumin, J.: Positioning of legal education and optimization of talent training mechanism in the context of China's rule of law. J. Law **36**(03), 42–51 (2015)
13. Zhang, H., Tao, J., Wu, Y.: Exploring project-based task-driven curriculum design. Comput. Teach. Educ. Inf. **1** (2020)
14. LiFang, H.: Reflections on the integration of innovation and entrepreneurship education into the whole process of talent cultivation. China Univ. Technol. (07), 89–91 (2018)
15. Bing, L., Chendi, S.: Analysis of innovation and entrepreneurship talent cultivation mode and innovation path in higher education under the background of 'internet+'. South. Agric. Mach. **49**(12), 10 (2018)
16. Zeng, B.: Study on the design of ESP curriculum of English and American contract law (2013)
17. George, T.E., Sydney, S.: What to Learn in Law School: An Introductory Reader in American Law. Peking University Press, Beijing (2017)
18. Long, L., Yi, L.: The humanistic legal education concept: a model for the cultivation of legal talents in high realm. China Law (02), 15–23 (2005)

Design and Implementation of Virtual Reality Experiment Project of Integrated Circuit Routing Algorithm

Zeping Lu[1,2], Genggeng Liu[1,2(✉)], Fuling Ye[1,2], and Wenzhong Guo[1,2]

[1] College of Computer and Data Science, Fuzhou University, Fuzhou, China
{luzeping,liugenggeng,guowenzhong}@fzu.edu.cn
[2] National Demonstration Center for Experimental Network Information Security and
Computer Technology Education, Fuzhou University, Fuzhou, China

Abstract. Given the lack of experimental teaching platforms and tools for integrated circuit (IC) related courses, this paper conducts research on the construction and teaching reform of IC series courses, and transforms the scientific research achievements and academic competition results of Fujian-Taiwan cooperation into virtual reality experimental cases focused on IC layout and routing. Practice shows that transforming the results of scientific research and competition into experiments can stimulate students' enthusiasm for scientific research and academic competitions in the field of IC, and cultivate students' abilities to solve problems of IC routing design. Moreover, the time for achievement transformation is effectively shortened, and the circular development of scientific research, subject competition, and teaching is achieved.

Keywords: Integrated circuit layout · Routing algorithms · Virtual reality experiment · Design rule constraints

1 Introduction

The "Several Policies for Promoting the High-Quality Development of the Integrated Circuit (IC) Industry and Software Industry in the New Era" issued by the State Council in 2020 emphasized that the IC industry and the software industry are the core of the information industry and are the key forces leading a new round of technological revolution and industrial transformation [1]. At present, there is a serious shortage of IC technology talents in our country [2]. To cultivate IC technical talents, who can design chips with superior performance and high yield, and master a wealth of theoretical knowledge, it is also necessary to enrich the experimental and practical experience in colleges and universities [3, 4].

2 Problems Existing in the Practical Teaching of "EDA Technology"

In response to the demand for IC circuit technology talents, Fuzhou University introduces the "EDA (Electronic Design Automatic) Technology" course in the training plan for students who major in Computer Science and Technology. Through theoretical learning and experimental teaching, it aims to enable students to understand the general steps and basic methods of analysis and design of the modern hardware system, to realize the current state of the forefront of IC development, to master basic innovation methods, to carry out engineering design and implementation, and to have the preliminary capability to independently develop IT products or systems and technical transformation [5–7]. In the practice teaching research of the "EDA Technology" course, it is found that there are the following problems.

2.1 Lack of Layout and Routing Experiments

In the EDA process, the layout and routing are key steps (as shown in Fig. 1), and its quality has a great impact on the final chip's good rate [8, 9]. Due to the current monopoly on some mainstream EDA tools on the market and the restriction of the usage of EDA tools in China, it is increasingly difficult to obtain relevant EDA tools as experimental tools for teaching. In consequence, the current practical teaching of "EDA Technology" lacks the key content of IC layout and routing, and student's understanding of it mostly stays at the theoretical level.

2.2 Difficulties in Operating Commercial Software

The development of the IC industry is characterized by rapid evolution and measurable progress. The current commercial software is highly specialized, complicated in operation, and does not provide data for learning. At present, there are few test circuit data available in academia, which can hardly satisfy the teaching needs.

2.3 Unaffordable Cost of Experiment

Commercial EDA tools are mostly used in industry due to their high price, while software functions applied for academia have great limitations and are not suitable for use in teaching scenes.

2.4 Non-intuitive Experimental Results

For the complex internal structure of IC chips, the wire width is as small as more than 100 nm, and there is a lack of a more intuitive and concise way for students to better understand the principles of IC routing.

In response to the above problems, this paper starts from the training goal of the Computer Science and Technology major, focuses on the design of IC routing algorithms, uses virtual simulation technology, and integrates the scientific research and competition results of Fujian-Taiwan cooperation to design and develop this experimental project. The implementation of the project helps students to understand the key principles of IC routing algorithms with a more concise and clear operation method. To cultivate students' abilities to learn autonomously and solve complex engineering problems such as IC routing, shorten the time for the transformation of high-level scientific research and competition results, and expand the depth and breadth of experimental teaching [10, 11].

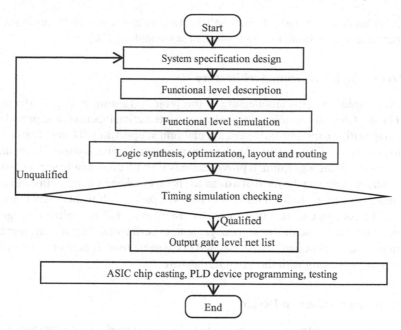

Fig. 1. The EDA design method flow.

3 Experimental Case Design and Implementation Scheme

Virtual simulation experiment teaching is an important part of the informatization construction of higher education and construction of experimental teaching demonstration centers [12]. Using virtual simulation technology, the virtual environment can be linked with objective reality, and an accurate and complete description of the various and complex information of objective reality can be made [13, 14]. It is conducive to further promoting the deep integration of information technology and higher education, and accelerating the construction and application of high-quality online education resources [15].

In 2018 and 2019, the team composed of teachers and students of our college won the third prize in the International Symposium on Physical Design (ISPD) academic competition for two consecutive years. The competition is organized by the International Symposium on Physical Design of Integrated Circuits. As of 2020, sixteen competitions have been held. In the competition, Cadence, one of the world's three major EDA companies, gave detailed routing propositions for practical problems the industry faced. Based on industrial circuit test data, it was required to design high-quality detailed routing results while considering various practical design constraints. The proposition has attracted many domestic and foreign scholars to carry out research.

This paper intends to transform the achievements of our institute in the above-mentioned ISPD competitions and the advanced scientific research achievements in related fields into virtual simulation experimental teaching project, which greatly shortens the time for cutting-edge technological achievements to be put into experimental teaching and narrows the distance between experimental teaching and real engineering practice. So that those experiments that can't do in reality can be realized in undergraduate experimental teaching through virtual simulation technology [16].

3.1 Overall Implementation Architecture

The overall implementation architecture of this project is shown in Fig. 2. The project adopts HTML, CSS, and JavaScript to realize web interaction functions and page design. The core simulation experimental operation platform adopts Unity3D and 3D simulation technology to build a 3D model of IC nets and experimental scene, and use C# language to realize the core routing algorithm. It provides Unity3D with event response processing of experimental operation in the form of a dynamic library and embeds the entire simulation experimental operation platform into the online web pages with WebGL technology for students. The background function of the website uses PHP to realize management and control functions such as user management, experimental data management, and experimental assessment and evaluation, and at the same time, it performs data storage and real-time interaction with the MySQL database.

3.2 Experimental Content Design

This experiment concentrates on the content of IC routing algorithms designation, including critical knowledge such as the common chip design rule constraints (DRC) in IC layout and routing, the selection and setting of the IC routing environment, the design of routing algorithms, and DRCs repair of nets. For the knowledge, several experimental parts based on students' autonomous operation, such as pre-experiment theoretical learning, preview modules, online testing, and net generation, are designed, whose steps are shown in Fig. 3.

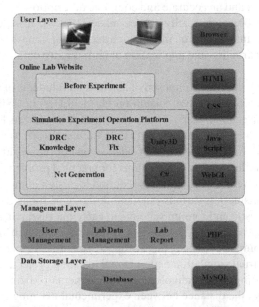

Fig. 2. The project's overall architecture diagram.

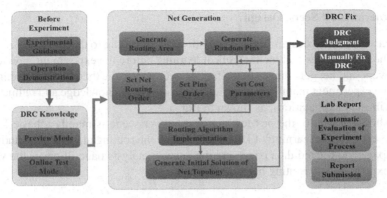

Fig. 3. The flow chart of the experiment.

The experiment completes the initial routing through the simulated router, which is simplified from the algorithm proposed in the related research [17–23]. The algorithm flow is shown in Fig. 4. Specifically, the algorithm selects any pin as the starting point and utilizes the single-source shortest path faster algorithm (SPFA) to find the shortest path from the starting point to other pins in turn. Each time the shortest path connecting a pin is obtained, this path is selected as a subtree of the Steiner tree, and the cost of the subtree in the routing graph is updated as 0. Then, the algorithm connects other pins. Repeat the above process until all the pins are connected to form a complete Steiner tree.

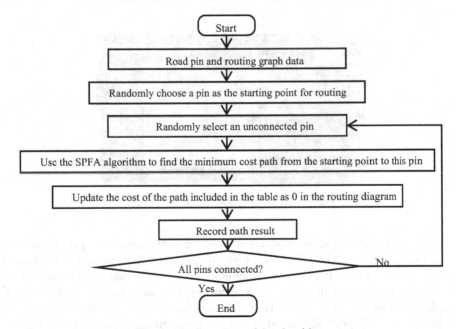

Fig. 4. The flow chart of the algorithm.

3.3 Experimental Scene Design

In this case, the scene design is reasonably divided according to the above experimental parts. The main scenes include theoretical learning before the experiment, preview and test answers, and net generation. In the form of web pages, the theoretical learning scene before the experiment mainly displays relevant theoretical knowledge and online videos of experimental explanations, as shown in Fig. 5.

As shown in Fig. 6, the preview and test answer scene is mainly a basic learning module set up for the learning of DRCs involved in the routing algorithm, including the answer page, the related data page, and the answer analysis page. It paves the way for part of experiments in routing net generation.

Fig. 5. The theoretical learning scene before the experiment.

Fig. 6. The preview and test answer scene.

In the net generation scene, students will use the core algorithm to practice routing operations, as shown in Fig. 7. It uses Unity3D to design the interactive interface of routing net parameter setting, net adjustment, constraint information, 3D routing nets, etc. The front-end interactive data is transferred into the back-end routing algorithm to calculate the routing results, which are displayed on the model interactive interface in the form of 3D nets. The net adjustment interface and constraint information interface are provided to assist students in repairing net constraints on the model interactive interface.

3.4 Automatic Assessment and Evaluation System for Experimental Results

The experimental project adopts the evaluation method of process assessment, and comprehensively assesses and evaluates the learning effect of students from four aspects: preview mode, online test, net generation, and experimental report, as shown in Table 1.

For the part of net generation, the system algorithm comprehensively considers various factors in the student's experiment process to weigh and obtain the score. These factors include the difficulty level, the completion time, and the complete accuracy of the final results of the experiment. The specific calculation standards are as follows.

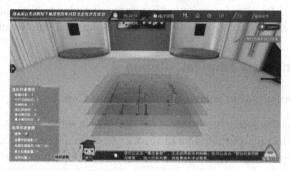

Fig. 7. The net generation scene.

Table 1. Experiment assessment and evaluation standard

Stage	Weight	Grading	Examination content
Preview mode	15%	20 Single-choice questions, 5 points for each question	The DRC knowledge
Online test	30%	10 multiple-choice questions, 10 points for each question	The DRC knowledge with higher difficulty
Net generation	30%	According to the correctness of the experimental steps, the completion degree of the experiment, the completion time of the experiment, and other indicators to evaluate and score	Application of the DRC knowledge in solving practical engineering problems
Lab report	25%	The results are given based on comprehensive consideration of the completeness and innovation of the lab report	Ability to record and analyze experimental process

Difficulty Level. Multiply the full score by the difficulty coefficient to get the score. The difficulty coefficients for "Easy", "Medium", and "Difficult" levels are 0.8, 0.9, and 1.0 respectively.

Completion Time. Multiply the score of difficulty level by the completion time factor. The factor starts from 1.0 and decreases by 0.1 for every half hour.

Completion Accuracy. Multiply the score of completion time by the accuracy coefficient to get the student's experimental score, denoted as *ScoreE*. The accuracy coefficient is the number of constraints repaired by the students divided by the total number of constraints. The computational formula of *ScoreE* is as follows:

$$ScoreE = 30 \times C_d \left(1.0 - \frac{Time}{0.5} \times 0.1 \right) \times \frac{x}{N} \tag{1}$$

where C_d is the difficulty coefficient, *Time* is the completion time in hours, x is the number of constraints fixed by the student, and N is the total number of constraints.

4   Experiment Case Implementation

4.1   The Implementation Process of Experimental Case Teaching

As a 4 class hours advanced experiment of the "EDA Technology" course, the experiment requires students to fully grasp the basic knowledge of the routing process, such as pins, tracks, vias, etc., to deeply understand the DRC problem of IC chips. Open online through virtual simulation, students can access the experimental platform through the Internet at any time for practical learning and skill training. The proposed experimental project can be set up with various modes and different levels of difficulty so that students can arrange experiments according to their knowledge accumulation and interests and their abilities to actively explore and practice learning independently is cultivated. Therefore, students can get a better education by their aptitude.

After the students complete all the experimental processes according to the experimental procedure (as shown in Fig. 8), including theoretical learning before the experiment, preview module, online test, and net generation, and submit the experimental results, the system will automatically give evaluation score according to the difficulty level, completion time and accuracy. Finally, the online experiment score can be obtained by weighting the evaluation score with the previous preview part, test part, etc.

In addition, students can complete the experimental report after class and submit it in the system for teachers to review it online. And the teachers can give the final experimental score to students by combining the online experimental score and the experimental report score.

4.2   Implementation Effect

The proposed experimental project is provided to third-year students majoring in Computer Science and Technology. It has been successfully used for 3 semesters, with a total of 247 students participating. And we analyzed and counted the feedback data of 99 students majoring in computer science, as shown in Table 2. It can be seen that most students can basically master relevant knowledge through the experiment, and more than half of them have developed an interest in in-depth research in the field of EDA during the experiment.

Students generally feedback the proposed experiment project can enable them to master the working principle and basic process of the router and repair the DRC of the routing net. And the design of experimental parts from simple to difficult, and the design of experimental content from theory to practice, can enable students to better grasp knowledge and stimulate their enthusiasm for research. Furter more, the interactive part of the simulation experiment allows students to fully understand the various violations of DRC, and practice the process of DRC repair in person so that students can masterly repair the routing net based on their DRC knowledge (Table 2).

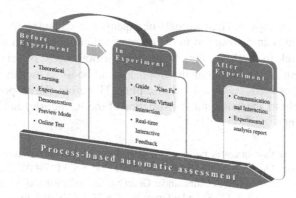

Fig. 8. The process of experiment implementation.

Table 2. Feedback data from students

	Rationality of experimental content	Divertingness of the experimental format	Satisfaction with the experimental operation experience	Mastery of the experimental knowledge	The degree of stimulation of students' research interest in the field of EDA
Num	86	67	25	97	56
Percentage	86.87%	67.68%	25.25%	97.98%	56.57%

The feedback of students can better summarize the new ideas and directions of the project in the future, effectively stimulate students' understanding and interest in cutting-edge disciplines, and stimulate their enthusiasm to participate in domestic and foreign competitions in the field of EDA.

At the same time, by expanding based on this experiment, this experimental project has been approved as a first-class course for provincial virtual simulation experiment teaching in 2021. The experimental teaching team has successfully applied for 1 provincial SRTP (Student Research Training Plan) and won 1 national second prize, 1 school first prize, and 1 school second prize in subject competitions.

5 Conclusion

In this paper, by using virtual simulation technology, the advanced scientific research and competition results of Fujian-Taiwan cooperation are transformed into experimental content, and the nano-scale IC routing process is designed as experimental interactive content. In the practice of analyzing and applying the typical DRC, students' ability to solve complex engineering problems independently is cultivated. We pay attention to the organic integration of ideological and political education into the curriculum, and help students effectively convert their cognition into an understanding of cutting-edge disciplines.

In the future, it is expected that through the expansion and open use of this experimental project, students can be inspired to obtain more scientific research and competition results to give back to teaching, thus realizing a virtuous cycle of scientific research, discipline competition, and teaching development, and boosting the development of the current nationally valued "IC" first-level discipline. Therefore, the proposed experimental project can help to accelerate the construction of the IC industry in China to get out of the predicament.

Acknowledgment. This work was partially supported by the National Natural Science Foundation of China under Grants No. 61877010, No. 11501114, No. 11271002, and No. 11141005, National Basic Research Program of China under Grant No. 2011CB808000, State Key Laboratory of Computer Architecture (ICT, CAS) under Grant No. CARCHB202014, Fujian Natural Science Funds under Grant No. 2019J01243, and Fuzhou University under Grants No. GXRC-20060 and No. XRC-1544.

References

1. Ministry of Industry and Information Technology. The first-level discipline of integrated circuits will be established to further strengthen the Demonstration School of Microelectronics. vol. 5, p. 1, Semiconductor Information (2019)
2. Ma, S., Shen, L., Wang, Y., Tang, Y., Tang, Z., Wang, Z.: Exploration on the construction of practice system for the training of integrated circuits design talent under the background of new engineering. Res. Explor. Lab. **41**(1), 206–210(2022)
3. Li, W., Fang, Y., Guo, Y., Ji, X., Xia, X., Zhang, C.: Research on virtual simulation in experimental teaching of integrated circuit series of courses. Exp. Sci. Technol. **15**(2), 74–76 (2017)
4. Hu, J.: Research on the training plan of integrated circuit professional talents. Heilongjiang Edu. (High. Educ. Res. Eval.) **11**, 89–90 (2020)
5. Gu, S., Du, D., Liu, Y., Ji, Z.: Exploration of teaching method of EDA course innovative experiment. Exp. Technol. Manag. **32**(003), 40–43 (2015)
6. Yin, S.: Exploration of multi-level progressive experiment teaching of integrated circuit specialty. Res. Exp. Lab. **38**(8), 166–168 (2019)
7. Yin, S.: Discussion on integrated circuit experiment teaching under the background of innovation. Res. Exp. Lab. **39**(7), 174–177 (2020)
8. Yang, X., Liu, D.: EDA Technology Foundation and Experimental Tutorial. Tsinghua University Press, Beijing (2010)

9. Xu, N., Hong, X.: Integrated Circuit Physical Design Theory and Algorithm. Tsinghua University Press, Beijing (2009)
10. Wu, Q., Peng, M., Li, J.: Experiment of CPU design based on open-source EDA software. Comput. Educ. **8**, 156–159 (2018)
11. Li, H.: EDA Software Integrated Management System. University of Electronic Science and Technology of China, Beijing (2015)
12. Li, P., Mao, C., Xu, J.: Construction of the national virtual simulation experiment teaching centers, improving the experimental teaching informatization in higher education. Res. Exp. Lab. **32**(11), 5–8 (2013)
13. Xu, W., Chen, Q., Ye, Y., Gu, G., Jin, Y.: Construction of teaching resources for computer virtual simulation experiment. Comput. Educ. **5**, 118–122 (2020)
14. Hu, Z., Wang, Y., Wang, C., Li, P.: Construction and thinking of virtual simulation experimental teaching center for civil engineering. Exp. Technol. Manag. **36**(10), 218–220(2019)
15. Zhao, X.: Exploration on the construction of virtual simulation teaching resources under the background of deep integration of production and education. China New Telecomm. **22**(12), 222–223 (2020)
16. Xiong, H.: Teaching characteristics of national virtual simulation experiment teaching project in new era. Exp. Technol. Manage. **36**(9), 1–4 (2019)
17. Liu, G., Zhuang, Z., Guo, W., Chen, G.: A high-performance x-architecture multilayer global router for VLSI. Acta Automatica Sinica **46**(1), 79–93 (2020)
18. Liu, G., Chen, Z., Zhuang, Z., Guo, W., Chen, G.: A unified algorithm based on HTS and self-adapting PSO for the construction of octagonal and rectilinear SMT. Soft Comput. **24**(6), 3943–3961 (2020)
19. Zhang, X., et al.: Mini delay: multi-strategy timing-aware layer assignment for advanced technology nodes. In: 2020 Design, Automation & Test in Europe Conference & Exhibition (DATE 2020), pp. 586–591 (2020)
20. Liu, G., Baom, C., Wang, X., Guo, W.,* Chen, G.: Multi-strategy delay-driven layer assignment for non-default-rule wiring techniques. Jisuanji Xuebao/Chin. J. Comput. **46**(4), 743–760(2023)
21. Liu, G., Wei, L., Xu, N*.: Multi-strategy layer assignment algorithm considering bus timing matching. Jisuanji Fuzhu Sheji Yu Tuxingxue Xuebao/J. Comput.-Aided Des. Comput. Graph. **34**(4), 545–551(2022)
22. Zhen, Z., Liu*, G., Ho, T.-Y., Yu, B., Guo, W.: TRADER: a practical track-assignment-based detailed router. In: Design, Automation and Test in Europe Conference and Exhibition (DATE 2022), pp. 766–771 (2022)
23. Liu, G., Zhang, X., Guo, W., Huang*, X., Liu, W.-H., Chao, K.-Y., Wang, T.-C.: Timing-aware layer assignment for advanced process technologies considering via pillars. IEEE Trans. Comput.-Aided Des. Integr. Circ. Syst. **41**(6), 1957–1970 (2022)

Reform and Practice of Programming Courses' Construction

Xiaohui Tan[✉], Zhiping Shi, Na Jiang, Jun Li, and Rui Wang

Information Engineering College Capital Normal University Beijing, Beijing, China
{xiaohuitan,shizp,jiangna,junmuzi,rwang04}@cnu.edu.cn

Abstract. The design of course group is an important part of major construction. The construction of course group should be closely focused on the professional talent training objectives. The cultivation of talents for artificial intelligence teachers specialty not only needs to develop students' ability to solve practical problems by applying the core technology in the field of artificial intelligence, but also needs to cultivate their theoretical knowledge, teaching practice and teaching ability of carrying out intelligent education. This paper analyzes how the programming course group plays its important supporting role in the process of talent training. The design method of the programming course group for AI teacher training is proposed. Besides we introduce the teaching practice and reform plan of the programming course group for AI teacher training in Capital Normal University.

Keywords: artificial intelligence teacher training program · programming course group · educational reform · teaching practice

1 Introduction

In recent years, the universities have actively dovetailed with national strategies on Artificial Intelligence (AI) development. Thoroughly implement the State Council's "New Generation of Artificial Intelligence Development Plan" [1] and "Action Plan for Artificial Intelligence Innovation in University" [2] published by the ministry of education. Data from the "2020 Artificial Intelligence Talent Training Research Report" show that there are 367 universities offering AI-oriented majors. The report of the 19th National Congress clearly proposed that artificial intelligence education should start from children, and the State Council's development plan for a new generation of AI also proposed to set up AI-related courses at the primary and secondary school and gradually promote programming education. The artificial Intelligence Normal Major cultivates senior scientific and technological talents and teachers with AI professional quality and cross-innovation ability. In the teaching of AI normal major, AI programming related courses require to be dynamic integrated and arranged as a whole. We should clarify the level of knowledge considering coherence and make the content rich and uncluttered. The aim of the reform is to improve students' comprehension and understanding. Our final goal is gradually improving students' problem solving skills, thus fostering innovative and application-oriented talents.

2 Design of Course Group

Course group refers to the collection of courses with certain relevance in teaching content. Such relevance can be a series of bridging courses within the same major, similar courses offered in different majors with different requirements, and the same courses offered by different teachers, institutions or majors. A relatively common course group refers to a coherent set of courses that belong to the same major and have sequential relationship. Course group is not only the natural unit of resource aggregation, but also the important foundation to maintain curriculum learning community. The construction of community helps to make tacit knowledge system explicit and organize individual knowledge together, which is not only important for the ecological evolution of teaching resources, but also for the improvement of talent cultivation quality. Under the framework of professional curriculum system, we can explore the articulation relationship between courses, equip reasonable teachers for course cluster construction, avoiding duplication or disconnection of course contents, making knowledge coherent and progressive, and thus improve teaching quality. Course group plays an important role in aggregating teaching resources and high quality sharing. It is one of the most important elements in sustaining the ecological dynamics of the teaching system. In the past year, Capital Normal University has carried out the construction of course group in the direction of artificial intelligence teacher training, and has achieved good results. This paper discusses and summarizes the exploration and practice of the construction of programming course group.

2.1 The Basic Goal of Course Group Construction

The construction of course group is a part of the specialty construction, and the construction of course group should be carried out closely focused on professional talent training objectives [3]. The AI normal major cultivates a new generation of innovative talents in the field of artificial intelligence. Graduates should master the basic theories, methods and technologies in the field of artificial intelligence, as well as the ability to apply core technologies in the field of artificial intelligence to solve practical problems, having lifelong learning ability and sustainable development capability. At the same time, normal university students have educational theoretical knowledge, teaching practice and the ability to carry out intelligent education. Besides, high-level scientific research and teaching ability is the most important ability for the students and these capabilities will ultimately provide support for the construction of China's education, science and technology, and intelligent society. The construction of course group should serve the goal of talent training, and should focus on the knowledge reorganization and knowledge integration of courses, which requires the redesign of teaching contents such as syllabus and experimental syllabus of individual courses. In terms of teaching objectives, the programming course group teaching is to make students proficient in a programming language, familiar with relevant development methods and tools, understanding object-oriented thinking and familiar with object-oriented programming techniques.

2.2 Course Group Framework

Artificial intelligence has now become one of the new focal of international competition, and it has become an inevitable trend for the future development of education to offer AI-related courses in primary and secondary schools. The gradual promotion of programming education and the promotion of AI teacher training has become an inevitable trend in the future educational development. Cultivation and improvement of programming ability is the key to the quality of AI teacher training majors. Programming courses have highly practical features [4]. Students are expected to master concepts as well as practical programming. From the point of view of teaching content, programming course teaching has the problem of complex content and disconnection between courses, and some students are easy to gradually lose confidence and interest in the process of learning. The existing teaching models of this kind of courses rarely reflect and summarize the differences between the results of previous course assessment. Few analysis and the achievement of students' learning objectives are clarified, so lacking of optimize of the subsequent teaching design and few efforts is to enhance the teaching effect through continuous improvement. Therefore, the related courses must be integrated and arranged, and the hierarchical relationship between knowledge and skills must be clarified, so that the knowledge points are coherent and progressive in teaching procedure. In the gradual improvement of students practical problem solving ability and improvement of students' understanding, and then we can train the future teachers with strong professional skills. In the teaching process, what is the most important is the technical training and ability training, including the training of students' practical ability, analysis and problem solving ability, writing and expression ability, cooperation ability and so on. We should emphasize the importance of practical teaching and formulate appropriate systematic teaching plans and training objectives for students. The construction of course group is conducive to the sharing of teaching resources and the improvement of teaching quality. Course group is not only the natural unit of resource aggregation, but also an important basis to maintain the curriculum learning community. Teaching resources can be shared among courses to avoid repeated construction. The teaching accumulation established by different courses from their own perspective can be used as reference and expansion of others. The contribution of teachers and students from different courses can create and refine some excellent works and improve the quality of teaching. The most important thing is that the construction of course group can establish a systematic training process. The training mode from shallow to deep and step by step is conducive to students' building of professional identity and the mode can solve the problem of difficult for entry and slow improvement during the learning process.

Combined with the relevant requirements of the national standard for undergraduate teaching quality, the core competencies of artificial intelligence teacher training are summarized and sorted out, integrated into the course group, and the overall framework of the program course group is designed, as shown in Fig. 1.

The teaching of the programming course group of normal major in artificial intelligence should be carried out to serve the realization of talent training objectives as well as the programming ability and teacher training skills. The required abilities need to achieve internal integration and equip the teaching process with the cultivation of ability by creating a practical platform for students. The programming course group created by the

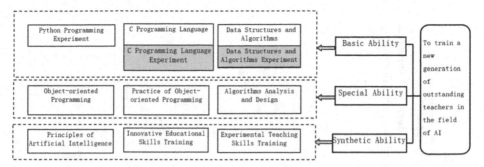

Fig. 1. Programming course group framework

Artificial Intelligence Teacher Training Program of Capital Normal University contains 11 courses, namely "Python Programming Experiment", "C Programming Language", "C Programming Experiment", "Data Structure and Algorithm", "Data Structure and Algorithm Experiment", "Object Oriented Programming", "Comprehensive Practice of Object Oriented Programming", "Algorithm Analysis and Design", "Principles of Artificial Intelligence", "Innovative Education Skills Training", and "Experimental Teaching Skills Training". These courses are all sequential in content with varying degrees of interconnection, and the major-related courses involve eight instructors. Graduates can work in the field of basic education in the teaching of technical courses, teaching management, teaching support, or pursue a master's degree in a related discipline. Figure 1 shows the framework of the programming course group for the AI teacher training program.

3   Course Group Construction and Practice

As the source of high-quality teacher training, the core characteristics of teacher training should be highlighted in the training of normal students under the background of artificial intelligence. In normal education, artificial intelligence-related knowledge and skills courses need to be introduced into the training of normal university students, and the ability of teachers to implement intelligent education needs to be cultivated.

3.1   Course Group Design

Teachers of artificial intelligence courses in primary and secondary schools should keep active in learning. For example, we should keep abreast of national and regional artificial intelligence development policies and take the initiative to use network resources to carry out autonomous learning of artificial intelligence knowledge [5]. In terms of attitude, it should be recognized that AI courses are an essential information technology foundation for future education to prepare for future changes. In terms of professional knowledge, in addition to learning disciplinary professional knowledge, modern teaching methods should be enriched. The most important thing is to improve practical knowledge through systematic process as "theoretical learning - practice application - reflection - practice again". In terms of professional ability, in addition to constantly improving their own

Table 1. The supporting matrix of course group for training requirements

Training Requirements / Courses	Practice teacher's ethics			Learn to teach		Learn to nurture		Learn to develop	
	Ethics norms	Educational sentiment	Academic literacy	teaching ability	Class guidance	Comprehensive education	Learn to reflect	Communication and collaboration	International vision
Python Programming Experiment	3	3	5	3	3	2	4	3	4
C Programming Language	3	3	5	4	3	2	5	4	3
Data Structure and Algorithm	3	3	5	4	4	3	4	4	3
Object Oriented Programming	3	3	5	5	4	3	4	4	3
Algorithm Analysis and Design	4	4	5	4	3	4	4	3	3
Principles of Artificial Intelligence	5	4	5	5	4	3	3	3	5
Innovative Education Skills Training	5	5	4	4	5	5	5	5	4
Experimental Teaching Skills Training	4	4	3	5	5	4	5	4	4

teaching ability, more important is to improve teaching research ability and practice. The teaching objectives for normal university students should be implemented through appropriate curriculum setting and educational approaches, so all courses and teaching activities should be carefully designed and rationally arranged to form a unified education and teaching system to ensure the realization of all teaching objectives. The construction of course group should be carried out around the training goal of artificial intelligence teachers. AI normal students in capital normal university should meet the teachers' professional graduation requirements. The four aspects should be covered as Practicing teacher ethics, learning to teach, learning to nurture, learning to develop. The training objectives are broken down into 8 requirements including teacher ethics, educational sentiment, subject knowledge, teaching ability, class guidance, comprehensive education, learning to reflect, communication and cooperation, etc., The objectives is decomposed into 23 graduation requirement index points. The different courses in the curriculum group have their own responsibilities and focus on the corresponding competencies, but they are closely focused on core professional skills and the development of teacher excellence ability. We regard the training requirements as a one-dimensional space, and the courses in the curriculum group as a one-dimensional space. This two-dimensional space can constitute the design space of the programming class course group, which make the correlation between the training objectives and the curriculum responsibilities. The support degree of the curriculum is described for the graduation requirements with 5 levels of intensity. A support matrix of course group for graduation requirements is formed, as shown in Table 1.

Programming courses aim to cultivate students' ability to "abstract" and "design" programming. Students accumulate rich programming experience and familiar with relevant programming languages, tools and platforms. Solid basic skills and strong practical ability can be learned to solve problems proactively and to be good at using the knowledge they have learned. In course design, we respect the learning rules, proceed from the simple to the deep, pay attention to practice, and link each other closely. The specific settings are shown in Table 2. The maturity of digital teaching resource platform provides a powerful guarantee for resource sharing. Compared with the large and complete resource library, the teaching resource platform which is related to the major, has the moderate scale, and has the curriculum internal correlation which is beneficial to promote the teaching development. In practical teaching application, course group with certain relevance should become an important carrier of digital teaching resource construction for courses sharing and optimization. In addition, in the construction of the application platform of digital teaching resources, attention should be paid to the continuous construction process of resource optimization and dynamic evolution, so as to fully mobilize the enthusiasm of teachers and students and promote the virtuous cycle development of shared teaching resources.

3.2 Practical Teaching Methods and Means

The cultivation of artificial intelligence normal university students needs to give consideration to the cultivation of innovation ability and normal university students' skills. Programming courses are very important for the development of students' professionalism, and they must be unique in teaching methods and means boldly strengthen on

Table 2. The curriculum of the programming course group

Course Name	Credits	Total Hours	The Bilingual State
Python Programming Experiment	3	5	3
C Programming Language	3	5	4
Data Structure and Algorithm	3	5	4
Object Oriented Programming	3	5	5
Algorithm Analysis and Design	4	5	4
Principles of Artificial Intelligence	4	5	5
Innovative Education Skills Training	5	4	4
Experimental Teaching Skills Training	4	3	5

experiment and innovativeness. In recent years, we take the opportunity of strengthening the practice reform of programming course group, and form the teaching method of combining experiment driven teaching with comprehensive practice. The traditional practical teaching of programming is generally uniform in its requirements, the content, the procedure etc., which restricts creative thinking of students with different foundation. We change the previous way, fully use the information platform in the students' experimental stage, and create an experimental teaching mode supported by a variety of media teaching resources and interactive learning. On the premise of giving full control to students' autonomy and aided by teacher-led learning, a multi-level independent experimental teaching mode is formed, which fully mobilizes students' enthusiasm for programming learning. Firstly, the teachers of each course re-divided the knowledge points of course and skills mastery, established a system of knowledge points based on "fragmentation". Then combined with the actual situation of our students, teachers recorded these "fragmented" knowledge points into practical micro-lesson videos with emphasis on the progressive relationship between knowledge points for students to watch and learn repeatedly. We realize online learning across time and space, and at the same time to prepare for the regularization of the epidemic [6]. In addition, on the basis of self-made practical micro-lesson videos, high-quality MOOC videos are also introduced to provide comprehensive online teaching resources to meet the learning needs of students at different levels. In the teaching process, case-based teaching are used throughout. Heuristic and research-based teaching methods are adopted to pay attention to cultivating students' programming innovation ability of independent learning and independent experiment. Students will improve their ability to organize seminars and develop good presentation skills through document preparation and comprehensive experiment defense. In terms of teaching methods, we aim to cultivate innovative and application-oriented teacher-training talents. By breaking the past practice of setting experiments by courses only, we establish a hierarchical experimental and practical teaching system. By means of "basic skills - comprehensive case –expanded practice" according to the new requirements of professional training, we comprehensively considerate the requirements of the programming course group for personnel training goals.

We build a practical teaching platform for students from the unified cases throughout each class and achieve the ability cultivation goals, as shown in Fig. 2.

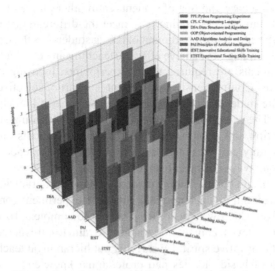

Fig. 2. Course competency development objectives

Firstly, basic skills are primary target [7]. This level covers basic programming knowledge, debugging techniques, syntax, algorithms, and verification experiments. The main purpose is to strengthen students' basic experimental skills and theoretical training, and gradually form the ability to connect with reality, analyze and solve problems, and lay a foundation for cultivating students' innovation ability. Secondly, comprehensive cases are taken as the main clue, and the case backgrounds of all courses are consistent, so as to reduce repeated understanding of application needs. Students are required to face simple engineering problems in the form of large assignments, and to complete the design, development, debugging and testing by themselves. Thirdly, to improve practice, mainly through the comprehensive practice in extra semester we achieve the teaching goal. Students are required to provide a practical process of integrated design, simulated products or scientific research. The extended practical connection places more emphasis on students' independent learning by research projects, extracurricular science and technology innovation activities, and subject competitions, etc. Students choose their own topics, build their own experimental platforms, design the implementation process, complete the tests, and finally pass the expert group defense assessment.

3.3 Hierarchical Practice Teaching

Learners use their existing knowledge and cognitive ability to learn new knowledge and use the new knowledge to build their own system of knowledge and ability. Because students have different levels of prior knowledge and cognitive abilities, it is impossible to meet the self-constructed needs of all students if all learners are confronted with no differences. 17% of our AI normal students come from Xinjiang or Tibet, and although in recent years minority students have completed their matriculation in language and basic subjects at the high school level in the high school class, there is still a big difference between their learning base and that of students from other places of origin.

The essence of multi-level teaching is to meet the differentiated needs of different students, which is the concrete embodiment of taking students as the learning main body. And that is the basic strategy to achieve effective teaching and efficient learning. Among them, basic experiments are required to do experiments, focusing on the training of students' basic skills. Comprehensive experiment is a part of selective experiment, pay attention to cultivate students' ability of comprehensive use of knowledge and problem solving capability. The extended experiment focuses on cultivating students' ability of application innovation and exploration spirit. Basic experiments and comprehensive experiments are mainly carried out in class exercises. The extended experiment was carried out in a group way of project team cooperation.

Figure 3 shows the practical teaching content system of program design course group at 3-level for artificial intelligence normal major. The experiment content of each level is longitudinally from shallow to deep, from simple to complex. To break through the boundary barriers of relevant courses horizontally, we aim to cultivate students' problem-solving ability and innovative spirit. By carrying out hierarchical teaching, students can have a solid grasp of basic theories and professional knowledge. At the same time, students with different foundations can have a sense of gain in the course practice, so as to stimulate students' interest in learning and improve their professional skills.

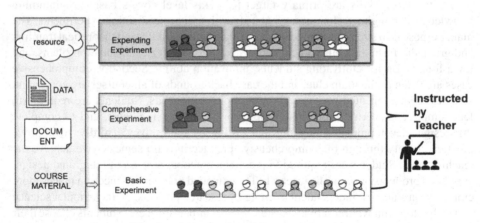

Fig. 3. Hierarchical teaching practice system

4   Teaching Reform of Programming Course Group

The course group construction is an iterative process, which needs to explore the improvement of teaching mode and method. Teachers are one of the core elements of teaching activities. A course cluster teacher group is formed by the course lead teachers, with a reasonable mix in terms of education, title and age. Experienced teachers and young teachers need to form a supportive relationship. The teacher in charge of the course cluster, mainly responsible for the construction and planning of the whole course cluster, as well as the organization of regular teaching communication. We actively promote the reform of "MOOC + Flipped class" teaching mode. Firstly, teachers are guided by the training objectives and take the syllabus as a framework to cut and optimize the teaching content, dissolve the knowledge content in a number of tasks. Then teachers develop an implementable independent pre-study task list. Through the analysis of the platform data, teachers can timely adjust the teaching strategy and personalized counseling for students. Finally, we effectively improve the teaching effect [8, 9] by flipped classes. Programming language and data structure algorithm classes use online assessment system within the course group, which provides online compiling, linking, running and discriminating functions. It can provide instant feedback on students' programming results and make more scientific and effective evaluation of students' ability.

The extension of flipped class requires students to work in groups to prototype and develop a mini-management system. The creation of a mini-management system, which runs through the different courses but has its own focus of requirements, thus avoiding the disadvantage of repeatedly understanding and starting from scratch for possibilities of progressive development. We emphasis on process-oriented examinations and the use of multidimensional evaluation. We integrate online and offline process evaluation and final exam evaluation for multi-dimensional assessment thus for evaluation to continuously teaching design improvement. According to the training objectives, we continuously improve and optimize the teaching design, and improve the teaching objectives and assessment as well as evaluation methods. Continuous teaching reform in a closed-loop mode, thus making the teaching methods more efficient, the teaching contents more rich and practical, and the teaching schedule more reasonable, thus continuously improving the students' professional skills and teaching and research abilities, and prompting them to become excellent teachers with excellent professional abilities. Continuous teaching reform in a closed-loop mode, can make the teaching methods more efficient, the teaching contents more rich and practical, and the teaching schedule more reasonable. So as to continuously improve the students' professional skills as well as teaching and research abilities to help them to become excellent teachers with excellent professional abilities.

5 Conclusion

The undergraduate normal major of artificial intelligence is an important base for cultivating high-level teachers with professional qualities of artificial intelligence. The training process also aims to equip students with the innovative practical ability to use the core technology of artificial intelligence to solve practical problems. Programming courses directly determine the quality of professional talents training. This paper introduces how to realize the course group construction to serve the cultivation goal from three aspects: course group design, construction and teaching reform. In the following teaching research work, we will further improve the construction of the course group according to the current accumulated teaching data, strengthen the continuous reform on iterative updating, further expand the scope of practice, deepen the content of practice, and explore the laws of the construction of the course group.

Acknowledgment. This work was supported by the Association of Fundamental Computing Education in Chinese Universities [grant number 2022-AFCEC-77].

References

1. State council of the People's Republic of China. New generation of artificial intelligence development plan [EB/OL]. http://www.gov.cn/zhengce/content/2017-07/20/content_5 211996.html Accessed 20 July 2017
2. Ministry of education of the people's republic of China. Notice of the ministry of education on action plan for artificial intelligence innovation in University" [EB/OL]. Official website of the ministry of education of the People's Republic of China. 04–03 2018. http://www.moe.gov.cn/srcsite/A16/s7062/201804/t20180410_332722.html Accessed 03 Jan 2019
3. Gao, Y., Zhao, P., Liao H.: Objective and path of application-oriented talents training in local universities. Chin. Univ. Sci. Technol. **3**, 52–54 (2017)
4. Zhang, X., Qu, Z., Zhang, L, Ma, X., Wang, H., Liu, X.: SI. Construction and practice of programming capability training system. Comput. Educ. **9**, 75–79 (2019)
5. Yu, S.: The future roles of AI teacher. Open Educ. Res. **24**(01), 16–28 (2018)
6. Zhang, S., Yang, H., Zhang, Y.: Discussion on online teaching mode of universities under the epidemic situation. China Mod. Educ. Equip. **2020**(11), 11–13 (2020)
7. Yang, Z., Xun, G.: How skills are formed: type discussion and pattern analysis. Res. Educ. Tsinghua Univ. **40**(05). 49–60 (2019)
8. Zeng, M., Li, G., Zhou, Q., et al.: From MOOC to SPIC: construction of a deep learning model. China Educ. Technol. **2015**(11). 28–34+53 (2015)
9. Zhan, Z., Li, X.: Blended learning: definition, strategies, Status and trends - a conversation with professor Curtis bunker, Indiana University, USA. China Educ. Technol. **2009**(12), 1–5 (2009)

Research on the Path of Building the Innovation and Entrepreneurship Education Ecosystem of Local Universities Based on the Big Data Platform

Lu Lu[✉]

Hainan Vocational University of Science and Technology, Haikou, China
365276735@qq.com

Abstract. The proliferation of Internet-based technologies has resulted in the availability of new forms of technical assistance for the development of talent. It does this by making education about innovation and entrepreneurship more data-driven, which in turn makes it possible for education about innovation and entrepreneurship to thrive in the modern day. Nevertheless, as the age of big data has emerged in the last few years, new problems have been presented to the process of talent nurturing in colleges and universities. Education in innovative business practices and entrepreneurship in colleges and universities has to be updated to meet the new standards set by the progression of society, the times, and the students' own personal growth. With this background in mind, the purpose of this article is to conduct an investigation into the present state of affairs regarding the building of an education system for innovation and entrepreneurship at colleges and universities. At addition to this, it explores the connection between big data and the establishment of an innovation and entrepreneurship education environment in schools like colleges and universities. It also suggests a roadmap for the establishment of an ecosystem for the teaching of innovation and entrepreneurship at local colleges and universities based on big data platforms. This serves to encourage the deep integration of big data technology with innovation and entrepreneurship education, which gives theoretical reference value for what has been referred to as the "innovation and entrepreneurship education ecosphere."

Keywords: Big data · Innovation and entrepreneurship education · Ecosystem · Path

1 Introduction

Scientific and technical revolutions have repeatedly shown that they are inevitable to spark a new educational revolution in human society. We have reached the big data age as shown by the rising use of science and technology in our daily lives. Examples include: the Internet, clouds, the Internet of Things, big data, and artificial intelligence. "In today's world, information technology innovation is evolving fast," General Secretary Xi Jinping said in a congratulations letter to the inaugural Digital China Construction Summit in

May 2018. Networking and intelligence are advancing at an accelerated pace. Thus, economic and social progress will be facilitated, and the national governance structure and ability for governing will be modernized. People's increasing aspirations for a better life are being met in this way. "Innovation in information technology is becoming more crucial". New educational revolutions are needed to meet the challenges posed by the technological revolution, and universities must adapt to the new features and demands of the growth of the big-data age in order to meet these challenges. At the same time, education and teaching methods need to be further reformed, with an emphasis on fostering a culture of creativity and entrepreneurship.

This research focuses on enhancing the quality of talent nurturing as the primary objective of furthering education and teaching reform at colleges and universities. As a research backdrop, it makes use of education in innovation and entrepreneurship, which is something that is present throughout the whole of the process of talent nurturing in colleges and universities. It places an emphasis on the fact that in this age of big data, when the revolution brought on by information technology significantly alters both the production methods and lifestyle choices of human civilization. At the same time, it has proposed new, more stringent aims and conditions for the development of talent in academic institutions such as colleges and universities. Education in innovation and entrepreneurship is given more emphasis in educational institutions like colleges and universities in order to keep up with the progression of the times. New difficulties have been presented to the process of talent nurturing in colleges and universities as a result of both the national growth and the personal development of students. As a result, it is essential to investigate the possibility of creating an innovation and entrepreneurship ecosystem at educational institutions like colleges and universities by using big data platforms.

2 Current Situation Analysis

The current situation of innovation and entrepreneurship education in colleges and universities in the era of big data.

College students are the primary focus of education programs that promote innovation and entrepreneurialism at schools like colleges and universities. Education in innovation and entrepreneurship has as its primary focus the cultivation of students' innovative and entrepreneurial consciousness at the collegiate level, the enhancement of students' innovative and entrepreneurial abilities, the recognition of the environment favorable to entrepreneurial endeavors, and the encouragement of students to delve deeper into their own entrepreneurial practices. To establish a system of education with the primary objective of developing individuals who are inventive, creative, and practical. Since the 1990s, colleges in China have been steadily increasing the priority they place on innovation and entrepreneurship education while also strengthening it. Efforts have been undertaken to study and design an innovative and entrepreneurial education system with Chinese features in terms of the curriculum system, faculty team, innovation competition, and entrepreneurial practice. As a result, this has led to some significant historical successes as well as some practical issues.

A. The innovation and entrepreneurship education system of colleges and universities is not landed.

In this day and age of big data, the educational experiences of students need to be "personalized" in order for them to be productive. Students have the ability to choose their instructors, classes, study groups, and any other component of their educational experience. As a result of this, educational institutions will be required to make modifications to their existing talent development system. This system encompasses everything from the management of educational programs to the management of laboratory equipment to the administration of systems for tracking and evaluating the progress of students. As a result, "students as the core" need to be the primary emphasis of any modifications. The teaching of innovation and entrepreneurship at our universities and other educational institutions is just getting started. It still lacks an overall and comprehensive plan, and it has a significant lack of expertise when it comes to building students' independent innovation capacity and cultivating innovative and entrepreneurial elite abilities. In education for innovation and entrepreneurship, there is a deficiency in the areas of goal formulation, the development of teams, the design of curricula and the selection of teachers, and the training of teachers. The management of education must not only improve the overall planning and resource integration of forces, but it must also construct and improve the top-level design of the education system for innovation and entrepreneurship as soon as is practically possible in accordance with the specifics of the local environment. This must be done in accordance with the specifics of the local environment.

B. The content structure of innovation and entrepreneurship education in colleges and universities is unreasonable.

The advent of the era of big data means that artificial intelligence will replace more traditional jobs, and new types of work will also emerge. The instructional content structure of colleges and universities has to adapt to the ever-changing technological landscape. There are now innovation and entrepreneurship departments or management teams at many colleges and universities, and courses linked to innovation and entrepreneurship education are being developed or established. Courses are still lacking in organization and rigor, which is a concern that many students face. College and university students who want to learn about entrepreneurship or innovation are limited to optional courses at certain institutions. In general, college students have a "poor participation rate" in innovation and entrepreneurship courses because of the courses' defective and illogical subject structures. In the meanwhile, many colleges and universities lack theoretical and practice courses on innovation and entrepreneurship. Entrepreneurial endeavors undertaken by students are often low-tech, low-success, and short-lived.

C. The teaching staff of innovation and entrepreneurship education in colleges and universities is not professional.

Artificial intelligence can now accomplish a great deal of previously remembered information thanks to the advent of big data. While classroom instruction is still necessary to impart certain information, it no longer has to be done in order to reach high levels of learning efficiency. As a result, college professors must confront and consider this issue in the age of big data. Also, how big data may be used to enhance classroom instruction. For innovation and entrepreneurship education, college teachers must have sufficient social experience and practical experience while having profound theoretical knowledge. Even still, according to the present state of the innovation and entrepreneurship faculty in China, the majority of professors are still unable to satisfy the educational demands of students at Chinese colleges and universities.

3 Problem Analysis

The challenge of building a university innovation and entrepreneurship education ecosystem in the era of big data.

It is critical that our institutions of higher learning, which have their roots in the People's Republic, remain committed to their essential mission of "building moral education" and to producing socialist builders and successors with Chinese features. The national big data strategy must always be the foundation for innovation and entrepreneurship education in colleges and universities, improving the capacity for talent training and serving as a driving force behind the modernization of the country. The first step is to teach college students about "big data" literacy. Because the technology behind big data is only going to become more prevalent in the next years, expanding students' knowledge of big data should become an essential component of curriculum for courses on innovation and entrepreneurship at schools like colleges and universities. On the one hand, schools should put more emphasis on introducing, training, and otherwise making students more experienced in the use of big data. In addition to that, it needs to heighten students' knowledge of big data. In addition to this, pupils' abilities to detect and make use of large amounts of data should be developed. On the other hand, students' political awareness of serving the nation should be raised by education about the hazards, rules, and ethics of big data, and their civilized rationality of big data life should be improved. This may be accomplished by teaching students about big data. Step two is making a concerted effort to locate and cultivate big data specialists. Since 2013, China has been working hard to put its big data strategy into action in order to keep up with the rising need for professionals skilled in handling large amounts of data. In 2015, the State Council made public the "Action Plan for Promoting Big Data Development," which they had previously drafted. A straightforward statement might read as follows: "innovate talent training mode and develop an excellent multi-level and multi-type big data talent training system." At the second collective study of the Central Political Bureau in 2017, Xi Jinping said that a "multi-level and multi-type big data talent team" needed to be created. Education focused on innovation and entrepreneurship is one of the most essential ways for schools and institutions to nurture talent in the field of big data. Not only does it improve the overall structure of the subject that is taught theoretically, but it also offers essential assistance to the instruction that is given practically. Thirdly, it encourages the establishment and growth of a big data platform for the teaching of innovative business practices and startup companies. One of the essential components of the national big data strategy is an initiative to spread awareness of the field of big data and encourage its use in educational settings. In addition, the building and development of a big data platform for the teaching of innovation and entrepreneurship in schools of higher education is just one component of the expansion of educational use of big data. In addition, if education in innovation and entrepreneurship is based on the development of big data, then this will encourage and drive the growth of big data across the whole education system. Students in colleges and universities are the driving force behind "mass entrepreneurship and innovation." The vitality of innovation and entrepreneurship among college students can only be unleashed via the effective promotion of the development of big data of innovation and entrepreneurship education in colleges and universities. This is the only way to push the growth of big data in education, which will in turn drive the development of big data on a national scale. Contribute to the development of the nation by contributing to the modernization of the educational system. In order to make the ideal of bringing prosperity to the nation through education and bringing strength to the country through education a reality.

4 Countermeasures and Suggestions

The dual-innovation education that is offered at schools of higher learning is the result of proactive innovation and reform in connection with the progression of the times, which has a very significant and vital practical importance. In the age of big data, the regional colleges and institutions that surround us need to likewise keep up with the trends. On the one hand, make the most of the opportunities that the big data technology provides. On the other side, there should be an expansion of the optimization route and technique of the dual innovation education ecosystem. This will better foster the growth of dual innovation education in the regional colleges and universities.

A. Use big data to achieve the integrated development of dual-creation education and professional education in local colleges and universities.

To begin, educational institutions in the immediate area, such as colleges and universities, must to proactively alter the prevalent notion of talent nurturing. Because the natural mix of college education that emphasizes dual innovation and professional education may more effectively foster the growth of colleges and universities within their own communities. A common understanding is necessary throughout the whole of the school's departments. They have to have a profound understanding of the relevance of integrating education in double innovation with professional education in tertiary institutions like colleges and universities. Attempts should be made to improve the manner of dual-innovation education offered at regional colleges and universities, with the primary emphasis being placed on the practical use of information technology. Encourage college students' innovative thinking, creative endeavors, and entrepreneurial spirit by cultivating these traits in them. Second, educational institutions such as colleges and universities need to put more effort into the building of a management system for college dual-innovation education. Using current information technology, actively construct a system that will merge dual-innovation education and professional education in the area's colleges and institutions.

Utilize the system promise to draw on the beneficial resources from all angles and include the present materials that are of a high grade for instruction. Continue to develop a method of management that is both scientific and reasonable for double-innovation education in higher education institutions. At the same time, it is necessary to make use of information technology in order to construct specialized teaching institutions for double-innovation education in colleges and universities. Additionally, it is necessary to organize and put into practice teaching and practice activities of double-innovation education in local colleges and universities in a manner that is targeted. The arduous process of double-innovation education at schools of higher learning may be made easier to manage with the help of advancements in information technology. Because of this, the double-innovation education offered at colleges and universities will become more practical. In addition to this, it will effectively encourage the organic merger of education in dual innovation and professional education in colleges and universities. In addition to this, it will further increase the active role that information technology plays in the growth process of the integration of two different cultures.

In other words, instructional materials should be built better. For this reason, it is vital to take into account the changing needs of students and construct a curriculum and instructional strategy that take into account these changes in student learning styles, cognitive skills, and thinking processes. This can be accomplished by combining the characteristics of the development of the times with the characteristics of the evolution of the times. Create educational resources for dual-innovation education that are suitable for use in the educational environment of nearby colleges and universities. Incorporate instructional content that emphasizes practical learning into the overall dual-innovation educational framework. Alter the conventional method of theoretical instruction, which consists of one-way communication. Change it to a method of interactive practical learning that is more diverse, multi-level, and multi-perspective, and that establishes the key position of students. Pay particular attention to representing the technological benefits of big data, since this is one of them. Allow big data to play a significant role in the development of the curriculum as well as the instructional approach, so that students may get increased levels of technological assistance.

B. Build a practical platform for dual-creation education in local colleges and universities.

At the moment, there is widespread concern across society over the dual-innovation education that is taking place in colleges and universities. The building of a platform, the provision of policy direction, and the provision of financial assistance have all been provided by various levels of government for the dual-innovation education that is being offered in the regional colleges and universities. At addition to this, the groundwork for the dual-innovation education in local colleges has been prepared, and favorable circumstances have been created. The educational institutions in the surrounding area, such as colleges and universities, have the opportunity to make the most of these advantageous circumstances by actively building a functional platform for dual-innovation education. Establish practice bases of a high grade and high quality for innovation and entrepreneurship among college students, and give additional possibilities for students to learn and practice in businesses. They are given the opportunity to get expertise in business ownership in accordance with the educational principle of dual innovation education that is practiced in colleges and universities. At the same time, we should make use of information technology to construct innovation laboratories in order to provide students the opportunity to articulate their requirements for innovation and put those requirements into practice. In order to offer students with knowledge and data pertaining to industries such as technology and the market, big data technologies should be used. College students may expand their worldview and develop their capacity for original thought by participating in activities that put their practical skills to use.

C. Strengthen the publicity of the dual-creation education policy of colleges and universities.

Encourage and fully back initiatives at local institutions to develop dual-innovation strategies, and do so vigorously. In order to establish a foundation for the advocacy of public policy, it is essential to make use of the informational and public relations resources made available by the government. Promote in a proactive manner, using network media and the technology of big data, the social impact and current value that is produced by the dual-innovation education offered at the regional colleges and universities. Participate actively in the function of benchmarking, as well as in the exhibition of representative photos. It is favorable to the establishment of accurate ideological guidance on college students' innovation and entrepreneurship to provide college students with direction in the area of innovation and entrepreneurship and to rectify the attitudes of college students in this area. At the beginning of their careers in innovation and entrepreneurship, it is helpful for college students to develop a healthy sense of social responsibility and a glorious mission in line with the times. In addition to this, it will foster a healthy social environment in which innovation and entrepreneurialism are highly valued across the board in the society. In addition, there should be a stronger emphasis placed on the building of new educational policies at local colleges as well as the reform of existing educational policies. The elimination of policy barriers that stand in the way of innovation and entrepreneurship on the part of college students will be accomplished through the development of various reward systems. This will allow the college students' entrepreneurial activities to be carried out without hiccups, which will, in turn, lead to an increase in the rate of success that entrepreneurship enjoys.

D. Build an interactive platform for innovation and entrepreneurship.

The activities of innovation and entrepreneurship carried out by students at universities have to be predicated on interactive collaboration, the incorporation of favorable resources, and the formation of synergistic effects. The management approach will serve as the foundation for the development of an interactive platform for fostering innovation and entrepreneurialism. Creating a social platform that allows for broad communication and engagement may be accomplished via the deployment of information technology in conjunction with big data technologies. On this platform, government functional institutions play their leading role, bringing together innovative enterprises, student innovation projects, university scientific research achievements, venture capital institutions, and university student entrepreneurship incubators around local universities. In this context, the above cooperative and interactive subjects carry out extensive communication under the guidance of functional departments, fully understand the innovation and entrepreneurship intentions and interests of all parties, through the digital information provided by big data, understand the market development dynamics, understand social needs, etc., so as to form various cooperation models on the basis of communication and understanding, provide data support and technical support, so as to integrate the high-quality resources of all aspects of society, and give full play to their own resource advantages to promote the further development of entrepreneurial projects.

E. Vigorously carry out innovative entrepreneurship competition activities.

Innovation and entrepreneurship need to do a good job in social demand survey, market development research, risk factor assessment, project feasibility investigation, etc. Therefore, college students need to have more opportunities for practical exercise in these areas, so that they can summarize their experience and improve their awareness.

Colleges and universities need to actively organize some innovative entrepreneurship competitions, encourage and improve students' participation through policies, guide college students to find entrepreneurial opportunities, seek innovative directions, and seek cooperation paths, and provide students with more practical training. In this process, the functional institutions of local colleges and universities should actively organize experts and scholars in this area to set up selection organizations, and comprehensively select innovative and entrepreneurial projects that adapt to the development of the times, have market development prospects, and are scientific and reasonable from the aspects of participating projects, development plans, implementation plans, organizational structures, and forms of cooperation. The nation's colleges and universities need to provide significant assistance by providing support in the form of policy support, budgetary support, resource integration, and operational direction. For college students, educational institutions like colleges and universities should serve as examples of successful innovation and entrepreneurship. Therefore, we are in a position to galvanize the enterprising spirit of college students and more effectively encourage the growth of dual-innovation education at educational institutions like colleges and universities.

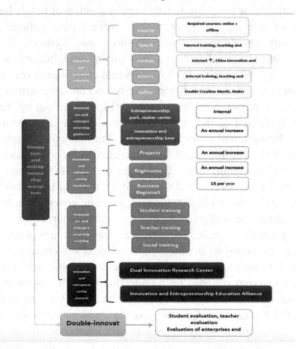

5   Path and Policy

Colleges have historically been tasked with the purpose and the social obligation of producing imaginative persons who are able to adapt and lead the evolution of the big data age. This responsibility has been passed down from generation to generation. In addition, the State Council wants to go on with the "Double Innovation" strategy, which calls for the growth of high-quality innovation as well as entrepreneurialism. It is also very vital to make further changes to education and teaching at higher education institutions like universities and colleges. In order to educate their students in innovation and entrepreneurship, local colleges and universities need to take the initiative to actively address current concerns and answer to the difficulties posed by the era of big data. To maintain one's relevance in today's world, it is very necessary to advocate for a comprehensive revision of the innovation and entrepreneurial talent development system.

A. Guided by educating people, optimize the top-level design of innovation and entrepreneurship education in local colleges and universities.

Education in innovation and entrepreneurship must constantly adhere to the proper orientation of teaching people in order for it to be provided at regional colleges and universities. It views the cultivation of students' innovative awareness as the main aim, together with the improvement of their practical skill and the enhancement of their feeling of social duty, and it takes moral education as its point of departure. The top-level design of education for innovation and entrepreneurship at colleges and universities is optimized, and "three penetrations" are required of students. To begin, there should be an increased emphasis on ideological and political education throughout. Even if the age of big data has made it easier for individuals to interact with one another and work together, it is still extremely important that ideological and political education be woven into the curriculum of innovation and entrepreneurship courses taught at schools of higher education. Develop in the vast majority of pupils abilities in innovation and entrepreneurship, as well as firmly held values and convictions, high-minded moral feelings, and healthy lives. Second, it is essential to make changes to the ways in which education and instruction are delivered. The age of big data has brought forth new expectations for the development of talent in educational institutions like colleges and universities. Education in innovation and entrepreneurship needs to undergo a more comprehensive overhaul at the various local institutions and universities. Education about innovation and entrepreneurship has to be included throughout the whole of the educational and instructional process at schools like colleges and universities. To create a synergy of education on innovation and entrepreneurship via the articulation of systems, the support of curricula, and the crossover of systems. Third, the development of innovation must be coordinated with the area economy. Nationally, provinces and regions are developing and putting into effect action plans to help spur entrepreneurialism and innovation in higher education. These plans aim to offer policy direction, financial assistance, and conducive circumstances for this kind of education to take place. On the one hand, it encourages the education of innovation and entrepreneurship that is taught in schools like colleges and universities to progressively transition from the classroom into practice. It continually improves the applicability and significance of education, both on campuses and in society as a whole. In addition, it encourages close collaboration between academic institutions and private sector businesses. Together we can establish an innovative and entrepreneurial education platform, share resources for teaching innovation and entrepreneurial skills and alter educational outcomes. This will help to ensure that our educational system is both secure and sustainable for future generations.

B. Practice-oriented, optimize the innovation and entrepreneurship education ecosystem of local colleges and universities.

The age of big data is also the period of an explosion in both information and knowledge. Both the pace of expansion in knowledge and the rate at which it is lost are accelerating at a rate that is quicker than in any preceding age. The growth of society and the march of time will be propelled forward by artificial intelligence. This indicates that education and instruction in higher education settings, such as colleges and universities, should not only convey information and skill training to students, but also foster students' core competency, core literacy, and hard technological exploration. Because of this, it is vital to consistently enhance the ecological environment of education about innovation and entrepreneurship at local colleges. Optimize your innovation and entrepreneurship education's practice-based curriculum first. In order to ensure that students are receiving a well-rounded education that emphasizes innovation and entrepreneurship, higher education institutions should create their curriculums scientifically to meet this need. Students' practical skills in theory application, market analysis, project creation, capital operation, decision-making command, and team communication should be continually improved via cross-fertilization and mutual promotion of instructional techniques and approaches. Another benefit is that "dual-innovation" space is encouraged. Collaborative education and an innovation and entrepreneurship incubation system are needed at local colleges and universities for innovation and entrepreneurship education. Make college and university campuses incubators, co-working spaces, as well as entrepreneurial centers for students. Students' creativity and entrepreneurship will benefit from this, as well as a management practice platform for the building of collaborative education mechanisms for academic affairs, academic staff, league committee, scientific research and employment. But on the other side, this can successfully overcome the challenges typically experienced by universities' innovation and entrepreneurship education, such as a shortage of space and funding and a dearth of projects and instructors.

C. Guided by "innovation", we will explore the big data application model of innovation and entrepreneurship education in local colleges and universities.

Education for creativity and entrepreneurship in the age of big data necessitates a macroscopic perspective of the whole age of big data. When looking at big data and its technologies from a microscopic point of view, it is more important to enhance innovation in teaching mode. Big data platforms should be actively built by colleges and institutions. Big data entrepreneurship scenarios need to be applied more widely and more quickly, as well as more timely, extensive, and rapid data collection on the current state of global university student innovation and entrepreneurship are all necessities. As a result of this, it will be possible to anticipate the future growth of innovation and entrepreneurship education in higher education institutions throughout the globe, particularly in the industrialized nations of Europe and the United States. A strong understanding of innovation and entrepreneurial education will be established as a result. Using big data management information systems for innovation and entrepreneurship education, universities can measure and control students' willingness to participate in innovation and entrepreneurship activities, as well as their adaptability and satisfaction with innovation and entrepreneurship activities. As a result, it is able to accurately analyze massive data on the engagement of instructors and students in innovative and entrepreneurial activities, as well as the rationale of innovation and entrepreneurship courses, and the practicality of education. All of these approaches aid colleges in keeping a close eye on and enforcing timely controls over the education process for innovation and entrepreneurship.

6 Epilogue

Schools and institutions in the area are benefiting from a large data supply mode, which is fueled by big data. On the one hand, colleges may use big data to create a variety of resource banks for fostering innovation and entrepreneurship. Using artificial intelligence, provide instructors and students with quick and easy access to knowledge. Universities and colleges, on the other hand, need to better prepare faculty and students to work with big data. Make sure they are always improving their understanding of big data and the technology that powers it. Aside from that, you may use it in your innovation and entrepreneurial activity. In addition to improving instructors' capacity to teach big data, this will also boost students' ability to innovate and start businesses using big data. Big data technology and innovation and entrepreneurship education can be better integrated via the use of this technology. This serves as a theoretical model for a "upgraded" innovation and entrepreneurship education environment.

Acknowledgment. This research was financially supported by 2021 Research Project of Higher Education and Teaching Reform in Hainan Province (Grant NO. Hnjg2021_98).

References

1. Drucker, P.: Management in a Time of Great Change. Trans. Zhu, Y. China Machine Press, Beijing (2019)
2. Christensen, C., et al.: The Task of Innovators. Trans. Hong, H. CITIC Publishing House, Beijing (2019)
3. Jianhua, L.: President's Point of View: University Reform and Future. Oriental Press Center, Shanghai (2018)
4. Da Xuan, F.: Education Renaissance under Globalization: Feng Da Xuan on higher education. Trans Wei, X.Y. Harbin University of Technology Press, Harbin, vol. 54 (2018)
5. Rogers, E.M.: Diffusion of innovation. Trans. Tang, X., Zheng, C., Zhang, Y. Electronic Industry Press, Beijing, vol. 449 (2016)
6. Christensen, C.: The Dilemma of Innovators. Trans. Hu, J. CITIC Press, Beijing (2014)
7. Elaine, E.: Imperfect System: Possibilities and Limitations of Reform. Trans. Chen, Y. China Renmin University Press, Beijing (2017)

Construct the Knowledge Graph of Information Security Introduction Course to Help Subject Teaching

Yanyan Zheng, Ying Chen[✉], and Linjun Wang

Department of Computer Science, Taizhou University, 605 Dongfang Avenue,
Linhai 317000, China
ychen222@foxmail.com

Abstract. With the rapid development of China's online courses and the national proposal of the task of intelligent education development, how to promote the deep integration between artificial intelligence and higher education, accelerate the higher education from digitization and networking to intelligence, improve the quality of online course construction, and promote the innovation and development of higher education has become an overall, long-term and strategic issue in the field of higher education question. As an important carrier of deep integration between artificial intelligence and higher education, online course knowledge graph is the core influencing factor of the development of intelligent education. In this paper, knowledge graph, an intelligent and efficient way of knowledge organization, is introduced into the teaching of information security introduction course. For the knowledge of "information security" course, a visual knowledge graph is constructed, and then the teaching resource platform of the course is formed.

Keywords: Knowledge graph · Intelligent education · Introduction to information security

1 Introduction

In the era of "Internet plus", the new generation of information technology represented by Internet, Internet of things, cloud computing, big data, artificial intelligence and block chain, promote the development of intelligent education in higher education, provide impetus and support for educational modernization, and bring opportunities and challenges to for the development of higher education [1]. Since 2017, the new generation of artificial intelligence development plan, colleges and universities artificial intelligence innovation action plan, China modern education modernization 2035 and other documents have been issued, supporting the development of intelligent education, promoting the deep integration of artificial intelligence and education, promoting the reform of learning environment, teaching methods, education management and evaluation [2]. Online learning platform effectively integrates modern information technology, and has been launched in colleges and universities for daily auxiliary teaching [3].

As the most basic unit of talent training system in colleges and universities, curriculum is the core element of specialty and discipline construction [4]. There are many knowledge points in the information security introduction course, and there are countless connections among them. After a semester of study, students can basically master all the knowledge points, but it is difficult to connect them and build them into a whole to form a complete knowledge system.

Knowledge graph is an intelligent and efficient way of knowledge organization. With the help of graph theory, statistics, modern information technology and other means, it can show the core structure of a certain field, the relationship between each node of the development history and the overall framework in a visual way. With its powerful semantic processing function and rapid analysis ability, knowledge graph has become an intelligent search and organization tool that can quickly and accurately obtain information resources, and has been widely used in finance, public security, telecommunications, medicine, agriculture, government affairs and other fields [5].

In the field of education, knowledge graph, as a visual representation of the structural relationship of subject knowledge points, can promote learners' cognition, understanding, memory and dissemination of knowledge content, and cultivate the application ability of new knowledge, so as to help them better complete knowledge construction and thinking training in the information age [6].

2   Construction of Knowledge Graph of Information Security Introduction Course

2.1   Overview of Knowledge Graph

Kant believes that knowledge and experience in human memory are stored in the form of graph, and only when new concepts and original knowledge concepts are connected can they produce meaning [7]. Using knowledge element association can help learners establish knowledge system, integrate and associate new knowledge with their own existing knowledge through systematic learning, practice, reflection and transformation, and finally internalize them into knowledge system that can be output independently. With the development of artificial intelligence to the stage of cognitive intelligence, subject knowledge graph, with its unique semantic relevance, knowledge reasoning and interpretability, is highly consistent with intelligent education, and plays an important role in the establishment of learner model, online learning platform and intelligent question answering system.

In 2012, the concept of knowledge graph was proposed by Google [8]. In recent years, knowledge graph has become a research hotspot in the field of artificial intelligence [9–11]. According to the differences of knowledge categories, knowledge graph can be divided into industry knowledge graph and general knowledge graph. The former is oriented to specific fields, such as educational knowledge graph, medical knowledge graph, financial knowledge graph, etc. The latter is popular, not oriented to specific fields, and belongs to encyclopedic knowledge graph, such as Yago, free base, Zhixin, etc. There is a complementary relationship between the two knowledge graphs. For example, the former can provide the latter with knowledge in specific fields, expand the latter's knowledge reserves and improve the quality of knowledge. The latter can provide the former with knowledge of other related fields, improve the knowledge coverage of the former, and enhance the knowledge service ability. As an industry knowledge graph, education knowledge graph is the cornerstone of the development of intelligent education [12].

With the help of education knowledge graph, the link relationship between knowledge can be reconstructed, and the network knowledge architecture of disciplines and specialties can be formed, which can effectively support flexible, accurate "teaching" and personality, lifelong "learning".

2.2 Construction of Knowledge Graph of Introduction to Information Security Course

The ontology based knowledge graph construction process of "Introduction to information security" course mainly includes OWL ontology construction and neo4j knowledge graph construction. The first part is to build a practical domain ontology of "Introduction to information security" by using the ontology tool protege; the second part is to use neo4j graphic database to store the related resources and semantic relations of "Introduction to information security" on the basis of the above ontology. Around these two parts, combined with the construction principles of knowledge graph, this paper finally constructs the knowledge graph of "Introduction to information security" course through five stages to form a more perfect domain knowledge graph. Figure 1 is the specific construction flow chart of the course knowledge graph.

1) Identify domain ontology: Referring to the information security introduction textbook compiled by Qi'anxin Institute of industry, the authoritative materials such as other relevant books and other teaching literature are collected. According to the purpose and demand of constructing the knowledge ontology of the information security introduction, the scope of ontology research field is determined and the relevant knowledge and terms are defined.

2) Searching available existing ontologies, that is, investigating the possibility of reusing existing ontologies Searching available existing ontologies, that is, investigating the possibility of reusing existing ontologies: At present, the field of introduction to information security is not mature, and the standard ontology library can be used directly. Therefore, building the ontology library of introduction to information security by hand is chosen.

3) List the important concepts in the field and summarize them: The related resources of "Introduction to information security" course are collected, and the concepts are extracted, duplication removed, semantically analyzed and merged to obtain domain terms.

For example, the extracted digital signature technology, identity recognition technology, etc. are the application realization of information authentication technology of information security. These concepts can be summed up as "application realization". According to this method, we finally summarize six knowledge sets: "research subject", "concept", "algorithm and principle", "research object", "application realization" and "instance".

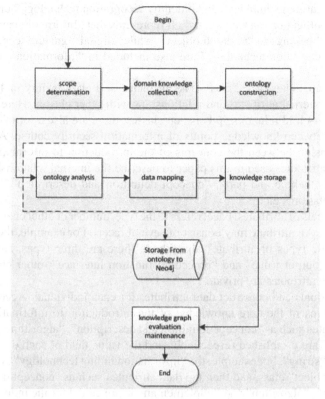

Fig. 1. Construction flow chart of the course knowledge graph

4) Define classes and their hierarchical relationships: The knowledge set summarized in the previous step is defined as "class", that is, "class" can be understood as containing several knowledge sets with the same characteristics. Starting from the goal of creating ontology of information security, the appropriate hierarchical relationship is selected on the premise of ensuring logic and practicability. There are two ways to construct class and hierarchy: top-down and bottom-up [8]. As the ontology of introduction to information security belongs to the mature field of information science, and the knowledge system has strong completeness, the top-down modeling method is adopted to construct the logical relationship of ontology, that is, first construct the top-level concept, and then gradually refine it down. The above six knowledge sets are defined as "research subject", "concept", "algorithm and principle", "research object", "application implementation" and "instance". And define the "research subject" class as a subclass of the top class, the remaining five classes are subclasses of the "research subject" class, and are of the same level relationship; then establish subclasses under each class, such as "research object" class, establish three subclasses of "information security technology", "information authentication technology", "information hiding technology", and create the third level class of

"digital signature technology" and "identity recognition technology" under the "information authentication technology". It represents that "Information authentication technology" belongs to "research object", while "digital signature technology" and "identity recognition technology" are also included in "information authentication technology".

5) Define the attributes of the class: The attributes of a class mainly include internal attributes, external attributes and relationships with other classes. Here, in addition to the parent-child relationship between classes, there are also a lot of logical relationships between knowledge points of information security course. According to the relationship between the concepts of the introduction to information security, the object attributes used in this paper to describe the internal relationship between classes are: "whole and part", "concept definition and description", "algorithm", "implementation", etc.

6) Defining facets of attributes: Facet refers to the type, number or other characteristics of an attribute. An attribute may consist of several facets. For example, there are static and dynamic types of attribute "algorithm"; there are three types, namely "input variable", "output value" and "procedure function interface"; other characteristics include that attributes are private.

7) Add individuals and construct data attributes for each individual: According to the characteristics of the core knowledge of the introduction to information security, data attributes such as "concept definition and description", "algorithm" and "implementation" are established respectively, and the value field of each data attribute is defined as "string". For example, the "information hiding technology" is added to the "research object" class, and then the data attributes such as "concept definition and description", "algorithm" and "implementation" are edited for the individual "information hiding technology". Among them, the specific description content of attribute "concept definition and description" is: "information hiding, also known as information camouflage, is to hide sensitive information by reducing some redundancy of the carrier, such as spatial redundancy, data redundancy, etc., so as to achieve a special purpose. Information hiding breaks the thinking category of traditional cryptography, and examines information security from a new perspective. Compared with the traditional encryption, information hiding is more covert. In information hiding, we can combine these two technologies. First, the secret information is encrypted and preprocessed, and then the information is hidden. The effect of confidentiality and imperceptibility of secret information is better. " The specific description of the algorithm is "LSB algorithm"; the specific description of the implementation is "input, output, implementation process".

2.3 Storage of Knowledge Graph of Introduction to Information Security

In this paper, we use the network knowledge base neo4j to store the knowledge graph, which can not only meet the storage of calculus knowledge, but also achieve the purpose of high-quality resource sharing by relying on the network. Neo4j is a graph database based on cypher language. It stores, processes, queries and presents data graphically. Each node of graph database has a directed edge pointing to the neighbor node, which makes it possible to traverse to the neighbor node in the case of O (1) time complexity, and the database stores the relationship between nodes separately, which is more conducive to improve the speed of graph traversal and search speed.

2.4 Realize the Web Front Display Interface

The knowledge graph application system can realize the functions of visualization display, intelligent search, Knowledge Q & A based on information security knowledge (Fig. 2).

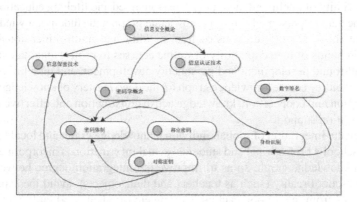

Fig. 2. Knowledge graph for information security courses

3 Construction of Knowledge Graph of Information Security Introduction Course

School education should actively promote the intersection and integration of students' own experience and various information from different channels, and cultivate students' knowledge creativity [13]. In the process of building knowledge graph of online courses, we need to establish the awareness of "open sharing of knowledge, collaborative innovation of interdisciplinary science", and build a knowledge graph at three levels of global, local and individual [14]. The global knowledge graph involves the knowledge of personnel training, including the entities (Concepts) and relationships carried by professional personnel training programs, and integrates the knowledge elements and relationships of disciplines, majors, colleges, teachers and industries. Individual knowledge graph involves students' knowledge, including the entities (Concepts) and relationships carried by students' individual and group characteristics.

As the core level of knowledge graph, local knowledge graph involves curriculum knowledge, including the entities (Concepts) and relationships carried by specific online courses. These three knowledge graphs are relatively independent and closely related. The above relationship is helpful to build and improve the knowledge graph of online courses by using the third-party knowledge library such as global knowledge graph and individual knowledge graph, and realize the "interconnection" knowledge network, provide a solid guarantee to the sharing of the three knowledge graphs, the co-construction of multi-party cooperation, the rapidity of organic reorganization of knowledge graph and the multi-dimensional integration of online course learning space. In addition, the above relationship helps to reduce the complexity of online course knowledge graph and improve the focus of online course knowledge graph construction.

Finally, with the help of the multi graph ablation system, we can improve the open, personalized and accurate education service level of online courses, meet the flexible, diverse, open, accurate and lifelong personalized education needs, and improve the integration ability of intelligent, networked, personalized and lifelong education system.

With the help of personnel training knowledge graph and student knowledge graph, through the above sharing, co construction, rapidity and multi-dimensional, we can solve the problems of the adaptability of online courses to professional talent training, students' all-round development and personality development, and give full play to the promotion of online course knowledge graph for the deep mastery of knowledge, learning communication and cooperation, knowledge active construction and effective migration ability cultivation support.

Through the integration of global, individual knowledge graph and local knowledge graph, the school's professional and students' actual information is incorporated into the curriculum knowledge graph, so as to improve the integration degree between online courses and school reality (such as teachers and their objects), avoid the separation of online courses from the school's actual learning environment, and build a harmonious and integrated platform of real space and cyberspace, which promote the construction of mixed curriculum, promote the identity transformation of teachers from dominator and instigator to director, helper, organizer and promoter, and enhance the initiative and innovation of students in the learning process. The continuous improvement of knowledge quality and reserves of knowledge graph can further optimize the learning community knowledge, improve the interactive communication and learning collaboration, build the efficiency of knowledge, and promote the construction of collaborative learning environment.

4   Conclusion

This paper discusses how to organically connect the knowledge points of the introduction to information security in the form of knowledge graph, and describes the specific steps of constructing the knowledge graph of the introduction to information security. In the teaching process, teachers can guide students to use the knowledge graph of the introduction to information security for efficient learning, so that students can understand the overall framework of the introduction to information security and know the origin of the knowledge points. In addition, through the combination of knowledge graph and big data machine learning, the goal of sharing high-quality educational resources is expected to better realize the use of knowledge graph of network knowledge base, which can help students acquire knowledge more efficiently, and help students carry out targeted learning through personalized learning recommendation.

Through the construction of the knowledge graph of online courses in Colleges and universities, we can form a knowledge architecture based on semantic network, consolidate the infrastructure for the development of intelligent education, support open, personalized and accurate education services, and provide solid support and reliable guarantee for the development of intelligent education.

Acknowledgments. The authors would like to acknowledge the technical environment provided by the Department of Computer Science, University of Taizhou. The funding from scientific research start-up project of Taizhou University is hereby acknowledged. Also, the authors thank family number for their unselfish dedication.

Disclosure of Interests. The authors have no competing interests to declare that are relevant to the content of this article.

References

1. Chen, L., Chen, Y.: On the characteristics of Chinese educational modernization in the age of wisdom. China Educ. Technol. **07**, 30–37 (2020)
2. Guo, H.: Construction of knowledge graph for the online course in colleges and universities based on intelligent education—a case study on Chinese medical history. China Educ. Technol. **02**, 123–130 (2021).
3. Wu, Y.-W., Sun, C.-H., Li, B.: Knowledge graph to aid subject teaching—a case study of basic analog electronics class in Universit. Softw. Guide **12**, 195–198 (2020)
4. Zhang, D.: Optimizing curriculum system and strengthening curriculum construction. China Univ. Teach. **12**, 10–12 (2018)
5. Tu, J., Xiao, J., Jiang, G.: Constructing the knowledge map of calculus to boost the construction of first class courses. China Univ. Teach. **11**, 33–37 (2020)
6. Zhao, L.-L., Fan, J.-R., Zhao, Y.-T., Tang, Y.-W., Zhong, S.-C.: The design and application of the learners' portrait model based on knowledge mapping —taking the "high school physics" Course as an example. Mod. Educ. Technol. **02**, 95–101 (2021)
7. Wan, H., Yu, S.: Learning cell-based construction of learning cognitive map. e-Educ. Res. **09**, 83–88 (2017)
8. Singhal, A.: Introducing the knowledge graph: things, not strings [EB/ OL]. https://google blog.blogspot.com/2012/05/introducing-knowledgegraph-things-not.html. Accessed 16 May 2012
9. He, L.: A Study on Systems and Applications of Scalable Knowledge Graph Serving. University of Science and Technology of China, Hefei (2018)
10. QI, G., Gao, H., Wu, T.: The Research advances of knowledge graph. Technol. Intell. Eng. **1**, 4–25 ((2017)
11. Ma, Z.-G., Ni, R.-Y., Yu, K.-H.: Recent advances, key techniques and future challenges of knowledge graph. Chinese J. Eng. **42**(10), 1254–1266(2020)
12. Deng, Z., Tang, S., Zhang, M., et al.: Overview of ontology. Acta Scientiarum Naturalium Universitatis Pekinensis **38**(5), 730–738 (2002)

Design on Experimental Dataset and Task for Teaching in Data Science and Machine Learning

Zhen Chen[1(✉)], Min Guo[1], Li-Rui Deng[1], Wen-Xun Zheng[2], Hao Wang[3],
Jia-hui Chang[1], Yi-song Zhang[1], Xiao-Dong Ma[1], Ying Gao[1], Hao-Yu Wang[1],
Xin Lu[4], Chao Li[1], Jin Zhou[1], and Shuang Shou Li[1]

[1] Tsinghua University, Beijing, China
zhenchen@tsinghua.edu.cn
[2] Ailibaba Group, Beijing, China
[3] Noyaxe Inc., Beijing, China
[4] PLS Inc., Beijing, China

Abstract. One of the key factor in teaching data science and machine learning is the well-prepared dataset. Although there are some well-known datasets, such as the MNIST, Fashion MNIST and ImageNet dataset are already used in teaching. To inspire students to learn more actively, it needs the instructors to design new experimental tasks and build dataset with the participation of the students. In this paper, we introduce our live examples to design experiments with hand-crafted dataset, crawling-base data, and live generated IoT data.

Keywords: Data Science · Machine Learning · Dataset · Performance evaluation

1 Introduction

1.1 Data Processing

Data science is the practice of using data to try to understand and solve real-world problems [1–4]. The concept of data science was put forward earlier in the last century. In the early stage, it has been in a tepid state due to the lack of data size, programming language, practical software tools, and the support of data analysis methodology.

In the 1980s, the advancement of data mining methods made the development of data science enter a new stage. Entering the 21st century, the field of data science has finally flourished due to the emergence of the ubiquity of Internet connection and mobile Internet, which has led to a sharp increase in the amount of data available. At the same time, with the fast cost reducing in the computing hardware and storage, organizations and enterprises are collecting and storing more data than ever before.

At the same time, in the aspect of the data analysis methodology, there have been breakthroughs in machine learning [5]. Machine learning techniques, especially deep learning [6, 7] have proven to be an efficient way to identify data patterns in practice.

W. Hong and G. Kanaparan (Eds.): ICCSE 2023, CCIS 2024, pp. 186–196, 2024.
https://doi.org/10.1007/978-981-97-0791-1_16

Fig. 1. Data processing steps

Machine learning technologies such as deep learning have a profound impact on the data science and technology industry. In deep learning, as more and more data are input into the Deep Neural Network, the effectiveness of deep learning has improved significantly.

As shown in Fig. 1, data science is flourish and has developed into a relatively comprehensive area. The common steps from data preparation, data management, data visualization and data analysis, a complete set of scientific and technological systems has been developed.

Since 2015, the course teaching group (CTG) has launched three courses about Big data and Machine Learning for teaching and training students in data science and machine learning. The main challenge in courses is the practice process and experiments design after theory learning. Hereafter we will introduce the principle and operation details about the dataset and experiments design in our courses.

1.2 Dataset

Dataset Used in DSML

Dataset is the key element in teaching data science and machine learning (DSML). Well-prepared dataset helps students to learn Machine learning Tasks and inspire themselves to explore the dataset space and to model the dataset with machine learning toolboxes. Although there are some well-known datasets, such as the MNIST [2], Fashion MNIST [1] and ImageNet [3] dataset already used in teaching. These datasets usually are used for toy examples or research purpose without the focus of real problems.

The need to use real data to inspire student to explore the technology frontier more actively requires the instructors to design brand-new course related experimental tasks and build their dataset with themselves, e.g., students participate in the data preparation stage.

In this paper, we introduce our three live examples to design experiments with hand-crafted dataset, crawler base data, and live generated IoT data. Our method shows with participation of student in dataset design, it helps students to learn more actively and more creatively which is helpful in improving the learning experience.

2 Experiment Dataset and Task Design

As the teaching goal in mind, we design three experimental tasks and the preparation of three different kinds of experimental dataset for teaching data science and machine learning.

The three kinds of datasets are introduced as follows:

(1) dataset for intelligent voice control task;
(2) dataset for helmet detect task;
(3) dataset for stock prices prediction task.

3 Intelligent Voice Control Experiment

Dataset for Intelligent Voice Control
This dataset is designed from real scenario with intelligent voice control devices. The intelligent voice-controlled devices are more and more popular as IoT gateway in Smart-House in recently years. The typical representative cases are Apple Home (with Siri), Amazon Echo (with Alexa), Xiaomi MI etc.

A set of typical voice directives in a well-designed intelligent voice-controlled devices are shown in Table 1. There are 24 directives includes the command to operate the device such as take phone call and play music in the Table.

Table 1. 24 Voice directives for device control.

Label	Content			
a	a	Bluetooth device start		
b	b	Bluetooth device take phone call	bb	Bluetooth device phone call
c	c	Bluetooth device answer phone call	cc	Bluetooth device answer call
d	d	Bluetooth device reject phone call		
e	e	Bluetooth device play music	ee	Bluetooth device music
f	f	Bluetooth device stop play music	ff	Bluetooth device stop music
g	g	Bluetooth device last music	gg	Bluetooth device last
h	h	Bluetooth device next	hh	Bluetooth device next music
i	i	Bluetooth device increase volume	ii	Bluetooth device increase sound
	iii	Bluetooth device volume up	iiii	Bluetooth device sound up
j	j	Bluetooth device decrease volume	jj	Bluetooth device decrease sound
k	k	Bluetooth device shutdown		
l	l	Bluetooth device battery notice	ll	Bluetooth device battery remained
	lll	Bluetooth device battery		

Handcrafted Data Description
We have collected about 400 students' voice note data. Each student recorded his or her voices with their mobile phone or laptop. Each student contributes the 24 directives' speech note. These data are voluntarily uploaded by students with privacy confirmed notice.

As speech note may leak some personal identification information, we anonymize the data by converting raw voices into spectrogram as shown in Fig. 2. This also includes the data preprocessing, as the raw data has several different formats. It takes time to handle different file formats, which is harmful for learn experience.

After the above data preprocessing, there are 2469 spectrogram pictures in dataset in total.

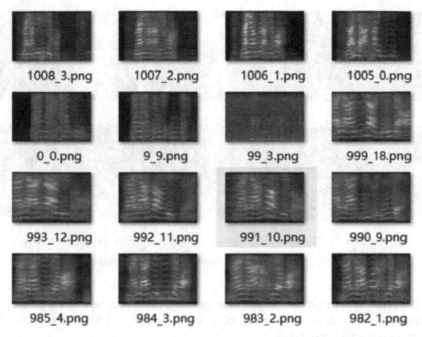

Fig. 2. Partial spectrogram dataset in intelligent voice control experiment.

Data Augmentation

Data augmentation is the common method used to expand the dataset larger in size, which is helpful to fight overfitting in the training process. The concrete approaches in data augmentation include adding random noise in images, random transformation such as image rotation, flipping, zooming etc. In the end, the size of dataset is multiplied with the factor of 6–8. The final results of data augmentation are shown in Fig. 3.

Intelligence Voice Control Task Design

Task design:

(1) Classification into 24 categories;
(2) F1-Score as metrics.

$$F_1 = \frac{precision \cdot recall}{precision + recall} \tag{1}$$

4 Helmet Detection Experiment

Helmet Dataset

The size of helmet dataset is 806 in total. Helmet Dataset includes three categories of photos. One is collected by taking photo by course group, the second is crawled in Internet, and the third is the pure photos of 7 brands. The different categories of pictures are stored in different directories as shown in Fig. 4.

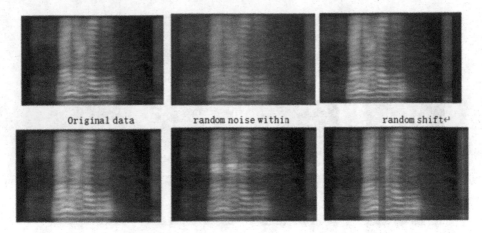

Fig. 3. Data augmentation with different methods.

Hand crafted: 216 photos, 72 students in class, each student wears a helmet and contribute the three photos: Front photo, Side-view photo and back-view photo. It is regular dataset with good definitions.

Collected Data: 200 photos with helmet wearied. With diversity of angles, colors and persons, and picture formats (*.jpg or *.png). Such dataset usually is not very in pixel level resolution.

Helmet only data: 390 with different sizes, seven brands of helmets. It is regular dataset with good definitions.

Fig. 4. Three kinds of data in helmet photo dataset.

Helmet Detection Task Design

As referred in Stanford HAI AI index report [13], TensorFlow2 remained by far the most popular open-source AI software library in 2021, which was followed by Keras, PyTorch and Scikit-learn. For this reason, TensorFlow2 is chosen as deep learning stack in our experiment tasks.

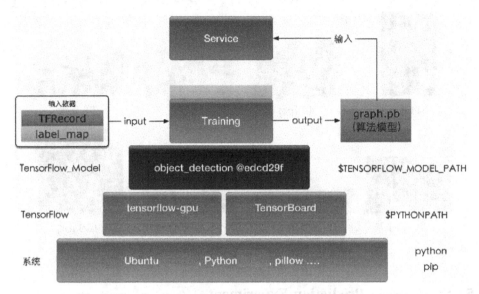

Fig. 5. Experimental environment with TensorFlow software stack.

Experimental Task Goal:
Detect the Objects in photos to find the person wear helmet or not.

(1) Step1. Preparation: Labeling the photo in train dataset, and train deep learning model.
    Install the requirement software and python library, the dependency in show in Fig. 5.
(2) Task steps:
       There are totally 6 steps in processing the data and train the deep learning model
    after the preparation.

Step 2. Convert: Convert the label_map and raw photos into TFRecord format for using in TensorFlow.

Step 3. Model Training: data input into training pipeline and save the checkpoint regularly.

Step 4. Model Evaluate: Using TensorBoard to visualize the training result.

Step 5. Model Export: frozen the model file when the accuracy reach requirement.

Step 6. Model Detect: Using test data to test object detection results.

Figure 5 shows the detection results of helmets and human in heading helmet from a student's task (Fig. 6).

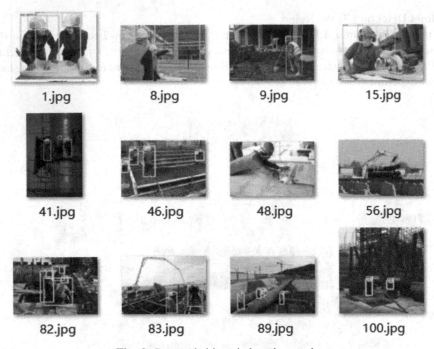

Fig. 6. Detected objects in learning results.

5 Stock Prices Prediction Experiment

Dataset for Stock Mid-Price Movement Prediction

As liquidity plays a vital role in the financial markets, the predicting of limit order book (LOB) by mining micro-structure of high frequency trading (HTF) is often considered a crucial task. LOB is a form of record listing all outstanding limit orders maintained by the exchange, which provides information on available limit order prices and their volumes. Based on these quantities, we provide a limit order book mid-price movement prediction (LOBMMP) dataset for empirical study on stock market as part of quant trading teaching courses.

Data Preparation

(1) Data gathering

To collect a more representative dataset on China stock market, we sampled 10 securities' data of 4 months' trading record (79 trading days in total) with Level-2 stock quote from both Shanghai Stock Exchange and Shenzhen Stock Exchange. The data then has been divided by continuous trading window, meaning the morning data(from 9:30am to 11:30 am) and afternoon data (from 1:00pm to 3:00pm). The daily data is stored in separated csv files and named with the form of '*snapshot_sym < xx > _date < yy > _am/pm.csv*', containing all 1521 csv files in total, as shown in Fig. 7.

(2) Feature enginering

In the dataset mentioned above, each row of data tables contains 31 attributes in different columns, 26 of which are features of snapshot data, with three types of information in LOB, as shown in Table 2.

For the purpose of avoiding information leaking, we masked the symbol name of security and exact trading day, keeping a sequential number as distinction. To further de-identify the symbol and standardize the price, we extract the split-adjusted factor of each security in all trading days and recalibrate their split-adjusted closing price. Next, we normalize all price data (ask/bid/mid/close) into movement ratio respect to adjusted closing price of previous trading day. For example, if the adjusted closing price of previous day was 50 and now best bid price was 50.05, it will be processed as 0.001 and 49.95 as -0.001.

(3) Data labeling

Last five columns of data provide prediction label, showing the different movement direction of mid-price in different time window. All though there are various types of weighted mid-price definition, we take the most succinct way to calculate by *(ask1 + bid1)/2*. The mid-price varied with ask and bid price is shown in Fig. 8.

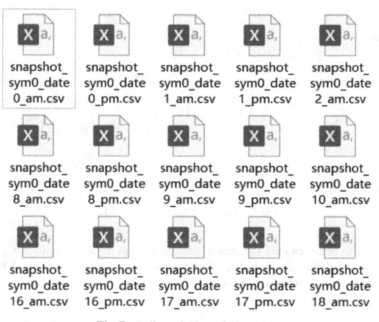

Fig. 7. Daily trade data of 10 stocks.

Table 2. List of provided features

Type	Feature	Description
basic	date	No. of trading date, from 0 to 78
	time	Time of snapshot
	sym	No. of security, from 0 to 9
price	Mid-price	Mid-price of this snapshot
	close	Latest closing price
	ask1–5	The first to fifth best ask price in LOB
	bid1–5	The first to fifth best bid price in LOB
volume	asize1–5	The volume of first to fifth best bid price in LOB
	bsize1–5	The volume of first to fifth best bid price in LOB
	amount	daily cumulative trading volume

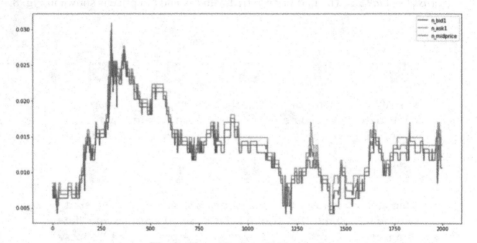

Fig. 8. The mid-price of bid and ask.

In order to better capture the movement momentum of the continuously changing stock price, we define the movement direction with $\varphi(x)$, and label with -1 for move down, 1 for move up, 0 for stationary.

$$\varphi(x) = \begin{cases} -1, & if \ x < -\alpha \\ 0, & if \ |x| \le \alpha \\ 1, & if \ x > \alpha \end{cases} \quad (2)$$

As volatility tends to grow larger with longer time window, we take $\alpha = 0.05\%$ when predicting movement on 5-tick and 10-tick time windows, and $\alpha = 0.1\%$ with 20, 40 and 60-tick time windows.

Stock Mid-Price Movement Prediction Task Design

This experiment was designed to help students with an empirical study on high frequency stock trading with data exploration. The key-point was encouraging student with feather engineering and model selection by enhancing their domain-specific knowledge.

Task steps:

(1) Understand the task;
(2) Exploratory Data Analysis;
(3) Data check with Python pandas;
(4) Trending predication with SVM (Supported Vector machine);
(5) Trending predicting with DNN (Deep Neural network).

The task benchmark metric is F-score within the test set. As in practical HFT (high-frequency trading) algorithm, the precision usually takes more important role than recall, for this reason we choose F-0.5 score as final result.

$$F_\beta = \left(1 + \beta^2\right) \cdot \frac{precision \cdot recall}{\beta^2 \cdot precision + recall} \tag{3}$$

6   Live Generated IoT Data

IoT Datasets

Most IoT device equipped with sensors including temperate, humidity, PM2.5 and light sensor etc. with fast and constantly connectivity, sensor data can be upload into the database in cloud and for further analytic use.

Our experiment uses raspberry Pi as the IoT devices and use DHT11 temperature sensors (Fig. 9).

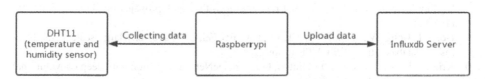

Fig. 9. Temperature data acquisition.

IoT Data Visualization Task Design:

This experiment helps students to understand the principle of IoT system and implement a simple IOT system.

Experimental process:

– Step 1. Use Raspberry Pi to collect the temperature and humidity data, which are obtained by DHT11 sensor;
– Step 2. Upload it to the server of Influxdb through wireless network;
– Step 3. Configure UI to view the data in the web side.

Experimental results:

The graph of data visualizing shows the real-time temperature and humidity on the web side of the server in the experimental scene.

7 Conclusion

In this paper, we introduce spectrogram data, helmet pictures, stock prices and IoT tasks to design experiments with hand-crafted dataset, crawler base data, and live generated IoT data. All these experiments are designed and made it possible by course teaching group, and are used to teach and train students in Data Science and Machine Learning within three real courses launched by CTG since 2015. The main contribution is let students to take part in the design of dataset generating, cleaning, and to targeted real problems in DSML domain, which inspires the students to learn more actively and have better learning experiences in mastering the knowledge of Data Science and Machine Learning.

References

1. Field Cady, Data Science: The Executive Summary - A Technical Book for Non-Technical Professionals, Wiley, Hoboken (2021)
2. Godsey, B.: Think Like a Data Scientist: Tackle the data science process step-by-step. Simon and Schuster (2017)
3. Cristina Mariani, M., et al.: Data Science in Theory and Practice, Techniques for Big Data Analytics and Complex Data Sets, 1st Edn, Wiley, Hoboken (2022)
4. Neal Fishman with Cole Stryker, Smarter Data Science - Succeeding with Enterprise-Grade Data and AI Projects, Wiley, Hoboken (2020)
5. Jordan, M.I., Mitchell, T.M.: Machine learning: trends, perspectives, and prospects. Science **349**(6245), 255–260 (2015)
6. Lecun, Y., Bengio, Y., Hinton, G.: Deep learning. Nature **521**(7553), 436–444 (2015)
7. Goodfellow, I., Bengio, Y., Courville, A.: Deep Learning. MIT Press, Cambridge (2016)
8. LeCun, Y., et al.: Handwritten digit recognition with a back-propagation network. In: NIPS (1989)
9. Deng, J., Dong, W., Socher, R., Li, L.J., Li, K., Fei-Fei, L.: ImageNet: a large-scale hierarchical image database. In: IEEE CVPR (2009)
10. Krizhevsky, A., Sutskever, I., Hinton, G.E.: ImageNet classification with deep convolutional neural networks. In: NIPS (2012)
11. Graves, A., et al.: Speech recognition with deep recurrent neural networks, In: ICASSP (2013)
12. Gao, H., et al.: Densely connected convolutional networks. In: CVPR (2017)
13. Stanford HAI. https://aiindex.stanford.edu/report/
14. Big data and machine intelligence. https://www.xuetangx.com/course/thu08091010085/18960834
15. Financial big data and quantitative analysis platform. https://www.icenter.tsinghua.edu.cn/dashboard/entry.html

Combined Problem-Based Learning in Computer Fundamentals Course

Changlong Gu and Xiaoying Li[✉]

College of Computer Science and Electronic Engineering, Hunan University,
Changsha 410012, China
{guchanglong,lixy}@hnu.edu.cn

Abstract. The computer fundamentals course is an important course aiming at cultivating students' computational thinking. In order to improve the course teaching effects, combined PBL, which is an effective instructional approach that can help students to acquire knowledge and to master skills, was employed from 2021's spring semester to 2023's spring semester. The role of the teacher has changed from indoctrinator to facilitator. The learning model has shifted from being teacher-centered to a student-centered approach. Teachers carefully prepared various problems, applied new teaching pattern throughout the whole teaching process and gathered students' reflections. Through these reflections, this model's teaching effectiveness was verified. On the basis of problem solving, the ability of computational thinking and collaborative learning of students was improved. Furthermore, the conclusion summarizes the main ideas, and further work perspectives.

Keywords: Problem-based learning · Computer fundamental course · Computational thinking · Collaborative learning

1 Introduction

With the development of new technology trends, such as information technology, communication technology, operation technology, internet of things, and artificial intelligence, the age of Industry 4.0 has arrived. It is changing, at a deep level, people's way of working, living, communicating and learning. As a result, computer fundamentals courses are facing many challenges related to teaching content, teaching method, and teaching with technology. Moreover, traditional teaching content and teaching methods cannot meet the needs of the new era. In fact, the teaching content needs to change from software operations to computational thinking. It should heighten students' computational thinking abilities to thinking like computer scientists, improve computer literacy, and provide students with professional knowledge and professional ability [1]. The learning effectivity of traditional teacher-centered teaching methods is not efficient and cannot achieve the goal of raising students' computational thinking awareness.

Problem based learning (PBL) is an instructional design principle that describes a learning scenario where students are engaged in solving meaningful real-world problems.

This process is generally divided into three stages: the problem analysis phase, learning knowledge and problem-solving phase, and reporting phase [2]. During the problem analysis phase, teachers interact with students, and together, they identify tasks to be accomplished, and lay down solutions that contribute to solving problems through acquiring new knowledge or applying existing knowledge. Regarding the stage of learning knowledge and problem solving, students learn with problems to be solved in mind. Therefore, students acquire knowledge on an individual basis or from peers through small-group discussions. In the reporting phase, students consolidate their learning through reflective writing.

PBL is consistent with constructivist learning theory. Problems provide a setting for students to build constructive knowledge and acquire problem-solving abilities. Also, PBL allow students to develop critical thinking and communication skills. Therefore, under PBL, students can actively participate, experience deeply, and establish their own learning methods for knowledge acquisition and understanding throughout the process. PBL is motivational, supports students' socialization, thinking, and self-regulation skills [3].

The flipped classroom was first used by Jonathan Bergmann and Aaron Sams, who were high school chemistry teachers from Colorado in 2006 [4]. In the flipped classroom method, the lecture happens out of class, while the practical application assignments, formerly known as homework, take place in the classroom [4]. The studies on the flipped classroom indicate that flipped classroom has a positive impact on students' learning and retention [5] and can improve students' critical thinking skills [6].

Collaborative learning is a form of group learning in which groups are formed around a central topic. As a result, group members exchange their experiences and opinions, discuss problems, request from each other a piece of advice, discuss with each other, help each other, construct knowledge together, and jointly accomplish learning goals. Collaborative learning is regarded as "suggesting a way of dealing with people which respects and highlights individual group members' abilities and contributions" [7].

In this paper, the authors present the new course content and a combined PBL teaching method which combining the PBL approach, the flipped classroom and the group collaborative learning. Additionally, the authors provide the collected students' reflections, summarize the results, and discuss the major issues to focus on when implementing such a model. As main contribution, this work depicts the effect of a combined PBL strategy in a university computer fundamentals course over students' learning. Moreover, it investigates a specific pedagogical approach aiming at assessing the validity and improving the quality of teaching and learning of the computer fundamentals course.

2   Status Analysis

2.1   Problems in the Teaching Content

Most existing teaching contents related to non-major computer fundamental course include several topics, namely, the introduction to computer composition and principle, the introduction to several commonly used software applications, or the learning of programming languages such as C, C + +, VB, or Java for the different non-majors. With the advent of the AI era, relying only on such content is no longer enough. Learners are eager to learn AI technology. Moreover, learners should be taught on how to use the computer as a tool, as well as to solve problems and to think like a computer scientist. For most non-major computer students who learn C/C + + /Java languages, due to the disconnect between what they have learned and the application of such knowledge into their respective majors, they can straightforwardly feel that they have "learned something useless". The programming language in the teaching content should be conducive to learn AI technology. However, the Python language is such a language, which is simple and easy to use, and can helps users focus on the solution to their real-world problem and not the structure or syntax of the problem [8]. It supports many libraries and has good computing ecology.

2.2 Problems in the Teaching Process

In traditional learning, teachers always impart knowledge in class and assign jobs with specific requirements or expected outcomes after class. Teachers always teach the same information to all students, even if their foundations and abilities are different [9]. In such a traditional paradigm, teachers are in charge of learning, while students passively receive knowledge from their teachers. Information is passed only from teachers to students, with little or no feedback from students to teachers. There is little to no communication or discussion among students. However, under such a course, over time, students can easily become tired or bored.

Students' problem solving and creative thinking skills are generally insufficient to meet job requirements. Therefore, when encountering a real-world problem, students are unable to arrive at a solution. Students often encounter various difficulties when completing a slightly more complex homework assignment. Many of them need to spend a lot of time completing their assignments, and some students may not finish their assignments on time. As the difficulty of the course increases, those students gradually lose their interest in the course.

Under the traditional teaching model, students do not have sufficient opportunities to develop their critical thinking and problem-solving skills due to limited learning time and the use of a teacher-centered model. The goal of a computer fundamentals course does not revolve only around learning knowledge, but more importantly around exercising the programming ability. Moreover, because the concept of programming requires many skills and a broad knowledge, students always give up at some point of the programming learning curve and the goals of the course are always missed.

3   Combined PBL in Computer Fundamental Course

A PBL approach combined with the flipped teaching method and collaborate learning method has been developed to improve the learning efficiency of computer fundamentals courses as well as to solve the drawbacks in the traditional teaching and learning model [10, 11]. Under such a combined approach, questions or tasks assigned by teachers are carried out in class and completed under the guidance of teachers. Additionally, some programming training is completed in class and students are requested to analyze these questions and to spare no effort in finding the solutions. As a result, students can identify what knowledge is necessary, and can acquire such knowledge by themselves or through cooperation with each other. Students learn by doing and study while practicing until they can solve these problems. Moreover, students need to communicate with teachers and peers in real time, which has as an outcome high students' interest in the course. Figure 1 depicts the differences between traditional learning and combined PBL.

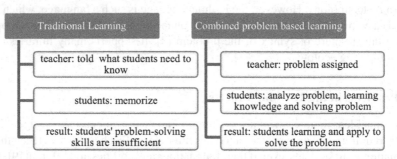

Fig. 1. Difference between traditional learning and combined PBL

In the combined approach the role of the teacher has changed from indoctrinator to facilitator [12], and the teaching mode has changed from "indoctrination" teaching to designing a motivating problem or question for students to investigate, as well as to guide them on how to learn. Throughout the entire process, teachers need to guide students' discussion, encourage students to think creatively, keep their interest at a high peak, provide analysis or pieces of advice, and evaluate students' learning abilities. Moreover, teachers always need to design specific learning resources or to provide existing ones. Additionally, teachers need to summarize the process of teaching and learning and assist in the process of building up students' collective knowledge with open-ended metacognitive questions [13]. An effective PBL-CT integration enhances teaching and learning besides improving students' computational thinking skills [14].

4 Introduction to Computing and Artificial Intelligence Course Descriptions

4.1 Course Setting

The computer fundamental course plays an important role in cultivating students' information literacy in universities. Such an affirmation makes more sense when considering the development of big data, cloud computing, internet of things, AI and other new technologies. As a result, the teaching contents and teaching modes of computer fundamental courses in universities are changing.

The course denoted as Introduction to Computing and Artificial Intelligence is a public basic course of information technology in Hunan University. This course is designed for freshmen students from non-computer majors to cultivate their computational thinking—since the 2020 fall semester. The teaching contents of this course include the Python language foundation, computational thinking and artificial intelligence algorithms and their applications. It can be divided into seven modules, as shown in Table 1. The Python language is used as the main programming tool to realize different thinking modes of computational thinking, which include computing system thinking, network thinking, data thinking, algorithm thinking and artificial intelligence thinking. These are viewed as the core components of computational thinking. Therefore, from the perspective of computational thinking, such a course is guided by artificial-intelligence-related problems and is taught through problem solving. As a result, students are being trained to master the solution consisting of traversing from a professional problem under a computing system to an algorithm first, then second to a program.

Table 1. Content of Introduction to computing and artificial

Module name	Description	Theory time	Experiment time
Overview of computing and computational thinking	History of computing, concepts of computational thinking	2 h	
Programming fundamentals	Python programming foundation	16 h	16 h
Computing system thinking	Mathematical Logic, Components of Computing Systems	2–4 h	2–4 h
Networking thinking	Internet, network spider, data parsing	2–4 h	2–4 h
Data thinking	Data management, data cleansing, data analysis and data visualization	4–10 h	4–8 h
Algorithm thinking	Classical algorithms	2–10 h	2–6 h
AI thinking	Machine learning, deep learning, large model applications	8 h	4 h

Different majors focused on different modules in their teaching, and the learning hours of each module were different.

4.2 Teaching Approach

In the 2020 fall semester, the traditional teacher-centered approach was used in the course. However, cultivation of computational thinking can be a difficult undertaking for some. For example, abstraction skills, decomposition skills, pattern recognition skills, programming skills, and logical reasoning skills are needed [15]. The teaching result was not satisfactory.

In the 2021 spring semester, a combined PBL approach was employed in the course. An online and offline blended teaching mode was adopted. Some parts of the concepts of computational thinking and artificial intelligence can be learned online, while the other parts are learned offline. Such a course emphasizes the cultivation of computational thinking ability, and the teaching method employed has also changed from "knowledge output" to "ability training". As a result, students are trained through PBL with intensive teaching and practice and learning by doing. Moreover, students conduct many standalone short problems and undergo problem-targeted training under team collaboration through teaching platform. They can practice through games in experimental class settings under a teacher's guidance. Therefore, through team training, students' cooperation consciousness and innovation ability are improved. Additionally, students' problem-solving ability using computational thinking is developed at multiple levels. Such a course will lay a foundation for students of various majors to design, construct and apply various computing systems to solve disciplinary problems in the future, as well as help learners improve their ability to interpret real-world systems and solve complex problems.

Multi-dimensional learning assessments is used to evaluate student's final score. This evaluation method reflects the learning process employed, such as short problems scores, student–student mutual evaluation scores, unit test scores, team comprehensive assignment scores, mid-term exam and final exam, as shown in Table 2. Considering Table 2, usual performance 1 usually groups together short problem scores in classroom performance and team comprehensive assignment score, while usual performance 2 consists of experiment scores, quiz scores and unit test scores.

Table 2. Evaluation method of computer fundamental course

Evaluation indicators		Percent of the total score	
Usual performance 1	short problem practices	10%	20%
	team comprehensive assignment	10%	
Usual performance 2	experiment	15%	30%
	quiz	5%	
	unit test	10%	
Midterm examination		10%	
Final examination		40%	

5   Combined PBL Implementation Descriptions

5.1   Planning

Non-computer-major students have enrolled in the Introduction to computing and artificial intelligence course since 2020 fall semester. Over 80% of them had no prior coding experience, according to a questionnaire survey of 721 freshmen in the fall semester of

2020. From the 2021 spring semester, the combined PBL method was adopted. In the 2021 spring semester, about 86 students enrolled in the Introduction to Computing and Artificial intelligence course participated willingly in the experiment.

Due to the zero-coding level of most students, we carefully prepared various problems for the course from a simple level to a complex one. The problems related to instructional design followed the same principle. These problems were classified into two types. One type was short problems, the second type was about large real-world problems. For each lecture class, we prepared about four short problems. Totally 60 short problems were prepared. Additionally, we prepared 4 large comprehensive problems from the real world for students to choose from. In the 2022 fall semester, the number of large problems added to 10, as shown in Table 3. Short problems were suitable for a single person to work on, while large problems were complex problems more suited for group collaborative learning activities.

Table 3. Evaluation method of computer fundamental course

Large problems	Part of Short problems
E-commerce marketing practice project - Construction and Evaluation of a model for predicting mobile phone sales	Currency conversion
Calculation and visualization of drug molecular fingerprints	Wheat on the chess board
Analysis of listed company stocks	Extracting information from ID card number
Analysis and management of large ancient poetry datasets	Caesar code encryption
Milk tea shop service system	Hurricane classification determination
Book management system	Mars rover statistics
Recruitment website information crawling and analysis	Random password generation
High quality film data acquisition and analysis	Word cloud production
Content crawling and analysis of literary works	Shooting curves of basketball drawing
Practical project for the development of Gobang game	Face detection

The course team teachers produced 66 micro lesson videos for students' preview and review. Those videos were published on the Educoder platform (https://www.edu coder.net). Educoder is a network teaching and learning platform that provides many functions, such as course creation, experiment creation, automatic score judgement, real-time evaluation, learning resource presence, and data statistics. Students can practice repeatedly on the platform. Additionally, the platform supports exercise banks and examination question banks, as well as examination functions, and digital teaching management. Teachers build and publish various course resources through the platform and track students' learning activities throughout the process. We create an online teaching course on the Educoder network platform, providing experiments and other learning resources. As a result, students can watch these videos from anywhere and at any time. Corresponding quizzes were also prepared with these videos. Courseware, exercises and unit tests were also prepared. We also created 15 learning guides, 20 courseware items, 16 experiments, 9 after-class exercises, and 6 tests. All of these teaching and learning resources were published on our online course in Educoder.

5.2 Implementation

At the beginning of the course, students were divided into groups. Each group consisted of three to four students. Students were required to preview the course content before the lecture class on the Educoder network platform according to the teacher's guidance plan. These learning resources include lecture videos, courseware, etc. As a result, students acquired basic knowledge or concepts before the lecture class.

The lecture class was divided into three parts, with each part having specific objective, namely, the preview test, problem-based learning, and the summary. A multiple-choice quiz was given onto the Educoder network platform at first, which would take about 5min. After the quiz, the Educoder automatically judged the answers and provided score statistics. The teacher could immediately check the score of each student and the statistical data of all the students on Educoder, including the highest score, the lowest score, the average score, the accuracy rate of each question, etc. The teacher then analyzed the different questions with students. Such process required around 5–10 min.

Then, the teacher introduced about short problems. Students discussed their understanding regarding a specific problem using flowcharts and discussed ideas and methods of solving problems in groups. They acquired the necessary knowledge by studying in a collaborative manner. When a group met difficulties, the teacher provided clues. However, students were required to program independently and complete their own summary reports. At the end of the class, students submitted their work on the Educoder, then the teacher summarized and displayed excellent work. After the class, students completed assignments and extended their knowledge and skills. Each student had to submit their learning report, which included the problem solution, program code and learning harvest. Following report submission, students gave a peer assessment to other students. From the peer assessment, students could learn different solutions to the same problems. The teaching process is shown in Fig. 2.

While in practice classes, students completed experiments on the Educoder platform. Unit tests were also conducted in practice classes to check students' performance. The measured students' performance could affect the future choice of the teacher's strategy.

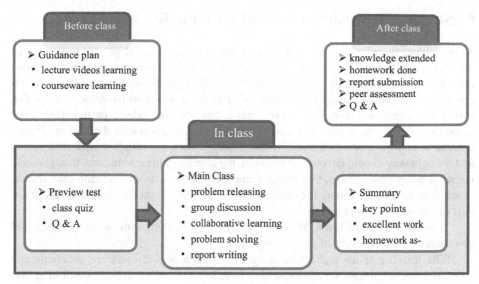

Fig. 2. Implementation of combined PBL approach

5.3 Team Comprehensive Training Problems

The large problems were assigned at the beginning of the semester. The large problems integrated multi-methods of computational thinking and required students to complete them in groups. Each group chose one large problem to design and implement according to their interest. Students could also choose another artificial intelligence problem according to their interest and ability.

When groups had determined the problem, the next step was to clarify the division of each group member. For example, one person in the group was responsible for scraping data from the website and saving the obtained data as a file, while the second person was responsible for data cleaning, sorting and analysis. The third group member was responsible for data visualization. Group members discussed what data to scrap from what website, as well as what kinds of analysis and visualization are suitable for the obtained data. Furthermore, as requirements, at least two analysis and visualization results were required to be displayed. Finally, other members used artificial intelligence model for modeling and prediction. Each member of the group then implemented his/her module with a Python program and combined it into a complete program. Finally, each group wrote a report that contained the description of all the work completed.

The large problem needed to be solved out of class. This required close cooperation among group members. If a student encountered difficulties, he/she could discuss and learn how to solve them in his/her group or seek help from the teacher. After all group reports had been submitted on Educoder, teachers gave scores to each group. The final score of the large problem was made of the scores related to coding, functions, and reports. Then, the teacher chose excellent works to review and share. This activity will further promote students' learning interests and abilities.

6 Students' Reflections and Analysis of the Teaching Effect

To investigate the effectiveness of the combined PBL approach adopted in the course in the spring semester of 2021, students' reflections from this course were gathered. Those reflections include the study status and effect, as well as group collaborative effect, which come from two questionnaires and students' large question report harvests. In week 7, a survey was conducted through a questionnaire. Seventy-six students participated in the questionnaire survey. In such questionnaire, there was an open-ended question "Please comment on your study this week." Nine students were not satisfied with their status and thought they should devote more time to the course. Fourteen students thought their learning status was average. Due to the complexity of the learning content, they should practice more. The remaining fifty-three students (70%) thought they had made progress. Part of the answers were as follows.

"It is better than last week. We have more communication with group members and give better play to the role of group cooperation."

"The learning status and effect are good. We can actively analyze problems and communicate with team members, which is reflected in more active questioning and communication with team members and master more list related knowledge."

"In this week's study, through many exchanges with teacher, teaching assistants and students in team, including the study of relevant videos before class, I found many deficiencies in my study."

Concerning the effect of teamwork towards the PBL approach in this course, about 82% of students thought it worked out, and were willing to communicate and help the students in the group. Figure 3 displays the response to the problem "Do you think teamwork has worked this week?".

Pre-class previews require students to learn specific knowledge before the class, which can reflect students' learning status and participation in learning. In the teaching survey of week 11, 91% of students carried out the pre-class preview. The group learning effectivity of the large problem was expressed from the students' group report harvests. The features of PBL such as creativity, collaboration and critical thinking impressed students deeply. Some reports written by students were as follows.

"This time, I have two harvests: one is the power of the team; the other is the power of innovation and creation - these two powers support us from facing the assignment requirements, to generating initial ideas, to the idea of from the skeleton to the full."

"In the teamwork, I have also gained and grown. What impressed me especially is the strong execution of my two teammates. Everyone has a clear division of labor, each performed their own duties and helped each other, which was the key to the success of our team."

Do you think teamwork has worked this week?

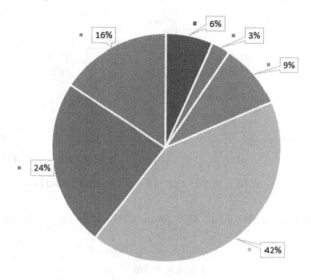

- ■ No, I'm introverted and don't like communication.
- ■ No, the crew didn't help me.
- ■ No, I can do it myself.
- ■ Yes, we learn from each other and communicate more.
- ■ Yes, if the team member reminds me, I will do it.
- ■ Yes, I am willing to take the initiative to communicate and help the students in the group.

Fig. 3. Pie chart of question about the effect of teamwork

To further investigate the effectiveness of the combined PBL approach, one class taught by the same teacher in the 2020 fall semester was compared with a class in the 2021 spring semester and a class in the 2023 spring semester. The number of people in the three classes is 70, 86, and 62, respectively. The final scores of the three classes are shown in Fig. 4. The 2020 fall semester did not adopt the combined PBL teaching method. These examinations were given according to the same teaching contents and for the same difficulty level. The passing rate of 2021 spring and 2023 spring semester's final scores were 93.3% and 100.0%, which were 0.7% and 7.4% higher than those of 2020 fall. Also, the excellence rate (90–100) of 2021 spring semester's and 2023 spring semester's final examination were 8.3% and 29%, which were 5.4% and 26.1% higher than 2020 fall semester's final scores. From the comparison of the average grades of the three semesters (see Fig. 5.), it can be seen that the grades are getting better and better, and to some extent, the teaching effect is getting better and better.

According to the curriculum teaching evaluation conducted by the university at the end of the two semesters, the students' satisfaction rate with the curriculum teaching effect has increased from 79.41% to 89%.

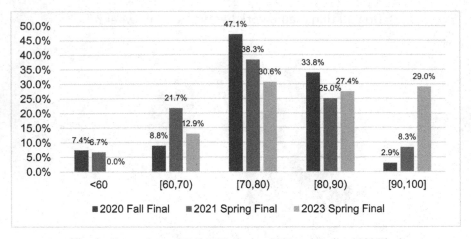

Fig. 4. Comparison of Fall 2020, Spring 2021 and Spring 2023 Final

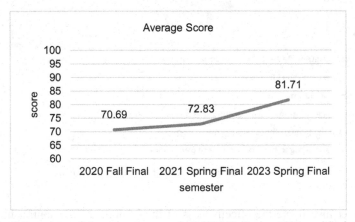

Fig. 5. Comparison of class average score in Fall 2020, Spring 2021, and Spring 2023

7   Conclusions

In the Introduction to Computing and Artificial Intelligence course, the teaching goal became to cultivate students' computational thinking ability based on problem solving. Through the teaching experience of using the combined PBL approach since 2021 spring semester, the effectiveness of combined PBL was proved. It enhanced students' initiative and enthusiasm for learning. Students' learning statuses were always well preserved. As a result, group learning promoted learning effectiveness, collaboration, critical thinking, and creativity.

Despite the potential benefits of incorporating a combined PBL approach in our computer fundamentals course, there are still limitations that may hinder its effectiveness and quality. One such limitation is the need for carefully crafted problems that progress from simple to complex. It is advisable to avoid incorporating too many specific grammatical details in problem design, as this knowledge can easily be acquired online and quickly resolved through student collaboration. Additionally, teachers must ensure that class progress remains on track to avoid delays in completing subsequent teaching tasks.

Although the combined PBL has achieved good results, 82% of respondents (Fig. 3) benefited from teamwork. However, there is still 18% who did not benefit from the application of the combined PBL method. In China, the Outline of the National Medium- and Long-Term Education Reform and Development Plan (2010–2020) points out that it is necessary to care of each student, respect the law of physical and mental development of students, and provide suitable education for each student [16](Han & Ye, 2017). There are differences in learning ability, hobbies, ways of thinking, cognitive characteristics, etc. Some methods should be adopted to help these students. In the future, personalized learning according to students' individual differences and learning needs should be carried out. It can help students to find learning styles adapted to them.

References

1. Wing, J.M.: Computational thinking. Commun. ACM **49**(3), 33–35 (2006)
2. Schmidt, H.G., Moust, J.H.: Factors affecting small-group tutorial learning: a review of research. Probl.-Based Learn.: Res. Perspect. Learn. Interact., 19–52 (2000)
3. Dilekli, Y.: Project-based learning. In: Paradigm shifts in 21st Century Teaching and Learning, pp. 53–68. IGI Global (2020)
4. Arnold-Garza, S.: The flipped classroom teaching model and its use for information literacy instruction. Commun. Inf. Lit. **8**(1), 9 (2014)
5. Mithun, S., Evans, N.: Impact of the flipped classroom on students' learning and retention in teaching programming. In: 2018 ASEE Annual Conference & Exposition (2018)
6. Davenport, C.E.: Evolution in student perceptions of a flipped classroom in a computer programming course. J. Coll. Sci. Teach. **47**(4), 30–35 (2018)
7. Laal, M., Laal, M.: Collaborative learning: what is it? Procedia Soc. Behav. Sci. **31**, 491–495 (2012)
8. Python Geeks. What is Python Programming Language? https://pythongeeks.org/what-is-python-programming-language
9. Berssanette, J.H., de Francisco, A.C.: Active learning in the context of the teaching/learning of computer programming: a systematic review. J. Inf. Technol. Educ. Res. **20**, 201 (2021)
10. Wang, G., Zhao, H., Guo, Y., Li, M.: Integration of flipped classroom and problem based learning model and its implementation in university programming course. In: 2019 14th International Conference on Computer Science & Education (ICCSE), pp. 606–610). IEEE (2019)
11. Chis, A.E., Moldovan, A.N., Murphy, L., Pathak, P., Muntean, C.H.: Investigating flipped classroom and problem-based learning in a programming module for computing conversion course. J. Educ. Technol. Soc. **21**(4), 232–247 (2018)
12. Frydenberg, M., Mentzer, K.: From engagement to empowerment: project-based learning in Python coding courses. In: EDISG Conference, Information Systems & Computing Academic Professionals (2020)
13. Yew, E.H., Goh, K.: Problem-based learning: an overview of its process and impact on learning. Health Prof. Educ. **2**(2), 75–79 (2016)
14. Saad, A., Zainudin, S.: A review of project-based learning (PBL) and computational thinking (CT) in teaching and learning. Learn. Motiv. **78**, 101802 (2022)

15. Yusoff, K.M., Ashaari, N.S., Wook, T.S.M.T., Ali, N.M.: Analysis on the requirements of computational thinking skills to overcome the difficulties in learning programming. Int. J. Adv. Comput. Sci. Appl. **11**(3) (2020)
16. Han, S., Ye, F.: China's education policy-making: a policy network perspective. J. Educ. Policy **32**(4), 389–413 (2017)

Computer-Aided Education Based on Research of Chinese Language Learning Behavior in Brunei Darussalam International High School from the Country-Specific Perspective

Shuxia Bi[1]([⊠]) and Huanhai Fang[2]

[1] Xiamen University, Xiamen 361005, China
932111610@qq.com
[2] Suqian University, Suqian 223800, China
fanghuanhai@xmu.edu.cn

Abstract. This paper selected an international school in Brunei as a research case, and used the Learning Behaviors Scale (LBS) to analyze the learning behaviors of learners in Chinese learning. According to statistics gathered by questionnaires, this essay analyzed the results via SPSS 22.0, and reported that when learning Chinese as a second language, all the four dimensions of learning motivation, attitude, attention and strategy were positively correlated with the learners' academic performance; differences in learning duration could lead to those in learning behaviors; differences also occurred in the learning behaviors between male and female students, i.e. boys performed weaker than girls in terms of the above four dimensions; there was a correlation between learners' language learning behaviors and their family languages, i.e. different family languages had an impact on all the four dimensions of learners' learning behaviors, among which difference between motivation and strategy was quite big; in addition, differences in religious beliefs did not affect learners' second language learning behaviors. Based on these research results, the paper advocates that the idea of computer-based education can be introduced to help students establish reasonable Chinese learning behaviors. At the same time, this study can provide several useful tips on international Chinese education integrated with computer technology.

Keywords: Chinese Language Education · Learning Behaviors · Computer Aided Education · Computer Science and Technology

1 Introduction

Language learning behaviors can be seen as parts of Basic Learning Behaviors or Stylistic Learning Behaviors. In recent years, scholars at home and abroad have begun to pay attention to the academic study regarding learners' language learning behaviors. McDermott et al. (1996) has developed the Learning Behaviors Scale (LBS). The LBS composed of 29 items also includes four dimensions of learning motivation, learning attitude, attention, and learning strategies. And it is suitable for testing the learning behaviors of learners of different ages, genders and ethnic groups.

Ehrman (1990) proposed that women could use learning strategies more efficiently and frequently than men in their learning, and had advantages in learning, communication and self-management. Finnemann's (1992) study showed that men and women tended to adopt different learning behaviors and the difference mainly lied in their choosing learning strategies in certain tasks. The survey conducted by Chambers (1995) reported that women had better social linguistic skills than men, which means women could show stronger abilities in mastering and applying a language when speaking, mainly in terms of fluency, vocabulary, spelling, etc. Kimura (2000) shared a similar viewpoint with Chamber in his survey and research, and he further found that compared with men, women could demonstrate better linguistic ability in language-memorizing and studying basic vocabulary. The findings of Durbrow, Schaefer and Jimerson (2001) also showed that factors affecting the students' academic performance were not only cognitive ability, but also attentions and anxieties they had in class. Riding, Grimley, Dahraei and Banner (2003) found that learners of verbal cognitive style and analytical cognitive style had better learning behaviors than those of other cognitive styles. However, they also claimed that a learner's gender was not significantly related to his learning behaviors, which contradicted with Chambers' and Kimura's study. Griffiths (2003) demonstrated that there was a positive correlation between the learners' language proficiency and their frequency of applying language learning strategies properly. Compared with the senior students, the learners of lower grade had some deficiencies in choosing language learning strategies. Oliver (2007) found that the average value of primary school students choosing and using learning strategies exceeded that of middle school students. Large numbers of studies conducted by Oxford (2008) reported that junior high school students used learning strategies even more frequently than those of senior high school.

Recent research on Chinese learning behaviors lacked the four dimensions of learning motivation, learning attitude, attention and learning strategies. It also failed to reach any reliable quantitative conclusions and could not provide the correct interpretation of learning behavior variables. In addition, there weren't enough feasible solutions to problems in students' learning behaviors, especially from the perspective of computer-based education. In view of this, this study selected an international school in Brunei as a research case and analyzed the learners' learning behaviors in the process of learning Chinese. At the same time, it is advocated here that the mode of computer-based education should be incorporated into the teaching of Chinese as a foreign language.

2 Research Design

2.1 Research Questions

- What is the relationship between the duration of Chinese language learning and Chinese language learning behaviors?
- What is the dynamic relationship between Chinese learners' genders and their learning behaviors?
- What is the relationship between Chinese language learners' learning behaviors and their home environment and family languages?
- What is the relationship between Chinese language learners' learning behaviors and their religious belief?

2.2   Research Framework

This study was mainly based on four theoretical assumptions. More specifically: 1) There is a correlation between the duration of language learning and learning behaviors. 2) There is a correlation between learners' genders and learning behaviors. 3) Learners' learning behaviors correlate with their home environment and family languages. 4) One's learning behaviors correlates with its religious belief.

In an attempt to find out both factors favorable and unfavorable to Chinese language teaching and learning, this study investigated and analyzed Chinese learning behaviors of students from one international school. The impact of learning behaviors on Chinese language learning was quantified in the form of questionnaire investigation. SPSS 22 was adopted to deal with the data gathered by questionnaire and the impact of different learning behaviors on learning outcome was finally analyzed via the method of systematic evaluation to find out the most effective learning behaviors. Under the guidance of the effective learning behaviors and through correcting and optimizing the improper learning behaviors, the students would be enabled to develop Chinese learning abilities in many ways and improve their learning performance. At the same time, the international Chinese education can be enhanced and promoted.

2.3   Participants

Founded in 1997, Jerudong International School of Brunei (JIS) is an IB World School fully accredited by Cambridge International Examinations (CIE), Edexcel and Assessment and Qualifications Alliance (AQA). Compared with local Brunei schools, Chinese language schools, and English language schools, Jerudong International School is characterized by multi-nationalities, various cultures, and greater mobility. It offers Chinese language courses including oral Chinese. The main purpose of these courses is to enable Chinese language learners to apply what they have learned in class to daily life and communication. Unlike other schools in Brunei, the majority of students from Jerudong International School arc non-native speakers of Chinese. For these language learners, the Chinese courses are only elective, which is different from the other Chinese language schools teaching Chinese as the first language.

Students in grades 7–11 taking Chinese courses in the Jerudong International School participated in this study. Ethnic Chinese students whose Chinese was poor or who did not speak Chinese as a first language were all included.

2.4   Data Collection

The questionnaire was composed of two parts, one was the basic background investigation of the students and the other was the structural investigation. The questionnaire was mainly based on the Learning Behaviors Scale (LBS) developed by McDermott, Green, Francis and Stott (1996). After synthesizing 29 basic learning behavior items of LBS, the author included the four basic dimensions and designed this questionnaire. The four basic dimensions, i.e., learning motivation, learning attitude, attention and learning strategy were adapted to test the learning behaviors of Chinese language learners of different ages, genders and ethnic groups. Factor analysis of the above four dimensions showed high consistency and test-retest reliability.

A total of 141 questionnaires were distributed and collected, with a collection rate of 100%.

3   Result Discussion

Adopting the software SPSS 22.0 as the basic analysis tool, this study calculated the mean and standard deviation of learning behaviors from different dimensions, and then determined the correlation coefficients. The difference test was used to determine the correlation coefficients between learning behaviors and academic performance of participants of different proficiency and genders. Correlation analysis and multiple regression analysis were used to investigate and analyze the impact of learning behaviors upon final academic performance.

Table 1. Correlation: learning duration & learning behaviors

		1-G; 2-F; 3-E; 4-D; 5-C	Motivation	Attitude	Attention	Strategy
Grades	Pearson correlation	1	−0.013	−0.079	0.127	0.143
	Significance (two tails)		.000	.000	.000	.000
	Numbers of participants	141	141	141	141	141
Motivation	Pearson correlation	−0.013	1	.549**	.588**	.227**
	Significance (two tails)	0.881		0	0	0.007
	Numbers of participants	141	141	141	141	141
Attitude	Pearson correlation	0.079	.549**	1	.670**	.486**
	Significance (two tails)	0.349	0		0	0
	Numbers of participants	141	141	141	141	141

(*continued*)

Table 1. (*continued*)

		1-G; 2-F; 3-E; 4-D; 5-C	Motivation	Attitude	Attention	Strategy
Attention	Pearson correlation	0.127	.588**	.670**	1	.478**
	Significance (two tails)	0.132	0	0		0
	Numbers of participants	141	141	141	141	141
Strategy	Pearson correlation	0.143	.227**	.486**	.478**	1
	Significance (two tails)	0.091	0.007	0	0	
	Numbers of participants	141	141	141	141	141

It can be seen from Table 1 that the Pearson correlation coefficients of study duration with learning motivation and learning attitude were −0.013 and −0.079 respectively, indicating that the longer study duration meant more proper learning attitude and stronger learning motivation; while the Pearson correlation coefficients of study duration with attention and learning strategy were 0.127 and 0.143 respectively, implying that the longer study length would lead to shorter attention span, so the learning strategy needed to be changed. Meanwhile, there was no significant difference in the correlation of length of study with learning motivation, learning attitude, attention and learning strategy of students of different ages. Therefore, there was a relatively obvious positive correlation of learning length with learning behaviors of motivation and attitude, and a significant negative correlation between that of attention and strategy.

As summarized in Table 2, the significance coefficients of gender differences for the learning motivation and strategies were 0.02 and 0.14 respectively, both of which were higher than 0.01; while those for learning attitude and attention were lower than 0.01. The data indicated that when it comes to the impact of learner's learning behaviors on academic performance, there was a certain correlation between gender differences and learners' learning attitude and attention. Female students could demonstrate more positive learning behaviors than male students. In terms of the impact of gender differences on learning behaviors, there was little difference between students of different grades. Whether from junior or senior high school, female students were all better than male students in language learning motivation, learning strategy, attention and learning attitude.

Table 2. Correlation: gender & learning behaviors

		1-Male 2-Female	Motivation	Attitude	Attention	Strategy
Grades	Pearson correlation	1	0.019	0.165	0.07	0.11
	Significance (two tails)		.002	.000	.000	.014
	Numbers of participants	141	141	141	141	141
Motivation	Pearson correlation	0.019	1	.549**	.588**	.227**
	Significance (two tails)	0.826		0	0	0.007
	Numbers of participants	141	141	141	141	141
Attitude	Pearson correlation	0.165	.549**	1	.670**	.486**
	Significance (two tails)	0.05	0		0	0
	Numbers of participants	141	141	141	141	141
Attention	Pearson correlation	0.07	.588**	.670**	1	.478**
	Significance (two tails)	0.409	0	0		0
	Numbers of participants	141	141	141	141	141
Strategy	Pearson correlation	0.11	.227**	.486**	.478**	1
	Significance (two tails)	0.194	0.007	0	0	
	Numbers of participants	141	141	141	141	141

Table 3 showed the Pearson correlation coefficients of home languages for learning motivation, learning attitude, attention and learning strategy were −0.051, −0.105, −0.193 and −00.128 respectively, indicating that when learning language there was an obvious correlation of a learner's home language with certain learning behaviors. More specifically, home languages had the greatest impact on learners' learning strategies and attention, followed by learning attitude and motivation. Although the last was the least affected, there was also some impact remained. In addition, there was no difference in the impact of home languages on learners of all grades and genders on this regard. From the survey, it can be concluded that the language environment is crucial for learners to learn Chinese. If there were family members who spoke Chinese at home, Chinese language learners could have a good learning atmosphere.

It is acknowledged that as the main part of human culture language and religion always complement each other, ultimately affecting the national psychology. However, such close relation between religion and language seems not exist in learning behaviors, as it was shown in Table 4 that obvious correlation of the main Chinese language learning behaviors was not found to be related with religious beliefs of the learners.

Table 3. Correlation: home languages & learning behaviors

		1-English 2-Chinese 3-Malay 4-Others	Motivation	Attitude	Attention	Strategy
Grades	Pearson correlation	1	−0.051	−0.105	−0.193	−0.128
	Significance (two tails)		.000	.0002	.0005	.000
	Numbers of participants	141	141	141	141	141
Motivation	Pearson correlation	−0.051	1	.549**	.588**	.227**
	Significance (two tails)	0.551		0	0	0.007
	Numbers of participants	141	141	141	141	141
Attitude	Pearson correlation	−0.105	.549**	1	.670**	.486**
	Significance (two tails)	0.216	0		0	0
	Numbers of participants	141	141	141	141	141
Attention	Pearson correlation	−.193*	.588**	.670**	1	.478**
	Significance (two tails)	0.022	0	0		0
	Numbers of participants	141	141	141	141	141
Strategy	Pearson correlation	−0.128	.227**	.486**	.478**	1
	Significance (two tails)	0.129	0.007	0	0	
	Numbers of participants	141	141	141	141	141

Table 4. Correlation: religions & learning behaviors

		1-Islam 2-Buddhism 3-Hinduism 4-Christianity 5-Others	Motivation	Attitude	Attention	Strategy
Grades	Pearson correlation	1	0.152	0.12	0.061	−0.069
	Significance (two tails)		0.345	0.142	0.475	0.414
	Numbers of participants	141	141	141	141	141
Motivation	Pearson correlation	0.152	1	.549**	.588**	.227**

(continued)

Table 4. (*continued*)

		1-Islam 2-Buddhism 3-Hinduism 4-Christianity 5-Others	Motivation	Attitude	Attention	Strategy
	Significance (two tails)	0.072		0	0	0.007
	Numbers of participants	141	141	141	141	141
Attitude	Pearson correlation	0.12	.549**	1	.670**	.486**
	Significance (two tails)	0.156	0		0	0
	Numbers of participants	141	141	141	141	141
Attention	Pearson correlation	0.061	.588**	.670**	1	.478**
	Significance (two tails)	0.475	0	0		0
	Numbers of participants	141	141	141	141	141
Strategy	Pearson correlation	−0.069	.227**	.486**	.478**	1
	Significance (two tails)	0.414	0.007	0	0	
	Numbers of participants	141	141	141	141	141

4   Conclusion

According to statistics gathered by questionnaire, this study analyzed the hypothesis through SPSS 22.0, and the results were as follows: 1) When learning Chinese as a second language, the four dimensions of learning behaviors positively correlated with learners' academic performance; 2) Differences in learning duration would give rise to those in learning behaviors; 3) There were also differences in learning behaviors of students of different genders. Compared with female students, male students were ill-performed in terms of the four dimensions; 4) Correlation could be found between language learning behaviors and home languages. Different home languages could affect learners' four dimension of learning behaviors, among which impact on motivation and strategy was the greatest; 5) Differences in religious beliefs would not affect Chinese language learners' language learning behaviors.

This study observed behaviors of students in learning Chinese language, analyzed differences in their Chinese learning behaviors via empirical method and reached to findings beneficial for teaching Chinese as a second language. In recent years, computer-based education has developed rapidly and has been recognized by many teachers and students. Now its focus has shifted from higher education institutions to primary, secondary and vocational schools, open teaching models are constantly being created. Against the background of the rapid development of integration of computer technology and language learning, Chinese language teachers should adjust their teaching strategies appropriately to better promote international Chinese education. According to the results of this research, it is proposed to introduce computer-aided instruction (CAI) and computer-assisted learning (CAL) into teaching Chinese as a foreign language. Table 1 showed a significant negative correlation between learning length and attention, implying that the longer study length would lead to shorter attention span, and the learning strategy needed to be changed, so CAI can be used in class to stimulate students' enthusiasm for learning. Table 2 indicated that female students could demonstrate more positive learning behaviors than male students. Accordingly, it is necessary to use CAI to design individualized teaching programs for male students that are different from female. Table 3 showed that a Chinese language environment is crucial for learners to learn Chinese. However, it is impossible for everyone to own a helpful learning atmosphere at home, and therefore the students could make full use of CAL system to solve that problem.

Acknowledgement. This work is supported by the Foundation of Center for Language Education and Cooperation (21YH019CX2). We are grateful to the workmates for their comments.

References

McDermott, P.A., Leigh, N.M., Perry, M.A.: Development and validation of the preschool learning behavior scale. Psychol. Sch. **39**(4), 353–365 (2002)

McDermott, P.A.: Learning behavior and intelligence as explanations for children's scholastic achievement. J. Sch. Psychol. **37**(3), 299–313 (1999)

McDermott, P.A.: Sex, race, class, and other demographics as explanations for children's ability and adjustment: a national appraisal. J. Sch. Psychol. **33**(1), 75–91 (1995)

McDermott, P.A.: National scales of differential learning behaviors among American children and adolescents. Sch. Psychol. Rev. **28**(2), 280–291 (1999)

Lakebrink, M.: Incremental validity of the learning behavior scale in special education evaluation. Dissertation, Eastern Illinois University (2014)

Canivez, G.L., Willenborg, E.: Replication of the learning behaviors scale factor structure with an independent sample. J. Psychoeducational Assess. **24**(2), 97–111 (2006)

Schaefer, B.A., Mcdermott, P.A.: Learning behavior and intelligence as explanations for children's scholastic achievement. J. Sch. Psychol. **37**(3), 299–313 (1999)

Riding, R.J., Grimley, M., Dahraei, H., Banner, G.: Cognitive style, working memory and learning behavior and attainment in school subjects. Br. J. Educ. Psychol. **73**, 149–169 (2003)

Rikoon, S.H., Mcdermott, P.A., Fantuzzo, J.W.: Approaches to learning among head start alumni: structure and validity of the learning behaviors scale. Sch. Psychol. Rev. **41**(3), 272–294 (2012)

Nishimura, K.: A study of school age children's affects in a learning behavior. Jpn. J. Educ. Psychol. **44**(4), 410–417 (1996)

Chapelle, C.: Construct definition and validity inquiry in SLA research. In: Bachman, L.F., Cohen, A.D. (eds.) Interfaces Between Second Language Acquisition and Language Testing Research, pp. 32–70. Cambridge University Press, Cambridge (1999)

Worrell, F.C., Vandiver, B.J., Watkins, M.W.: Construct validity of the learning behavior scale with an independent sample of students. Psychol. Sch. **38**(3), 207–215 (2001)

Durbrow, E.H., Schaefer, B.A., Jimerson, S.R.: Learning-related behaviors versus cognitive ability in the academic performance of Vincentian children. Br. J. Educ. Psychol. **71**, 471–483 (2001)

Kormos, J., Csizér, K.: Age-related differences in the motivation of learning English as a foreign language: attitudes, selves, and motivated learning behavior. Lang. Learn. **58**(2), 327–355 (2008)

Embedded Computing Course Design for Internet of Things and Smart Things Applications

Zhen Chen[1(✉)], Tian-Xiao Lin[2], Yi-Song Zhang[1], Xiao-Dong Ma[1], Min Guo[1], Yu-Xiang Lin[2], Fan Li[1], Wei Ran Lin[1], and Shuang Shou Li[1]

[1] Tsinghua University, Beijing, China
zhenchen@tsinghua.edu.cn
[2] Guanglun Electronic Technology, Beijing, China

Abstract. With the rapid advancement of IoT technology, IoT education has emerged as a new challenge in university education. A course named "Smart Hardware and Intelligent Systems" is designed to target for undergraduate students in IoT education. The course content includes the mastery of embedding computing hardware, scene-based programming methods, IoT communication technologies and cloud services, design thinking in smart product etc. The course teaching methods combine lectures, hands-on experiments, case studies, and creative design. The course creates a comprehensive and self-directed learning environment for students. The AIOE hardware is also introduced to remove the barriers to learning embedded computing and facilitate the development of IoT application in this course.

Keywords: Embedded Computing · Internet of Things · Microcontrollers · Smart Hardware · IoT Education · Industry-University Convergence

1 Introduction

1.1 Internet of Things (IoT)

Today, as the computing and communication technology advance, intelligence and connectivity are ubiquitous. Internet of Things (IoT) and edge cloud services are widely used. IoT is supposed to become the next "major productivity booster" propelling rapid global development and constitutes a trillion-dollar market. The IoT industry stands as a strategic highland in the current world economy and technological development, with nations investing substantial resources in IoT research and exploration. This is an unprecedented opportunity for the IoT developers [1].

Characterized by making everything intelligent and connected, Masayoshi Son of SoftBank Corporation in Japan also asserted that IoT applications will lead the next technological explosion. It won't be long before the number of connected IoT devices reaches one trillion [6].

W. Hong and G. Kanaparan (Eds.): ICCSE 2023, CCIS 2024, pp. 221–233, 2024.
https://doi.org/10.1007/978-981-97-0791-1_19

IoT products span a range of applications, from sensors and controllers to cloud computing, serving various fields like smart homes, transportation and logistics, environmental protection, public safety, smart buildings, industrial monitoring, personal health, and more.

It is believed that IoT can enhance economic efficiency, significantly reduce costs, and provide technological impetus for global economic recovery. The extensive usage of IoT can become another driving power for economic development, hence offering a vast potential for industry development.

1.2   Fragmentation Problems in IoT Applications

Due to the constraint posed by fragmentation in IoT applications, there is some obstacles remained in IoT development. This is because that IoT endpoint devices come in a wide variety of forms and functions, with lower production volume (i.e., "small quantities with great diversity").

The fragmentation issue in IoT applications is evident in diverse industries and application domains, such as wide variations in types and functions, and significant differences in performance. Fragmentation problem not only complicates development, incurs development costs, and impedes future scalability and maintenance, but also presents a shortcoming of "small quantities with great diversity" in the supply chain. IoT products development has problems such as low sales volumes and a low return on investment, which dampens capital to enter the IoT field and hinders the pace of IoT development.

1.3   Limitations of IoT Education

With the rapid advancement of IoT, there is a significant talent gap in the IoT industry, leading universities worldwide to introduce IoT education programs, creating a vast market for IoT education and training. IoT industry has become a hub for innovative and entrepreneurial education, providing a practice platform for students to show their capabilities and creativities. Consequently, how to conduct effective IoT education has become a new challenge in university education.

The fragmentation problems in IoT applications also have negative impact in IoT education and training. From a technical perspective, IoT is about connecting embedded applications to the Internet. IoT development demands a deep technical stack. Consider that a student interested in IoT development, the student needs to know the knowledge of operating systems, embedded programming, Internet programming, embedding hardware, debugging. This accumulates high learning costs.

Moreover, as mentioned before, IoT product development is costly with low return, making it challenging for companies to afford high salaries for engineers. Compared to the Internet industry, IoT development has become a task with high learning effort, low earnings, which making it difficult to attract the talent students. Without a qualified workforce, industry development is hampered.

In the education side, there is a substantial population of students and makers, without a major in electronical engineering or computer sciences, software engineering etc., who may not be interested in acquiring fully electronic, computing and programming knowledge. They are more interested in rapidly realizing their creative ideas and hope to produce practical products with simple programming with quick learning.

1.4 Industry-Education Convergence

With the proposal of "deepening industry-education convergence" in China, an increasing number of universities have adopted the "industry-education convergence practice" in their educational models. To enhance the quality of talent cultivation, universities are collaborating with enterprises. Both parties rely on their core resources and advantages, adhere to the "win-win" principle, and share common responsibilities. Industry-education research integration serves as a bridge for communication between universities and industries, reinforcing the functions of both sides. Furthermore, industry-education cooperation can provide valuable support for university graduates' future career planning. It can stimulate students' creativity and innovation, create opportunities for combining career planning with learning, and promote the healthy development of lifelong education [3].

2 Course Contents and Structure

2.1 Course Objectives

For the needs of smart life, work, study, health, transportation, environment and other fields, our course explores the future direction of smart hardware products combined with social needs and technological development trends. Our course will strengthen the education of basic knowledge and innovative concepts of innovation and entrepreneurship through innovative practice models.

Based on well-chosen IoT experimental platforms, such as AIOE hardware Education System etc., students can be instructed to finish the design demo of intelligent hardware product prototypes more quickly.

2.2 Course Team Group

This course is collaboratively developed by experienced educators from Tsinghua University and senior engineers from Guanglun Electronic Technology, with a strong emphasis on "industry-education convergence."

The contents of course include: Smart things, intelligent hardware architecture, Internet of things and communication technology in IoT, Internet of everything and cloud services, Design Thinking in smart product, smart agriculture etc.

2.3 Course Content of Each Section

2.3.1 Section 1

Section 1 includes cutting-edge information in the industry, a brief introduction to the C language required for embedded development boards, hardware libraries and development boards, AIOE Studio/KEIL-ARM development tools, firmware download guidance. Two hardware development experiments are designed to help students quickly get started.

2.3.2 Section 2

Section 2 combines design thinking to guide design concepts of innovative product and meet the needs of various application scenes. Section 2 also introduces the TreeOS Zero software architecture and explain the methods based on scene-based programming techniques to make the development process of intelligent hardware products more efficient and flexible. Students practice the experiments with automatic timing from network to consolidate the learning in teaching content (Fig. 1).

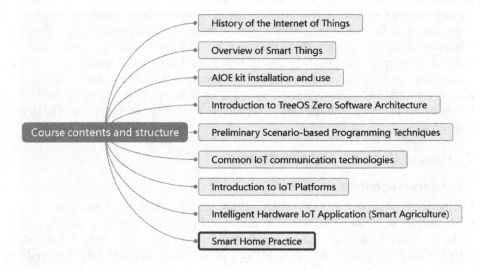

Fig. 1. Course contents

2.3.3 Section 3

Based on AIOE hardware architecture, new programming methods is learned in Sect. 3. Section 3 also introduces serial communication, RFID technology, and scene-based programming methods through relevant experiments. Students practice with the hardware platform to integrate various technologies, and improve development efficiency.

2.3.4 Section 4

Section 4 introduces basic IoT communication technologies, IoT cloud platforms, and learn the IoT Studio of Alibaba Cloud IoT platform. With a mobile phone, students practice the "WiFi Colorful Lighting Scenario" experiment to achieve the control of colored lights through the WiFi network. Smart agriculture application is used as the typical IoT application scenario to explain the principle and method of various components in a IoT product development and implementation.

2.3.5 Section 5

Section 5 gives the Smart-Home Controller as an example (see Sect. 3.1). Firstly, students are divided into small groups, brainstorm to form their own creative designs in group level. Then students are guided to select specific hardware components and complete their own product demoes. Finally, students present their creative design demo, and teachers provide their feedback and suggestions for each group respectively.

2.4 AIOE Developer Suite for Course Experiments

First and foremost, to attract more talent to participate in IoT development, it is essential to simplify IoT software and hardware development, lower the learning and development thresholds, and reduce the costs. In this context, the AIOE hardware (referred to as the "Smart Hardware Library" hereinafter) has been developed [4]. This is a low-complexity, application-focused intelligent hardware suites which are targeted for embedded system teaching and training, IoT product development and innovative design competitions.

2.4.1 Design Objectives

AIOE is an IoT practical training suites based on innovative technology, designed to provide a practical environment for professional and non-professional students, makers, and electronics enthusiasts. It aims to offer hands-on experience and practical development training, enabling students to better understand knowledge through practice, keep updated to the latest IoT technologies and applications, rapidly enhance their practical development and problem-solving abilities. This system aims to contribute to the growth and popularization of the IoT industry.

2.4.2 Key Innovations

First, a "network-based multi-core" embedded system hardware architecture establishes a new "hardware parallel multi-threading" working mechanism, greatly simplifying application code development. Due to the advantages of separation software-hardware, task decoupling, modularization, and cross-platform compatibility, this system is well-suited hardware for maker education.

Second, "Scene-Based Programming" [5] with a "Zero-Core Component System" divides an application development into various scenes, which represents a human-computer interaction interface or a control process. This division simplifies complex applications into concise, visual scene modules. Scenes are categorized as main or sub-scenes, forming a tree-like structure. All scenes follow a unified programming architecture. This programming method is easy for beginners to grasp.

2.4.3 System Components

The AIOE hardware library used in this course consists of nearly 100 electronic building blocks, covering various aspects such as sensors, control devices, communication, data collection, and human-computer interaction. Students can gain hands-on experience and learn a wide range of advanced hardware knowledge, providing a foundation for smart hardware development.

Additionally, this course gives the 9 simulated IoT applications, including Wi-Fi smart lights, Bluetooth electronic scales, shared washing machines, smart door locks, food traceability, smart manhole covers, smart mining, smart homes, and smart agriculture. These applications integrate IoT technology into the practical cases, covering the aspects of IoT with the view of "cloud, pipe and endpoint". These applications serve as valuable examples for students to observe, adapt, and enhance their understanding of smart hardware development methods.

2.4.4 System Features

- Simplifying the IoT development by using electronic building blocks, especially for IoT applications, to accelerate the practical electronic innovations.
- Unified standard interfaces eliminate the messy and confusing use of jumper wires and breadboards.
- Black-box electronic building blocks eliminate the complexities of microcontrollers, interrupts, I2C, SPI, and other low-level driver programs. Students do not need to understand hardware details, enabling "zero driver" development. Building IoT systems with plug-and-play building blocks makes development easier.
- Automatically generated code eliminates the burdensome low-level development, achieving a complete "software-hardware separation." Students can accomplish smart product with a few lines of code. An example is provided in Appendix A.
- "Scene-based Programming" allows students to easily grasp business logic development, even without learning complex operating systems knowledge. It let them to develop complex application systems with "zero-core" hardware. For example, the final course assignment shown in Sect. 3.1, has a moderate complexity, but students can complete it well in a day.
- The hardware library meets creative needs, allowing various innovative combinations and enhancing the fun of learning. It also prepares the hardware foundation for complex applications.
- The 9 simulated IoT applications, which has practical applications scenarios, provide not only example codes, but also the business implementation. The experience of practical implementation can accelerate students' mastery of smart hardware development methods.

2.5 AIOE Developer Suite for Smart Agriculture

China is a country with a large population of 1.4 billion people. Since 2016, the Chinese government has clearly put forward the requirement of vigorously promoting "Internet plus modern agriculture". Smart agricultural technology is an important part of "Internet plus modern agriculture". By integrating agriculture and information technology, real-time monitoring and analysis of farmland data can be achieved, helping farmers make scientific decisions, optimize planting structures, apply fertilizers, irrigate and control pests and diseases reasonably, and improve crop yield and quality.

2.5.1 Intelligent Greenhouse for Smart Agriculture

The modern agricultural greenhouse control has the characteristics of strong system detection ability and rich control equipment. It also has the following functions: real-time greenhouse environmental monitoring, intelligent alarm system, intelligent control system, and mobile client (Fig. 2).

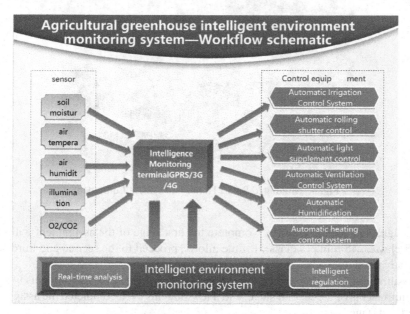

Fig. 2. Intelligent greenhouse workflow

The intelligent environmental monitoring system connects various sensors and control systems through integrated monitoring terminals. The values collected by various sensors and the operating status of various control devices within are the multiple environmental factors of this system. When the composed of multiple factor conditions are triggered, various actions corresponding to the conditions are executed. When the intelligent rule engine detects that the exception still exists after a specified time, other solutions are taken based on the current data and status of each factor. The rule engine can automatically execute various actions according to the setting.

3 Course Homework and Projects

3.1 Course Assignment - Simulated Smart Home Controller

This course assignment is based on the "AIOE Smart Hardware Library" and primarily focuses on assessing students' proficiency in programming skills, and innovation using the AIOE hardware platform.

The AIOE hardware for experiments includes AIOE1001 host board, AIOE3015 LCD human-machine interaction module, AIOE5014 temperature and humidity sensor module, AIOE6001 relay module, AIOE5042 collision sensor, AIOE3014 eight-digit display (for device status indication), as shown below (Fig. 3):

Fig. 3. Simulated Smart Home Experiment Equipment

Assignment Requirements. Complete the first stage of the assignment within one day (8 classes, 45 min per class). If time allows, proceed to the second and third stages of the advanced questions.

Assignment Completion Status. All students completed the assignments to satisfy the requirements of the second stage, and a few students even completed the assignments in the third stage.

After course learning, students from different majors, grades, and varying skill levels have mastered the ability to design IoT application by using the AIOE hardware (Table 1).

3.2   On-Site Visit Course

This course arranges 2 h on-site visit to Beijing medicinal botanical garden, which is located in the northwest side of Beijing city. This visit helps students to learn the greenhouse control in smart agricultural for IoT practice. The practical smart agriculture application includes following functions: real-time greenhouse environmental monitoring, intelligent alarm system, intelligent control system, and mobile client (Fig. 4).

This smart agriculture application system helps tropical medicinal plants in the greenhouse to flower, grow, bear fruit and sow normally in Beijing's subtropical climate area, and to have normal yields. This is especial important in the summer and winter time in Beijing city.

3.3   Innovation Idea and Creative Design in Course Project

Taking the Simulated Smart Home Controller as an example, students brainstormed in groups to form their own group creative designs. Instruct students to select specific

Table 1. Content of course assignment.

Stage	Task	Purpose
First Stage	Display and modify the clock calendar on the LCD screen Collect environmental temperature and humidity and display in real-time Trigger sound and light alarms when the temperature exceeds a certain value or collision sensor detects an event Manually control four relays' switches Allow deactivation of the alarm	Evaluate mastery of AIOE Studio usage, TreeOS Zero basic program structure, module usage, scene analysis, and basic code writing skills
Second Stage	Increase the number of controlled devices to 12 (device names listed below) and enable manual selection and display of device on/off status on the LCD. Simulate these 12 devices using 4 relays and an 8-digit display Controllable Device names: 1. Living Room Ceiling Light, 2. Living Room Air Conditioner, 3. Master Bedroom Ceiling Light, 4. Master Bedroom Air Conditioner, 5. Secondary Bedroom Ceiling Light, 6. Secondary Bedroom Air Conditioner, 7. Study Room Ceiling Light, 8. Study Room Curtains, 9. Corridor Aisle Light, 10. Bathroom Fan, 11. Balcony Curtains, 12. Kitchen Fan	Enhance understanding of complex scene analysis methods and lay the foundation for building more complex applications
Third Stage	Add full automation function: For each device, set manual/auto mode switching; Each device can have individual on/off times (hour: minute), and in auto mode, the device operates automatically according to these settings	Evaluate students' comprehensive application skills and innovation. [Hint: You can use the time calculation functions provided by TreeOS_timelib.h]

hardware components to complete their own designs. Students complete the group creative design with their group members, includes presentation, value proposal, sketch graph and implementation plan etc. In their demo presentation, all teacher will give their comments on project design. The following include four group design idea and their implementation plan with AIOE.

Fig. 4. Smart Agriculture application in Beijing medicinal botanical garden.

4   Course Project in Innovation Design with AIOE

There are totally 20 students in our course and have their four creative ideas to redesign the smart things include smart backpack design, smart food fresh box, smart seating and smart gaming peripherals (Spirit). The details design and implementation plan are not included here due to the space limitation.

5   Future Work

With a focus on industry-education convergence, we plan to further develop the course in the following aspects:

1) Provide more programming language supported, such as Python (or MicroPython), JavaScript, C++, and others, to facilitate the learning process for students.
2) Provide more comprehensive teaching materials for both teachers and students, such as experimental guidance instructions and operating procedures etc.
3) Expand the hardware library to offer students more choices for realizing IoT products and applications.
4) Establish automatic inventory system for hardware library, enabling teachers, students, and off-campus learners to conveniently borrow hardware resources.
5) Encouraging more professionals from industry to participate and contribute to the development of the course and its related resources.

6 Conclusion

Combining the innovation through industry-education convergence, this paper introduces a course design for IoT education based on a smart hardware library. The course teaching group, consisting of members from university educators and industrial developers, collectively design teaching objectives, content frameworks, as well as the affiliated exercises, assignments, and course projects. The course combines lectures, hands-on experiments, case studies, on-site visiting, which creates a self-directed learning environment for students. The AIOE hardware is used to remove the barriers in learning hardware and development. This course is also open to students from various majors, and all students completed the course project, and engaged in the brainstorming sessions to generating some fresh creative ideas for smart products. Students from various disciplines can proficiently utilize scene-based programming to develop practical, moderately complex smart products based on AIOE hardware building blocks. The feedback from questionnaire indicate that students gained a deeper understanding of IoT development after the course.

Appendix A: A Simple Practice Example

Functionality: Read temperature and humidity values from the environment and display them in real-time on an LCD.

Experimental hardware includes: AIOE1001 host, AIOE3015 LCD human-machine interaction module, AIOE5014 temperature and humidity sensor module, as shown below (Fig. 5):

Fig. 5. Temperature and Humidity Display Experiment Equipment

Experiment procedure:

1) Following the hardware connection diagram, configure using AIOE Studio software (as shown below) to generate a Keil software project (the MCU model of the mainboard is STM32F103RCT6) (Fig. 6):

Fig. 6. AIOE Studio Configuration for this Project

2) The project contents are as shown below (Fig. 7):

Fig. 7. Software Project Contents for this Project

3) In the *GlobalTask_EventTimer_scan()* function, which is the event task triggered by the timer (executed every second), insert the two lines of code as follows (Fig. 8):

```
void GlobalTask_EventTimer_scan(void)
{
  AIOE3015_show_i32(0,0,tOFF, AIOE5014_temperature_value);
  AIOE3015_show_i32(0,2,tOFF, AIOE5014_humidity_value);
}
```

Fig. 8. Code for Displaying Temperature and Humidity Values

Here, *AIOE5014_temperature_value* and *AIOE5014_humidity_value* are the temperature and humidity values that are automatically updated every second and are defined in the AIOE5014_API module (Fig. 9).

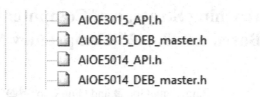

Fig. 9. API Functions

4) Compile, download the generated *.hex* file to the MCU, and start the application.

This project's functionality can be implemented with a few lines of code, making it very convenient, even for beginners.

References

1. Song, H.: Internet of Everything Key Technologies, Practical Applications and Security of IoT. World Scientific Publishing Co. Pte. Ltd., December 2022. https://doi.org/10.1142/12526
2. Hong, W., Li, C., Wang, Q. (eds.): Technology-Inspired Smart Learning for Future Education. CCIS, vol. 1216. Springer, Singapore (2020). https://doi.org/10.1007/978-981-15-5390-5
3. Yu, Z., et al.: One case of THOUGHT: industry-university converged education practice on open source. In: Hong, W., Weng, Y. (eds.) Computer Science and Education. CCIS, vol. 1813, pp. 289–303. Springer, Singapore (2023). https://doi.org/10.1007/978-981-99-2449-3_26
4. Introduction to scene-based programming with AIOE. http://www.treeos.com/index.php?m=content&c=index&a=show&catid=1&id=183. Accessed 29 Oct 2023
5. AIOE developer suite document. http://www.treeos.com/uploadfile/2017/0717/201707170154 32427.pdf. Accessed 29 Oct 2023
6. IoT explosion. http://itech.ifeng.com/44477879/news.shtml?from=timeline. Accessed 29 Oct 2023

A Teaching Strategy of Computer Courses Based on "3 + 2" Competency Model

Pingzhang Gou and Qing Cao(✉)

College of Computer Science and Engineering, Northwest Normal University, Lanzhou, China
Caoqing_1002@163.com

Abstract. The concept of "competency-based learning" is proposed in the CC2020 report, which provides a new guidance for the training of computer professionals. This paper first analyzes the role of the concept in the teaching process and puts forward the "3 + 2" competency model. The model updates students' cognitive structure twice through three teaching processes, so as to attain the three-dimensional competency training covering knowledge, skills and dispositions. Then, under the guidance of this model, the teaching strategy for computer courses is proposed which adopts the way of "Learning Maps", uses MOOC to realize students 'personalized learning, uses task-based teaching to realize students 'participatory learning, and realizes the improvement of students 'comprehensive literacy through cooperation and discussion. Finally, taking *Python Language Programming* as an example, two classes of first-year computer majors were selected for comparative experiments. The improvement of students' competency in the dimension of knowledge and skills was quantitatively analyzed by comparing their scores, and the cultivation effect of students' competency in the dimension of dispositions was analyzed by interviews. The result showed that the teaching strategy proposed in this paper can improve students' competency level and get a good teaching effect.

Keywords: Competency Model · Teaching Strategy · Computer Course · MOOC

1 Introduction

The Harvard Dictionary of Competency [1] gives the following definition of competency: Competency is the effective "things" that a person must show in his work. These "things" include behavior, motivation, knowledge, and skills related to the job. In the field of education, success in career preparation usually requires students to develop three qualities: knowledge, skills, and dispositions, so competency must link these three essential dimensions.

The concept of "Competency-based learning" proposed in the CC2020 report emphasizes the cultivation of students from three dimensions of knowledge, skills and dispositions [2]. Knowledge dimension focuses on "what is it", including the core concepts, notions and content of computer science. Skills dimension focuses on "how to use it" which includes the high-level thinking ability to apply computer science knowledge and the practical ability to operate and design computer software and hardware. Dispositions dimension focuses on "why is it" which refers to the emotional capacity, behavior, and attitude towards the completion of the task. The teaching concept of "competency-based learning" proposed in the CC2020 report pointed out the direction for the training of computer professionals. However, the CC2020 report did not give a teaching practice plan on how to cultivate students 'competency combined with specific courses.

The purpose of this paper is to explore the impact of the concept of "competency-based learning" on the computer courses teaching. In the actual teaching activities, how to cultivate students from the three dimensions of knowledge, skills and dispositions? How does the concept of "competency-based learning" help to set the teaching objectives of computer courses? How should teaching strategies be designed to achieve a balance between competency training objectives and curriculum characteristics?

2 Methodology

2.1 "3 + 2" Competency Model

The process of students rushing toward competency on the "runway" of classroom learning is dynamic, continuous and constantly adjusted [3]. CC2020 divides competency into three dimensions: knowledge, skills and dispositions, and puts forward relevant learning requirements for students in a step-by-step way. With the advancement of teaching, students will gradually realize two cognitive structure updates from knowledge to skills and from skills to dispositions, and finally realize the cultivation of competency.

The two updates of students' cognitive structure can be regarded as the stage results of teaching activities, and the overall teaching activities can be divided into three teaching processes. In the process of ability improvement, students acquire the basic knowledge and successfully apply it to become their personal ability, completing the first update of cognitive structure from knowledge to skills. In the process of literacy improvement, the acquired knowledge and skills are internalized into personal qualities such as values and professional attitudes, and the second cognitive structure update from skills to qualities is completed. In the feedback adjustment process, students, as independent individuals, evaluate and reflect on their own initiative, grasp their own learning progress, and provide reference for subsequent learning.

Through the above analysis, the concept of "competency-based learning" proposed in the CC2020 report is implemented in the curriculum teaching activities, and the "3 + 2" competency model is formed, which corresponds to the two updates of students 'cognitive structure, and three teaching processes of ability improvement, literacy improvement and feedback adjustment. As shown in Fig. 1.

Firstly, students establish a cognitive structure related to the course content through memorization and understanding of knowledge. Through the training with specific tasks, students can improve their ability to analyze and solve tasks with knowledge, improve their ability from knowledge dimension to skill dimension, and complete the first update of cognitive structure.

After that, with specific tasks constructed based on real situations, students have a high sense of participation and a sense of mission to solve problems. In the process of exploring solutions, students 'initiative, creativity and professionalism are exercised,

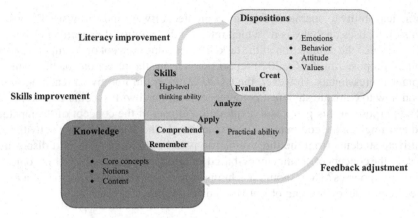

Fig. 1. "3 + 2" competency model.

and their literacy is improved from skills dimension to dispositions dimension, and the second update of cognitive structure is completed.

With the successful solution of specific tasks, students evaluate the completion of the program and their overall performance, and enter the feedback adjustment process. Students take the assessment results as the reference of phased learning, reposition their own professional level, think about the future career development path, and then adjust the learning pace and content spontaneously. The overall teaching activity which includes three processes from knowledge to skills improvement, from skills to dispositions improvement and from dispositions to knowledge feedback adjustment, finally realize the cultivation of students' competency.

2.2 Design Three Dimensions Objectives Based on "3 + 2" Competency Model

Goals setting should conform to the changes of the students' cognitive structure in the process of learning. The "3 + 2" competency model regards the two updates of students' cognitive structure as the phased results of teaching activities. Therefore, the design of curriculum teaching objectives should first consider what kind of learning effect students should achieve from knowledge to skills and from skills to dispositions. Moreover, the knowledge is the foundation of all ability and accomplishment [4]. When designing teaching objectives, it is necessary to examine the degree of students' knowledge mastery.

In this paper, the curriculum teaching objective is designed into three levels: knowledge objective, ability objective and literacy objective. From the perspective of computer courses, the knowledge goal focuses on the mastery of basic knowledge of the subject, including the basic principles of computer, programming basis, computer network and other subject knowledge as well as mathematics, statistics and other interdisciplinary basic knowledge. Knowledge objectives require students to have a specific understanding about computer courses and realize the "know-what". The ability goal focuses on students' proficiency in computer, the main tool for solving problems, and the thinking training in the process of solving tasks. It is dedicated to cultivating higher-order abilities such as mathematical thinking, computational thinking and engineering thinking.

In the face of complex problems in real situations, students can use the knowledge and skills they have mastered to solve problems and realize the "know-how". Literacy goals focus on the emotional tendencies, behaviors and attitudes displayed by students in the process of task achievement, such as responsibility, professionalism, conscientiousness, initiative, etc., and realize "know-why".

2.3 Design Teaching Strategy Based on "3 + 2" Competency Model

Computer courses are generally characterized by high abstraction and high requirements for practical ability [5]. Therefore, in the actual teaching process of computer courses, we should fully consider the differences in cognitive basis and ability level among students, so as to realize students' personalized learning and participatory learning.

The "3 + 2" competency model provides directions for the improvement of teaching strategies. For students, the degree of understanding and mastering knowledge in the initial learning stage determines the construction of students' cognitive structure, and whether students can understand and master knowledge is affected by their own original cognitive foundation and ability basis. Therefore, it is crucial to emphasize personalized learning in the process of building cognitive structures for students. It is difficult to truly personalize teaching with traditional offline class teaching methods, and MOOC has significant advantages in this regard. In this study, MOOC is chosen to replace one-to-many teaching by offline teachers, so as to give students full initiative in learning. MOOC is characterized by fragmentation and the differentiation of learning progress, and its disadvantage is the consistency of learning content [6]. In order to improve this shortcoming, this paper introduces the concept of "Learning Maps" and divides students into two levels: "zero-basis learners" and "basic learners" according to the difference of students' cognitive basis and ability level. Different MOOC "Learning Maps" are set according to the level differences, and students can choose their own paths to complete the learning process according to the maps.

The process of ability improvement emphasizes students' practical operation, application of knowledge in practice. Task-based teaching in this part can provide students with more practical opportunities and realize students' participatory learning. Task-based teaching plays an important role in the whole teaching strategy. On the one hand, it connects the MOOC learning stage and helps students build richer links with their knowledge system in the process of analyzing and solving tasks. On the other hand, it can link up the subsequent teamwork and pave the way for students to enter a higher level of learning. The task content should arouse the resonance of students' own experience world, start from the real experience world that students can easily understand, start from cases or problems, and lead to new abstract knowledge together with the abstract knowledge already learned.

The process of literacy improvement focuses on students' assessment and reflection, shaping values and obtaining learning feedback in communication. Cooperation and discussion is one of the most effective forms of communication. Students enter the process of competency shaping on the dispositions dimension while they are trained by multiple tasks, solve large-scale complex engineering problems through teamwork. Students face the challenges brought by the task together and exercise the ability to resist pressure for the future; Find the most suitable role in the division of labor and cooperation, laying the foundation for future career development; Integrate themselves into the social environment of interpersonal communication through the communication with members; Stimulate their own sense of responsibility and mission in the process of task solving; When students succeed against all odds, they will have a more positive attitude towards the future. The overall teaching strategy is shown in Fig. 2.

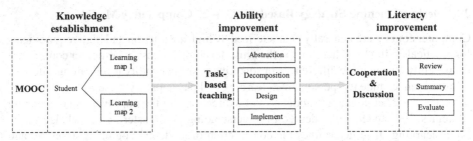

Fig. 2. The teaching strategy based on "3 + 2" competency model.

2.4 Teaching Implementation

This paper takes the *Python Language Programming* in the fall semester of 2022 as the object to carry out practical teaching, which is a required major course for first-year in computer science and technology. Table 1 shows the basic information of this course.

Table 1. Overview of *Python Language Programming*.

Item	Illustration
Name of course	Python Language Programming
Semester	Fall semester 2022
Total class time	48
Knowledge	Basic Python syntax; Program flow control; Basic data type; Common built-in functions; Branch and loop program structure; Character string; Regular expression; The concept of object-oriented; Python module; Python module; Package; The concept of frame;
Abilities	Define and use functions; Define and use classes; Debug; Read and modify files; Crawl data;
Literacies	Sense of responsibility, patriotism, Professional ethics, Engineering ethics

Figure 3 is a diagrammatic drawing of the "Learning Maps" while students use MOOC for personalized learning. It should be noted that the purpose of the Learning Maps are to provide learning guidance, and students can still adjust the order according to their own learning ability.

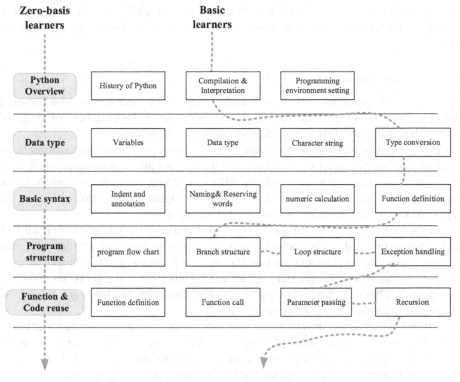

Fig. 3. A diagrammatic drawing of the "Learning Maps".

Tracking the progress of students' MOOC learning, design the course task list with the pre-set competency goals as shown in Table 2. According to the scale and difficulty, the task is divided into two types: individual task and teamwork task.

Table 2. A task list for *Python Language Programming*.

Task type	Content
Individual task	Using the Monte Carlo method to solve PI
	Draw the Koch curve
Teamwork task	Count the word frequency of characters in *A Dream of Red Mansions*
	Draw the multi-level radar chart
	China excellent tourist city ranking crawler

The study began in the fall semester of 2022 and ended in the current semester with a total of 16 teaching weeks. The experimental group selected 46 students from Class 1 of Grade 2022, and the control group selected 50 students from Class 2 of Grade 2022. The experimental group used the teaching strategy based on the "3 + 2" competency model, while the control group still used the traditional teaching method. In order to reflect the relative accuracy of teaching data, the teachers of the two groups were the same.

2.5 Teaching Evaluation

The method of quantitative evaluation and qualitative evaluation is used to evaluate the cultivation effect of students' competency, that is, the improvement of students' knowledge, skills and dispositions. Specific design is as follows:

In the dimension of knowledge, formative evaluation and summative assessment are used to evaluate the effect of students' MOOC learning and task demonstration. Five online tests are designed to test students 'MOOC learning effect, mainly assessing the mastery of basic knowledge such as Python syntax, program flow control, and basic data types. At the end of the semester, there will be a final exam.

In the skills dimension, design 3 task demonstrations, including 1 individual task and 2 teamwork tasks. Each student or team representative will present their task solution ideas, the implementation process, and the problems and challenges encountered. Teachers give comprehensive grades to students from five aspects: task completion degree, scheme design, programming ability, teamwork and language expression. Detailed evaluation scheme as shown in Table 3.

In the dimension of dispositions, interviews are used to investigate students' attitudes towards course learning, career planning and values. The interviews were conducted around the following three aspects: the first is students' feelings about *Python Language Programming*, focusing on students' expression of learning interests and course difficulty. The second is students' understanding of programming, focusing on whether students have the consciousness of combining theory with practice and solving problems with programming ideas. The last part is students' understanding of computer industry, focusing on students' career intention and career planning.

Table 3. The detailed evaluation scheme.

Evaluation method	Weight	Evaluation content
Formative evaluation A_1	λ_1: 40%	5 Online test scores
		3 Task demonstration scores
Summative assessment A_2	λ_2: 60%	Final examination

Final score $= A1\lambda1 + A2\lambda2$.

3 Results

3.1 Analysis of Students' Academic Performance

The online test scores, task demonstration scores and final scores of 96 people in experimental group and control group are counted. The results shows that the average score of the experimental group is 88.7 points, slightly higher than the average score of the control group is 85.3 points. This indicates that the learning effect of the students in the experimental group on the two dimensions of competency knowledge and skills is better than that of the control group. Further, the score distribution range of class members is counted, as shown in Fig. 4.

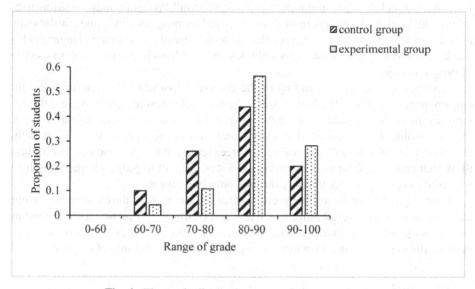

Fig. 4. The grade distribution range of class members.

On the whole, the grade of the students in the two classes is normally distributed. According to the standards of 60–70 points qualified, 70–80 points good, and more than 80 points excellent, the results show that 39 students in the experimental group achieved excellent rating, accounting for 84.78%, and 32 students in the control group obtained excellent rating, accounting for 64%. Compared with the control group, the excellence rate of the experimental group increased by 32.47%. The results further show that the teaching strategy proposed in this paper can improve students' competence in knowledge and skills dimensions.

3.2 Analysis of Students' Interview Results

After the end of the semester, 20 students were randomly selected from the experimental group for interview. The interview results are summarized as follows:

First, how students feel about *Python Language Programming*. Among the 20 interviewees, they all mentioned "understand" and "feel interesting", and students considered that learning through MOOC has reduced the difficulty of courses. 18 students thought that cooperation and discussion were necessary. They believe that in teamwork tasks, communication with team members can often emerge different perspectives, which is often the birth of new ideas, new ideas, new solutions. At the same time, some students said that in cooperation, because they did not want to affect the work progress of other members, they would urge themselves to ensure that they completed the assigned work within the specified time. This shows that task-based teaching, cooperation and discussion can not only give students the opportunity to fully apply knowledge and exercise skills, but also help train students' way of thinking and shape students' values.

Secondly, students' understanding of programming learning. More than half of the interviewees said that "programming is not that difficult", "programming is starting to be interesting", "many problems in life can be solved by programming" and similar opinions. From these words, it can be seen that students' fear of programming languages has weakened, and they can consciously rethink some problems in life from the perspective of programming.

Finally, students' understanding of the computer industry. When asked about the employment thoughts of the interviewees, the male interviewees generally said that the work in the computer industry is challenging and has a sense of accomplishment, and they are willing to engage in related work, and their future study will be closer to the technical level. The female interviewees' career intention is not obvious, most of them think that computer courses are abstract, and it is difficult to judge whether they have the ability to engage in the industry through only one course.

It can be seen from the interview content that the members of the experimental group have expressed their interest attitude, sense of responsibility, professional understanding and career planning. It indicates that the teaching strategy proposed in this paper can achieve the improvement of students' competency in the dimension of dispositions.

4   Conclusions

Based on the concept of "competency-based learning" proposed in the CC2020 report, this paper explores the improvement direction of teaching strategies for computer courses, highlighting the personalized learning of students, the advanced thinking training, and the long-term professional development. From the results of empirical research, the teaching strategy based on the "3 + 2" competency model proposed in this paper can play a role in cultivating students' competency and has certain reference value. However, the research still has shortcomings. On the one hand, the sample number of students selected in the empirical research stage is small; on the other hand, there are many computer courses, and the *Python Language Programming* selected in this paper can only be used as a representative of programming courses. In the future, the author will do more research and exploration on the integration of the proposed teaching improvement strategy of computer courses with other professional courses.

Acknowledgements. This research was supported by the Education Research Project of AFCEC (Grant Nos 2022-AFCEC-143, 2023-AFCEC-451) and the Northwest Normal University 2023 Curriculum Assessment Reform Project (Grant No.202320051259) and the 2023 Graduate Teaching Casebook Construction Project of Northwest Normal University (Grant No. 2023YAL014).

References

1. Harvard.   https://www.campusservices.harvard.edu/system/files/documents/1865/harvard_c ompetency_dictionary_complete.pdf. Accessed 26 Sept 2023
2. Computing Curricula 2020. https://www.acm.org/binaries/content/assets/education/curricula-recommendations/cc2020.pdf. Accessed 03 Oct 2023
3. Zhang, M.: The impact of ACM/IEEE CC2020 competency model on the development of computer education in China. Comput. Educ. **2023**(04), 3–8+14 (2023)
4. Chang, L.: Link CC2020 and engineering education accreditation standards with competency literacy model. Chinese Univ. Teach. **2023**(03), 52–55+79 (2023)
5. Shi, Z.: Case analysis and enlightenment of computational thinking training in American universities. Comput. Educ. **2020**(1), 177–180 (2020)
6. Wang, C.: A study on Influencing factors of college students' online learning burnout in MOOC environment. J. Henan Univ. (Soc. Sci. Edn.) **63**(03), 120–125+156 (2019)

A Preliminary Study on University Computer Basic Curriculum Reform Aimed at Cultivating Computational Thinking from the Perspective of Smart Education

Niefang Yu[1,2,3], Yiwen Liu[1,2,3]([✉]), Xiaoning Peng[1,2,3], Xiaomei Li[1,2,3], and Youmin Lu[1,2,3]

[1] School of Computer and Artificial Intelligence, Huaihua University, Huaihua 418000, Hunan, People's Republic of China
lyw@hhtc.edu.cn

[2] Key Laboratory of Wuling-Mountain Health Big Data Intelligent Processing and Application in Hunan Province Universities, Huaihua 418000, Hunan, People's Republic of China

[3] Key Laboratory of Intelligent Control Technology for Wuling-Mountain Ecological Agriculture in Hunan Province, Huaihua 418000, Hunan, People's Republic of China

Abstract. With the rapid advancement of information technology such as artificial intelligence, cloud computing, big data, virtual reality, etc., in the context of the deep integration of information technology and education and teaching, smart classroom has set off a new round of revolution. Based on this background, this paper discuss how to cultivate students' computational thinking in a smart education environment, and explore the cultivation of computational thinking in basic university computer courses from three aspects: before class, during class, and after class in smart classrooms. In the background of smart education, only by comprehensively cultivating students' computational thinking that we can achieve more results in the future. Thereby improving students' ability to comprehensively apply computer technology.

Keywords: Artificial Intelligence · Smart Education · Computational Thinking

1 Introduction

Following the development of information technology, the concept of smart education that has emerged in the field of education is gradually entering a wider public. Smart education takes advantage of certain technical means to build an intelligent teaching environment to promote the teaching and learning of teachers and students, and plays an active role in the reform of education and teaching mode.

In the context of smart education, almost all technologies will exhibit characteristics of sharing, interaction, and collaboration. If necessary, traditional educational models can be changed through the use of information technology. Smart education It is a significant change in the form of education and learning itself, and will also have a

W. Hong and G. Kanaparan (Eds.): ICCSE 2023, CCIS 2024, pp. 244–254, 2024.
https://doi.org/10.1007/978-981-97-0791-1_21

significant impact on the transformation of education form. Education informatization it plays a very important role in transforming educational ideas and deepening education reform. From the perspective of future development models, this will also be an inevitable choice to achieve leapfrog development in education.

With the promotion of artificial intelligence,the importance of computational thinking education is becoming increasingly prominent. How to make university computer basic courses aim at cultivating computational thinking with five key sub capabilities, and how to improve students' computer application ability to adapt to the current employment environment. A series of suggestions and countermeasures are given by pointing out the problems in the basic computer curriculum in our universities [1].

2 The Current Status and Problems of University Computer Basic Course Teaching in the Context of Smart Education

2.1 Few Class Hour

The class hours of the basic computer course at our university has been adjusted to 48 h, which leads to insufficient classroom teaching time for teachers and less practice time for students. At the same time, there is not so much time left for teachers to interact with students, and teachers can not able to take good care of all students, which is resulting in unsatisfactory teaching effect.

2.2 Students Foundations Are Quiet Different

Due to the different places where students come from,their basic computer ability is also various, and their subjective experience of learning this course is also very diverse. Some students feel that they have learned too little, while others feel that they can not keep up with the rate of progress, so it is hard for teachers to cater to students of vastly different levels and at different levels and at different paces.

2.3 Lack of Computational Thinking

In actual teaching, teachers pay less attention to the cultivation of students' thinking activities in the programming design process. As a result, students face a new problem alone and are unable to apply the programming language they have learned to design and solve the problem. It is necessary to train students to use computational thinking to analyze problems and solve problems encountered in real life.

2.4 Single Digital Resource

Under the context of artificial intelligence, the digital learning method has become the most effective learning method. Rich teaching resources can guide students to efficiently participate in learning activities and form good study habits, thereby which can be used to improve the teaching effectiveness of computer courses.

2.5 Personalized Learning is Not Enough

In the process of practical computer teaching, teachers need to understand students' real academic conditions, abilities and qualities, and arrange different learning tasks according to the different students. Students need to be clear about practical goals, ability goals, and value goals, so that they can teach according to their abilities.

2.6 The Assessment Mechanism is Not Rich Enough

At present, the assessment mechanism for basic computer courses combines daily performance, computer operation, and theoretical knowledge exams to comprehensively evaluate students' learning effectiveness. It has always been the teacher who evaluates students' grades. In the context of smart education, it is now possible to consider incorporating student mutual evaluation into students' grades, enriching the ways of evaluating grades.

3 Relevant Concepts and Connotations

3.1 Smart Education and Smart Classroom

After experiencing two waves of "focusing on human knowledge" and "the rise of machine learning," artificial intelligence research is about to usher in a third wave of "interpretive and general artificial intelligence technology" [2]. The field of education is changing under the influence and penetration of the wave of artificial intelligence research. The education informatization process is a process of comprehensively promoting digital awareness, digital thinking, and digital capabilities [3]. However, smart education is the high-end form of educational informatization development, and smart classroom is also an important vehicle for smart education.

Smart education refers to the use of artificial intelligence and other technologies for differentiating teaching design, dynamical adjustment of teaching strategies, and reflection on teachers' own teaching standards through intelligent teaching and research activities.

The true essence of smart education is to build an ecological learning environment that integrates technology, based on the principles of precision, individuality, optimization, collaboration, thinking, and creation, allowing teachers to use highly effective teaching methods, allowing learners to obtain suitable personalized learning services and beautiful development experiences, making it possible from impossible, from small abilities to great abilities, and thus cultivating good personality traits and strong action abilities Talents with good thinking qualities and deep creative potential.

Smart classroom generally refers to an intelligent classroom teaching environment constructed by using Internet of Things technology, cloud computing, and network technology. Guided by advanced teaching and learning theories, which is supported by appropriate information technology and learning resources, and data analysis and mining technology as basic methods to construct learning tasks, further promoting the development of intellectual abilities and the emergence of intelligent action in a learning environment.

3.2   Computational Thinking

Computational thinking is a thinking process that is not limited to the field of computer science and scientists, and it should be a basic skill for everyone. Its essence is that people understand the thinking methods and thinking activities of natural and social systems. It is a systematic process.Through the basic processes of organization, analysis, simplification, abstraction, modeling, recursion, and traceability, scientific tools are used to carry out abstract simulation and seek the optimal solution of the problem. In 2016, the American Association of Computer Science Teachers updated the definition of computational thinking in "K-12 Computer Science Standards" (K-12 Computer Science Standards): computational thinking is a problem-solving methodology that can be extended from the field of computer science to all disciplines, providing a unique method for analyzing and developing problems that can be solved through computational methods. Computational thinking focuses on abstraction, automation, and analysis, and is a core element of the broader discipline of computer science. It is the core task and fundamental goal of computer science education to cultivate the ability of computational thinking.

Computational thinking is a way of using basic concepts in computer science to solve problems, design systems, and understand human behavior. It covers a wide range of thinking tools in the field of computer science.

Computational thinking is not only a concept and idea adapted to computer science, but also a perspective widely applied in work, learning, life, organization, and analysis of problems. Computational thinking believes that when we encounter problems, we should consider whether we can formulate them so that we can use the power of computers to solve them.

This article will refer to the 14 authoritative definitions of computational thinking that are frequently used domestically and internationally for word frequency statistics, and the constituent elements will be modeled as sub abilities. Five key sub abilities of computational thinking have been identified, namely abstract modeling, algorithm design, automation, problem decomposition, and problem transfer. The computer teaching reform of our school will also revolve around its five key sub abilities, integrating computational thinking and problem recognition sub abilities to form the complete process of problem-solving, as shown in the following Fig. 1:

The names and descriptions of the five sub abilities of computational thinking are as follows:

a. Problem Identification and Decomposition Ability

Able to identify complex problems from the real world, break them down into several small, manageable problems, and evaluate whether these problems are suitable for solving using computational thinking methods.

b. Abstract Modeling Ability

Identify common attributes of things and extract core features of the problem. Able to extract general patterns for problem-solving and reduce complexity. Capable of modeling phenomena and processes, designing simulation systems.

c. Algorithm Design Ability

Master the basic elements including algorithms, variables, parallelism, control structures. Be able to formulate a series of orderly steps to solve problems or achieve certain goals. Also be able to find the optimal path among multiple solutions.

d. Automation Capability

Ability to develop solutions through programming or use computers to complete monotonous and repetitive tasks. Ability to create computational works for practical purposes or to solve social problems. Ability to improve existing programming works through testing and debugging.

e. Problem transfer ability

Can summarize and transfer existing problem-solving processes and methods to other problem-solving approaches.

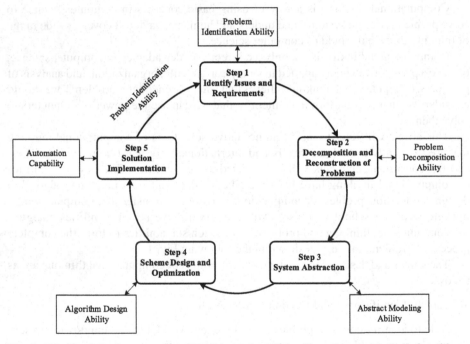

Fig. 1. Distribution of computational thinking sub abilities from the perspective of problem-solving

3.3 The Advantages of Cultivating Computational Thinking in Smart Classrooms

The key to the development of computational thinking is to immerse students in a rich learning environment that includes the right tools and a collaborative environment. Smart classrooms relies on technologies such as the Internet, mobile device terminals, and network cloud platforms, etc., and have the characteristics of personalized cooperation, rich tools, and three-dimensional learning resources, and provides supporting conditions for problem analysis.

The cultivation of computational thinking needs a long period of accumulation, and teachers need to carry out rich teaching activities so that students' computational thinking can be cultivated in teaching activities. Smart classrooms can collect teaching data and learning activity data before, during and after class, and perform big data analysis on the data to focus on the process of teaching and learning, so as to make teaching activities more effective according to ability.

Smart classrooms pays attention to exploratory and cooperative teaching methods, which can subtly cultivate students' computational thinking. Students' research activities require the help and support of teachers to find solutions to problems. The process of solving problems is the process of generating intelligence and developing computational thinking.

4 Construction of a Smart Classroom Teaching Model for Computational Thinking Cultivation

In the background of smart classroom, it is necessary to sort out the content in traditional classrooms, and then better play a leading role in the construction process. And in the future, new organizational methods and ideas will be used for teaching. Continuously guide students to think in the process of imparting knowledge to them.

In this way, students can gradually establish a way of computational thinking. The teacher needs to first summarize the internal unit knowledge, then effectively sort out the internal computational thinking content, and effectively introduce the thinking points, in order to ultimately turn the teaching of knowledge into the teaching of thinking. In a smart classroom, teachers can adopt a teacher-student discussion approach during class, allowing every student to participate in the learning process and effectively summarize the problem through their presentation and guidance. In the actual design process of the program, it is necessary to effectively explain the ideas, and then conduct a comprehensive analysis of the problem, and understand how to explain the ideas from a computer perspective.

The construction of a smart classroom teaching model for the cultivation of computational thinking is divided into three stages: "before class, during class, and after class". The three stages are a circular process in normal teaching, and all the data obtained during this period also supports the preparation, attendance, and after-school guidance for the next class.

4.1 Before Class

According to the teaching objectives and difficulties of the course, the teacher conducts academic analysis based on the students' existing experience, and promoting learning materials such as videos and courseware to stimulate students' interest in learning by making questionnaires, posting quizzes, and uploading guidance resources, etc. Using the online teaching platform of smart classroom to make students learn, ask questions, and trigger students' thinking. Teachers can monitor and review students' learning results in real time on the cloud and export analysis reports, including the number of times students have studied, the length of time they have watched, and the accuracy rate of the test. At the same time, they can also promptly remind students who did not take part in the test as soon as possible. Teachers can design lesson plans suitable for students and prepare corresponding teaching resources based on academic analysis data generated in the cloud [4].

4.2 In Class

When organizing teaching, teachers should make full use of interactive functions in smart classrooms, such as question-and-answer methods (raising hands, random selection, quick answers), test methods (voting, questionnaire, question-and-answer, testing), and evaluation methods (teacher evaluation, mutual evaluation), etc., to facilitate students' learning activities to facilitate the effective achievement of teaching goals. The data analysis generated in the classroom can also help teachers effectively improve teaching design and carry out targeted one-on-one tutoring after class [5].

In the evaluation process, the Smart Education Cloud Platform integrates cloud technology and big data technology. In this intelligent teaching network environment, teaching evaluation is more objective and timely, and teaching management is more efficient. Communication between teachers and students and students is made more convenient through back-office information feedback on the platform, and teachers can keep abreast of students' learning dynamics and participation in learning in a timely manner [6].

4.3 After Class

Teachers examines some of the student's work. Unqualified assignments can be called back to the students for re-assessment until the assessment criteria are met. In addition, teachers can use their mobile phones to shake their names through the Pocket Cloud Classroom to let students respond to questions and help students consolidate and expand their knowledge.

Based on before class and in class data analysis and students' classroom activities, teachers promote hierarchical personalized extracurricular development resources for each student to consolidate students' learning outcomes. This not only allows students with spare time to learn to broaden their horizons, but also enables poor students to consolidate their knowledge and gain progress, thus meeting the differentiated learning needs of students.

5 Practice of Teaching Models

Schematic diagram of a smart classroom teaching model oriented to the cultivation of computational thinking as shown in Fig. 2.

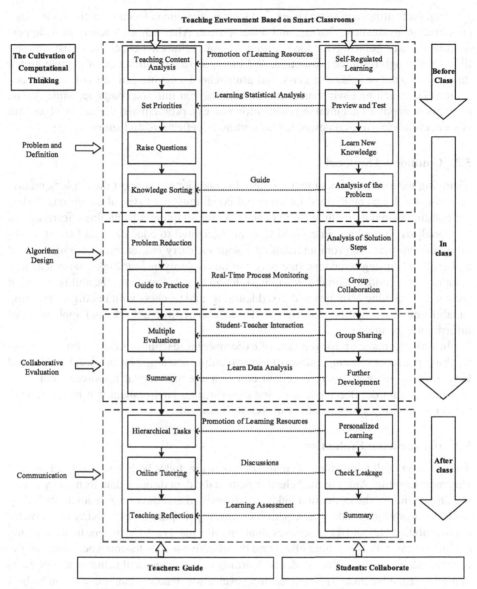

Fig. 2. Schematic diagram of a smart classroom teaching model oriented to the cultivation of computational thinking

5.1 Operating Process

In the teaching environment of smart classrooms, before class, the teachers conduct targeted digital situation analysis on students to carry out accurate promotion of learning resources and personalized teaching. In the classroom, teachers design problems, drive the teaching process with problems, and design teaching activities by inspiring, guiding, motivating, and supervising. Students participate in teaching activities through cooperation, evaluation, sharing, and development. After-school teachers provide personalized study guidance for the learning situation. Students check for omissions and fill gaps through resource promotion, and incorporate the cultivation of computational thinking into the pre-class, in-class, and after-school teaching activities of smart classrooms. The teaching environment can be summarized into four parts according to the students' computational thinking cultivation process: problem and definition, algorithm design, collaborative evaluation, learning transfer, reflection, and summary.

5.2 Conditional Support

Changing the teaching model requires certain conditions to support the implementation process, which can be divided into internal conditions and external conditions. External conditions mainly include next generation mobile Internet technology, learning big data analysis technology, intelligent terminals oriented to education, and smart teaching platforms that can promote teaching resources, carry out teaching activities,record and analyze learning behaviors. Internal conditions mainly include high-quality teaching resources that confirm learners' learning styles and have clear goals, the ability to design reasonable teaching activities with fixed learning, and teachers with intelligent teaching capabilities such as problem design, real-time classroom feedback, and application of information technology.

In order to make up for the lack of experimental teaching resources on our online teaching platform, our university will use two online teaching platforms, EduCoder and ChaoXing, to integrate more excellent course and experimental resources from other universities, and develop a teaching and experimental environment that is in line with the actual learning situation of our university's students.

5.3 Instructional Evaluation

The teaching evaluation index of smart classrooms includes both teachers' teaching and students' learning. Analyze the behavior behind the data through data formed by teaching and learning. The evaluation index are diversified and three-dimensional, including students' learning attitude, participation in learning, inquiry ability, ability to problem-solving ability, etc., and the process evaluation is the main one. On the one hand, teaching evaluation can reflect teaching effect and the effectiveness of teaching activities, on the other hand, it can also reflect students' learning effectiveness and achievement of goals in intellectual education. Through teaching evaluation, teachers can reflect on and adjust their teaching strategies to improve teaching methods. Students promptly find out the problems in their studies through teaching evaluation, and make up for the deficiencies in a targeted way.

Students' works can not only be evaluated by teachers, but also add a section for mutual evaluation among students, enriching the diversity of teaching evaluation.

5.4 Changes in the Status of Teachers

Teachers use various information technology and equipment to design teaching resources, teaching plans and implementation plans according to teaching goals, teaching environment, and the needs of teaching subjects, and should effectively promote learning resources according to students' personalized, fragmented, and mobile learning needs. Due to the openness and diversity of artificial intelligence, cross-school cooperation and cross-classroom cooperation have become the new normal in education, breaking the time, space, and geographical restrictions of teacher teamwork. In an intelligent learning environment, teachers need to acquire new knowledge or new skills, and their roles will change because of learners. Teacher groups work together to study teaching content and teaching methods, and continue to innovate.

In Short, By analyzing the connotation of smart classrooms, we can improve the teaching mode and refine the ability to cultivate computational thinking into five sub abilities during the teaching process. As shown in Fig. 3.

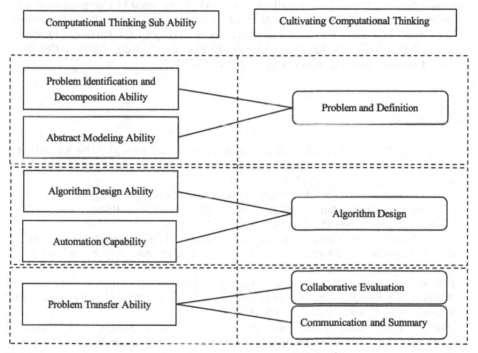

Fig. 3. Schematic diagram of the combination of computational thinking sub ability and intelligent classroom teaching mode

6 Summary

Smart education is an inevitable product of the rapid development of educational informatization. The smart classroom teaching model of cultivating computational thinking has broken through the drawbacks of previous classroom teaching and has been better integrated the cultivation of computational thinking into it. In the whole teaching process, teachers should not only impart of knowledge, but also guide students to learn. This kind of seeking process can internalize computational thinking into a way of thinking for students, which helps improve students' ability to solve problems.

In basic computer course teaching in universities, attention should be paid to the training of computational thinking ability and the improvement of application ability, making it a basic literacy for solving practical problems. The training of computational thinking not only requires teachers to have solid basic knowledge and good thinking abilities, but also to have certain educational and teaching abilities and methods. Therefore, teachers should establish correct teaching concepts, adopt appropriate teaching methods, and flexibly arrange teaching content and methods according to the situation. Only in this way can we cultivate high-quality students who meet the needs of society, have innovative consciousness, innovative spirit, and strong innovative ability.

Acknowledgment. We are very thankful that this study is supported by Computer Basic Education Teaching Research Project of the National Association of Computer Basic Education in Colleges and Universities "Exploration and Analysis of Ideological and Political Education in Computer Basic Courses of Art Universities in The Era of Self-Media" (2021-AFCEC-257); Huaihua University Teaching Reform Project (HHXYJG-202305).

References

1. Wang, Y.W., Wang, Y.R., Li, Y.X., et al.: Countermeasures and suggestions for improving the quality of online education during the epidemic prevention and control period. Chin. Med. Educ. Technol., 119–124, 128 (2020)
2. National Science and Technology Council: The national artificial intelligence research and development strategic plan [EB/OL], 24 March 2017. http://www.360doc.com/content/16/1015/20/37334461_598685262.shtml
3. Online Searcher. From digitization, through digitalization, to digital transformation [EB/OL] (2019). https://www.infotoday.com/OnlineSearcher/Articles/Features/From-Digitization-Through-Digitalization-to-Digital-Transformation-129664.shtmlPageNum=1
4. Petrovica, S., Anohina-Naumeca, A., Kikans, A.: Definition and validation of the subset of SCORM requirements for the enhanced reusability of learning content in learning management systems. Appl. Comput. Syst. 25(2) (2020)
5. Zheng, C.X.: Organization and Implementation of Classroom Teaching in Flipped Classroom Teaching: Take Engineering Training Heat Treatment Teaching as an Example, University Education, pp. 58–60, March 2020
6. Zablocki, É., Ben-Younes, H., et al.: Explainability of deep vision-based autonomous driving systems: review and challenges. Int. J. Comput. Vis. 130(10), 2425–2452 (2022)

Design and Application of Formative Evaluation in the Artificial Intelligence Course

Ping Zhong, Chengyang Zhu, Guihua Duan, Yu Sheng[✉], and Wanchun Jiang

Central South University, Changsha 410083, China
shengyu@csu.edu.cn

Abstract. Artificial intelligence course is an essential fundamental compulsory course for information majors. Current assessment methods of the course lead students to focus solely on their final grades rather than the knowledge itself, failing to provide effective information for students to improve their comprehensive qualities. This paper first analyzes the appropriateness of applying formative evaluation to the artificial intelligence course. Subsequently, it adopts the integrated design concept of "teaching-learning-evaluating' and a three-step design procedure of "objectives-tasks-evaluation", using the example of the School of Computer Science and Engineering at Central South University throughout the whole process. Implementing formative evaluation in the artificial intelligence course, promoting evaluation as a means of teaching and an impetus in learning, is conducive to cultivating advanced skills in students, which is an effective approach for nurturing innovative talents in the era of intelligence.

Keywords: Formative Evaluation · Artificial intelligence Course · Students-centered

1 Introduction

One of the core concepts in the accreditation standards for engineering education is student-centered educational principle. A crucial aspect of being student-centered is the effective use of assessment for learning, enabling students to learn how to learn. Any "student-centered" approach that doesn't empower students to learn how to learn is not genuinely student-centered. Formative evaluation focuses on the ongoing process-based outcomes throughout the entire period of instructional activities, provides a diverse and comprehensive evaluation of students' learning, offering timely feedback and summarization of their progress to cultivate students' comprehensive application skills and self-directed learning abilities [1]. Unlike summative evaluation, such as end-of-term exams, which serves as an assessment of educational outcomes for prior instructional activities.

Any learning assessment activity, regardless of when it occurs during the teaching process, who designs it, where it is implemented, how it is conducted, or the extent of its coverage, as long as the information collected is used for diagnosing, analyzing, and improving both the teaching by educators and the learning by students, then it constitutes

W. Hong and G. Kanaparan (Eds.): ICCSE 2023, CCIS 2024, pp. 255–260, 2024.
https://doi.org/10.1007/978-981-97-0791-1_22

formative evaluation [2]. However, due to various reasons, many teachers in China often misconstrue or misinterpret formative evaluation by its literal meaning, which is primarily reflected in equating formative evaluation with post-lesson quizzes or incentive systems, prioritizing "evaluation standards" over the "formative" process, oversimplifying formative evaluation as a singular assessment method, utilizing excessively narrow evaluation strategies, and neglecting the comprehensive and systemic nature of evaluation strategies. These misunderstandings are likely to impact teachers' pedagogical perspectives and students' development.

Artificial intelligence is a new technological scientific discipline that explores the simulation, extension, and expansion of human intelligence. It's also a core subject in professional education. How to integrate formative evaluation into the popular field of artificial intelligence teaching is a topic worthy of exploration and research [3]. This paper first analyzes the characteristics of formative evaluation and extensively details the specific implementation of formative evaluation within the curriculum of artificial intelligence. Conducting formative evaluation in artificial intelligence courses drives evaluation-based teaching and learning enhancement.

2 Characteristics of Formative Evaluation

The essential characteristic of formative evaluation is that the collected information is primarily used for improvement. It should not be simply equated with routine score-keeping [4]. Teachers must grasp the essential nature of formative assessment, deeply analyze regular assignments, examine the students' learning process. This involves both acknowledging their achievements and progress while objectively identify gaps and shortcomings in relation to the learning objectives, adjusting the teaching and learning based on the analysis of reasons. Only when routine assignments and tests are used as a foundation for educational improvement can they genuinely fulfill the role that formative evaluation is supposed to play.

(1) Purpose of Evaluation: Formative evaluation places more emphasis on individual feedback and the achievement of stage-specific learning goals, particularly knowledge and skill-based objectives, whose outcomes are not used for cumulative purposes or as the basis for summative evaluation.

(2) Evaluation Process: Formative evaluation is an ongoing evaluation of students during the teaching process, utilizing the gathered information for improvement. It delves into the strengths and weaknesses of students during the learning process or the pursuit of goal achievement, allowing teachers to adjust instructional activities accordingly.

(3) Evaluation Methods: The methods are diverse, including teacher classroom observations, student self-assessment and learning notes, peer evaluation and group work, assignments and experiments, in-class tests, and presentations. Emphasis is placed on quantitative evaluation tools.

(4) Evaluaiton Feedback: During the evaluation, evaluators provide the evaluated individuals with instructive feedback regarding their performance, behavior, abilities and facilitating feedback like reference materials, examples, discussions, reflections to aid them in improvement and optimization of their work performance. Feedback should be timely, specific, constructive, and respectful of privacy.

3   Concrete Implementation of Formative Evaluation in Artificial Intelligence Course

With the advancement and breakthroughs in core technologies such as deep learning and machine vision, artificial intelligence has entered a new phase of development, stepping into a "golden era." Formative evaluation in the context of an artificial intelligence course is akin to reinforcement learning based on human feedback, guiding the intelligent agent to interact with the environment, learning strategies to maximize rewards or achieve specific goals. To enhance student learning outcomes, around the educational objectives of artificial intelligence, formative evaluation is employed to align teacher's instructional activities with students' learning situation, forming an integrated approach of teaching, learning, and evaluation.

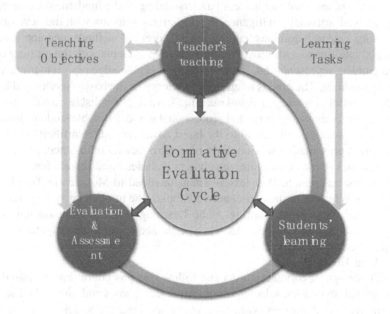

Fig. 1. "Teaching-Learning-Evaluation" integration.

3.1   "Teaching-Learning-Evaluation" Integration

In the concept of "Teaching-Learning-Evaluation" integration, teacher's classroom instruction, students' learning progress, formative assessment complement and dynamically respond to each other, as shown in Fig. 1. Students receive guidance during assessment process while teachers adjust teaching strategies based on assessment results. Here, we adopt a new teaching model where the focus shifts from teaching-centered to student-centered, transitions from knowledge delivery to capabilities achievement, striving for continuous improvement.

3.2 Implementation Process

The specific implementation process of formative assessment in the artificial intelligence course consists of three steps:

(1) **Educational Objectives**

The educational objectives encompass three dimensions: knowledge and skills, processes and methods, emotional attitudes and values, concretely describe abstract capability achievement on these three dimensions of knowledge, skills, and emotions. Subsequently, evaluation objectives are determined based on these three-dimensional educational goals (such as what should be known, what can be accomplished, and what should be developed). This provides directional guidance for designing formative tasks and implementing formative evaluation.

The objectives of the artificial intelligence course are diverse [5]. The course aims to provide students with an in-depth understanding of the fundamental concepts and principles of artificial intelligence. It familiarizes students with the developmental trajectory, research domains, cutting-edge theoretical methods, and applications of artificial intelligence. Moreover, it aims to equip students with the mastery of common problem representation, search techniques, knowledge representation, and reasoning methods. The goal is to ensure proficiency in the basic theories and methods of computational intelligence and machine learning, establishing a solid theoretical foundation for engaging in related professional work. To enable students to combine in-class knowledge and extend to the latest advancements in artificial intelligence, specialized presentation sessions have been introduced. For instance, when covering search topics in the curriculum, the content includes blind search, heuristic search, and adversarial search. Post-lesson extensions lead to Montecarlo Tree Search in AlphaGo. When lecturing neural network topics, the in-class knowledge spans from MP models, perceptron learning, Hebb Learning, and Backpropagation Learning to convolutional neural networks. The specialized research investigates large-scale models based on transformers.

(2) **Teaching Tasks**

The design of formative tasks can follow this procedure: Firstly, based on the educational objectives, select appropriate project themes and established scenarios, design task combinations within the major teaching units. Then, design specific evaluation tasks according to the actual teaching content and evaluation objectives, which involves formulating task requirements, providing clear and explicit task instructions, determining feasible evaluation methods based on actual conditions. Finally, build evaluation rules, breaking down evaluation objectives in specific tasks into observable and measurable behavioral performance objectives. Considering that artificial intelligence courses are often conducted in project-based and collaborative formats, grading rules need to account for both individual and collective evaluations. Individual grading rules are directed at individual behavioral performances, which can not only give summarizing grade targeting at student's overall performance, but also utilize itemized grading rules to quantify complex performance that include numerous critical factors. Collective evaluations are directed towards team/collaborative group/class, usually giving evaluation to collective outputs like group work, collectively accomplished project documents, or assembled AI kits.

After determining evaluation components with the help of checklists, performance inventories, grade scales, and basic element analysis scales, it is further necessary to decompose evaluation objectives within specific tasks into observable, evaluable performance criteria, preparing for the evaluation implementation.

For instance, in our artificial intelligence course, students need to conduct topic research in groups where teachers clarify tasks for each student to ensure clear divisions of work. Additionally, to differentiate between different levels, three tiers are proposed: 1) direct translation of literature or internet search for existing knowledge, demonstrating a certain level of research ability; 2) capable of implementing existing solutions through programming, showcasing practical skills; 3) proposing viable new ideas based on existing solutions, indicating innovative capabilities. These three tiers increase in difficulty progressively.

Tasks should be more specific and explicit than the objectives. For example, for students choosing the neural network topic, the teacher will provide classic papers on transformers and the official website of the ChatGPT large model. We can divide the subject into four aspects: 1). Historical Development (research background, industry evolution); 2). Data and Computing Power (basics, preparation); 3). Model Principles/Key Technologies; 4). Applications and Societal Impact (challenges and opportunities). Each aspect will contain four to five guiding questions, prompting students to think in a question-based and heuristic manner.

When considering the historical development of large-scale models, how to approach the following questions:

1. Definition and development of natural language processing (NLP)? Development of large language models (LLM)?
2. Typical tasks in NLP? What task does ChatGPT perform? Besides conversational abilities, what are its distinguishing features?
3. Core members of the ChatGPT team? What backgrounds do OpenAI employees possess?
4. History of OpenAI? Why it is OpenAI that developed ChatGPT? Are there any other large-scale models?
5. Evaluation of ChatGPT by AI scholars, including Ilya Sutskever, Stuart Russell, Yann LeCun, and others.

(3) **Evaluation Feedback**

The implementation of formative evaluation needs to align with the teaching/project implementation process. Data collection methods (such as questionnaires, assignments, reports, notes, etc.) should be determined based on selected evaluation method. Following the analysis of evaluation results, teachers should conduct timely attribution processing, provide feedback to students in a reasonable manner and make appropriate teaching interventions [6]. Students should actively reflect under teacher guidance, adjust their learning status and strategies. The implementation of evaluation should follow two principles: 1) comprehensiveness - evaluation criteria should cover all levels that students can reach, provide differentiated descriptions for different dimensions of performance, focus on and highlight the differences across these dimensions during the evaluation implementation. 2) accuracy - evaluation criteria for each dimension and each evaluation indicator should be clear and precise, allowing distinction between different behavioral performance levels, enabling evaluators to understand what and how to evaluate. Simultaneously, the criteria should make students aware of the gap between their current level and a higher level, guiding them towards further development."

For instance, during student presentations on their research topics, feedback is provided based on the three tiers of task. For the first tier, it focuses on how well they read literature, the comprehensiveness of their research, their understanding of both domestic and international research status, familiarity with basic and latest approaches, and the logical structure of presentation. The second tier examines whether students utilize open-source code or develop their own, use public datasets or simulated data, etc. The third tier analyzes whether proposal of new ideas is feasible, the motivation and evidence are established.

4   Conclusion

Effective teaching hinges on evaluation taking the lead. Formative evaluation involves recurrent, comprehensive, and in-depth evaluations of learners' progress during their learning journey. It constitutes a systematic and dynamic process aimed at helping learners promptly correct errors, improve study methods, boost academic performance, and enhance self-awareness. This paper takes the example of specialized research within an artificial intelligence course to elaborately illustrate the implementation process of guiding students through their specialized presentations using formative evaluation. Evaluation represents solely a stage-specific outcome, while students are continually evolving. Hence, teachers need to adjust themselves constantly, viewing students through a developmental lens, facilitating students to learn self-reflection, improve confidence and learning abilities through the evaluation process.

Acknowldgement. This work was supported in part by the Education and Teaching Reform Research Project of Central South University (2021JY031 and 2022JY042), Innovation and Entrepreneurship Education Teaching Reform Research Project of Central South University (2021CG038).

References

1. Tsipianitis, D., Mandellos, G.: The value of formative evaluation in an education program. Int. J. Appl. Syst. Stud. **9**(4), 381–388 (2022)
2. Chen, Z.X., Jiao, J.L., Hu, K.X.: Formative assessment as an online instruction intervention: student engagement, outcomes, and perceptions. Int. J. Dist. Educ. Technol. **19**(1), 1–16 (2021)
3. Luo, D.S., Li, W.X., Deng, Z.H.: Teaching reform and practice of artificial intelligence course in Peking University. Comput. Educ. (10), 3–8 (2019)
4. Zhan, Z.H., Yao, J.J., Wu, Q.Y., Huang, B.B.: The design and application of performance evaluation in artificial intelligence courses. **32**(5), 32–41 (2022)
5. Yuan, Y.: Quantitative analysis of Chinese classroom teaching activity under the background of artificial intelligence. Educ. Inf. Technol. **27**(8), 11161–11177 (2022)
6. Ikejiri, R.: Development and formative evaluation of a learning game for overcoming typical difficulties in historical thinking. In: Proceedings of International Conference of the Learning Sciences, ICLS, pp. 1952–1953, Japan (2022)

Teaching Reform to Computer System Fundamentals (RISC-V Version) for Developing Students' Computer System Capabilities

Xing Liu, Qing Wang, Wenjie Zhu, Xinyi Zhang, and Menglin Chen[✉]

School of Computer Science and Artificial Intelligence,
Wuhan University of Technology, Wuhan, China
{liu.xing,1442459023,325967,325945,chenmenglin428}@whut.edu.cn

Abstract. Currently, most college students majoring in computer science in China have studied the computer science courses such as C language programming, compiling principles, digital logic circuit, computer organization and system architecture. However, many of them cannot specifically state how a C program runs inside the computer when they graduate. A key reason for this phenomenon is because these courses are taught independently, and lack coherence and continuity with each other. Consequently, the students are lack of computer system capabilities. To solve this problem, we offered a course named "Computer System Fundamentals (RISC-V version)" in Wuhan University of Technology. This course integrates the knowledge from different software and hardware courses so as to improve the students' computer system capabilities. Specifically, this course designs a representative C program example, and then uses this example to investigate how a program runs inside the computer from the high-level application layer to the low-level hardware layer. First, it guides the students to explore how a C program is converted into assembly code; Then, it discusses how the assembly code is translated into machine code; Next, it introduces how the machine code is stored in the memory system; Finally, it investigates how to design a RISC-V CPU to run the machine code in the memory system. This course can help the students understand the correlation between software and hardware, and enhance the ability to analyze a computer problem from a global system perspective. The course has been offered in the computer science major of Wuhan University of Technology for 4 years and has been greatly welcomed by the students. The survey results also show this course has effectively improved the students' computer system capabilities.

Keywords: Computer system fundamentals · RISC-V · Computer system capability · Teaching and education

Supported by Ministry of Education of China (MOE) & Intel Industry-University Cooperation Collaborative Education Project (Grant No. 220900015192812, 220800015230202) and National innovation and entrepreneurship training program for college students (Grant No. 202310497051).

1   Introduction

Computer system capability refers to the ability to integrate different hardware and software knowledge so as to enable the students majoring in computer science to develop a computer project or analyze a computer problem from a global system perspective, rather than a limited local perspective. In the past years, the computer system capability has been recognized by the Steering Committee on Computer Education of the Ministry of Education of China as an important ability that the students majoring in computer science should cultivate [9].

Currently, many Chinese universities have conducted teaching reform to cultivate the students' computer system capabilities. A mainstream teaching reform method is to build a cross-curricular theoretical and practical teaching system which involves four key computer science courses "digital logic, computer organization, operating system and compiling principle". Through this teaching reform, the students can understand how to design a CPU, an OS and a compiler independently. Moreover, they master the skills to run the developed CPU, OS and compiler on one computer platform [6,12]. In addition to the above work, some research work integrates the new teaching concepts such as new engineering and OBE into the system capability training, thereby enhancing the effect of system capability reform [7,10]. Some other research efforts focus on evaluating the effects of computer system capability reforms, e.g., Zhang et al. propose a multi-subject and multi-dimensional hierarchical teaching evaluation system dedicated to computer system ability training and the multi-dimensional evaluation results show that the evaluation system proposed is effective and provides a reference for teaching evaluation [11].

At Wuhan University of Technology, we also launched the teaching reform work aiming at cultivating the students' computer system capabilities since several years ago [3,4]. And we have implemented two kinds of reform proposals. This first one is to build a cross-curricular teaching system by integrating four core computer science courses "digital logic, computer organization, operating system and compiling principle", and this reform plan is similar to that of the other universities [6,12]. The other is to build a cross-curricular teaching system by integrating three courses "C language programming, assembly programming and computer organization", and this reform proposal aims to help the students understand clearly how a program runs inside the computer from the high-level application layer to the low-level hardware layer. Regarding the second reform proposal, we have offered a new course named "Computer System Fundamentals (RISC-V version)", and this article introduces the teaching work of this course.

The contribution of this paper is as follows: First, it introduces the software and hardware tools which can be used for the RISC-V teaching. These tools have been tested in practice for several years and can bring great convenience to teaching work. Second, a representative program example is used throughout the course teaching. This example can help the students understand the course knowledge more intuitively. Moreover, it can increase the students' study interest. Third, this course integrates different software and hardware knowledge

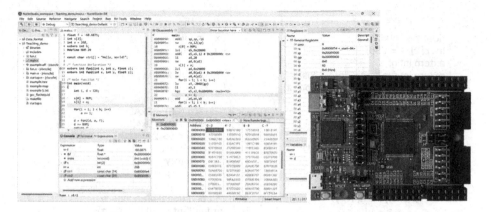

Fig. 1. The Nuclei RISC-V IDE and RV-STAR teaching board.

ranging from the upper application layer to the lower hardware layer, and this can help develop the students' computer systems capabilities.

The organization of this paper is as follows: In Sect. 2, the instruction set and supporting software and hardware tools used for the teaching work of this course are introduced. In Sect. 3, the representative program example which is used throughout the course is presented. In Sect. 4, the teaching contents and teaching plan of this course are illustrated. In Sect. 5 and Sect. 6, the theoretical teaching work and experimental teaching work of this course are investigated respectively. In Sect. 7, a survey to this course is conducted. In Sect. 8, a discussion to the teaching work of this course is presented. Finally in Sect. 9, the conclusion is given.

2 Instruction Set and Development Tools

Since this course involves the compiling from source code to machine code, it is necessary to determine which instruction set to be used in this course. Currently, the mainstream instruction sets include x86, ARM, MIPS, RISC-V, etc. In this course, the RISC-V instruction set is chosen since it is a completely open instruction set architecture (ISA) that is freely available to academia and industry [8].

After the instruction set is determined, it also needs to select the corresponding RISC-V compiler, IDE tools, teaching development board and SDK software package. Through our research, we decide to chose Nuclei's RISC-V series open-source software tools for the teaching work [2].

The Nuclei RISC-V series software includes the compiler, the IDE, the SDK and also the development board. The Nuclei RISC-V compiler is improved based on the RISC-V GNU tool chain, and it can be used to compile the high-level program to the assembly code and machine code. The Nuclei IDE is developed based on the MCU Eclipse IDE, and it can be used to debug the program

```
/* source file 1: main.c */
float f = -60.6875;
int s[2], a = 268;
extern int b;
extern int fun1(int x, int y, float z);
extern int fun2(int x, int y, float z);

int main(void)   {
    int i, d = 260;

    /* variable assignment */
    s[1] = a;

    /* loop execution */
    for(i = 1; i < b; i++)
            a += i;

    /* function call */
    d = fun2(d, a, f);
    d += 20;
    return d;
}
```

```
/* source file 2: fun.c */
extern int a;
int b = 60;

int fun1(int x, int y, float z)
{
    char *p = (char *)&a;
    *(p + 6) = 0xA9;
    *(p + 7) = 0x42;
    a = a >> 2;

    return y;
}

/* conditional branches */
int fun2(int x, int y, float z)
{
    if(x < y)
            return 256;
    else
            return a;
}
```

Fig. 2. A representative C sample program used for teaching work.

and monitor the run-time status of the program. The Nuclei RISC-V development boards include CM32M433R-START, RV-STAR, Nuclei DDR200T, Nuclei MCU200T, etc. In our work, the RV-STAR board, which is equipped with the RISC-V GD32VF103 MCU, is chosen as the teaching evaluation board since it is cheap, easy to use, and also has small size [1]. In Fig. 1, the Nuclei RISC-V IDE and RV-STAR teaching board are depicted. The other Nuclei open source software include nuclei-sdk, nuclei-linux-sdk, freeloader, buildroot and so on. These software resources provide greater convenience for the RISC-V teaching work.

3   Teaching Example Design

To specifically describe the process of translating a C program into assembly code and machine code, a representative C program example needs to be designed. This example should be as concise as possible, since it is more conducive to teaching in this way. However, it also needs to be representative, that is, it needs to cover most common operations in C programs, including variable assignment, loop operation, conditional branches, function calls, arithmetic and logical operations, etc.

In our teaching work, we designed a sample C program as is shown in Fig. 2. In the follow-up work, we use this program as the example to describe how a program runs inside a computer, including how the C program is translated into assembly code, how the assembly code is further translated into machine code, and also how the machine code is executed by the CPU to realize its functionality.

Table 1. Theoretical teaching contents and teaching plan (software part)

Title	Contents	Credits
Data representation	- Data representation of float and integer. - How data is stored in memory.	2
Instruction set and programming language	- Instruction set introduction (x86, arm, mips, risc-v) - The features of RISC-V instruction set - How to design an instruction set (basically introduction). - How to program by machine code - Machine language, assembly language and high-level languages	6
Program compilation and executable file analysis	- GNU toolchains, and compiling operations. - Analysis of executable file (ELF format, binutils, objdump, objcopy, nm, etc.) - How the machine code is stored in the memory - project management (makefile, etc.) - RISC-V IDE (compilation, debug, etc.)	5
RISC-V assembly code	- RISC-V assembly code - Assembly code of variable assignment, loop operation, function call, conditional branch, arithmetic and logical operations - Stack and heap, context saving	7
RISC-V machine code	- How assembly code is translated to machine code? - RISC-V compact machine code - RISC-V instruction format analysis	4
startup code	- Analysis of C program startup code	2
Linking principle	- GNU linker script (program sections) - Linking principle (static link, dynamic link, etc.)	6

4   Teaching Contents and Teaching Plan

This course has 80 credit hours, including 48 theoretical credit hours and 32 experimental credit hours. In Table 1, Table 2 and Table 3, the teaching contents and teaching plan of this course are introduced.

The theoretical teaching work of this course contains the following contents: (1) Introduction to the basic knowledge such as data representation, instruction set and programming languages. This knowledge lays the foundation for the next step of program analysis. (2) Analysis of program executing process (software part). This teaching work uses a C program as an example to explain how the C program is translated into the assembly code and machine code. First, the GNU compiler and binutils tools are used to compile the C program and generate the assembly code and machine code of this program. Then, the function of each assembly statement is analyzed to help the students understand how the C program implements its function through assembly code. Next, the way to translate the assembly code into machine code is discussed. Finally, the program linking principle including the dynamic linking and static linking is discussed. (3) Analysis of program executing process (hardware part). The software-part work has taught the students how to generate the machine code. Next, we need to teach the students to design a hardware system to store and run the machine code. First, the structure of the memory system is introduced. And then, how the machine code is stored in the memory system is explained. Next, how to design a single-cycle and multi-cycle RISC-V CPU to run the machine code is investigated.

Table 2. Theoretical teaching contents and teaching plan (hardware part)

Title	Contents	Credits
Memory system	- How the instructions and data are stored in the memory? - The structure of memory system. - Memory address, memory capacity extension. - Connection between memory system and CPU.	6
RISC-V single-cycle CPU design	- SoC system for CPU run-time environment - Introduction to functional components of CPU datapath - How to design the datapath of single-cycle RISC-V CPU? - How to design the controller of single-cycle RISC-V CPU?	6
RISC-V multi-cycle CPU design	- How to design the controller of multi-cycle RISC-V CPU? - How to design the datapath of multi-cycle RISC-V CPU?	4

The experimental teaching work contains two parts: software experiments and hardware experiments. (1) The objective of the software experiments is to help the students understand the translation process from C language to machine code, and two lab exercises are designed to achieve this objective. This first one requires the students to develop an assembler to achieve automatic translation from assembly code to machine code. To complete this task, the students should deeply understand the relationship between assembly code and machine code. The second one requires the students to solve the software problems from the machine-code level, e.g., fixing program bugs by modifying the machine code directly without the necessity of changing the source code. This exercise requires the students to understand the whole translation process from the high-level C language to the low-level machine code. (2) The hardware experiment aims to design a multi-cycle RISC-V CPU, and then use this CPU to run the machine-code instructions generated by the previous software project. This experiment aims to integrate both software and hardware system. As for the development of CPU, two development tools are provided. One is the simulation tool Logisim [5], and the other is the hardware-programmable FPGA. The software simulation tools are more flexible, easy to use and allows the students to make more attempts and innovations. However, it is not a real hardware circuit, and lacks some features of the real-world physical hardware. Therefore, in our teaching work, we first teach the students to use the simulation tools Logisim to design the circuits and learn design methods. And then, we further teach the students to use the hardware FPGA to implement the designed proposal. By this way, the advantages of both software simulation and hardware implementation can be integrated.

Table 3. Experimental teaching contents and teaching plan

Title	Contents	Credits
Lab1: Assembler development	Develop a RISC-V assembler to translate the RV32I assemble codes to machine codes	8
Lab2: Machine-code-level program development	When a program has some programming bugs, fix these bugs by directly changing machine codes, with no necessity to modify the source code	4
Lab3: RISC-V CPU development based on Logisim	Use the Logisim simulation tool to design a multi-cycle RISC-V CPU, which can support most RV32I instructions.	8
Lab4: RISC-V CPU development based on FPGA	Use the FPGA platform to design a multi-cycle RISC-V CPU, which can support most RV32I instructions	12

5 Theoretical Teaching Work

The theoretical teaching content mainly includes the program compilation, the assembly code analysis, the machine code analysis and the CPU design.

5.1   Program Compilation and Executable File Analysis

The sample program can be compiled into an ELF (Executable and Linkable Format) file by the GNU compiler. Then, the ELF file can be analyzed by the binutils tools such as objdump, nm and objcopy to get the information such as the addresses of the variables and functions in the program, the assembly code and machine code of the program, as is depicted in Fig. 3. These information lays the foundation for the following program analysis.

5.2   Assembly Code Analysis

By analyzing the assembly code, the students can understand how each statement of a C program implements its function inside the computer.

Since variable assignment, loop operation, conditional branches and function call are the most commonly used C statements, we focus on analyzing the assembly code of these statements in this course.

Variable Assignment. There is a variable assignment statement in the sample program "s[1] = a", and its function is realized by the assembly codes as follows:

- 8000066: 20000737   lui a4,0x20000
- 800006a: 00472703   lw a4,4(a4)
- 800006e: c3d8   sw a4,4(a5)

The *lui* instruction is used to get the base address of RAM. The *lw* instruction reads the value of variable a from memory space and puts it into register $a4$. The *sw* further writes the value of register $a4$ to the memory space of variable $s[1]$. By this way, the assignment operation is completed. In Fig. 4, the above process is depicted.

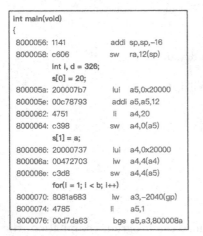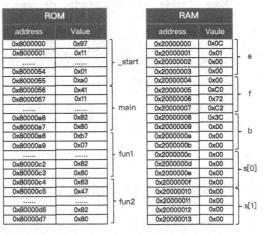

Fig. 3. The basic program information generated by using binutils tools.

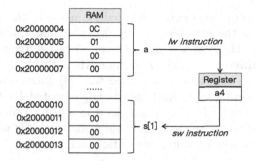

Fig. 4. The implementation of variable assignment statement in the sample program.

Loop Operation. The sample example also has a loop statement "for(i = 1; i < b; i++) a += i", and its function is realized by the assembly statements as follows:

- 8000070: 8081a683   lw a3,-2040(gp) # 20000008 <b>
- 8000074: 4785   li a5,1
- 8000076: 00d7da63   bge a5,a3,800008a <main+0x34>
- 800007a: 973e   add a4,a4,a5
- 800007c: 0785   addi a5,a5,1
- 800007e: fed79ee3   bne a5,a3,800007a <main+0x24>
- 8000082: 200007b7   lui a5,0x20000
- 8000086: 00e7a223   sw a4,4(a5) # 20000004 <a>

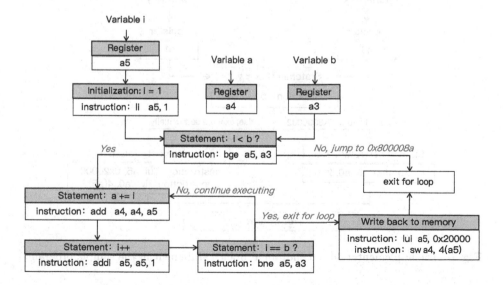

Fig. 5. The implementation of loop execution statement in the sample program.

The implementation of loop operation usually consists of three steps: (1) Assign the initial values to the variables. In the sample program, the variables i, a, and b are placed in the registers $a5$, $a4$, and $a3$ respectively, and the value of variable i is initialized to 1. (2) Determine when the loop ends. And this is implemented by two instructions: *bge* and *bne*. (3) Increment the count value and perform loop operations. And this is implemented by the *addi* and *add* instructions respectively. In Fig. 5, the loop executing process of the sample example is depicted. Note that the final value of variable a needs to be written back to the memory when the loop execution ends.

Conditional Branches. The conditional branch statement in the sample example is as follows:

- if(x < y) return 256;
- else   return a;

and its function is realized by the assembly code as follows:

- 80000c4: 00b54763   blt a0,a1,80000d2 <fun2+0xe>
- 80000c8: 200007b7   lui a5,0x20000
- 80000cc: 0047a503   lw a0,4(a5) # 20000004 <a>
- 80000d0: 8082   ret
- 80000d2: 10000513   li a0,256
- 80000d6: 8082   ret

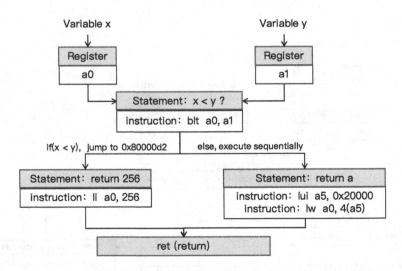

Fig. 6. The implementation of conditional branch statement in the sample program.

The *blt* instruction is used to implement the *if* conditional statement. When the comparison condition is satisfied, the program will jump to the address 0x80000d2, and execute a *li* instruction to perform the operation "return 256". Otherwise, the program runs sequentially, and execute two instructions *lui* and *lw* to perform the operation "return a". Note that all return values need to be placed in register *a*0 before the program returns. In Fig. 6, the conditional branch operation of the sample example is depicted.

Function Call. The sample example also has a function call statement "d = fun2(d, a, f)", and it's implemented in the computer by the assembly code as follows:

- 800008a: 200007b7   lui a5,0x20000
- 800008e: 0007a603   lw a2,0(a5) # 20000000 <f>
- 8000092: 200007b7   lui a5,0x20000
- 8000096: 0047a583   lw a1,4(a5) # 20000004 <a>
- 800009a: 14600513   li a0,326
- 800009e: 201d   jal 80000c4 <fun2>

The first two instructions *lui* and *lw* are used to pass the value of parameter *f* to register *a*2. The following two instructions *lui* and *lw* are used to pass the value of parameter *a* to register *a*1. The *li* instruction is used to pass the value of parameter *d* to register *a*0. Through the above operations, the sub-function *fun2* can take the parameter values of *x*, *y* and *z* from the registers *a*0, *a*1 and *a*2, respectively. In Fig. 7, the above parameter passing process is depicted.

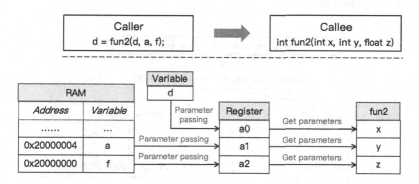

Fig. 7. The implementation of function parameter passing in the sample program.

After completing the above parameter passing operation, the function call can be executed by a *jal* instruction. This instruction first saves the address of the next instruction into register *x*1, and then modifies the PC to jump to the sub-function. When the sub-function runs to the end, it will execute a *ret* instruction, and this instruction will pass the value of register *x*1 to the PC pointer, thus allowing the program to return to the function breakpoint to continue the previous execution. In Fig. 8, the above context saving and context restoration process of *jal* instruction is depicted.

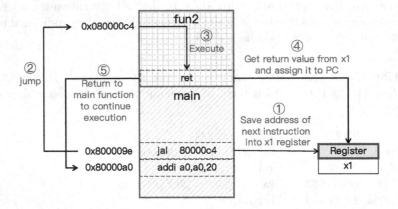

Fig. 8. The implementation of function context saving in the sample program.

5.3 Machine Code Analysis

By analyzing the assembly codes, the students can understand how the C language statement is implemented at the low-level of the computer. Next, this course guides the students to explore how the assembly code is further translated into machine code.

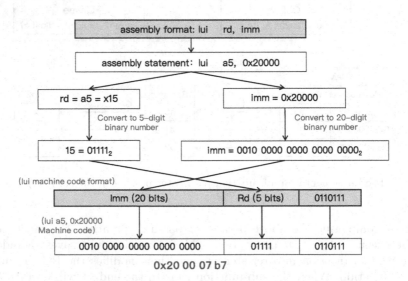

Fig. 9. The way to translate the assembly code into machine code (*lui* instruction).

Taking the *lui* instruction as an example, the assembly format of *lui* instruction is "lui rd, imm", and the 32-bit instruction format of *lui* instruction is "imm(20-bits) | rd(5-bits) | 0110111 (opcode)". Suppose a specific *lui* instruction instance is "lui r5, 0x20", then it can know that $rd = 5, imm = 20$. By converting the values of rd and imm into 5-bit and 20-bit machine code respectively, the machine code of "lui r5, 0x20" can be generated, as is shown in Fig. 9.

5.4   RISC-V CPU Design

With the above teaching work, the students can understand the whole process of translating a C program into the machine code. Next, we need to focus on the hardware system and guide the students to investigate how to design a CPU to execute these machine codes.

Currently, there are many textbooks on CPU design, so this paper does not discuss this topic in detail. Overall, The teaching work of CPU design can be divided into the following steps: (1) Design the single-cycle CPU firstly, including the design of datapath and controller of this CPU. (2) Extend the functionality of the single-cycle CPU to make it become a multi-cycle or pipelined CPU.

6   Experimental Teaching Work

This section presents the experimental teaching work of this course. The experiments consists of four lab exercises. The first two exercises focus on the software development, and aims to examine whether the students have mastered the principle of translating a high-level C program to the low-level machine code. The latter two exercises focus on the hardware design, and aims to examine the students' ability to design and implement a RISC-V CPU.

6.1   Lab Exercise 1: Assembler Development

This lab exercise requires the students to develop an assembler which can automatically translate the RV32I assembly code to the machine code. The students can use any programming language, and the experimental results are tested by comparing the machine code generated by the assembler with the machine code produced by the standard RISC-V GCC compiler.

6.2   Lab Exercise 2: Machine-Code-Level Project Development

This lab exercise requires the students to solve some engineering problems from the machine-code level rather than the source-code level, e.g., when the program has some programming bugs, the students are required to correct these bugs directly by modifying the machine code instead of the source code. To complete this task, the students need to clearly understand the translation process from C language to machine code.

In our teaching work, we assume that there is a programming bug in the sample program, and the statement:

– d = fun2(d, a, f);

should be modified to:

– b += a;
– d = fun1(d, b, f);

Then, the students are required to perform this modification by modifying the machine code directly, without making any change to the source code.

To complete this work, the students need to change the called function from $fun2$ to $fun1$, which involves the modification to the machine code of jal instruction. The students also need to change the function parameter from variable a to variable b, which involves the modification to the machine code of lw instruction. Additionally, they also need to insert a new statement "b += a" before the function call. To achieve this, they need to make the program jump to a free memory space, and then add the machine code of "b += a" in this space. Later, they need to add another "jump" instruction to make the program jump back to the breakpoints to continue the original execution process.

6.3   Lab Exercise 3: RISC-V CPU Development Based on Logisim

This lab exercise requires the students to develop a single-cycle RISC-V CPU which supports 21 instructions by using Logisim software. First, the students need to use Logisim to implement the CPU components such as ALU, Regfile and controller. Then, they need to connect different circuit components to build a RISC-V CPU. Later, they need to load some instructions and data into the instruction memory and data memory respectively, and run the Logisim simulation to verify whether the designed CPU's functionality is correct or not. In Fig. 10, an example of a CPU designed based on Logisim is shown.

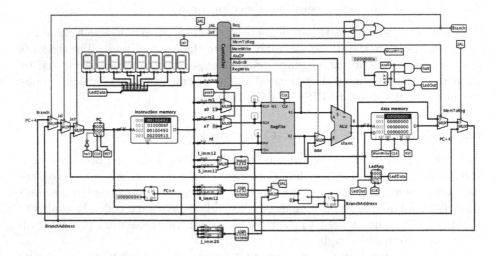

Fig. 10. RISC-V CPU developed based on Logisim software.

6.4   Lab Exercise 4: RISC-V CPU Development Based on FPGA

This lab exercise requires the students to develop a multi-cycle RISC-V CPU which supports 21 instructions based on the FPGA platform, and it requires the students to complete the following tasks: First, the students need to design an SoC system which consists of CPU, memory system and general-purpose input and output (GPIO). This SoC system can provide a testing environment to verify whether the functionality of the designed CPU is correct or not. Then, the students need to use FPGA to design a single-cycle CPU that supports 21 instructions. Later, they should expand the circuit functions of the single-cycle CPU to make it become a multi-cycle CPU.

7   Course Survey and Feedback

We survey the teaching effect of this course from the following aspects: (1) Whether the students can complete the experimental tasks of this course independently? Regarding this topic, the data shows that the proportion of the students who can complete the four lab exercises is 94%, 98%, 90% and 84% respectively. This result is in line with our expectations. (2) Whether the students can clearly state the complete executing process of a program in the computer? For this topic, the survey results show that 96% students are able to do this, which shows our teaching work has achieved positive results. (3) Are the students enthusiastic about taking this course? To understand this, we counted the number of students who intend to take this course in the past three years, and the result shows that the average number reaches about 300 each year, which far exceeds the scheduled capacity of this course. And this proves that the students are highly interested in the courses.

8   Discussion

Currently in China, many teaching reform programs for college computer science majors strive to enhance the correlation and cohesion of different computer software and hardware courses so as to improve the students' computer system capabilities, e.g., many teaching reforms focus on integrating the knowledge of OS, compiler and CPU to enable the students to build a microcomputer independently.

These reform efforts are very effective. However, they neglect to integrate the high-level programs with the underlying technologies (OS, CPU, compiler, etc.). Consequently, many students lack an in-depth understanding of how a high-level program runs inside the computer.

In this paper, we present our teaching work which aims to solve the above problem. We design a representative C program and then use it as the example to investigate how a program runs inside the computer from the high-level application layer to the low-level hardware layer. This way of teaching can improve the students' study interest, and enhance the students' ability in understanding and applying the computer knowledge comprehensively.

9   Conclusion

This paper presents the teaching work of the course "Computer System Fundamentals (RISC-V version)" in Wuhan University of Technology. This course aims to enhance the coherence of knowledge in different hardware and software courses by guiding the students to understand how a C program runs inside the computer from the high-level program layer to the low-level hardware layer. This course has been offered at Wuhan University of Technology for 4 years, and the course survey results indicate that it has effectively improved the students' computer system capabilities.

The teaching work of this course has given us the following enlightenment: (1) It is important to offer a comprehensive course in the computer science college which can integrate the knowledge of different software and hardware courses, and this way of teaching can significantly improve the students' computer system capabilities. (2) Using a specific sample example to teach throughout the whole course can increase the students' interest in learning. (3) Effective experimental teaching tools can greatly improve the quality of teaching.

For the ongoing work, we will further integrate the knowledge of the operating system course into this course, for the purpose of enhancing the coherence of knowledge in more computer science courses.

Acknowledgements. Our thanks to Prof. Zhihu Tan with Huazhong University of Science and Technology in providing the Logisim design of RISC-V CPU to us for the teaching work.

References

1. Nuclei RV-STAR development board, October 2023. https://doc.nucleisys.com/nuclei_board_labs/hw/hw.html
2. Open source software for Nuclei system technology, a professional RISC-V processor IP company, October 2023. https://github.com/Nuclei-Software
3. Liu, X., Fu, L., Rao, W., Lin, X., Liao, M., Shi, B.: Multi-cycle CPU design with FPGA for teaching of computer organization principle. In: 2019 14th International Conference on Computer Science & Education (ICCSE), pp. 472–477. IEEE (2019)
4. Liu, X., Tian, J., Li, Y., Xiong, S., Rao, W., Yuan, J.: Instructional design of computer system fundamentals for cultivating students' computer system ability. In: 2021 16th International Conference on Computer Science & Education (ICCSE), pp. 311–316. IEEE (2021)
5. Logisim: a graphical tool for designing and simulating logic circuits, October 2023. http://www.cburch.com/logisim
6. Mao, Y., Feng, Y., Cheng, D., Xie, Q.: Computer curriculum system reform based on system ability training. In: 2016 11th International Conference on Computer Science & Education (ICCSE), pp. 907–910. IEEE (2016)
7. Shuying, C., Lei, C.: Reform and research of computer professional curriculum system based on systematic capability training under the background of emerging engineering education. In: 2018 13th International Conference on Computer Science & Education (ICCSE), pp. 1–5. IEEE (2018)

8. Waterman, E.A., Krste Asanovic, R.V.F.: The RISC-V instruction set manual, volume I: user-level ISA, document version 20191213, December 2019. https:// riscv.org/technical/specifications/
9. Yuan, C., Gao, X., Chen, Y., Bao, Y.: Teaching undergraduates to build real computer systems. Commun. ACM **64**(11), 48–49 (2021)
10. Yuan, H., Sun, W., Chen, Y.: Computer system capability hardware course group construction based on OBE. In: Proceedings of the 5th International Conference on Distance Education and Learning, pp. 85–88 (2020)
11. Zhang, W., Wang, R., Tang, Y., Yuan, E., Wu, Y., Wang, Z.: Research on teaching evaluation of courses based on computer system ability training. In: Zeng, J., Qin, P., Jing, W., Song, X., Lu, Z. (eds.) ICPCSEE 2021. CCIS, vol. 1452, pp. 434–442. Springer, Singapore (2021). https://doi.org/10.1007/978-981-16-5943-0_35
12. Zhang, Y., Chen, X., An, X., Lu, J., Li, X., Zhou, X.: Building step-by-step practical curriculum system for computer systemic ability training. In: Proceedings of the ACM Turing 50th Celebration Conference-China, pp. 1–6 (2017)

AI-Assisted Project-Based Learning and Exploration in the Field of Electronic Information Engineering Majors

Li Yu, Ming-Wei Wu$^{(\boxtimes)}$, Gang Cen, Yong-Xin Xi$^{(\boxtimes)}$, Xin Yan, and Tian-Hao Qiu

School of Information and Electronic Engineering, Zhejiang University of Science and Technology, Hangzhou 310023, China
wumingwei2004@aliyun.com, 770045043@qq.com

Abstract. Artificial intelligence (AI) is advancing rapidly and finding its way into various industries. Universities are placing a high priority on incorporating AI into professional education. However, for students who are not majoring in AI, applying AI technology to projects can be challenging. To foster the development of application-oriented talents in the AI era, this article presents an illustrative example of project-based learning that focuses on the use of AI tools for assisted education in the context of blind navigation vehicles. The project specifically concentrates on core AI applications, such as pedestrian detection using Raspberry Pi and line tracking for blind navigation. Voice broadcasting is employed to facilitate interaction with visually impaired individuals. The project is carried out in teams, with an emphasis on utilizing user-friendly AI tools for project-based education and practical experimentation. By integrating theory and practice, students have the opportunity to enhance their practical skills, deepen their understanding of AI, strengthen teamwork, improve communication skills, and foster innovative thinking.

Keywords: Artificial Intelligence · Project-Based Education · Team Collaboration

1 Introduction

In recent years, with the rapid advancement of the digital economy, artificial intelligence (AI) has undergone extensive cross-disciplinary integration with various fields [1]. Its deep integration into diverse application scenarios has become

This work is supported by National Undergraduate Innovation and Entrepreneurship Training Program (Grant No. 202311057011), Zhejiang University of Science and Technology (ZUST) Teacher's Professional Growth Community Project 2023, ZUST Top Undergraduate Courses Development Project 2022-k4, 2020 Zhejiang Provincial-level Top Undergraduate Courses (Zhejiang Provincial Department of Education General Office Notice (2021) No. 195).

increasingly evident. Among the disciplines that heavily rely on AI are communication and electronic engineering. Consequently, it becomes imperative to integrate AI technology into the curriculum of educational institutions. However, non-AI majors often face challenges due to the lack of systematic learning in AI courses [2] or limited resources, confusing and hindered progress in applying AI methods to enhance their project capabilities. Recognizing this issue, universities need to go beyond theoretical courses and address the growing demand for applied talents in society. In response, our project team has proposed an intelligent solution for blind navigation vehicles, employing project-based learning that utilizes AI tools to facilitate practical learning [3].

2 Teaching Project Plan Design

2.1 Objectives and Requirements

The project-based practice aims to nurture application-oriented talents who are adaptable to the AI era [4]. This approach entails equipping students with the skills to apply theoretical knowledge gained from their major courses using user-friendly AI tools, as illustrated in Fig. 1.

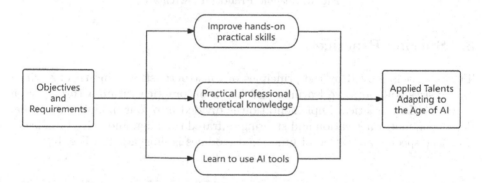

Fig. 1. Project Practice Objectives and Requirements Chart

2.2 Practical Process

Project teaching will be practiced from the overall process shown in Fig. 2, first by mastering professional knowledge and organizing a team, then by division of labor and cooperation, specific practice, and finally by practical application simulation. The specific practice will be divided into three modules: learning to call AI tools, learning to develop Raspberry Pi, and learning to hardware the car, as shown in Fig. 3.

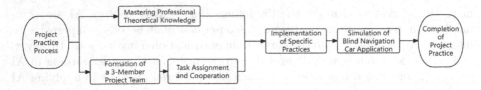

Fig. 2. Overall Flow Chart of Project Practice

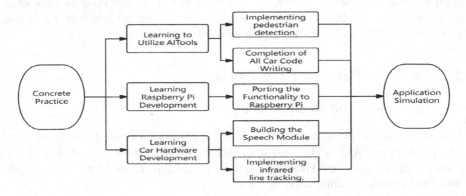

Fig. 3. Specific Practice Flow Chart

3   Specific Practice

The project is guided by the principles of constructivist learning theory, which emphasizes collaborative learning and hands-on practice within a three-person team [4]. The practical implementation is divided into four modules: AI visual detection, motor activation and steering, infrared tracking, and voice broadcasting. The specific allocation of functional modules is illustrated in Fig. 4.

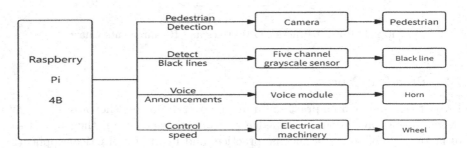

Fig. 4. Specific module distribution

3.1   AI Visual Detection Module

This module enables students to learn how to call pedestrian detection database [6] to identify pedestrians and master the ability to call simple artificial intelligence tools.

Students need to understand that the key principle of pedestrian visual detection is to determine whether there are pedestrians by extracting the features from the image. These features can be the shape, texture, color, etc., of the pedestrian image. The commonly used feature extraction method is grayscale image conversion. In this paper, the Haar feature extraction method is used for detection, which is realized by combining the Haar feature with the Adaboost algorithm.

The Haar feature is used to represent the light and dark changes of the pixel values of pedestrians in a local range, and the integration graph technique is combined to accelerate the training of a cascade classifier. The representation of Haar features is shown in Fig. 5, 6, 7 and 8.

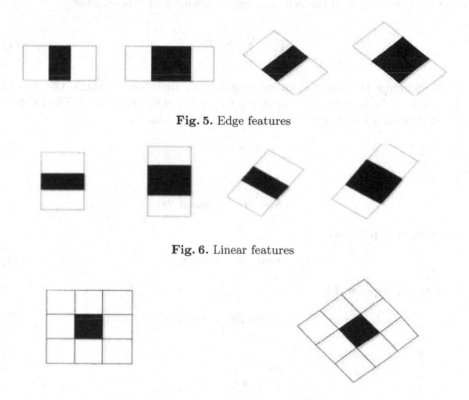

Fig. 5. Edge features

Fig. 6. Linear features

Fig. 7. Center surround

Fig. 8. Diagonal features

Haar features reflect the grayscale change of the image, but it needs to calculate a lot of rectangles, to speed up the calculation, it is generally necessary to use the integral channel method. Useful information is stored in the integral feature map, and the value on the point (x, y) is the sum of the gray value of the upper left corner of the point gray map and the part surrounded by the point (x, y). Assume that the grayscale image here is, and its integral image is, both have the same size and the relationship between I and I' is as follows:

$$I' = \sum_{i=0}^{i \leq x} \sum_{j=0}^{j \leq y} I(i, j) \tag{1}$$

After obtaining the integral image according to the above formula, the sum of the pixels in the area can be calculated through certain operations. The integral diagram is shown in Fig. 9. Where the integral of point a is:

$$I_a = Sum(Ra). \tag{2}$$

the integral of point b is:

$$I_b = Sum(Ra) + Sum(Rb). \tag{3}$$

the integral of point c is:

$$I_c = Sum(Ra) + Sum(Rc). \tag{4}$$

the integral of point d is:

$$I_d = Sum(Ra) + Sum(Rb) + Sum(Rc) + Sum(Rd) \tag{5}$$

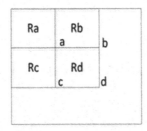

Fig. 9. Integration simplification diagram

and

$$Sum(Rd) = I_a + I_a - (I_b + I_c) \qquad (6)$$

The eigenvalues can be obtained by calculating the rectangular endpoints of the integral graph. After students master the principle of the Haar feature, they can begin to write the pedestrian detection program. The pedestrian detection program of the system uses Haar features to train samples calculate the integral graph, and construct a classifier. The main ideas are shown in Fig. 10.

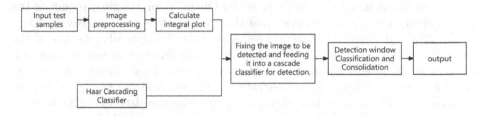

Fig. 10. Pedestrian detection sequence diagram

The AI tool employed by students is a pedestrian detection classifier based on Haar features, implemented using OpenCV. For junior-level students with a foundational understanding, the pre-trained Haar cascade library within OpenCV is a suitable choice. The Haar pedestrian detection cascade classifier, such as the haarcascade-fullbody.xml file depicted in Fig. 11, can be invoked by students to enable pedestrian detection functionality in their projects. Furthermore, students can efficiently leverage pre-trained cascade classifiers to accomplish other elementary AI functions, including facial detection, eye detection, and smile detection.

haarcascade_eye.xml	2023/8/17 18:19	xmlfile	334 KB
haarcascade_eye_tree_eyeglasses.xml	2023/8/17 18:19	xmlfile	588 KB
haarcascade_frontalcatface.xml	2023/8/17 18:19	xmlfile	402 KB
haarcascade_frontalcatface_extended.xml	2023/8/17 18:19	xmlfile	374 KB
haarcascade_frontalface_alt.xml	2023/8/17 18:19	xmlfile	661 KB
haarcascade_frontalface_alt_tree.xml	2023/8/17 18:19	xmlfile	2,627 KB
haarcascade_frontalface_alt2.xml	2023/8/17 18:19	xmlfile	528 KB
haarcascade_frontalface_default.xml	2023/8/17 18:19	xmlfile	909 KB
haarcascade_fullbody.xml	2023/8/17 18:19	xmlfile	466 KB
haarcascade_lefteye_2splits.xml	2023/8/17 18:19	xmlfile	191 KB
haarcascade_license_plate_rus_16stages.xml	2023/8/17 18:19	xmlfile	47 KB
haarcascade_lowerbody.xml	2023/8/17 18:19	xmlfile	387 KB
haarcascade_profileface.xml	2023/8/17 18:19	xmlfile	810 KB
haarcascade_righteye_2splits.xml	2023/8/17 18:19	xmlfile	192 KB
haarcascade_russian_plate_number.xml	2023/8/17 18:19	xmlfile	74 KB
haarcascade_smile.xml	2023/8/17 18:19	xmlfile	185 KB
haarcascade_upperbody.xml	2023/8/17 18:19	xmlfile	768 KB

Fig. 11. The XML file for pedestrian detection after training

For senior-level students with a strong grounding, independent dataset training to achieve pedestrian detection is recommended. The subsequent delineates the fundamental steps involved in training the object detection classifier: First of all, training necessitates a substantial collection of positive and negative samples. Positive samples encompass image regions containing the target object, while negative samples comprise image regions devoid of the target object. Students are required to partition the training dataset into training and testing sets, subsequently converting them into XML format. Then, students can utilize the CascadeClassifier function provided by OpenCV for training, requiring the pre-configuration of parameters such as Haar feature type and quantity, positive-to-negative sample ratio, learning rate, and more. Additionally, the size of the student's training dataset significantly impacts the duration of the training process, typically ranging from several hours to several days. Finally, the trained cascade classifier XML file, as illustrated in the selected file in Fig. 11, can be utilized by students to detect objects. By utilizing the detectMultiScale function provided by OpenCV, students can obtain the detected object's position and size. Ultimately, students can seamlessly integrate the trained AI detection classifier into their projects.

The specific code for invoking this simple AI tool is illustrated in Fig. 12. In consideration of computational resource limitations, the classifier once debugged and integrated with the trained samples, is initially tested on a PC platform. Following this validation, it is then transferred to the directory within the Linux system where students will be developing their programs.

```
def face_detect_demo(image):
    global count
    gray = cv.cvtColor(image, cv.COLOR_BGR2GRAY)
    face_detector = cv.CascadeClassifier("/home/pi/Desktop/Test/haarcascade_fulbody.xml")
    faces = face_detector.detectMultiScale(gray,scaleFactor = 1.1,minNeighbors = 5)#BCKUP: SF 1.2 mN 6
    count = len(faces)
    for x, y, w, h in faces:
        cv.rectangle(image, (x, y), (x+w, y+h), (0, 0, 255), 2)
        count += 1  # 累计人数
        # 把统计人数显示出来
        cv.putText(image, '{}'.format(count), (x, y-7), 3, 1.2, (0, 0, 255), 2)
    cv.imshow("result", image)
```

Fig. 12. The schematic illustration of the program that invokes the AI tool

To display the picture in real-time, students need to try to call the camera to get the picture. The image is first converted to a grayscale image, the purpose is to reduce the amount of computer calculation. Then pedestrian detection can be started. The whole process involves recognizing the new picture according to the training data. The detection value will be a list, and each of the four variables in the table are x, y, height, and width. In this project, the detected pedestrians are represented as a list, where the size of the list indicates the number of pedestrians. The position of each pedestrian in the image is represented by four parameters: (x, y, height, width). Here, x and y represent the coordinates of the top-left corner of the pedestrian, height indicates the height of the pedestrian, and width represents the width of the pedestrian. With this information, the precise position and size of each pedestrian in the image can be determined. To see the detection results more directly, students can frame the information. Through the real-time detection screen obtained from the computer terminal connected to the Raspberry PI, the face information when pedestrians are close to them is detected, as shown in Fig. 13.

Fig. 13. Real-time detection picture

3.2 Motor Starting and Steering Module

This module allows students to master the ability to control the motor starting and steering and learn to use the wheel speed difference to fine-tune the steering means.

Students need to create a car direction Run class RobotDirection, initialize the motor and instantiate the object part program before running, create 6 functions in the class to set 6 states of the two-way motor of TB6612, and then set the motion state of the car with 6 states. Including the left motor and the right motor for forward, reverse, and stop. Then use the function to set the running state of the car, including forward, backward, left, right, and stationary.

After the students have finished loading the car and have a certain understanding of the compiler, they can realize the basic control of the car by learning relevant knowledge. Students can begin using the library function to judge the car's data. First, students let the car move forward for some time, and judge the returned data of the left and right wheel speed and the number of rotation laps. Then students directly observe the data, they can find: that even in the setting of the same speed, the left and right wheel speeds still appear to have a lot of strange differences, and are unstable. On this basis, students can use Python to fit scattered points, save and input data through text documents, and obtain the image as shown in Fig. 14(a) and Fig. 14(b). Figure 14(a) is the fitting value of the rotation angle of the left and right wheels, and Fig. 14(b) is the fitting image of the left and right wheel speed.

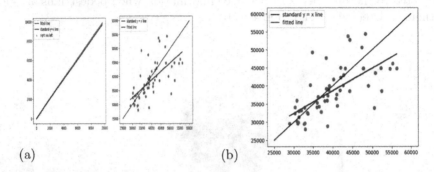

(a)   (b)

Fig. 14. Wheel Rotation Angle and Wheel Velocity Fitting Diagrams

The picture on the right is a point diagram of the rotation speed of the left and right wheels measured by the tachometer. The horizontal axis represents the rotation speed of the left wheel, and the vertical axis represents the rotation speed of the right wheel. The unit is r/10 min. The red dot represents the rotation speed of the left and right wheels when the set speed is the same. The point where the wheel speed error ratio exceeds (the point with a large error), the black line represents the theoretical curve (the left wheel speed is equal to the right wheel speed: y = x), the dark blue represents the fitted curve, and its equation is viewed as y = x − 5000, it can be found that the left and right wheel speeds returned by the speedometer are unreliable and have errors.

3.3 Infrared Tracking Module

This module enables students to master the ability to use infrared sensors and apply infrared tracking. The main idea of the infrared tracking program of this module is shown in Fig. 15.

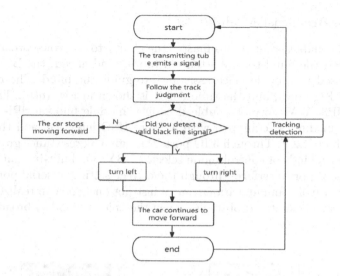

Fig. 15. Flowchart of the tracking program

Students need to understand that the infrared sensor equipped with the car system is a digital sensor, and the output state is 0, 1, that is, the high level and low level in the digital circuit, the sensor has four pins, namely VCC (positive power supply), GND (negative power supply), OUT (output signal) and LED (infrared emitter control pin). The sensor does not detect the black line, the sensor status is light, and the level output is 0, the sensor detects the black line, the sensor status is light off, the level output is: 1, infrared sensor detection reflection distance is 1 mm–25 mm applicable, and not easy to be interfered by external signals, when the infrared ray irradiates the measured object, and receives the reflected light, the optical signal is converted into electrical signal, and finally OUT foot output low level to the Raspberry PI, and the Raspberry PI receives the infrared tracking command through code communication, We will use the tracking function in Infrared class. The specific analysis is as follows: The host instruction is parsed in the Communication-decode function. When infrared tracking instruction is identified, the value of the function mode loop flag bit CRUISING-FLAG is changed, and the value of the function mode loop flag bit is compared to enter a different function mode.

After changing the value of the loop flag bit, it is checked in the main loop to enter different functional modes; The communication function in the Socket class, Bluetooth communication and network cable, WiFi communication, etc., is started by thread, and the communication will call the instruction parsing function, that is, the communication instruction parsing function and the main loop function and the PS2 control function are running at the same time, at this time, the program will call the infrared tracking function, and initialize the infrared sensor. Enable the infrared tracking function.

3.4 Voice Broadcast Module

This module enables students to master the ability to use voice broadcasting.

To remind the blind to pay attention to the road ahead, the BY8301 voice module is used to provide voice assistance to guide the blind. The real object is shown in Fig. 16(a), and the tube Angle is shown in Fig. 16(b). The module supports MP3, WAV format double decoding, module built-in SPI-FLASH as the storage medium is equipped with a Micro USB interface, and the working voltage is about 4.2 V. Through 3 IO ports through 3.3k resistance ground or not connected to 8 kinds of control mode selection, BY8301 built-in standard asynchronous serial port interface, through the correct setting of serial port parameters and the use of communication control instructions, you can realize when the navigation car encountered obstacles when the voice reminder, broadcast voice can also be synthesized.

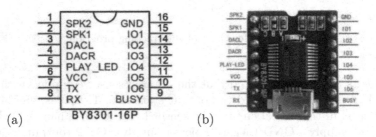

(a)   (b)

Fig. 16. Schematic diagram of module pins and Physical diagram of the module

4 Simulation Test

The students simulated a blind person moving indoors. The movement methods included straight driving and turning on the horizontal plane. The navigation vehicle navigated in front of the experimenter. The test was conducted through passive traction. The navigation vehicle was intercepted from 2 s, 6 s, and 6 s during the infrared tracking process. The operation situation at 10 s is shown in Fig. 17. It also simulates the situation of encountering pedestrians blocking the road during navigation. At this time, the voice module will broadcast to remind the tester of the road conditions ahead and the direction of the car's upcoming movement, and then the car turns.

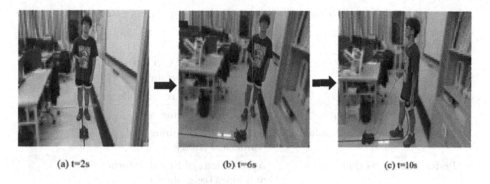

(a) t=2s   (b) t=6s   (c) t=10s

Fig. 17. Guided test

Test results: The navigation vehicle did not deviate from the track during indoor tracking. After multiple tests, the route recognition rate reached 97%. The performance of the infrared sensor was good; the visual obstacle avoidance distance from the vehicle body was 1 m–2.5 m and the camera elevation angle was 15°–75°. When a single pedestrian is detected in the vehicle, the detection is correct, and the navigation vehicle will perform normal obstacle avoidance and voice broadcast operations. Under the same circumstances, when multiple pedestrians are detected, the navigation vehicle can still operate normally for obstacle avoidance and voice broadcast operations. However, there were errors in the detected number of pedestrians, and the number of errors was small. Through the construction of the above four modules, the students realized the visual pedestrian detection, line patrol navigation, and voice reminder functions of the navigation vehicle, and completed the functional realization of the project. This not only applied the professional knowledge of communication and electronic engineering in practice but was also supplemented by the call of artificial intelligence tools to complete the objectives and requirements of the project.

5   Related Knowledge Points and Technical Points

The practical implementation of an AI-assisted intelligent blind navigation vehicle, with the aid of artificial intelligence tools, is carried out through a project-based learning approach. Taking the field of communication engineering as an exemplar, this approach presents a tangible manifestation of the relevant knowledge derived from specialized courses [5]. The corresponding relationship between the technical points and the involved professional courses is illustrated in Table 1. As evident from the aforementioned table, the required professional courses for this project span over multiple semesters. Therefore, this project can be promoted as an in-class specialized teaching program, serving as a coursework and graduation project topic for students.

Table 1. Relevant technologies and corresponding courses.

Technique	Course	Semester
Circuit Design	Fundamentals of Circuits and Electronics Laboratory	3
Infrared Sensors	Principles of Microcontrollers	3
Raspberry Pi Development	Embedded Systems	4
Line Following CodeDevelopment	Python Programming and Numerical Analysis	5
Pedestrian Detection	Applications of Smart Internet of ThingsTechnologies	6

6   Preliminary Results and Prospects for Promotion

Based on their practical experience in this project, students have actively pursued technological innovation initiatives. Some have successfully sought and obtained support for their project outcomes through the "2023 National Undergraduate Innovation and Entrepreneurship Training Program." Additionally, participating students have showcased their projects in various competitions, including physics competitions and the Internet+. Notably, one student attained a Class A provincial third prize in a physics competition.

After proposing the use of simple AI tools to assist in the implementation of project-based learning in the field of electronic information, we conducted a questionnaire survey [7] among a total of 29 students, including students from the 2018 to 2022 cohorts of the electronic information major and international students majoring in electronic information. Among the surveyed students, 34.49% had limited knowledge of AI, and 24.14% were unclear about it, as shown in Fig. 18(a). Only 28% of the students were aware that their major offered courses in AI, as shown in Fig. 18(b). Figure 18(a) shows an Understanding of AI in Statistical Graphs and Fig. 18(b) is the Percentage Distribution of AI Courses Offered.

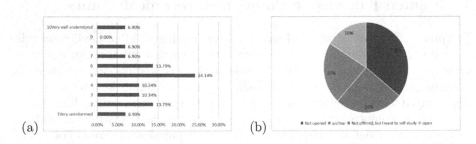

(a)   (b)

Fig. 18. Statistical Chart of Percentages of AI Understanding and Course Offerings

However, after gaining a basic understanding of the integration of AI into different disciplines, 86.2% of the students expressed a willingness to engage in self-study, as shown in Fig. 19(a). Among these self-study enthusiasts, 79.3% felt that the difficulty of learning the content of two different majors within four years was substantial, as shown in Fig. 19(b). Figure 19(a) Statistical Graphs Depicting Students' Self-Learning Willingness and Fig. 19(b) is Statistical Graphs Depicting the Intention to Pursue Dual Majors Simultaneously.

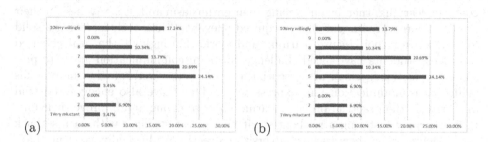

Fig. 19. Statistics on students' willingness to self-study and dual major intention

However, after learning about the practical project of an intelligent blind navigation vehicle built with the assistance of AI tools, 86.2% of the students expressed confidence in engaging in simple applications of AI, as shown in Fig. 20(a). If the school were to offer professional knowledge teaching using this project, 89.65% of the students would be interested in taking such a course and would be willing to utilize this project for extracurricular practical activities or even as part of their graduation design, as shown in Fig. 20(b). Figure 20(a) Confidence in the Application of AI - Statistical Graph and Fig. 20(b) is Student Interest in Project-based Courses - Statistical Graph.

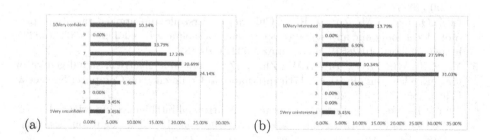

Fig. 20. AI application confidence and student interest in project courses statistics

Based on the feedback from the questionnaire survey, it was found that project-based learning in the field of electronic information, assisted by AI, has received positive affirmation and strong support from students majoring in electronic information. This finding holds significant implications for its promotion and implementation.

7   Conclusion

Through project-based practices in education assisted by artificial intelligence, students have been able to integrate theory with practical applications [8], gaining a deeper understanding of their field of study. They have experienced the joy of applying their knowledge, which has sparked their interest and motivation to continue learning, thereby enhancing their enthusiasm and proactiveness in their studies. Moreover, students have acquired relevant technical skills, laying a solid foundation for their future learning and work. Throughout the project-based practices, students have faced challenges in team communication and interpersonal interactions, which are essential for cultivating well-rounded individuals skilled in communication and expression [4]. They have also encountered trial and error in the practical process, learning how to debug and improve their mistakes, thereby fostering a resilient spirit that grows stronger with each setback and teaching them how to face adversity correctly. Additionally, students have integrated knowledge and skills from multiple disciplines in their practical applications, fostering their interdisciplinary thinking and developing their overall abilities [8], ultimately nurturing their innovative capabilities.

References

1. Wang, J.P.: Research on interdisciplinary integration model based on educational artificial intelligence support. China Educ. Technol. Equip. (17), 10–11+16 (2021)
2. Ge, D.Y., Wei, J.J.: Research on the development of online teaching capabilities of university teachers in the era of artificial intelligence. Res. Continuing Educ. (11), 23–27 (2023)
3. Ren, L.J.: Research on the integration strategy of artificial intelligence and discipline based on project-based teaching. Primary Secondary Sch. Audio-Visu. Educ. (04), 88–90 (2023)
4. Li, Z.Q., Chi, Z.M., Zhang, R.N.: Cultivating versatile and applied talents to promote local economic and social development. Democracy Legal Times (005) (2022). https://doi.org/10.28579/n.cnki.nmzfz.2022.001448
5. Ye, Z.R., Wu, M.W., Tao, H.W., Zhang, Z.: A portable electrical signal generator for active learning. In: IEEE 17th International Conference on Computer Science & Education (ICCSE) (2022)
6. Chu, J.L., Xie, Z.X.: Design and practice of artificial intelligence experiential learning activities for cultivating literacy: a case study on "Facial Recognition" teaching. J. Digit. Educ. Primary Secondary Sch. 10, 35–39 (2023)
7. Jiang, M.L., Zhu, J.L., Chen, J., Wu, M.W., Wu, J.Q.: Research on experimental teaching of communication principles based on visible light communication. In: IEEE 16th International Conference on Computer Science & Education (ICCSE), Lancaster, pp. 1019–1023. IEEE (2021)
8. Liang, Y.W., Wu, M.W., Pan, Z.S., Cen, G.: Information and communication technology-enabled active learning in a college physics experiment. In: IEEE 16th International Conference on Computer Science & Education (ICCSE), Lancaster, pp. 1014–1018. IEEE (2021)

Online Learning and MOOCs

Evaluation of Students' Performance with Facial Capture Avatars in Online English Instruction

Yu Qiu[1,2,3], Gang Wang[1,2,3(✉)], and Qianxi Zhang[1,2,3]

[1] School of Computing and Data Engineering, Ningbo Tech University, Ningbo, China
smile588@sina.com, qianxi.zhang@nottingham.edu.cn
[2] School of Design, University of Nottingham, Nottingham, UK
[3] Department of Architecture and Engineering, University of Nottingham, Ningbo, People's Republic of China

Abstract. This article evaluates the possibility of deploying virtual avatars on personal devices in online English instruction, as well as the impact on student-teacher interaction and tacit truancy issues. Based on the correlation analysis and linear regression analysis of the data acquired from the distributed questionnaires, it is possible to conclude that there may be no statistical association between avatars and student-teacher interaction. However, avatars have a positive effect on reducing truancy. Therefore, we consider that the utilization of virtual avatars in computer-assisted language learning provides an innovative and promising method for online instruction.

Keywords: facial capture · virtual avatars · student-teacher interaction · tacit truancy

1 Introduction

In the context of the unpredictable expansion and development of the COVID-19 pandemic, online education has emerged as one of the most popular and indispensable means for accessing educational resources. There are primarily two methods for delivering distance education: synchronously and asynchronously [1]. With the aid of educational resources, such as books and pre-recorded videos, asynchronous learning is student-driven. The majority of MOOCs, such as Chinese University MOOCs and Coursera, have embraced this methodology. Globally, the most commonly used form of distance learning is the synchronous approach, which entails switching the teaching setting to an online classroom and is relatively similar to the traditional offline learning environment.

In College English, language skills are developed through interaction with teachers, other students, and learning resources [2]. In conventional face-to-face instruction, teacher-student interaction can be incorporated into knowledge points, courseware, and quizzes, all of which can be accomplished effectively via eye contact, verbal, or even physical activities [3]. But when the social distancing restrictions were encountered unexpectedly, teachers began adopting platforms such as Zoom, DingTalk, and Tencent Meetings to communicate in real-time with students as part of virtual deliveries.

Although nearly every video conferencing platform has classroom simulation and interaction functions as part of personal response systems, such as check-in, questioning, in-class tests, and even questionnaires, the teacher cannot identify whether students are sleepy, sleeping, or leaving midway through the session [4, 5]. That is to say, in a synchronous approach to online teaching, if the teacher expects students to turn on the camera to assess student performance and ensure quality instruction, but the students strongly refuse the request, there is little the teacher can do in front of the screen. Under such circumstances, it is also usual to encounter situations in which the instructor opens the floor for questions but no student responds, contributing to the unpleasantness of uncomfortable silence, and the tactics employed by the teacher in response to such situations are frequently ineffectual [1]. This circumstance frequently results in distractions and even tacit truancy (a form of mental absenteeism in which students participate negatively in classroom instruction) [6].

Pavlov et al. [2] investigated the impact of webcam on collaboration in online second language instruction. According to the responses of the students to the question "How do EFL students perceive the use of the camera?" About 70% of the students would turn on the camera when asked to do so by the teacher but would turn it off otherwise. Just 19% of the students stated they often turn on the camera. When asked why they turn cameras off, students talk about their study environment: "I need to leave the study place" (64%), "I do not want others to see me" (60%), "I am not alone in the room" (45%). Importantly, 35% of students say that when their cameras are turned off, they can concentrate better and get distracted less. This response might be connected with the feeling that the study environment factors do not influence them when their cameras are off. As they feel shy, 50% of students prefer to turn cameras off, and 47% of respondents say they feel uncomfortable when they are being watched by many others. Low English proficiency is a reason to turn off cameras for only 8% of students. It is evident from the data that, for both objective and subjective reasons, students' webcams are switched off the majority of the time in online teaching environments, making it hard for teachers to communicate with students via the camera.

Peterson's research [7] indicates that "of the many network technologies now being utilized in computer-assisted language learning (hereinafter referred to as 'CALL'), immersive virtual environments appear to hold great potential as learning tools." and "the application of virtual worlds in CALL offers new opportunities to engage learners in the kind of interaction that may facilitate the development of second language competences." Therefore, if we can establish a virtual world in the online classroom in which the students can show their virtual avatars through the webcams, their motivation to turn on the camera may be boosted.

Today, virtual YouTubers (Vtubers) that use computer-generated virtual avatars are gaining popularity throughout the globe. Numerous VTubers have demonstrated their commercial values in the live-streaming market and have amassed a sizable following on a range of social platforms, e.g., YouTube, Niconico, and Bilibili [8]. To capture movement, real-time motion capture software or technology is frequently (though not always) employed. Students can utilize Vtuber's implementation technology to conceal their true faces while displaying their dynamic avatars in the virtual world through the camera. The vast majority of laptops and desktops are equipped with RGB-D cameras, which can be deployed to track facial movement in real-time without complicated preprocessing and modeling [9]. In addition, iPhones equipped with Face-ID and the Huawei Mate30 Pro can capture facial motions using a True Depth camera and a ToF 3D camera, achieving a nearly identical result, so that learners can map their facial emotions onto their avatars in the virtual world with low-cost and ubiquitous hardware.

To investigate the following research questions, we distributed a questionnaire through the Questionnaire Star platform to examine online English learning among college students.

1. Can the utilization of a real-time virtual avatar enhance teacher-student interaction?
2. Can the usage of virtual avatars in real time alleviate the problem of tacit truancy?

2 Research Methodology

2.1 Participants

The questionnaire was distributed via the Questionnaire Star platform, in the form of a QR code and URL link for direct access without verification, and placed in the class social software groups of the School of Data and some school-level student organization social groups as well as some influential private WeChat platform accounts of NingboTech University. Therefore, all the participants were undergraduate students of NingboTech University. The questionnaire was available from 10 to 12 May.

2.2 Questionnaire

The questionnaire was administered in Chinese. In the questionnaire, the participants were asked 10 questions. Questions 1 and 2 were constructed as single-answer, multiple-choice questions with an "other" answer option or comment area to determine the type of English course the participants were enrolled in as their major and during the online teaching time. Question 4 was a multiple-choice question that addressed why students were reluctant to turn on the camera. The other seven questions assessed students' opinions toward the usage of cameras and virtual avatars in the virtual classroom using a 5-point Likert scale, with responses ranging from "strongly disapprove" (one point) to "strongly agree" (five points). Particularly, in question 7, participants were asked if they would be willing to turn on the camera if only a virtual avatar was shown, and we provided a brief explanation of how virtual avatars (2D/3D models that capture facial movements through the camera and map them to the virtual world in real-time through facial motion capture software, without displaying realistic faces and scenes) are driven for those with limited knowledge of it.

3 Results

3.1 Basic Data

In our survey, a total of 63 responses were received. One response was disqualified since the respondent indicated on the questionnaire that he did not attend English courses. Therefore, 62 undergraduate students in NBT from 8 of the 10 second-level colleges, excluding the School of Design and the School of Material Science and Engineering, participated in this study. During the time from April 12, 2022, to April 24, 2022, they all attended online English-related college courses.

The reliability coefficient of the scale questions is 0.637, and the quality of the study data reliability is acceptable.

3.2 Perception of Some Reasons for Closing the Camera

For the question " What do you suppose are the reasons for students' unwillingness to turn on the camera", Table 1 illustrates student replies.

In the "Other" option, one participant stated that it was unnecessary to enable the camera.

As shown in Table 1, the goodness-of-fit test was significant (chi = 43.065, p < 0.001), indicating that there is a substantial variation in the proportion of selected items. Specifically, the response rates and prevalence rates for two items, "Need to leave" and "Inconvenient to turn on the camera in public areas", were significantly higher.

Table 1. Response and Popularity Rate

Categories	Response		Popularity Rate ($n = 62$)
	n	*Response rate*	
Need to leave	22	28.57%	35.48%
Inconvenient to turn on the camera in public	34	44.16%	54.84%
Better focus when the camera is turned off	12	15.58%	19.35%
No camera or damaged camera	8	10.39%	12.90%
Other:	1	1.30%	1.61%
Total	77	100%	124.19%
Goodness of fit: $\chi^2 = 43.065\ p = 0.000$			

3.3 Correlation Analysis of Virtual Avatar and Interaction

As shown in Fig. 1 (the horizontal coordinate corresponds to the relevant score on a five-level scale, while the vertical coordinate represents the frequency), the data deviate significantly from normality, and the contours of the columns exhibit imperfect bell-shaped characteristics. Given the short sample size, such typical characteristics are generally accepted. The data in Fig. 2 fulfill normality, and the distribution of several columns can be represented by a bell-shaped normal curve. Therefore, it is reasonable to infer that the data conform to the normal distribution.

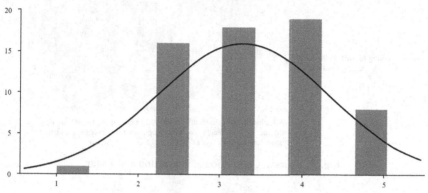

Fig. 1. Histogram of the question about interaction

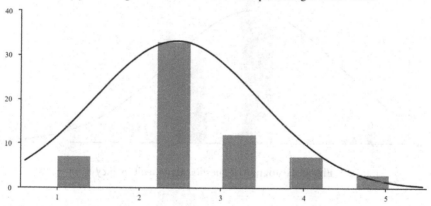

Fig. 2. Histogram of the question about presenting avatar

According to Fig. 3, the correlation coefficient value between closing the camera and displaying a virtual avatar is 0.21, which is near to 0. Save for that, the p-value is $0.103 > 0.05$, showing that there is no correlation between the two variables.

3.4 Regression Analysis of Avatars and Tacit Truancy

Figure 4 demonstrates that the data conform to a normal distribution.

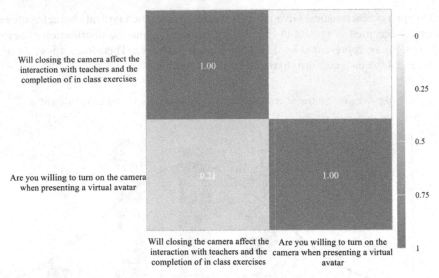

Fig. 3. Pearson Correlation of interaction and avatar

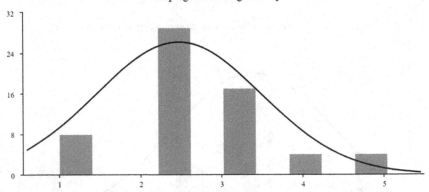

Fig. 4. Histogram of question about tacit truancy

According to Fig. 5, the correlation coefficient between using avatars and tacit truancy is 0.34, and the computed p-value is $0.008 < 0.05$, indicating that they have a significant positive correlation.

From Table 2, it can be seen that the model equation is: restricting tacit truancy = $1.632 + 0.341$*presenting avatar, and the model R-squared value is 0.112, indicating that presenting avatar can explain 11.2% of the cause of change in restricting tacit truancy. The model passed the F-test (F = 7.588, p = $0.008 < 0.05$), which means that presenting avatars must have an influential relationship with the restricting tacit truancy, and the final specific analysis shows that the regression coefficient value of is 0.341 (t = 2.755, p = $0.008 < 0.01$), meaning that the avatar will have a significant positive

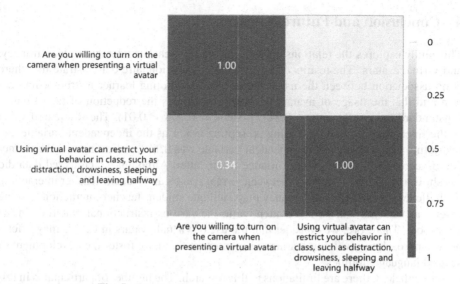

Fig. 5. Pearson Correlation of avatar and tacit truancy

influence relationship on restricting tacit truancy. In conclusion, it can be demonstrated that presenting avatars will have a significant positive effect on restricting tacit truancy in online English instruction.

Table 2. Parameter Estimates (Summary)

	Coefficients	95% CI	VIF
Constant	1.632** (4.989)	0.991 ~ 2.274	–
present avatar	0.341** (2.755)	0.098 ~ 0.583	1.000
n	62		
R^2	0.112		
Adj. R^2	0.097		
F Value	$F(1,60) = 7.588, p = 0.008$		
Dependent Variable: restrict tacit truancy			
D-W: 1.916			
$* p < 0.05 ** p < 0.01$ t statistics in parentheses			

4 Conclusion and Future Research

This study explores the relationship between student-teacher interaction, tacit truancy, and virtual avatars. The results of the distributed questionnaire demonstrate that there is no association between the use of avatars and promoting learner-instructor interaction and that the usage of avatars positively influences the reduction of tacit truancy (unstandardized coefficients = 0.341, p-value = 0.008 < 0.01). The R-squared value of the linear regression model using presenting avatar as the independent variable and restricting tacit truancy as the dependent variable was 0.112, indicating that the former could account for 11.2% of the variance in the latter. Although the collected data did not show a statistical correlation between virtual avatars and student-teacher interaction, we believe that reducing tacit truancy may facilitate student-teacher interaction to some extent, as students will be more attentive to the various instructional materials in the classroom. Therefore, we consider that the use of virtual avatars in CALL may offer a novel approach to involving learners in interaction that may foster the development of second language abilities.

Nonetheless, there are limitations to this research. The number of participants in this study was limited, the sample size was too small, and the sample was unbalanced since no data were obtained from two of the ten schools, while the School of Computer and Data Engineering and the School of Business had significantly more participants. In addition, due to timing constraints, the online questionnaire was only available for three days. Given these constraints, a longitudinal study may be a viable way to investigate avatars and interaction as well as tacit truancy in further exploration. Except for that, although we established the viability of utilizing personal devices such as laptops and smartphones for facial motion capture in the introduction section, more work is intended. At present, few video conferencing platforms natively support the use of webcams to build real-time avatars. The current solution is to use separate specialized software for motion capture and then send the created avatar to platforms as a data stream, which platforms presume is received from the camera but is a software simulation of a virtual camera. Such a procedure is too cumbersome and complex to be acceptable to the general population. In future research, we believe it is vital to enhance the research methodology and simplify the use of virtual avatars. Furthermore, we also consider whether the features of the avatars would influence student-teacher interaction, like the tendency of students with more attractive models to express themselves in the virtual world via, for example, asking and responding to questions. Additionally, our study was conducted in a synchronous context; in the future, it may be conceivable to evaluate student performance in an asynchronous context [10]. The overall objective is to maximize the possibilities of avatars in CALL for remote education.

Acknowledgment. This paper is supported by Zhejiang Provincial Natural Science Foundation of China (LQ20F020006), Zhejiang Provincial Philosophy and Social Science Planning Project (22NDQN291YB), Research and Creation Project of Zhejiang Provincial Department of Culture and Tourism (2020KZY003), in part by Ningbo Natural Science Foundation under Grant 2023J280, in part by Ningbo Key R&D Program (No. 2023Z231).

References

1. Prattico, F.G., Shabkhoslati, J.A., Shaghaghi, N., Lamberti, F.: Bot undercover: on the use of conversational agents to stimulate teacher-students interaction in remote learning. In: 2022 IEEE Conference on Virtual Reality and 3D User Interfaces Abstracts and Workshops (VRW), Christchurch, New Zealand, pp. 277–282, March 2022
2. Pavlov, V., Smirnova, N., Nuzhnaia, E.: Beyond the avatar: using video cameras to achieve effective collaboration in an online second language classroom. J. Univ. Teach. Learn. Pract. **18**(7), 228–243 (2021)
3. Ma, C.: Analysis of problems and strategies of online teaching in universities and colleges during the period of epidemic prevention and control. China Modern Educ. Equip. **7**, 14–16 (2020)
4. Wang, H., Li, Z., Luo, X.: Study on the learners' performance evaluation in online teaching with personal response systems. In: 2021 16th International Conference on Computer Science & Education (ICCSE), Lancaster, United Kingdom, pp. 3–7, August 2021
5. Han, Y., Wang, X.B., Guo, Y.H.: Study on monitoring system of learning situation in online teaching based on deep learning. Henan Sci. Technol. **40**(3), 19–21 (2021)
6. Guo, Y.F.: Beyond the deviant behavior: a sociological analysis of college students' tacit truancy. J. Bingtuan Educ. Inst. **30**(3), 54–60 (2020)
7. Peterson, M.: Learning interaction in an avatar-based virtual environment: a preliminary study. PacCALL J. **1**(1), 12 (2005)
8. Xu, S.: The research on applying artificial intelligence technology to virtual YouTuber. In: 2021 IEEE International Conference on Robotics, Automation and Artificial Intelligence (RAAI), pp. 10–14, April 2021
9. Ren, H., Zhang, X.: Efficient facial reconstruction and real-time expression for VR interaction using RGB-D videos. In: Cai, Y., van Joolingen, W., Veermans, K. (eds.) Virtual and Augmented Reality, Simulation and Serious Games for Education. GMSE, pp. 177–188. Springer, Singapore (2021). https://doi.org/10.1007/978-981-16-1361-6_14
10. Yu, H., Hu, J.: A multilevel regression analysis of computer-mediated communication in synchronous and asynchronous contexts and digital reading achievement in Japanese students. Interact. Learn. Environ., 1–15 (2022)
11. The SPSSAU project: SPSSAU (Version 22.0). [Online Application Software] (2022). https://www.spssau.com

An Education-Oriented Collaborative Code Hosting Platform for Programming Courses

Yao Liu, Tianran Liu, Chaopeng Yi, Yuepeng Xu, Ming Gao, Wei Wang[⊠], and Aoying Zhou

School of Data Science and Engineering, East China Normal University, Shanghai, China
liuyao@cc.ecnu.edu.cn, {51215903077,51265903044, 51265903002}@stu.ecnu.edu.cn, {mgao,wwang, ayzhou}@dase.ecnu.edu.cn

Abstract. Online practicing platforms and open-source communities have enriched teachers and students with abundant teaching resources and convenient practicing environments. However, the designs of these platforms cannot fully meet the demands of educational scenarios, particularly in programming courses. To address challenges such as code collaboration, homework management, and configuration of practicing environment, this paper introduces an intelligent code hosting and project collaboration platform known as ShuiShan Code Park, which explores a new educational model based on collaboration. Specifically, it introduces team collaboration into teaching, and centers education around repositories. Furthermore, ShuiShan Code Park enhances the educational experience in multiple dimensions including the code similarity comparison, point-based ranking, enhanced Markdown, and Tianhe containers-based practicing. Detailed cases of ShuiShan Code Park's applications effectively demonstrate its optimization of educational scenarios. Feedback from students highlights the practical value of Shuishan Code Park.

Keywords: Programming Courses · Code Hosting · Project Collaboration · Online Practicing

1 Introduction

In the present era, the field of education is undergoing a rapid evolution driven by advancements in computer and data science [1, 2]. Despite the abundant resources and practical opportunities that online practicing platforms and open-source code management communities have provided for education, existing educational tools still face particular challenges in meeting the specific needs of programming courses [3, 4]. These challenges include the inability to effectively compare students' code similarity and cultivate students' collaborative spirit.

To establish a teaching platform that supports students to collaborate on projects, we have deeply customized the open-source project Gitea [5] to construct a versatile, shareable, and accessible educational platform called Shuishan Code Park. The central objective of this paper is to introduce the intelligent code hosting and project collaboration platform, Shuishan Code Park, as a critical sub-platform within the new generation, fully integrated online learning platform known as Shuishan Online. This platform is designed for intelligent code hosting and creative collaboration tailored for educational purposes [6]. We will deeply explore the overall structure and main features of Shuishan Code Park, as well as its practical application in the field of education. From the current background of computer science online education, our research has made the following contributions.

(1) Collaboration-based education platform design: Propose an online course teaching scheme based on Shuishan Code Park.
(2) Implementation and optimization for education scenarios: Address specific optimizations and implementations aimed at solving real-world educational challenges.
(3) Application cases: Present practical application cases of Shuishan Code Park and demonstrate its practical value in the educational scene.

2 Requirement Analysis

With the rapid advancement of information technology, there is a growing demand for personalized education, leading to the emergence of numerous online educational platforms. Existing online open course learning platforms such as Chinese University MOOC provide teachers and students with a consistent digital learning medium that supports comprehensive learning and self-assessment [7, 8]. Online practice platforms represented by Alibaba Cloud use cloud technology to promote online collaboration in computer education. It extends the concept and method of massive online practice by providing a convenient online operational environment and abundant practical resources [9–11]. Open-source communities like GitHub Classroom and Gitee for universities not only serve as major centers for technical exchanges but also offer code management and collaboration solutions for the educational scene.

The above platforms help teachers carry out computer teaching work more conveniently from all aspects, which is crucial to the ecological construction of computer educational practice. However, facing complex and dynamic educational demands, there is still room for improvement regarding close collaboration between teachers and students, the process of homework transfer, experimental environment configuration, and effective support for different educational scenarios [12, 13]. Drawing from the strengths of related education platforms and accumulated practical experience in computer teaching, Shuishan Code Park has identified four core requirements for online computer teaching platforms: cloud storage for students' codes; cultivation of students' team collaboration skills; efficient interaction between teachers and students; and a platform for student to practice.

3 Collaboration-Based Education Platform Design

Cloud storage plays a crucial role in computer education [14, 15]. Migrating students' homework codes to the cloud not only avoids code loss but also makes the presentation of students' outstanding work more convenient. Additionally, teachers can perform assessment analysis and provide guidance based on students' behavioral data stored in the cloud. Developing collaborative skills is a key focus in computer education, as teams harness the collective intelligence of individuals, thereby enhancing the quality and impact of projects. However, traditional storage methods like cloud drives often lead to issues such as file conflicts and version management during the collaboration process. Introducing code management tools can effectively solve these problems. Combining the cultivation of students' teamwork awareness and skills by employing code management tools can better promote teamwork and enhance students' overall capabilities.

3.1 The Overall Architecture Design of Shuishan Code Park

The code hosting process has many similarities to education [16]. For example, the "Organization" feature of the open-source code management project Gitea proves highly practical for managing team members, allocating permissions, and overseeing and governing multiple repositories. These functionalities have significant similarities with management in educational scenes.

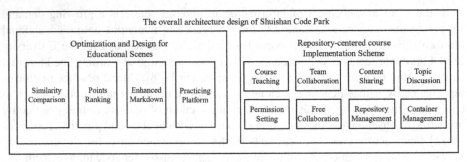

Fig. 1. The overall architecture design of Shuishan Code Park

Therefore, based on Gitea, we combined platform characteristics and educational ideas to deeply customize an intelligent code hosting and project collaboration platform for educational scenarios——Shuishan Code Park. Its overall architecture design is depicted in Fig. 1.

3.2 Repository-Centered Course Implementation Scheme

To solve the problems of long cycles, cumbersome processes, and confusion of homework in the process of collecting programming course homework. As is depicted in Fig. 2, Shuishan Code Park designs course teaching and implements various behavioral patterns in the educational scene with the repository as the central medium.

In the educational scenario, teachers post homework requirements in the topic section of the student-readable repository and upload relevant materials to this repository, through which students can quickly check the homework requirements. Teachers can manage students' access rights to the code repository based on different homework

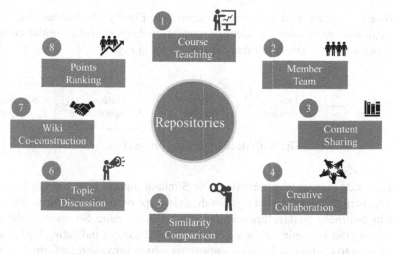

Fig. 2. Repository-centered course teaching design

types. If individual homework is posted, students can only manage their code repositories, and students cannot read other students' repositories. If the homework is assigned to a team, the teacher can divide the students into multiple teams. Members of each team can read and write the team's repository together, but cannot access the repositories of other teams. Through this approach, independence between teams is guaranteed, as well as smooth collaboration and communication within the team.

4   Implementation and Optimization for Education Scenarios

In the educational scene, catering to the personalized needs of both teachers and students is of great importance. To achieve real-time code evaluation and feedback, cultivate students' learning motivation and enthusiasm, and simplify teacher-student communication, interaction, and cooperation, Shuishan Code Park has been optimized in multiple aspects, such as learning analysis in Sects. 4.1 & 4.2 and learning experience in Sects. 4.3 & 4.4, according to the teaching practice.

4.1   Code Similarity Comparison Module

In the context of programming courses, a significant number of students work on the same homework, which may lead to code similarity issues. Therefore, a code similarity comparison module has been introduced to detect such anomalies [17, 18]. This module employs different comparison logic based on the homework type: open-ended homework is checked for similarity among students, while standard homework is evaluated for consistency with the provided solutions, thereby enhancing assessment accuracy.

When teachers launch a similarity detection for a specific homework, the code similarity comparison module traverses every student's codes in the repositories of the course. Subsequently, redundant content like comments are removed based on code type to improve the accuracy of similarity comparisons. Finally, the Simhash algorithm is used to calculate similarity and identify students with excessively similar codes. The whole process of code similarity detection is shown in Fig. 3.

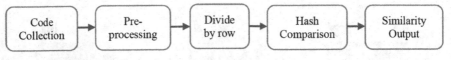

Fig. 3. Code similarity comparison process

During code similarity comparison, the Simhash algorithm is used to map textual data to fixed-length binary encodings. Simhash is a type of locality-sensitive hashing that reduces high-dimensional feature vectors to a single hash value. Similarity is determined by calculating the Hamming distance, with smaller distances indicating higher similarity. Compared to traditional hashing algorithms, which provide no information beyond inequality of original content, the hash signatures generated by Simhash can represent the similarity of the original content partially, making it more suitable for comparing the similarity.

4.2 Points Ranking Module

The Points ranking module aims to quantify students' learning processes through their various interactions in Shuishan Code Park, motivating them with points and fostering a sense of competition. Students' course points are calculated based on comprehensive classroom behavior data such as the number of submissions, questions, and answers. Teachers have the flexibility to customize points allocation strategies based on their educational needs and assign different weights to various metrics. To ensure that students' learning interests are not adversely affected, educational psychology factors are considered, and behavioral data is normalized, with adjustments made to the minimum points threshold. Specifically, each student's performance data is compared with the class average data, and the result is mapped to the range between the minimum score and full marks. The formula for calculating a student's score is as follows:

$$score = \sum \left(\frac{behavior_i}{maxbehavior_i - minbehavior_i} \times weight_i \right) \times = 1(100 - threshold) + threshold \quad (1)$$

4.3 Enhanced Markdown

To enhance communication and collaboration between teachers and students, the platform has undergone optimizations for everyday teaching. Markdown support in educational scenarios has certain limitations, prompting enhancements for it. For instance, educational scenarios often involve complex mathematical equations and different text styles to emphasize key content, teachers and students need more diverse presentation methods to help students understand and remember. Shuishan Code Park has strengthened Markdown support, allowing the use of LaTeX syntax for mathematical equations and HTML syntax for modifying font, color, background, and more. This enables teachers and students to rapidly compose and present formulas, documents, and other contents, facilitating better clarification and communication. Here are some examples of Markdown enhancement in Table 1.

Table 1. Examples of Markdown enhancement

Code	Effect
<font color = "#FF0000">Text</font>	font color
<font face = "Arial">Text</font>	font type
<table><tr><td bgcolor = #008080>Text</td></tr ></table>	back color
$$ \sum_{i = 0}^N\ $$	sum
$$ \frac{a}{b}\ $$	fraction

4.4 Online Practicing Module Based on Tianhe Containers

To simplify students' code-based practice, the platform has integrated with Tianhe containers, the national high-performance computing environment based on Tianhe supercomputer, to address environment configuration and monitoring issues [19, 20]. This environment not only deploys the necessary programming software to meet students' requirements but also provides teachers with container management functionality to better monitor students' progress in online practice. Accordingly, the module supports two roles: teachers and students, with its architecture depicted in Fig. 4.

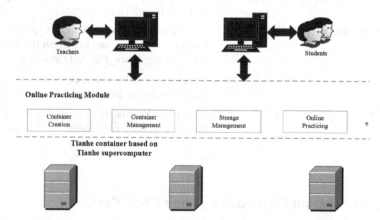

Fig. 4. Architecture of the online practicing module based on Tianhe containers

Through the online practicing module, students can create and manage their containers. During online practice, they can effortlessly write and run their codes without the need for environment configuration. Saved codes are not lost even when the containers are deleted; instead, they are stored on Tianhe server, allowing students to continue editing them in subsequent container creations.

In addition to having all the functions of students, teachers also have functions such as multiple container creation, container management, and storage management. Teachers can view the container status of all students on the container management interface, take appropriate measures in response to exceptional cases, and concurrently monitor the practicing progress of individual users on Tianhe platform.

To realize the online practicing functionality, a set of interfaces interacting with the Starlight system (Tianhe supercomputer's container management system) has been developed within Shuishan Code Park, as illustrated in Table 2. Through these interfaces, users can log into the Starlight system and perform operations such as creating and managing containers.

Table 2. Interfaces for online practicing functionality

Interface function	Request method	Purpose
GetLongTermToken	POST	Obtain a long-term token through this interface to gain access to login to Tianhe supercomputer
CreateJobJupyter	POST	Request the creation of a Jupyter container on Tianhe supercomputer and receive information such as JobId, Name, Work_Dir, CreatedAt, and a URL to access the container
GetRunningJobs	GET	Retrieve the usage details of all containers, including information like JobId, Name, Work_Dir, and CreatedAt
DeleteRunningJobById	DELETE	Delete a specified container corresponding to a given ID through this interface
GetRunningJobDetail	POST	View detailed information about a specific container corresponding to a given ID, including JobId, Name, Work_Dir, and CreatedAt
IsAvailable	POST	Check the availability of a container corresponding to a specific ID via this interface
IsExistDir	GET	Determine the existence of a specified user directory within a container through this interface

5 The Application Cases of Shuishan Code Park

Since the release of the Shuishan Code Park platform in 2019, it has seen the participation of dozens of courses, serving thousands of teachers and students, including over 3,000 repositories, comments, and about 500,000 behaviors. The data reflects a high level of enthusiasm and proactivity among students for self-learning on the platform.

In the following sections, we will delve into the platform's application within the context of the "Fundamentals of Computer Science and Programming Course ". This course is a required public course for non-computer science majors. Through the learning of fundamental programming syntax and algorithm design with basic control structures, it aims to comprehensively enhance students' computer literacy and programming thinking, fostering their ability to utilize tools for practical problem-solving.

5.1 Case 1: The Application of Code Learning Analysis

The first case is related to learning analysis. In programming courses, a practical component is indispensable, which consists of targeted unit homework and comprehensive projects designed to enhance theoretical learning. Unit homework provides real-time feedback to assess teaching effectiveness and develop students' fundamental programming thinking. Comprehensive projects, on the other hand, nurture students' abilities to identify problems and employ computers to solve them. Students are required to complete the entire process, including topic selection, problem description, algorithm design, program implementation, testing, and optimization.

Teachers have a strong demand for real-time assessment and feedback in the context of the above practical work, then the code similarity comparison module came into being. In this module, teachers initiate similarity checks for a particular homework and calculate the degree of similarity among submissions. If the similarity of a student's codes significantly exceeds the class average, the module highlights such instances by marking them in red, as illustrated in the query page depicted in Fig. 5. Additionally, to enhance the precision of similarity calculations, an option to exclude binary files has been implemented, considering that non-text characters may be present in some specific homework. The module also supports both single-file and branch-wide comparisons,

Fig. 5. Code similarity comparison

allowing teachers to provide detailed feedback at a micro-level for individual tasks as well as assess the overall quality of the entire homework at a macro-level.

Figure 6 shows the points ranking for learning behavior in programming courses. This module provides a quantitative standard for teachers to analyze students' course interaction in real time, thereby increasing the persuasiveness of student course evaluation.

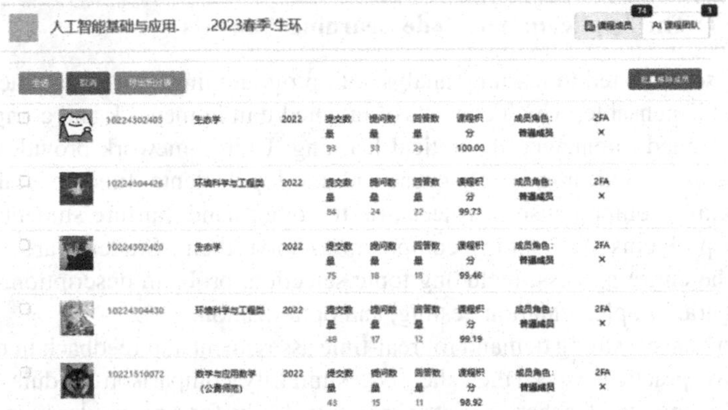

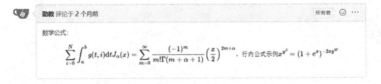

Fig. 6. Points ranking

5.2 Case 2: The Application of Learning Experience

The second case is about learning experience. As shown in Fig. 7, teachers and students can quickly write and display code, formulas, and other content with the enhanced markdown statements mentioned above, so as to improving collaboration and expression efficiency.

数学公式:

$$\sum_{i=0}^{N}\int_a^b g(t,i)dt J_\alpha(x) = \sum_{m=0}^{\infty}\frac{(-1)^m}{m!\Gamma(m+\alpha+1)}\left(\frac{x}{2}\right)^{2m+\alpha},\ \text{行内公式示例} x^{y^2}=(1+e^x)^{-2xy^w}$$

Fig. 7. Markdown enhancement

The online practicing module, developed in conjunction with Shuishan Code Park and Tianhe supercomputer, has established a bridge between the online education cloud platform and high-performance computer, thus expanding the applicability of computer education. Based on the characteristics of programming courses, this module offers features suited for different roles within the educational context.

In the practicing module, students are relieved of configuring their environments manually, as they can now complete coding and execution tasks directly through a web interface. Teachers can prepare code snippets in advance for student's exercises, diversifying the teaching methods in computer courses and reducing students' learning curve.

Within the container, students can engage in online practice using Jupyter Notebook or upload files for practical work. As depicted in Fig. 8, while coding, they can write code directly within code blocks. A notable difference from traditional practice is the support for incremental execution, which enables students to inspect variable states during code execution, facilitating timely identification of issues.

Fig. 8. Online Jupyter Notebook practice

Through the online practicing module, teachers have real-time oversight of the operational status of all containers. They possess the authority to create multiple containers, refresh them, or delete redundant containers to ensure system efficiency and cleanliness. Furthermore, teachers have access to the Starlight system for comprehensive management of all user-stored files.

5.3 Case 3: Questionnaire Feedback

The integration of Shuishan Code Park into programming courses has brought about a more organized course structure. This development enables teachers to interact more effectively with their students during the learning process. Simultaneously, students can hone their coding skills within the platform and collaborate with team members to complete code repositories. In Table 3, we present the results of a survey conducted to assess students' experiences with the use of Shuishan Code Park.

The survey indicates that 90.57% of students express their approval of the user experience with Shuishan Code Park, and 94.34% of students perceive the educational outcomes achieved within Shuishan Code Park as excellent. The feedback from students reflects their great enthusiasm for the Shuishan Code Park educational platform, which offers an excellent user experience and contributes significantly to enhancing the effectiveness of programming courses.

Table 3. Shuishan Code Park questionnaire feedback

Level	Platform experience	Teaching effect
Excellent	35.85%	52.83%
Good	54.72%	41.51%
Fair	9.43%	5.66%
Poor	0.00%	0.00%

6 Conclusion

This article has provided a detailed exploration of Shuishan Code Park, an intelligent code hosting and project collaboration platform for computer education. Shuishan Code Park aligns itself with the configuration of a practicing environment, promoting collaborative online teaching. It harnesses students' enthusiasm, encouraging cooperative coding for creative innovation. The platform collects and analyzes students' learning behaviors, paving the way for educational model enhancements to address teaching challenges.

Shuishan Code Park has undergone real-life testing in selected university computer courses. In the future, Shuishan Code Park will envision an expansion of its services to encompass more computer science courses and disciplines, thereby providing a comprehensive educational experience for students. Furthermore, the platform aims to integrate personalized education based on the analysis of learning behaviors. By leveraging big data and more AI algorithms, Shuishan Code Park will be able to provide customized learning pathways and resource recommendations for each student, which will lead to more efficient knowledge absorption, higher engagement, and better learning outcomes ultimately.

Acknowledgments. This work was supported in part by the National Natural Science Foundation of China under Grant 42375146, and in part by the Ministry of Education's University-Industry Collaborative Education Program under Grant 202102511018.

References

1. Crompton, H., Burke, D., Gregory, H.K.: The use of mobile learning in PK-12 education: a systematic review. Comput. Educ. **110**, 51–63 (2017)
2. Nikolopoulou, K., Gialamas, V., Lavidas, K., et al.: Teachers' readiness to adopt mobile learning in classrooms: a study in Greece. Technol. Knowl. Learn. **26**, 53–77 (2020)
3. Liu, Q.: The application of visual teaching resources in Chinese teaching in schools for the deaf*. In: Proceedings of the 5th International Conference on Economics, Management, Law and Education (EMLE 2019) (2019)
4. Dong, J., Zhang, C., Hou, D., et al.: Teaching reform and practice of computer application course in material science and engineering based on "Internet+". Curric. Teach. Methodol. **6**(8) (2023)
5. Gitea: Git with a cup of tea. https://github.com/go-gitea/gitea

6. Wang, W., Lu, X.S., Huang, B., et al.: Shuishan online: constructing and teaching with a data-driven learning platform. In: IEEE International Conference on Engineering, Technology, and Education, pp. 1–8. IEEE (2021)
7. Hao, H., Lihjen, J., Dandan, Q.: Take a MOOC and then drop: a systematic review of mooc engagement pattern and dropout factor. Heliyon 9(4), 1–12 (2023)
8. Michael, Y., Anindya, R., Meghan, P., et al.: AI-assisted analysis of content, structure, and sentiment in MOOC discussion forums. Front. Educ. 8, 1250846 (2023)
9. Ma, J.: The online teaching practice of the tunnel engineering during the COVID-19 pandemic. Sci. J. Educ. 11(3), 93–103 (2023)
10. Tondeur, J., Howard, S.K., Scherer, R., Siddiq, F.: Untangling the great online transition: a network model of teachers' experiences with online practices. Comput. Educ. 203, 104866 (2023)
11. Hashlamoun, A.N., Daouk, L.: Information technology teachers' perceptions of the benefits and efficacy of using online communities of practice when teaching computer skills classes. Educ. Inf. Technol. 25(6), 5753–5770 (2020)
12. Zhao, X.Y., Wang, Z.Q., Jiang, J.J., et al.: Stratified and Diversified Teaching of Graduate Algorithm Course. DEStech Publications (2018)
13. Sunil, S., Suajatha, S., Jayalakshmi, J., et al.: 122.4: breaking barriers in transplant coordination training: a developing country's experience with online education initiative. Transplantation 107(10S1), 23–24 (2023)
14. Lei, Y., Wei, T.: Research on the construction of examination system based on cloud storage in open education environment. Adv. Comput. Signals Syst. 7(7), 123–128 (2023)
15. Han, P.Y., Liu, C.Y., Wang, J.H., et al.: Research on data encryption system and technology for cloud storage. J. Commun. 41(08), 55–65 (2020)
16. Cao, Y., Li, H., Wang, X.F., et al.: Exploration on practical teaching of software development courses based on github open source platform. Guide Sci. Educ. 16, 112–115 (2023)
17. Liu, S., Wu, Y.J., Shen, L.W., et al.: An approach for recommending issue resolutions based on code contexts similarity analysis. Comput. Appl. Softw. 39(06), 21–28+102 (2022)
18. Yu, Z., Cao, R., Tang, Q., et al.: Order matters: semantic-aware neural networks for binary code similarity detection. In: Proceedings of the AAAI Conference on Artificial Intelligence, vol. 34, no. 01 (2020)
19. Min, W., Bin, W., Jing, S., et al.: Analysis of the applicability of Tianhe-1 supercomputer in the field of meteorology. In: Advances in Meteorological Science and Technology (2012)
20. Liu, J., Shi, Y.Z., Yang, B., et al.: Parallel algorithm libraries for tianhe supercomputers. Chin. J. Comput. Phys. 1–13 (2023)

Practical Teaching Reform of Programming Courses Based on Online Coding Platforms

Guowu Yuan[1,2] 🆔, Kun Yue[1,2(✉)] 🆔, and Kuang Hu[1,2]

[1] School of Information Science and Engineering, Yunnan University,
Kunming 650504, Yunnan, China
kyue@ynu.edu.cn
[2] Yunnan Key Laboratory of Intelligent Systems and Computing,
Kunming 650504, Yunnan, China

Abstract. Programming proficiency stands as one of the most vital competencies for students majoring in computer-related disciplines. This paper scrutinizes the issues prevailing in the cultivation of programming skills. Notably, it emphasizes an imbalance in teaching, whereby concepts and syntax receive undue attention while hands-on programming experiences are inadequately incorporated. Furthermore, the absence of standardized assessment mechanisms and avenues for advanced students to enhance their skills compounds these challenges. To augment students' programming capabilities, we have established an online coding platform, facilitating a practical teaching reform in programming courses guided by "learning, practicing, certification and competing". "Learning" entails knowledge learning, "practicing" involves extensive programming practicing, "certification" signifies reaching programming competency standards, and "competing" denotes participation in programming competitions to enhance skill sets. Over seven years, this implementation has markedly improved students' programming prowess. It has also led to advancements in certified software professional (CSP) and various programming competition outcomes, effectively embodying the "promoting learning and teaching through competitions" philosophy.

Keywords: Programming · Online Coding Platform · Competition · CSP Certification

1 Introduction

Computer science has emerged as one of the most popular fields of higher education, with undergraduate enrollment in computer-related programs accounting for approximately 15% of total undergraduate admissions annually. In this context, developing four core competencies—computational thinking, algorithm design and analysis, programming, and system expertise—has become essential for students in computer-related disciplines [1, 2]. Among these competencies, programming skills, which form the foundation of computer engineering education, represent a core requirement for computer science professionals at various levels [3]. Therefore, enhancing the quality of education related to programming skills has emerged as a pivotal concern in the construction of modern computer science programs and is a crucial element of cultivating outstanding engineers through the Education and Training Program 2.0.

Programming courses encompass essential core subjects such as high-level language programming, data structures, algorithm design and analysis, object-oriented programming, and more. These are considered fundamental core courses for computer majors, aiming to develop students' computational thinking. The educational objective is to teach students how to analyze, design, and validate scientific and engineering problems computationally. While traditional teaching methods have yielded some positive results, they still suffer from inadequacies such as insufficient student preparation, an overemphasis on syntax at the expense of application, a lack of problem-solving and analytical thinking in programming, and inadequate practical programming training.

With the evolution of computer science from a focus on computation to a focus on data, and a growing emphasis on practical engineering and learning capabilities, practical programming courses face new challenges regarding teaching methods, content, and effectiveness. These include challenges related to nurturing students' skills in open-source development, cloud-based computing, and iterative programming design. In recent years, these topics have become hot issues in developing new engineering disciplines in computer science and curriculum reforms.

Efforts in the development of programming experiment platforms, the construction of corresponding case libraries, and the creation of Massive Open Online Courses (MOOCs) focused on computational thinking have received increasing attention. Reference [7] discusses the construction of innovative practical platforms at various levels, including basic programming experiments, professional system development, enterprise practical training for engineering applications, and independent research and innovation. Reference [8] provides insights and results related to curriculum reform focusing on code style and grade statistics. Reference [9] outlines the construction of a MOOC for C programming and practical teaching methods. While these studies provide valuable insights for curriculum reform and online teaching in programming courses, they fail to fully meet the functional requirements for online programming and practical innovation platforms, particularly in code hosting, version control, automatic code execution, and online code editing.

The open-source framework GitLab [10] offers code hosting and version control features similar to GitHub, with the added advantage of providing the platform as an open-source project, allowing users to download the GitLab source code and deploy it as a standalone GitLab service on their private clouds. GitLab includes built-in support for continuous integration, encompassing automated code testing and building. GitLab offers a built-in Web Integrated Development Environment (WebIDE) with extensive online code editing capabilities. Utilizing the community edition of GitLab maintained by the open-source community and deploying it in private clouds can meet the requirements for an online programming and practical innovation platform in four key areas [11]: code hosting, version control, automatic code execution, and online code editing.

Drawing from accumulated experience in teaching core courses for computer science and public elective programming courses at Yunnan University, as well as innovations in professional development, we have focused on developing online programming plat-forms based on the GitLab open-source framework. This has driven the upgrading and transformation of practical teaching modes, guided by "learning, practicing, achieving, and competing." This paper presents the foundational concepts and critical technologies behind this platform's development, along with insights into the "learning, practicing, certification and competing" approach. It aims to provide valuable reference material for professionals in similar departments engaged in curriculum development and educational reforms.

2   Building the Online Programming Platform

2.1   The Foundational Concepts of Online Programming Platform Construction

(1) Adopting the Outcome-Based Education (OBE) Model and Embracing the CST 4 CSE Educational Philosophy

In the teaching of programming courses within computer-related programs, an explo-ration of comprehensive professional reform is essential. We propose the CST 4 CSE (Computer Science Technology for Computer Science Education) educational philoso-phy based on the OBE teaching model. This philosophy focuses on engineering practical skills and effectively utilizes cloud computing, open-source programming, and related tools and technologies. It aims to create a practical platform for programming courses, with the primary goal of developing students' programming and implementation capa-bilities. This platform incorporates real-world applications and cases, guiding students to learn by doing and encouraging them to use a top-down approach to solving real prob-lems through programming. In this way, it supports the broader objectives of computer education.

(2) Goal-Oriented Instruction and a Shift in the Teaching Model for Programming Courses

Breaking down programming course objectives into specific tasks, each correspond-ing to a knowledge point, is key to our transformation. Teachers evaluate students based on completing these tasks, aligning their achievement of knowledge points with their performance. This shift in the teaching model aims to align student exam scores with developing their programming skills. We explore several strategies to achieve this goal:

Knowledge Points and Task-Driven Teaching Content: Shifting the focus from tra-ditional content-centered teaching to knowledge-point-based teaching, we incorporate an understanding of knowledge points into programming tasks.

Student-Centered Classroom Learning: Fostering an active learning model with the goal of programming tasks, we encourage students to form project groups or teams for cooperative work. In this process, the role of the teacher transitions from being a knowledge lecturer to a student learning guide, flipping the teaching model from being "teacher-centered" to "student-centered."

Assessment Based on Practical Skills: Using the online programming platform, we move away from paper-based examinations, transitioning to ongoing assessments of stu-dents' progress through programming tasks and team project performance. This approach aims to cultivate students' engineering and practical skills.

(3) **Building an Online Programming Platform Based on the GitLab Open-Source Framework**

Incorporating open-source programming platforms from the industry into practical teaching in programming courses aligns with our educational philosophy. Leveraging the GitLab framework, we construct an online programming platform. The essential technical requirements and features encompass:

Code Sharing Between Teachers and Students (Code Talk): The platform must facilitate code hosting and version control.

Interactive Coding Among Teachers and Students, and Students Themselves (Code Interaction): The platform should allow code execution.

Collaborative Development and Code Cooperation (Code Cooperation): The platform should support project collaboration.

2.2 Key Technologies in Building the Online Programming Platform

Presently, mainstream online Integrated Development Environments (IDEs) do not fully support real-time online programming in several back-end languages such as Java, C, and Python. To address this, we have established a GitLab executor cluster to provide a real-time compilation and execution environment for code edited within online IDEs. This encompasses the entire process of code editing, version control, and code execution for online programming learning. Below, we detail the critical technologies associated with the deployment and configuration of the GitLab executor and Docker containers:

(1) **Deployment and Configuration of the GitLab Executor**

The GitLab executor is installed as a daemon on the host operating system, with the capability to install it as a Docker service on a standalone Docker host or within Kubernetes clusters. Additionally, it can be configured for horizontal automatic scaling using Docker Machine.

(2) **Docker Containers**

The Docker executor calls Docker containers on the host to manage processes. Depending on the Docker image requirements defined in continuous integration scripts, it starts Docker containers on the host to execute project code. The Shell executor directly uses the host's shell to execute project code. To address the issue of parallel execution when multiple programming languages are involved, we specify the necessary Docker images within the continuous integration script. Furthermore, we utilize Docker technology for GPU server virtualization and install GitLab executors based on Shell executors on GPU servers. This configuration enables GPU servers to use local user privileges for GPU access, allowing projects to share the same shell. Through Docker technology, we virtually isolate GPU servers, avoiding the monopolization of GPUs and safeguarding servers against malicious code. Docker containers act as execution "sandboxes," preventing any harmful impact on the server.

3 "Learning-Practicing-Certification-Competing" Practical Teaching Reform

The concept of "learning through competition and enhancing education through competition" refers to effectively improving the quality of student learning and the teaching skills of instructors through participation in competitions. Among computer-related programs, programming competitions are the most widely held academic contests. Employing the "Learn-Practice-Achieve-Compete" philosophy, we aim to promote the learning of computer science and programming. To foster a culture of "learning through competition and enhancing education through competition" among computer science students, we have implemented the following strategies:

3.1 Knowledge Acquisition

Addressing the challenge of students placing a heavy emphasis on theoretical concepts and syntax rather than practical programming and experiencing a lack of enthusiasm and motivation in learning, we guide students to engage in inquiry-based and personalized learning. This approach fosters independent thinking and problem-solving skills, reflecting the cutting-edge, contemporary, and innovative nature of the curriculum. We focus on integrating knowledge to develop students' comprehensive problem-solving abilities and advanced thinking skills. Furthermore, we emphasize applying knowledge in practical scenarios and complex settings, thereby bridging the gap between course content and real-world applications and elevating the course's level of sophistication and challenge.

(1) **Curricular Reform:** In transforming our teaching content, we emphasize cultivating specialized thinking that aligns with the entire academic framework. We introduce foundational content from subsequent courses, such as data structures in generic programming, on top of the primary programming languages. This approach helps nurture a general mindset within the profession, emphasizing the development of computational thinking and the ability to tackle complex engineering problems. Academic advancements are the backdrop for case studies, linking theoretical knowledge to practical, real-world applications. Simultaneously, we integrate values into course topics and case studies, guiding students to use their acquired knowledge to address real societal problems and cultivate a scientific and artisan spirit.

(2) **Teaching Resources:** We leverage information technology resources to integrate technology into teaching deeply. Using recommendation systems and online assessment technologies, we ensure that technology covers all teaching aspects. Over the years, we have accumulated numerous course materials, examples, and exercises, forming a repository of course knowledge resources. We combine research achievements to create a network of course knowledge, building an adaptive assisted learning platform to provide intelligent and personalized education based on platform resources.

(3) **Teaching Methods:** We employ a task-based approach before, during, and after the class, creating a closed-loop teaching cycle. Before class, we assign basic knowledge learning tasks and exercises, allowing students to prepare through online platforms.

In the classroom, we focus on explaining challenging issues, enhancing teacher-student interaction, adopting a flipped approach, and increasing classroom engagement. Through in-class exercises, we establish rapid feedback on practical learning. After class, we connect with subject competitions to explore the depth and complexity of the course, fostering students' comprehensive problem-solving abilities, and increasing the course's level of challenge. This ensures student-centered and stratified teaching.

These reforms represent our commitment to achieving the "Learning-Practicing-Certification-Competing" approach, making our curriculum cutting-edge, responsive to the ever-changing field of computer science, and fostering students' enthusiasm for learning, problem-solving, and innovation.

3.2 Practical Skill Refinement

In addressing the issue of a disconnect between theoretical and practical aspects of programming courses and the lack of active student participation in the classroom, we've reformed the approach to programming course experiments in the following ways:

(1) Basic Programming Experiments

These experiments primarily verify individual knowledge points and are designed to provide students with extensive practice. They aim to ensure that students grasp the various knowledge points covered in class, understand commonly used programming development environments, and acquire basic debugging skills. We've adopted an Online Judge platform for all basic programming experiments. After students submit their code, the server compiles it and runs it through black-box testing using test data, immediately providing a score for the submitted code. Based on the evaluation scores, the system offers feedback on algorithm efficiency and code formatting issues. This encourages students to refine their code for improved efficiency and compliance with coding standards. Additionally, students can view their code scores and ranking in the class, fostering a sense of competition and enthusiasm for programming.

(2) Comprehensive and Design-Oriented Programming Experiments

In the early stages of the laboratory curriculum, we ensure that each experiment builds upon the previous ones. The experiments aim to lead students to the development of a practical small system. Guided by well-defined project requirements, we assist students in understanding the learning context and connecting it with theoretical principles. Through continuous trial and error, iterative implementation, and refinement, students work towards creating a final project.

In the later weeks of the lab course, we introduce challenging projects with greater complexity and workload. These projects require the collaboration of 3–5 students, and the groups are given time to present their work, allowing for comprehensive grading.

(3) Assessment Reform

The traditional paper-based final exam of programming courses disproportionately weighted fundamental concepts, downplaying hands-on skills. To address this issue, we have introduced computer-based testing. The weighting of memory-based questions like multiple choice and fill-in-the-blank is reduced to less than 30%, while over 70% involve on-computer programming tasks. This approach ensures that students passing the course exhibit a certain level of hands-on programming competency.

3.3 Achievement Certification

Similar to how the English CET4/CET6 exams measure English proficiency among Chinese university students, we hope to assess and compare students' programming skills nationally. This certification also aims to showcase our students' comprehensive programming abilities to potential employers and promote employment opportunities.

As a result, Yunnan University has been conducting the prestigious CCF (China Computer Federation) Certified Software Professional (CSP) exam and the Ministry of Industry and Information Technology's National Computer Technology and Software Professional Qualification (Intermediate Level, mainly for Software Designers) exam since 2017.

(1) CCF CSP Certification

The CCF Certified Software Professional is a nationally recognized professional qualification in computer science [11, 12]. We have included a practical course, "Program Design Ability Test," in the curriculum. To graduate, undergraduate students majoring in computer science and technology must achieve a CSP certification score above the minimum standard set by the college for that academic year. This measure ensures that the programming abilities of all computer science students meet the minimum industry requirements, preventing the production of subpar talent.

(2) National Computer Technology and Software Professional Qualification (Intermediate Level) Exam

This exam, organized by the Ministry of Human Resources and Social Security and the Ministry of Industry and Information Technology, is a nationally recognized examination. The certification is part of a unified plan for the national vocational qualification certificate system and is valid nationwide. In the corporate world, it can substitute for professional title evaluations.

We have introduced a practical course, "Industry Certification," in the curriculum. Currently, this is an elective course, and students who pass the software exam receive academic credits. This measure has been in place for five years, with the pass rate for the National Computer Technology and Software Professional Qualification (Intermediate Level), primarily for software designers, increasing from less than 10% in the first five years to 41.7% in 2022.

3.4 Competition Enhancement

For students who excel in their programming courses and achieve certification, we have organized advanced training to provide these outstanding students with further development opportunities. This initiative aims to enhance their skills, present a platform for their growth, and serve as a model for their peers.

Starting from the fall semester of 2021, we introduced a course named "Algorithm and Programming Competition Advancement." This course is scheduled on weekends with four sessions per week. It provides students systematic training on standard algorithms used in programming competitions and organizes weekly competitions to elevate their skills further. This additional training and competition participation not only advance the abilities of these high-achieving students but also showcase a pathway for their development. Additionally, it serves as a model for their peers (Fig. 1).

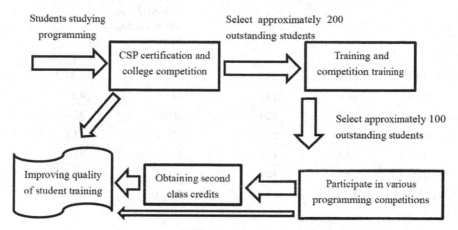

Fig. 1. Basic process of programming competition selection and training.

These students have actively participated in a variety of programming competitions, including the National Software and Information Technology Talent Contest (Blue Bridge Cup), the International Collegiate Programming Contest (ICPC), the China National Computer Contest (CNCC) - Group Programming Ladder Tournament, the China Computer Federation (CCF) National College Computer System and Programming Contest, among others. Their involvement in these diverse competitions has significantly furthered their programming capabilities.

Through the aforementioned initiatives, we have successfully placed students at the center of their learning process. By promoting self-directed learning, collaborative learning, and creative learning and leveraging digital resources and tools, we have guided the learning journey toward a more profound understanding. These reforms aim to continually enhance the quality of computer science education, giving our students a significant advantage in their careers and further academic pursuits, such as graduate studies.

4 Implementation Effectiveness

4.1 Organizational Success in Certified Software Professional (CSP)

Due to outstanding efforts in organizing the CCF CSP certification, Yunnan University has organized 21 certifications since 2017, involving more than 3,500 students. In May 2018, Yunnan University became one of the first 39 institutions authorized to offer CCF

CSP certifications. In July 2018, July 2019, and January 2023, Yunnan University was awarded the title of "Excellent Unit for CSP Certification" on three occasions.

Table 1. Comparison of CSP certification results in the past 7 years.

Certification time	Certification serial number	National average score	Average score of undergraduate students in computer science and technology at Yunnan University	Difference with national average score
Sep. 2017	11th	138	92.3	−32.7
Sep. 2018	14th	144	148.5	4.5
Sep. 2019	17th	129	164.8	35.8
Sep. 2020	20th	143	170.1	27.1
Sep. 2021	23th	152	185.3	33.3
Sep. 2022	27th	149	179.4	30.4
Sep. 2023	31th	154	191.6	37.6

We have extracted the results of certifications conducted in September each year from 2017 to 2023, as shown in Table 1. The platform established for practical programming education has led to a substantial improvement in the average scores of undergraduate students majoring in Computer Science and Technology. Moreover, the gap between their scores and the national average has notably narrowed. In the September 2021 certification, Yunnan University ranked 23rd among the top 30 CSP institutions in the country (based on overall average scores). In the March 2022 certification, Yunnan University secured the 16th position among the top 300 CSP institutions in the nation (based on average scores for institutions with over 300 participating students) and the 19th position among CSP's top 30 institutions (based on overall average scores).

4.2 Significant Improvement in Programming Competition Awards

In recent years, we have organized our students' participation in various programming competitions, including the National Software and Information Technology Talent Competition in the Software Category (Blue Bridge Cup) from 2019 to 2023, the Collegiate Computer Systems & Programming Contest (CCSP), the Team Programming Ladder Tournament from 2019 to 2023 and International Collegiate Programming Contest (ICPC) from 2022 to 2023. The details of these awards are presented in Table 2. It is evident that through platform development and the corresponding educational reforms, we have achieved a significant increase in awards across these three categories of programming competitions, ranking prominently among universities in the southwestern region of China.

Table 2. Comparison of Program Design Competition Results.

Name of Programming Competition	2020	2021	2022	2023
National Software and Information Technology Talent Competition in the Software Category (Blue Bridge Cup)	2 national second prizes and 16 third prizes; 29 provincial-level first prizes	2 national second prizes and 10 national third prizes; 21 provincial-level first prizes	2 national second prizes and 7 national third prizes; 17 provincial-level first prizes	6 national second prizes and 8 national third prizes; 16 provincial-level first prizes
Collegiate Computer Systems & Programming Contest (CCSP)	1 silver award in the Southwest division	2 gold awards and 5 silver awards in the Southwest division	2 silver awards in the national finals, 2 gold awards in the Southwest region, and 5 silver awards	Not yet held
Team Programming Ladder Tournament	No participating	1 national second prize and 1 Yunnan Provincial special prize	1 national second prize and 2 Yunnan Province special prizes	2 national second prizes and 2 Yunnan Province special prizes
International Collegiate Programming Contest (ICPC)	No participating	No participating	1 national silver award and 3 bronze awards	2 national silver awards and 4 bronze awards

5 Conclusion

In our pursuit of enhancing students' programming capabilities, this article has outlined the implementation of practical programming education reforms based on the constructed online programming platform. Guided by the principle of "learning, practicing, certification and competing", these reforms have been implemented for seven years. During this time, students' programming skills have markedly improved, as evidenced by their performance in software certification exams and various programming competitions. These efforts have successfully achieved the objective of fostering learning through competition and improving teaching through competition. Our ongoing work includes continued platform refinement, extensive integration into programming courses, further advancement in educational reforms, and providing a foundation for research in related fields.

Acknowledgments. This work is supported by Research Project on Undergraduate Education and Teaching Reform in Yunnan Province, China (No. JG2023234) and High Quality Curriculum Construction Project for Graduate Students in Yunnan Province, China (SJYZKC20211117).

References

1. Yuan, G., Yang, X., Yue, K., et al.: Building and practice of excellent talents training system in computer science and technology. Softw. Guide **19**(02), 160–163 (2020)
2. Yuan, G., Kong, B., Jiang, M., et al.: Research on the construction of computer science and technology undergraduate curriculum group. Softw. Guide (Educ. Technol.) **15**(11), 42–43 (2016)
3. Zhao, M., Xu, T., Zhang, W., et al.: Exploration of teaching reform for programming courses under the background of new engineering. Comput. Educ. (02), 149–152 (2023)
4. ACM, IEEE CS. Computer Engineering Curricula 2016 (2017). https://www.acm.org/binaries/content/assets/education/ce2016-final-report.pdf. http://www.acm.org/binaries/content/assets/education/ce2016-final-report-chinese.pdf
5. Guo, W., Wu, G., Chen, J., et al.: Think for improving computer education. Comput. Educ. **281**(5), 74–90 (2018)
6. Zheng, Q., Wu, C., Cui, X., et al.: Construction of multi-level practical and innovative platform for IT majors. Exp. Technol. Manag. **33**(5), 7–9+20 (2016)
7. Xu, W., Chen, K., Ma, J., et al.: A preliminary exploration of the online teaching reform of computer professional program design course. Softw. Guide **19**(12), 181–184 (2021)
8. Zhao, Y., Wang, J., Zhou, L., et al.: Construction of MOOC designed with c language programming guided by computational thinking. Exp. Technol. Manag. **35**(4), 147–150 (2018)
9. GitLab. https://GitLab.com/GitLab-com/#content-body
10. Yue, K., Hu, K., Yuan, G., et al.: Construction of online programming platform under open source framework and educational reform in practice. Softw. Guide **22**(03), 212–216 (2023)
11. Yuan, G., Yue, K., Yang, X., et al.: Research on improving student programming skills through CSP certification. Softw. Guide **19**(12), 14–18 (2020)
12. CCF CSP Computer Software Capability Certification. https://cspro.org/

Exploration and Research on Ideological and Political Education in Course Operating Systems and Security

Hong Song[✉], Ping Zhong, Yu Sheng, and Weiping Wang

Central South University, Changsha 410083, China

{songhong,ping.zhong,shengyu,wpwang}@csu.edu.cn

Abstract. Based on the training objectives of information security professionals and the course objectives of Operating Systems and Security, this paper explores the cultivation of awareness, emotion, and connotation of information security professionals and constructs a new teaching mode integrating the new three teaching centers of students' developing, students' learning, and learning effectiveness. Using the new teaching mode, the college personnel training can achieve three objective dimensions, including knowledge transfer, skill development, and value guidance. Also the paper analyzes the effectiveness of new teaching mode, and can provide a beneficial exploration in information security talents training with independent innovation ability.

Keywords: Operating Systems and Security · Information Security · Course Ideological and Political Education

1 Introduction

Currently, with the continuous coverage of computers and networks, as well as the widespread application of network resources and services, network security incidents have also occurred frequently. Malicious network attacks target critical information infrastructure, network application software, etc. They are increasingly showing characteristics of concealment, complexity, nationalization, diffusion, and intelligence. Facing the increasingly severe complex network security situation, the teachers in universities should continuously reform teaching methods and means to improve the quality of talent and to cultivate socialist successors who can shoulder historical missions.

As the core course for the students majoring in information security, Operating Systems and Security includes operating system security design, security mechanisms, security models, security architectures and other contents. The course aims focus on students' understanding of the basic principles and implementation mechanisms of various security models, and promoting students the understanding of various core technologies and theories of system security protection. Also enhancing students' practical and innovative abilities is the goal of the course.

W. Hong and G. Kanaparan (Eds.): ICCSE 2023, CCIS 2024, pp. 327–335, 2024.
https://doi.org/10.1007/978-981-97-0791-1_28

The ideological and political reform aimed at the information security profession can be divided into two aspects. On the one hand, it is committed to explore the construction of an ideological and political system for professional talent cultivation. In [1], the authors explore the effective combination of ideological and political courses and courses on the quality, ability, and knowledge of cyberspace security professionals. In [2], the authors use implementation of engineering certification, and form a vertical and horizontal construction method of professional ideological and political education. They integrate ideological and political elements sense of social responsibility into professional knowledge of professional talent cultivation, and build an information security professional ideological and political system from point to surface. In [3], authors focus on cultivating strong defenders and guardians of national cyberspace security building a strong cyber power by using Five in One information security talent training model, which are thinking, learning, practical abilities, competition, and aspirations. These studies and practices have laid a solid foundation for the cultivation of information security professionals with both moral and professional abilities. It also constructs a systematic framework for ideological and political education in professional courses.

On the other hand, reformation focuses more on the ideological and political teaching of specific professional courses and the organic integration of professional knowledge and ideological and political elements. Authors in [4, 5] explore the elements and resources of ideological and political education in cryptography courses, as well as exploring the implementation methods of ideological and political elements such as humanistic quality education, value orientation, and ideological quality in the curriculum. Moral education elements and social practice are analyzed and extended in the course of Information Security Technology [6]. The authors in [6] also research on the second classroom and other links in order to achieve the unity of knowledge transmission and value guidance in professional courses. Based on the theory of reverse instructional design, the authors in [7] construct a systematic process of curriculum ideological and political design for problem-based learning. The systematic process starts from five aspects, such as curriculum front-end design, hierarchical curriculum ideological and political teaching objectives, rational evaluation, diversified learning activities, and teaching feedback. In [8, 9], content security courses are analyzed from the aspects of the positioning of the course in the information security curriculum system and the training objectives of cyberspace security majors. And the authors explore how to introduce ideological and political content into actual classroom teaching.

As operating system security is the core component of computer systems, and the course is the key foundation for cyberspace security, network application security, and business information system security. It is necessary to carry out teaching reform to improve students' practice ability. Without operating system security, the upper level system is a fragmented and insecure entity.

At the same time, Operating Systems and Security is a highly practical course which emphasizes comprehensive application of technology and knowledge. The teaching reform should consider the basic task of cultivating morality and talents in universities, and the goal of cultivating information security professionals. And in order to cultivating excellent talents with both morality and talent, we also need to introduce ideological and political education into core courses, as well as value-oriented content and professional knowledge content. Thus, the effect of moistening things silently can be achieved throughout the entire teaching and education process.

2 Implementation Processes

2.1 Analysis of the Ideological and Political Characteristics of Curriculum

The course Operating System and Security is the main course to enhance the professional skills of cyberspace security students, and it is also an important carrier for cultivating network security professionals to know, understand and internalize the awareness of network sovereignty. And the course Operating Systems and Security mainly explores the mechanisms, means, and methods of ensuring network and computer system security from the bottom system level. As we all know that operating system security is the foundation of the entire computer system and even the entire cyberspace security. If the computer manager can't ensure the security of Operating Systems, there would be no cyberspace security. Facing with the complex network security situation, we can easily be found that there are inevitably rich ideological and political elements in the course of Operating Systems and Security.

However, what ideological and political elements should be highlighted in the curriculum, so that students can quickly absorb and deeply understand, and truly influence their actions and quality, it is the primary issue to be solved in the ideological and political teaching process of the course Operating Systems and Security. Therefore, the first key issue is to fully explore the ideological and political elements of consciousness, emotion, and connotation in the curriculum. Also, we need to analyze the needs and goals of ideological and political education based on the characteristics, knowledge system, and experimental requirements of the Operating Systems and Security curriculum.

2.2 Research on the Integrated Teaching Model of Ideological and Political Curriculum and Professional Knowledge

The traditional teaching model adopts the Three Center Model, which is centered on Textbook, Teacher and Class. This teaching model emphasizes teacher's preaching and solving doubts. Generally, the traditional teaching model is centered on teachers, and teachers instill knowledge in one direction. This results in the neglect of students' learning initiative throughout the entire learning process. In the modern teaching process, teachers also actively explore methods such as role exchange, thematic discussions, problem summaries, and topic guidance to unleash students' subjective learning ability. However, the sense of integration and interest still need to be further improved.

With the advent of the information revolution, the traditional Three Center Model has transformed into a new student-centered Three Center Model. The new Three Center Model includes three core perspectives, which are student development-centered, student learning-centered, and learning effectiveness-centered. This learning model emphasizes generating learning, guiding students to discover and construct knowledge independently, creating a favorable learning environment, improving the quality of learning, and enabling various types of students to achieve success.

Therefore, how to organically integrate the ideological and political elements of the curriculum in the teaching process of the new three centers, so that students can receive the guidance of consciousness, the transmission of emotions, and the guidance of value silently, is the second key problem that needs to be solved. Adopting appropriate teaching methods, stimulating students' enthusiasm for learning and creation, and achieving the dual penetration of holographic ideological and political elements and professional knowledge is an important research goal.

2.3 Research on the Construction of a Multi Directional Teaching Evaluation System

Integrating ideological and political theory into professional courses, organically integrating professional knowledge with ideological and political theory, and achieving the educational role of integrating knowledge transmission, skill cultivation, and value guidance in professional courses, is the main purpose of integrating ideological and political elements into professional course teaching. However, after the introduction of ideological and political education, the teaching content, methods, and forms of the original professional courses have increased, and process monitoring and teaching effectiveness evaluation also need to be adjusted and supplemented accordingly to adapt to changes in teaching content and methods.

Therefore, the third key issue is to study a multi-dimensional teaching evaluation system after integrating ideological and political theory, forming a corresponding collaborative education system framework, assisting in the structured and continuous monitoring of the teaching process, promoting each other with the teaching process, and forming a beneficial closed loop for cultivating professional talents.

3 Work Measures

3.1 Overall Implementation Plan

The overall implementation plan is shown in Fig. 1. According to the research content, the main research content consists of an analysis of the characteristics of curriculum ideological and political education, a study on the integration of curriculum ideological and political education and professional knowledge teaching mode, and a study on the construction of a multi-dimensional teaching evaluation system. The three parts are organically unified.

Firstly, through the diagnosis of academic situation, analyze the knowledge content and ideological and political characteristics of professional courses, construct knowledge from cognitive, ability, and quality goals, and analyze the consciousness, emotion, and connotation goals in the course.

Secondly, we will study how to integrate ideological and political education in the process of imparting professional knowledge. Based on the three student-centered centers, we will introduce the BOPPPS teaching model and multi-modal teaching method. As a result, we propose the teaching model of integrating knowledge imparting, skill cultivation and value guidance in professional classroom teaching.

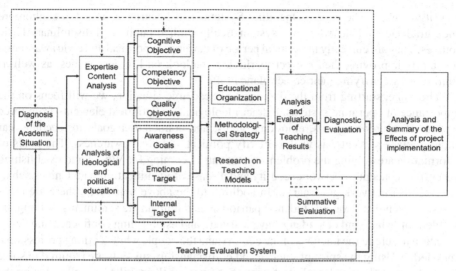

Fig. 1. Schematic diagram of overall implementation

Thirdly, diagnostic and summative evaluations are conducted based on the teaching effectiveness. And the evaluation results are fed back to the teaching organization and method strategy research, goal analysis, and learning situation diagnosis. Based on the evaluation results, adjustments are made to form a positive closed-loop and continuously improve the teaching effectiveness.

Finally, the new teaching method will be applied to the teaching process of the course Operating Systems and Security. We analyze the effectiveness of project implementation, and make improvements based on the implementation effect to achieve holographic knowledge penetration and improve the quality of innovative professional talent cultivation.

3.2 Analysis of the Characteristics of Ideological and Political Elements in Curriculum

Because the operating system is the first layer and the core software in a computer system, it is responsible for controlling and managing the entire computer software and hardware resources and coordinating their work. Any computer cannot do without the operating system. Without the security of the operating system, the upper level software will be the castle on the sand pile. The course Operating Systems and Security is based on the characteristics of operating systems. By teaching the basic principles and security design of operating systems, it explores mechanisms, models, and evaluations to ensure operating system security. On April 23, 2018, an article, which titled The Pain of a Big Country Without a Self-Developed Operating System in Science and Technology Daily, stated that constructing a self-Operating System is one of the core technologies in China. This highlights the importance of operating systems for the development of China. Developing our own Operating System is an urgent task for China. There is a wealth of ideological and political education nurtured in the teaching of operating systems and security courses. The course Operating Systems and Security is aimed at sophomore undergraduate students who have systematically studied public and disciplinary basic courses. They are currently in a critical period of developing political and civic awareness, constantly improving their correct worldview, outlook on life, and values, as well as continuously clarifying their career plans in life.

Therefore, starting from the diagnosis of academic situation, we will focus on the importance of operating systems, extract ideological and political elements from three aspects of awareness goals, emotional goals, and connotation goals for second year undergraduate students, as well as clarify political and civic awareness. The goals of reformation are solving the problem of students' Learning for Whom and establishing the correct concept of network security and a sense of identification with Chinese characteristics of network governance. In addition to the above objectives, there are other goals, including cultivating students' patriotism and humanistic sentiments, solving the problem of 'what kind of students have learned', and establishing confidence and determination to defend the interests of the country and the people while learning professional knowledge. Using the spirit of science and craftsmanship, students are required to solve the problem of "how to learn", and striving to improve their skills, as well as laying the foundation for better serving the country and society.

3.3 The Integrated Teaching Model of Ideological and Political Education and Professional Knowledge in Curriculum

The high integration of ideological and political elements in the curriculum and the teaching of professional knowledge can stimulate students' enthusiasm for learning and creation, and achieve the dual penetration of holographic knowledge and ideological and political education. Therefore, in the process of imparting professional knowledge, appropriate teaching methods and BOPPPS models are introduced to establish a teaching model that integrates knowledge imparting, skill cultivation and value guidance. The aims are guiding students to independently discover and construct knowledge, creating a new "student-centered" three center environment, and stimulating the learning motivation of students at all levels.

The BOPPPS model is a teaching model that is oriented towards educational goals and student-centered. It is divided into six teaching stages: course introduction, learning objectives, prediction, participatory learning, post testing, and summary. It is a closed-loop feedback course design model that emphasizes teaching interaction and reflection, and is also one of the most effective design models for teachers in teaching design and classroom teaching.

After using BOPPS model to extract ideological and political elements from each knowledge point of the course Operating Systems and Security, we analyze the technical representation methods of visual, listening, speaking, and touching images, audio, video, etc.. And we introduce appropriate multi-modal teaching methods for the knowledge points and organize the entire teaching process to form a trinity teaching model of knowledge imparting, skill cultivation and value guidance. The new teaching model can achieve the organic integration of ideological and political courses with professional knowledge, as well as cultivating talents for the consolidation of national information infrastructure construction.

We design each of teaching points. Firstly, in the introduction section of this course, we introduce a video of the founder of Linux, and instill the idea that "such a simple studio can create the popular operating system Linux that is loved by everyone" by visiting his studio through the video. This process will highlight the guidance of values and humanistic sentiments of the Undergraduates. The spirit, even in an average external environment, great success can still be achieved, will inspire the students to pursue a sense of creative achievement. Secondly, by analyzing the position of operating systems in computer systems and the importance attached by the state to operating systems, we can find that learning operating systems is very important, as it can help the country break free from the current situation of being constrained by others and stimulate students' patriotism and political consciousness. Once again, in the process of teaching the functional principles of various operating systems, introduce on-site images from current life, such as scheduling sites and industrial control sites, to stimulate students' ability to discover and solve problems. Thus, the organic integration of ideological and political education and professional knowledge is achieved.

3.4 The Construction of a Multi Directional Teaching Evaluation System

An effective teaching evaluation system and feedback mechanism can further expand the effectiveness of teaching reform and stimulate students' learning. Evaluate the teaching results from two aspects: diagnostic evaluation and summative evaluation, and provide real-time feedback to the entire process of teaching design and implementation, forming an effective closed-loop of the teaching evaluation system. Establish a multi-dimensional teaching evaluation system from aspects such as classroom performance, research reports, and practical abilities. We use Regular grades for timely assessment of students' mastery of the knowledge points in this class and Experimental examination for assessment of students' ability to analyze and solve problems, as well as the design and implementation of innovative ideas. We also use Knowledge expansion for students' ability of discovering, analyzing, and solving problems. In order to assess their scientific research and innovative thinking, we can use Knowledge expansion. Besides these measures, Classroom analysis and reviews of daily life are be used to examine the teaching effectiveness of ideological and political courses and Final Exam are be used to evaluate students' degree of understanding and mastering knowledge, as well as their comprehensive ability.

At last, Test is adopted to evaluate the effectiveness of reform in practice. We try to identify problems in a timely manner for improvement and optimization. At the same time, we adjust the reform details in real-time according to the professional training plan. After completing each stage of the task, questionnaire survey and application effect analyses are used to summarize the reformation methods, further improving and promoting their application.

4 Result Analysis

The ideological and political construction reform of the course Operating Systems and Security has been implemented in the course teaching and practical teaching process of the past two semesters. Students have shown more active classroom performance and are able to conduct targeted discussions based on the questions raised by the teacher. After class, further communication with the teacher and students has been conducted, and experimental verification has been conducted, resulting in the formation of relevant research reports.

At the same time, in order to further strengthen their learning of operating systems and security courses, students have independently formed interest groups. From the final exam results, over 98% of students in 2022–2023 can successfully pass the exam, with an excellent rate of over 59%. The proportion of excellent exam scores has in-creased compared to 2021–2022, while the number of failed students has decreased compared to 2021–2022, and the distribution pattern is basically normal; Explain that students have improved their mastery of the knowledge points in the course and their ability to analyze and solve problems.

5   Conclusion

Starting from the teaching objectives, the ideological and political construction reform of the course Operating Systems and Security explores the ideological and political characteristics elements. We analyze and excavate the ideological and political elements in the course, construct a teaching mode of the course Operating Systems and Security that integrates consciousness, emotion and connotation, as well as the new three centers of teaching, to achieve three dimensions of goals in the education and teaching process. The reformation results shows that new idea and new integrated method will cultivate high-quality comprehensive talents with comprehensive development of morality and talent, as well as providing certain reference value for the ideological and political reform of other professional courses.

Acknowledgments. This study was funded by teaching reform projects of Central South University (grant number 2022KCSZ015, 2022CG013).

Disclosure of Interests.   The authors have no competing interests to declare that are relevant to the content of this article.

References

1. Zhang, W., Huang, H., Chen, Y.: Discussion on ideological and political construction of cyberspace security courses in the new engineering. Guide Sci. Educ. (3), 81–83 (2020)
2. Lai, Y., Liu, J., Yang, Z., Zhuang, J.: The construction method of professional ideological and political system for information security. Comput. Educ. (08), 46–49 (2020)
3. Guo, W., Zhang, Y., Dong, C.: Exploration of the "Five in One" information security talent training model under the background of the network power strategy. Chin. Univ. Teach. (10), 21–24 (2020)
4. Han, M.: Research on information security course integrating ideological and political education under the cultivation system of "Three Aspects of Education". Guide Sci. Educ. (26), 38–39 (2020)

5. Guo, Y., Jiang, M., Xiao, J., Sun, M.: Exploration on the construction of information security professional courses from the perspective of curriculum ideology. J. Langfang Normal Univ. (Nat. Sci. Ed.) **21**(02), 100–103 (2021)
6. Si, J.: Exploration and practice of political education in professional and technical courses. Comput. Era (02), 92–94 (2020)
7. Li, J., Cao, J., Zhang, Y., Zhang, M., Li, H.: Reverse teaching design of curriculum ideological and political in information security major - Take the wireless communication network security course of Xidian university as an example. Chin. J. Netw. Inf. Secur. **7**(03), 166–174 (2021)
8. Su, Z., Zhang, G., Hu, D.: Research on ideological and political teaching of content security course in complex network environment. Comput. Educ. (07), 42–46 (2021)
9. Yuan, Y., Nie, X.: Research on the ideological and political construction of cyberspace security professional courses targeting multidirectional training objectives. Comput. Educ. (09), 37–41 (2021)

An Instructive Video Locating System for Hybrid Teaching with MOOC

Tian Song[(✉)], Mengdie Li, and Wentian Zhao

Beijing Institute of Technology, Beijing 100081, China
songtian@bit.edu.cn

Abstract. The rapid growth of Massive Open Online Courses (MOOCs) has revolutionized the education landscape by providing accessible and flexible learning opportunities. However, with the emergence of hybrid learning models, how to integrate MOOC into traditional classroom environments and effectively utilize MOOC video content in face-to-face teaching has become a current challenge. To solve this problem, we propose an instructive video locating system for MOOC hybrid teaching. The system analyzes teacher instructions and leverages technologies such as speech recognition, text segmentation, and natural language processing to easily locate relevant video clips in MOOC courses, enhancing the blended teaching experience. We conducted experiments using educational videos in MOOC online courses. The results show that the system can accurately locate video clips based on text queries. Compared with manual searches, the accuracy rate exceeds 85%, which significantly improves the efficiency of merging and supplementing multimedia content. The video locating system proposed in this article seamlessly integrates MOOC resources into the physical classroom through intelligent information retrieval, which not only enhances teaching flexibility and enriches hybrid teaching, but also lowers the technical threshold for teachers to use video assistance. This innovative application has great potential to promote the development and application of hybrid learning models in the education field.

Keywords: MOOC · hybrid teaching · educational technology · educational video retrieval · speech recognition · text segmentation

1 Introduction

With the rapid development of science and technology and the continuous growth of economy, the application of information technology in the field of education has become increasingly widespread. Among them, MOOC, as a product of modern mobile Internet technology, has gradually become popular and has become an important direction for the reform of education and teaching in colleges and universities. The popularization and application of MOOCs not only effectively solve the shortcomings of a single course in traditional classroom teaching and the disconnect between theory and practice, but also provide students with a

© The Author(s), under exclusive license to Springer Nature Singapore Pte Ltd. 2024
W. Hong and G. Kanaparan (Eds.): ICCSE 2023, CCIS 2024, pp. 336–346, 2024.
https://doi.org/10.1007/978-981-97-0791-1_29

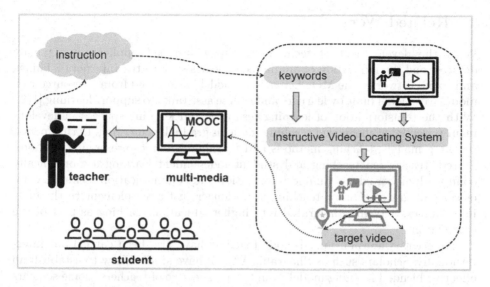

Fig. 1. Schematic Diagram of MOOC Video Locating System for Hybrid Teaching.

large number of high-quality teaching resources and enhance their self-study abilities. However, an important function in traditional schooling is the experience of face-to-face communication between students and between students and teachers. This kind of face-to-face contact, communication and feeling cannot be completely replaced by any high-tech means. This also determines that MOOCs cannot completely replace the traditional face-to-face teaching model.

In order to solve this problem, the hybrid teaching model emerged. This model combines the advantages of offline classroom teaching and online MOOCs, taking advantage of MOOCs' high flexibility in separation of teachers and students, separation of time and space, and separation of teaching. At the same time, it can flexibly select and combine all teaching elements according to the teaching objectives. Give full play to the leading role of teachers in leading, inspiring and monitoring the teaching process. In the context of the hybrid teaching model, this paper proposes a MOOC video locating system for hybrid teaching(see Fig. 1). The system combines speech recognition, text segmentation and other technologies to achieve instant video locating in the classroom by analyzing the instructions of teachers or students to improve the efficiency and convenience of video teaching. Experimental results show that the system can effectively improve the accuracy and efficiency of video locating, while reducing the cost and threshold of hybrid teaching. This innovative system is of great significance in promoting the development and application of blended teaching. It not only further optimizes teaching methods and improves teaching quality, but also reduces teaching costs and expands the scope of teaching. The successful application of this system will effectively promote the development and popularization of blended teaching in the education field.

2   Related Work

With the development of technology, the widespread application of smart devices, and the innovation of online technologies such as the Internet of Things and social networks, the MOOC teaching model has evolved from a resource-rich model to a model built by learners and course assistants to support learning [1, 2]. With the transformation of learning resources and learning space, the development potential of the hybrid teaching model is gradually emerging. In this model, teaching models, teaching methods and teaching resources are organically integrated; teacher-led teaching and student independent learning are organically combined; higher education and information and communication technology are closely integrated. Online teaching is no longer just a supplement to the original courses, it begins Integrated into higher education teaching as part of the curriculum.

Different studies on mixed-mode teaching have also been carried out internationally. Scholars such as Shaarani, A.S. [3] have studied how to establish an effective blended learning model from the perspective of teachers. Some scholars have also discussed the factors that affect the usage rate of online learning learners from a technical perspective. It is believed that the application of mobile devices enhances the convenience and accessibility of learning and broadens the field for the development of online learning. Research by scholars such as So, H.J. [4] shows that high-quality cooperative learning can not only increase learners' social interaction, but also reduce learners' psychological distance, thereby overcoming the loneliness of learning and providing more emotional support and motivation for students' learning participation. Howard J. Klein [5] and other scholars conducted quasi-experimental studies on the factors that affect students' learning motivation and outcomes under online and offline hybrid course models and traditional course models, and found that learning under blended learning conditions Students are more motivated to learn, have higher cognitive engagement, and have higher course grades. At the same time, blended teaching has been applied in different ways internationally. For example, the Hong Kong University of Science and Technology in Canada uses MOOC to carry out hybrid courses on and off campus to realize Internet-assisted teaching. In addition, the IMITATE project of the Massachusetts Institute of Technology in the United States has established a hybrid system for teacher professional training based on MOOC and has achieved good results.

However, there are still certain problems in the implementation process of blended teaching [6–8]. First of all, under this model, it is difficult to make in-depth comprehensive use of online and offline learning resources. For example, after some schools offer courses online, there are differences in resources and offline classes, making it difficult to form a complete teaching system. Secondly, teachers need to improve their level of using network technology to implement hybrid teaching [9,10]. Finally, some videos or online courseware emphasize visual expression but ignore student learning efficiency and interactivity [11,12]. This article proposes a MOOC video locating system for hybrid teaching. Through the precise locating of MOOC videos, it can not only enhance students' sense of participation and interactivity, but also teachers can flexibly select and combine all teaching elements according to the teaching objectives to give full play to Teachers play a leading role in leading, inspiring, and monitoring the teaching process, thereby improving the quality and effectiveness of teaching. The system can also integrate online and offline teaching resources, including online MOOC videos, offline classroom teaching, digital resources, teachers inside and outside the school, etc., to achieve collaborative teaching and innovative teaching. Through different hybrid teaching models, teachers can better guide students to innovative thinking and practice, realize diversified teaching models, and meet the learning needs of different students and the teaching needs of teachers.

3   Method

3.1   System Working Principle

This system utilizes various cutting-edge natural language processing and information retrieval technologies to efficiently locate educational video content for teachers. It leverages automatic speech recognition techniques [13] to transcribe voiced audio in videos into timed subtitle texts. The subtitle statements are then semantically segmented using text tiling algorithms [14] that calculate lexical and syntactic similarity to determine precise boundaries between concepts. These enriched segmented subtitles are fed into distributed search engine indices [15, 16] for robust querying and retrieval.

When teachers issue search instructions in the classroom, the system first preprocesses the input instructions and extracts the core keywords or phrases using natural language processing technology. Next, the system will search for subtitle fragments closely related to these keywords through a distributed search engine in the established video resource library. In this process, the system will use advanced technologies such as deep learning and machine learning to measure the degree of correlation between each subtitle segment and the target keyword based on factors such as semantic similarity and contextual matching, and sort these candidate segments according to their correlation size.

Specifically, the processed subtitle text will be split into multiple elements, each of which will be connected to a specific time point in its corresponding original video. At the same time, each subtitle segment will also contain a unique identifier, which is the URL, to point to the video file where it is located. In this way, the system can establish a cross linking structure within the index, so that each subtitle text can be directly mapped to its specific location. When teachers or students initiate search requests, the system will analyze the query conditions based on their needs and extract key information, such as keywords, topics, etc. Then, the system will search for subtitle clips related to these information in the index and find corresponding video clips based on their association relationships. Due to the fact that each subtitle contains timestamp information, the system can quickly and accurately locate the target segment that meets the requirements and extract it from the original video for users to watch. This efficient retrieval and positioning method not only greatly improves the speed of obtaining teaching resources, but also provides users with a more intuitive and vivid learning experience.

By properly utilizing automation technology in this system, the positioning of teaching resources can be effectively changed from laborious manual processes to a relaxed and convenient experience. Teachers can then focus solely on promoting students' knowledge absorption, without being limited by the need to search for appropriate content. At the same time, students can also achieve more efficient self-learning through personalized learning paths and materials.

Overall, this comprehensive system provides innovative solutions for blended learning models based on intelligent positioning of online educational videos. As long as its functionality continues to be improved, the system can significantly improve the efficiency of large-scale hybrid teaching methods. It not only makes it easier for teachers to prepare lesson plans by actively recommending content that matches learning needs, but also enhances interactive discussions between students and teachers, bringing deeper levels of participation to learning. With the continuous enhancement of artificial intelligence and big data processing capabilities, the optimization potential of this system is even more infinite. It not only helps traditional teachers better carry out blended teaching, but also creates strong support for mobile learning and intelligent classrooms. In summary, this system will greatly promote the development of blended learning models.

3.2   Model Architecture Diagram

The following is the framework diagram of our proposed MOOC video locating system (see Fig. 2).

The first part of the system is the speech recognition module, whose main task is to extract textual information from spoken language. The principle is mainly to use advanced signal processing technology and machine learning algorithms to analyze and understand the speaker's speech features, thereby achieving automatic conversion from speech to text. Next, the system enters the audio extraction process, which involves extracting audio data from a video stream. During this process, the system will separate the sound part from the video file for further processing and analysis. Subsequently, the extracted audio information will be fed into the subtitle generation module, whose task is to generate visual subtitle text based on the audio information. In order to ensure the quality of subtitles, the system usually adopts advanced audio processing technologies such as speech synthesis and recognition, as well as intelligent semantic understanding methods to ensure that the generated subtitle content is consistent with the actual pronunciation. Then, the generated subtitle text will be sent to the subtitle segmentation module for processing. Here, the system will divide the entire subtitle into individual words or phrases to facilitate subsequent indexing and search operations. It should be noted that subtitle segmentation is a complex process that takes into account various factors such as semantics and grammar to ensure that the resulting substring has good readability and semantic integrity. After the above stages are completed, the system will build a video index library with a search engine, and the preprocessed subtitle files will be added to the search engine. At the same time, this library records the mapping relationship between important keywords extracted from each video and the URL and timestamp of the video, used for indexing and retrieving video clips. After receiving teacher instruction requests, the system will use natural language processing technology to deeply analyze the instructions and extract key query words from them. Subsequently, it will use the previously established video index library to conduct full-text matching searches based on the semantic similarity between query words and keywords. The search results will be sorted based on matching degree. The most relevant subtitle segments will be ranked first, extracting their URL to the original video and the start and end time positions of the matching segments in the video. This completes the entire process of linking from teacher needs to video solutions, providing precise and efficient content support for teachers.

The various modules mentioned above have worked closely together to build a complete video content retrieval system. This system fully utilizes human-computer interaction technologies such as speech recognition, information extraction, and semantic understanding, achieving full process automation from teacher input to relevant video clip output. Compared to the traditional method of manually searching for teaching videos, this system significantly improves the efficiency of teachers in preparing classroom teaching resources. It constructs a rich video index library through deep preprocessing of classic videos. When a teacher proposes a topic concept in the classroom, the system can provide as many matching video clips as possible in just a few seconds, helping the teacher carry out the explanation smoothly. At the same time, the system also takes into account the increasing scale of the index library as video content continues to accumulate. It adopts a distributed architecture, improving the efficiency and scalability of video matching. In the future, it is possible to add adaptive capabilities to the indexer based on the data used by teachers, so that the retrieval results are closer to actual needs. In summary, the video content retrieval system utilizes advanced artificial intelligence and voice processing technology to provide efficient and convenient classroom services for teachers. It is expected to change the traditional manual search teaching mode and help build a more comprehensive blended teaching system.

3.3   Advantages and Innovations

By leveraging cutting-edge speech recognition and natural language processing techniques, the system is able to efficiently locate and retrieve educational video resources. It automatically transcribes speech to text via subtitles, and further segments.

This intelligent preprocessing lays the foundation for fast and precise content matching. When teachers provide instructions, the system analyzes keywords and matches them to indexed subtitle segments using distributed search engines. This powerful matching ability allows accurate pinpointing of highly relevant video clips related to the learning objectives outlined.

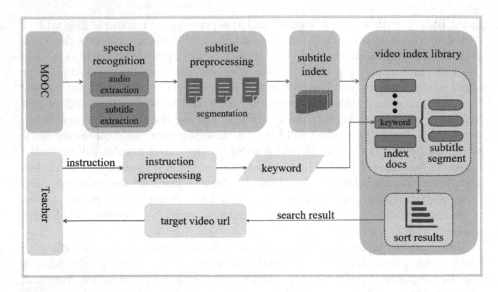

Fig. 2. Architecture Diagram of MOOC Video Locating System for Hybrid Teaching.

Through continual enhancement of the underlying linguistic models, the system is designed to maintain high accuracy in its segmentation and matching capabilities over time. Leveraging vast amounts of training data optimizes the relevance of retrieval results.

By connecting matched snippets back to their original videos and timestamps, teachers and students can immediately jump to target segments, skipping straight to the most pertinent information without wasteful searching. This saves valuable classroom time that can instead be dedicated to active learning.

The personalized and automated location of learning resources according to individual needs fosters a customized educational experience for all. Teachers gain back time through effortless content preparation, allowing them to focus more on instructional methods and student engagement. Learners benefit from optimized access to knowledge tailored to their learning pathways.

With its intelligent, efficient and user-centered design, the proposed system promises to significantly enhance hybrid learning models. It holds the potential to revolutionize how blended teaching and studying are conducted at a large scale through augmented educator productivity and learner experience.

4   Experiment

4.1   Experimental Setup

To evaluate the proposed system, we conducted a controlled user study with the following experimental setup:

Dataset: To thoroughly assess the performance of the proposed system, a carefully curated dataset was compiled containing educational video resources. The dataset consisted of 10 video lectures sourced from renowned MOOC platforms teaching fundamental and advanced concepts in Computer Science. The lectures encompassed a wide range of typical lengths commonly found in online courses, from 5–15 min, to evaluate performance under varying conditions. The lectures represented the diverse topics covered in Computer Science curricula, including programming languages, operating systems, algorithms, databases, machine learning and more. Both introductory and advanced technical videos were included to test the system's ability to retrieve segments matching queries of differing difficulties. All videos underwent the full pipeline of the proposed system, including speech recognition, subtitle generation and natural language processing before indexing. The experimental dataset is shown in Table 1.

Table 1. Experimental Dataset.

VideoName	VideoTheme	KnowledgePoint 1	KnowledgePoint 2	KnowledgePoint 3	duration
video-1	Operating System	Process Management	File System	Process Management	10 mins
video-2	Data Structure	Linear List	Tree Structure	Graph Structure	7 mins
video-3	Computer Network	OSI Reference Model	TCP/IP Protocol	LAN	6 mins
video-4	Web Page Design	HTML	CSS	JavaScript	8 mins
video-5	Algorithm Analysis	Time Complexity	Space Complexity	Asymptotic Notation	9 mins
video-6	Database Principles	Relational Model	SQL Language	Transaction Management	11 mins
video-7	Cyber Security	Hacking Techniques	Authentication	Encryption	13 mins
video-8	Machine Learning	Unsupervised Learning	Supervised Learning	Applications	15 mins
video-9	Computer Graphics	2D Graphics	3D Graphics	Rendering	8 mins
video-10	Software Engineering	Agile methodology	DevOps	waterfall model	9 mins

Participants: 20 educators with substantial education experience voluntarily participated in the rigorous evaluation of the proposed system. Their familiarity with classroom instruction and analysis of video lessons ensured reliable assessment.

Experimental Design: A within-subjects study design was adopted where each participant underwent identical procedures. This within-group comparison strengthened validity of obtained results.

Procedure: Participants were first introduced to system functionalities. They then watched pre-selected educational videos covering various topics and lengths. For each video, participants formulated sample instruction queries simulating real classroom needs. The system localized matching segments which participants appraised for relevance on a 5-point Likert scale.

Post-Study Survey: Upon experiment completion, participants provided demographic information and responded to a questionnaire measuring perceived usability, satisfaction and areas for improvement on standardized constructs. Open-ended feedback was also elicited.

Data Collection: Objective performance data included accuracy rates of video localization across different query types and content domains. Subjective rating scores and open comments comprised the qualitative dataset.

This controlled process with randomized sample ensured unbiased collection of both quantitative and qualitative insights from experienced users. Repeated evaluation by each minimized confounding and yield robust conclusions regarding system effectiveness. Valuable feedback was also gained for future optimization.

4.2 Evaluation Indicators

To effectively evaluate the performance of the proposed video localization system, we defined three main evaluation metrics: location accuracy, retrieval relevance, and user experience.

Location accuracy measures how precisely the system can pinpoint the targeted video segments within a video based on user queries. Test participants were asked to judge if the located segment fully matches the given time or content. We calculated the accuracy rate for each video by taking the number of correctly located segments divided by the total number of segments.

Retrieval relevance assesses how well the search results allow users to understand the video content. After viewing retrieval outputs, participants assigned a rating between 1 to 5 to indicate their comprehension level. The average relevance score across participant ratings reflected the overall retrieval quality.

User experience examines different usability aspects from the users' perspective. A questionnaire investigated interface design, workflow, ease of use and satisfaction level using Likert scale questions. This provided a quantitative analysis of how the system was received by participants.

To evaluate the metrics, we conducted a user study using a dataset of 10 educational videos. The results were recorded and analyzed to demonstrate the performance of our video localization system. We believe these comprehensive metrics allow a multidimensional assessment of the system and identify areas for potential improvement.

4.3 Experimental Results

The experimental results are shown in Table 2. The experimental results are shown in Table 2. Participants submitted a total of 100 queries in 10 sample videos, covering different themes, video length, video keywords, and complexity. Relatively speaking, the accuracy of query positioning for videos below 10 min is higher than that for videos within the range of 10 to 15 min, but the average accuracy is still over 85%. In addition, compared to the accuracy of basic queries related to entry-level concepts, the accuracy of more professional intermediate and advanced queries is slightly lower. These results demonstrate the technical effectiveness of the proposed MOOC video localization system in accurately locating relevant segments under different experimental conditions. This framework is expected to enhance hybrid learning models by optimizing the retrieval of online educational content.

Table 2. Experimental Result.

Input Video	keyword	Accurate Segments	Accuracy Rate	Average Relevance
video-1	Process Management	3	85%	4.4
video-2	Linear List	4	87%	4.5
video-3	TCP/IP Protocol	3	95%	4.7
video-4	CSS	2	85%	4.4
video-5	Time Complexity	4	89%	4.5
video-6	Transaction Management	4	88%	4.6
video-7	Supervised Learning	3	86%	4.5
video-8	2D Graphics	2	85%	4.4
video-9	waterfall model	3	91%	4.6
video-10	Software Engineering	4	93%	4.6

5 Conclusion

This paper proposes a MOOC video locating system to address key challenges in hybrid teaching models. Specifically, existing hybrid teaching approaches struggle with efficiently locating and accessing relevant video resources from the massive amounts of educational content available online.

The proposed system aims to solve these issues through its innovative architecture and integrated technologies. It applies cutting-edge techniques like speech recognition, natural language processing and distributed information retrieval to understand teaching instructions and pinpoint matching video segments with high precision.

Extensive experiments were conducted to evaluate the system performance. The results demonstrate that the average accuracy of video localization is very high, significantly outperforming manual search. This confirms the technical viability of the proposed approach.

Additionally, user studies in the form of feedback surveys and interviews were carried out with participants who utilized the system. The findings reveal overwhelming satisfaction levels amongst teachers and learners regarding the user experience offered. They highlighted the major improvements in learning efficiency and convenience brought by the system.

Based on the promising experimental and user study outcomes, it can be concluded that the MOOC video locating system has the potential for wide adoption and application in hybrid education models. By seamlessly integrating diverse online resources, it offers learners personalized learning pathways and saves valuable time typically spent searching for content.

In summary, this research lays the foundation for more engaging, flexible and optimized blended teaching paradigms through advanced application of technologies to enrich online and classroom learning experiences. Its outcomes also suggest future research directions in this important domain.

Acknowledgement. This work was supported by the grants of the following program: National Natural Science Foundation of China (NSFC, No. 62077004, 62177005)

References

1. Kop, R., Fournier, H., Mak, J.S.F.: A pedagogy of abundance or a pedagogy to support human beings? Participant support on massive open online courses. Int. Rev. Res. Open Distrib. Learn. **12**(7), 74–93 (2011)
2. Zhang, Q., Chen, Q., Li, Y., Liu, J., Wang, W.: Sequence model with self-adaptive sliding window for efficient spoken document segmentation. In: 2021 IEEE Automatic Speech Recognition and Understanding Workshop (ASRU), pp. 411–418. IEEE (2021)
3. Shaarani, A.S., Bakar, N.: A new flipped learning engagement model to teach programming course. Int. J. Adv. Comput. Sci. Appl. **12**(9), 57–65 (2021)
4. So, H.-J., Brush, T.A.: Student perceptions of collaborative learning, social presence and satisfaction in a blended learning environment: relationships and critical factors. Comput. Educ. **51**(1), 318–336 (2008)
5. Klein, H.J., Noe, R.A., Wang, C.: Motivation to learn and course outcomes: the impact of delivery mode, learning goal orientation, and perceived barriers and enablers. Pers. Psychol. **59**(3), 665–702 (2006)
6. Kop, R.: The challenges to connectivist learning on open online networks: learning experiences during a massive open online course. Int. Rev. Res. Open Distrib. Learn. **12**(3), 19–38 (2011)
7. Reich, J., Ruipérez-Valiente, J.A.: The MOOC pivot. Science **363**(6423), 130–131 (2019)
8. Breslow, L., Pritchard, D.E., DeBoer, J., Stump, G.S., Ho, A.D., Seaton, D.T.: Studying learning in the worldwide classroom research into edX's first MOOC. Res. Pract. Assess. **8**, 13–25 (2013)
9. Pappano, L.: The year of the MOOC. The New York Times, 2(12) (2012)
10. Jordan, K.: Initial trends in enrolment and completion of massive open online courses. Int. Rev. Res. Open Distrib. Learn. **15**(1), 133–160 (2014)
11. Margaryan, A., Bianco, M., Littlejohn, A.: Instructional quality of massive open online courses (MOOCs). Comput. Educ. **80**, 77–83 (2015)
12. Mary, S., Julie, J., Jennifer, G.: Teaching evidence based practice and research through blended learning to undergraduate midwifery students from a practice based perspective. Nurse Educ. Pract. **14**(2), 220–224 (2014)
13. Zheng, R., Chen, J., Ma, M., Huang, L.: Fused acoustic and text encoding for multimodal bilingual pretraining and speech translation (2021)
14. Hearst, M.A.: Text tiling: segmenting text into multi-paragraph subtopic passages. Comput. Linguist. **23**(1), 33–64 (1997)
15. Robertson, S.E., Jones, K.S.: Relevance weighting of search terms. J. Am. Soc. Inf. Sci. **27**(3), 129–146 (1976)
16. Mikolov, T., Chen, K., Corrado, G., Dean, J.: Efficient estimation of word representations in vector space. arXiv preprint arXiv:1301.3781 (2013)

ExpT: Online Action Detection via Exemplar-Enhanced Transformer for Secondary School Experimental Evaluation

Haomiao Yuan[ID], Zhichao Zheng[ID], Yanhui Gu[ID], Junsheng Zhou[ID], and Yi Chen[(✉)][ID]

Nanjing Normal University, Nanjing 210023, Jiangsu, China
{222202008,zhengzhichao,gu,zhoujs,cs_chenyi}@njnu.edu.cn

Abstract. Secondary school experimental evaluation is an essential component of secondary school science education. However, it faces several challenges, including obstacles to precise assessment within limited time and the presence of inconsistent evaluation criteria. Hence, it has become imperative to explore and harness artificial intelligence technology to improve secondary school experimental evaluation. Yet existing applicable online action detection (OAD) algorithms are hindered by limitation to historical context and inefficiency, leading to setbacks in realistic experimental evaluations. Based on this, we present **Ex**emplar-enhanced **T**ransformer (ExpT), a real-time mechanism for online action detection that more accurately and efficiently assesses the experiments conducted by students. By leveraging exemplars through temporal cross attention, the ExpT model provides complementary guidance for modeling temporal dependencies, along with the reduction of excessive attention. We evaluate ExpT on two realistic chemistry experiment datasets for online action detection, and it significantly outperforms all existing methods.

Keywords: Secondary school experimental evaluation · online action detection · transformer · temporal cross attention

1 Introduction

Secondary school experimental evaluation is an indispensable pillar of science education, nurturing students' experimental skills and honing their hands-on expertise. It serves as a cornerstone in the edifice of quality teaching. Nevertheless, the prevailing model of secondary school experimental evaluation grapples with a myriad of issues. These encompass the challenge of rendering precise assessments within the confines of limited time and the perennial issue of inconsistent evaluation criteria. In light of these pressing concerns, it is paramount to

Supported by the Natural Science Foundation of China (Nos. 62377029, 22033002).

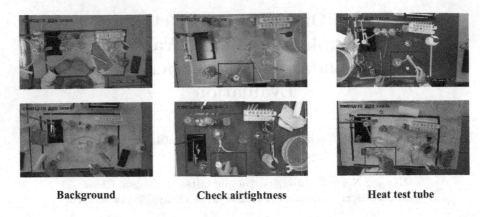

Background   **Check airtightness**   **Heat test tube**

Fig. 1. Examples in realistic chemistry experiments. Each category contains multiple instances and each instance exhibits unique appearance and motion characteristic. For instance, in the category "Checking airtightness", there is an action of holding a test tube with both hands, while in the category "Heat test tube", the action of heating a test tube with an alcohol lamp appears, which are boxed in the figure.

harness the transformative potential of artificial intelligence (AI) technology. AI has the capacity to conduct real-time analysis and evaluation of student experiments, laying the foundation for a comprehensive and standardized evaluation framework. This paper aims to explore and utilize AI to enhance secondary school experimental evaluation, ultimately improving the quality and outcomes of science education.

To tackle these challenges, our approach revolves around harnessing online action detection algorithms [7] for a groundbreaking transformation of experimental evaluation. Online action detection is specifically tailored to identify ongoing actions in videos without relying on future information. Recently, this task has garnered increasing attention due to its diverse potential applications in real-world scenarios, such as autonomous driving [15,32], video surveillance [23], and anomaly detection [19,20]. However, existing methodologies [7,28–30,33] predominantly focus on modeling long-term dependencies, which can lead to overfitting to scene-related cues. Additionally, an overreliance on attention mechanisms to enhance temporal modeling may significantly reduce efficiency and prove counterproductive in practical scenarios.

As shown in Fig. 1, we observe that in real-world experiments, each step (category) contains multiple instances that exhibit unique appearance and motion characteristic. We discover that incorporating exemplary frames as guidance can step outside the confines of the historical context and more effectively identify dynamic changes in video clips. Furthermore, a producive online action detection algorithm should always be efficient. Through the augmentation by exemplars, the costly or insufficient temporal attentions can be reduced, without harming the performance. To this end, we propose Exemplar-enhanced Transformer (ExpT), an real-time mechanism for online action detection that can accurately and rapidly evaluate the experiments made by students. To demonstrate the efficacy of ExpT, it is validated on two realistic chemistry experiment datasets and it achieves the state-of-the-art performance for online action detection.

2 Related Work

Online Action Detection. Online Action Detection (OAD) is designed to promptly identify frames in an untrimmed video stream. Unlike offline video tasks that have access to all frames, OAD can only utilize gradually accumulated historical frames at each moment. Some methods [3,6,10,11,28,31] rely solely on recent video frames spanning a few seconds as contextual information for the current frame. However, these approaches might overlook vital information in long-term historical frames, potentially limiting performance. To tackle this, TRN [29] utilizes LSTM [13] to memorize all historical information, although it has limitations in modeling long dependencies. Recently, LSTR [30] explores both long-term and short-term memories using Transformer [27], significantly enhancing action identification performance at the current frame by globally attending to long-term history. Going beyond the exploration of historical information, certain methods [28,33] attempt to overcome causal constraints by anticipating the future. For instance, OadTR [28] combines predicted future information with the current feature to identify ongoing actions. In this paper, ExpT leverages exemplars in a straightforward manner to enhance temporal modeling, achieving significant performance improvements over other methods.

Transformers for Action Understanding. Transformers have achieved groundbreaking success in NLP [8,21] and have found applications in computer vision tasks such as image recognition [9,26] and object detection [4]. Recent research has further expanded the use of Transformers to address temporal modeling tasks in videos, encompassing areas like action recognition [1,5,18,22] and temporal action localization [17,24], yielding promising results. However, the efficiency of these specialized methods is often constrained by computational and memory requirements. Our exemplar-augmented model intervenes to alleviate this constraint by reducing the computational and memory demands of temporal attention without compromising performance.

3 Methodology

3.1 Task Definition

In the context of this task, the goal is to instantaneously identify actions occurring in real-time within a video stream that may encompass multiple actions. We denote the input streaming video as $V = i_t t = -T^0$, where $i0$ represents the current frame chunk to be classified. The action category of the current frame chunk i_0 is represented by y_0, where $y_0 \in 0, 1, ..., C$, with C being the total number of action categories, and index 0 indicating the background category.

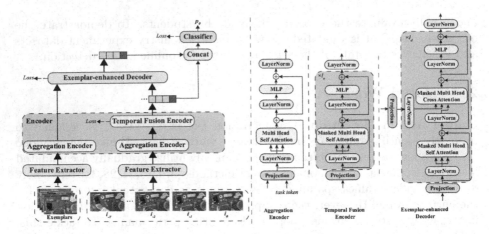

Fig. 2. Illustration of the proposed Exemplar-enhanced Transformer (ExpT). The Aggregation Encoder processes the input streaming video and exemplars by attaching a task token to the visual features to consolidate feature representations. Following this, the video sequence undergoes the Temporal Fusion Encoder, aiming to capture extended historical temporal dependencies. Finally, the Exemplar-enhanced Decoder utilizes exemplary features to further enhance temporal understanding through temporal cross-attention.

3.2   Architecture

The architecture of Exemplar-enhanced Transformer (ExpT) is illustrated in Fig. 2. It utilizes an encoder-decoder architecture to process long-term memory and exemplars for the identification of current actions. The Aggregation Encoder is introduced to improve the quality of long-range video representations and enhancing exemplary features. Then the Temporal Fusion Encoder is designed to model temporal dependencies in the video sequences. ExpT also employs our presented key component Exemplar-enhanced Decoder that conducts interaction between memory and exemplars in an iterative loop.

Aggregation Encoder. Given a streaming video $V = {i_t}{t = -T}^{0}$, the feature extractor [25] converts it into a 1D feature sequence by collapsing the spatial dimensions. Following this, an extra linear projection layer further transforms each vectorized frame chunk feature into a D-dimensional feature space, yielding $F = {f_t}_{t=-T}^{0} \in \mathbb{R}^{(T+1) \times D}$.

In the Aggregation Encoder, a task token $t \in \mathbb{R}^D$ is introduced to the embedded feature sequence F for the creation of the combined token feature sequence. It is crucial to highlight that this token is utilized to acquire global discriminative features pertinent to the online action detection task. Subsequently, we apply position encoding E^{pos} to the sequence to retain positional information:

$$\tilde{f}_t = \text{Concat}(f_t, t) + E_t^{pos} \tag{1}$$

Now we get the feature sequence $\tilde{F} \in \mathbb{R}^{(T+1) \times 2 \times D}$, which is further to perform the Multi Head Self Attention(MHSA):

$$\hat{F} = \text{MHSA}(\text{LN}(\tilde{F})) + \tilde{F} \tag{2}$$

where $\text{LN}(\cdot)$ indicates layer normalization [2] and residual connections [12] are also applied. $\hat{F}$ is then dropped before feeding to the MLP, and the output of the Aggregation Encoder is formulated as:

$$\bar{F} = \text{LN}(\text{MLP}(\text{LN}(\hat{F})) + \hat{F}) \tag{3}$$

Finally, we extract the token from the sequence, yielding the aggregated video representation $X \in \mathbb{R}^{(T+1) \times D}$. Similarly, the Aggregation Encoder is employed to refine exemplars. When considering action instances within the same category, we select instances with distinctive appearance characteristics and clear motion patterns as exemplars representing that category. Using the K-means clustering algorithm [14] for each category, we perform clustering and obtain M exemplary features denoted as $F^e = [f^e_{c,1}, f^e_{c,2}, ..., f^e_{c,M}]^C_{c=0} \in \mathbb{R}^{(C+1) \times M \times D}$. Subsequently, we follow the same procedures to aggregate exemplary representation, resulting in $X^e \in \mathbb{R}^{(C+1) \times D}$.

Temporal Fusion Encoder. To effectively determine the category label of the current frame, leveraging rich contextual cues from neighboring frames is crucial. The Temporal Fusion Encoder is designed to capture temporal evolution by dynamically aggregating local features. Additionally, we introduce a directional attention mask [27] to the video representation X to ensure that each frame in the representation can only depend on its preceding frames. This approach enables predictions for all frames in the sequence as if they are the most recent ones. Due to the incoherence between exemplars, our focus is on modeling the video sequence. The output of the l_e-layer Temporal Fusion Encoder is denoted as X^{enc}.

Exemplar-Enhanced Decoder. So far, we have generated video features $\tilde{X}$ and exemplary features X_e. The current frame, however, is limited to the video clip and can not go beyond history. Thus, the Exemplar-enhanced Decoder is designed to further reinforce the effect of temporal modeling and make it more robust.

The video features are firstly fed into a Masked MHSA layer:

$$\tilde{X} = \text{MHSA}(\text{LN}(X^{enc})) + X^{enc} \tag{4}$$

Then, there is a Masked Multi Head Cross Attention (MHCA) layer, where $\hat{X}$ as a query condition dynamically extracts new semantics from exemplary features.

$$\hat{X} = \text{MHCA}(\text{LN}(\tilde{X}, \text{LN}(X^e), \text{LN}(X^e))) + \tilde{X} \tag{5}$$

$$\bar{X} = \text{MLP}(\text{LN}(\hat{X})) + \hat{X} \tag{6}$$

$$X^{dec} = \text{LN}(\bar{X}^{(\ell_d)}) \tag{7}$$

Finally we concatenate the current index of the output by the decoder and encoder, followed by a classifier to obtain the classification score p_0 as the result of online action detection.

3.3   Training

Our ExpT model relies on action steps of interaction between video and exemplars to predict the current action. These steps are utilized as auxiliary information to benefit action detection.

For the X^{enc} generated by the encoder, we feed it to a classifier to generate the action probabilities $P^{enc} = \{[p_{t,0}^{enc}, p_{t,1}^{enc}, ..., p_{t,C}^{enc}]\}_{t=-T}^{0}$. We calculate the cross-entropy loss to guide the learning process:

$$\mathcal{L}_{enc} = -\sum_{t=-T}^{0}\sum_{c=0}^{C} y_{t,c}\log(p_{t,c}^{enc}) \tag{8}$$

Similarly, the output of the decoder also has a corresponding loss $\mathcal{L}_{dec}$. In addtion, the final output of the ExpT is the key to correctly discriminate between different action categories. The classification loss $\mathcal{L}$ is formulated as:

$$\mathcal{L}_{cls} = -\sum_{c=0}^{C} y_{0,c}\log(p_{0,c}) \tag{9}$$

Therefore, the final joint training loss is:

$$\mathcal{L} = \lambda_a\mathcal{L}_{enc} + \lambda_b\mathcal{L}_{dec} + \mathcal{L}_{cls} \tag{10}$$

where $\lambda_a = 0.7$ and $\lambda_b = 0.5$ are the balance coefficients.

4   Experiments

4.1   Setups

Datasets. To demonstrate the effectiveness of ExpT in Secondary school experimental evaluation, We carry out experiments on two realistic chemistry experiment datasets. Oxygen Experiment dataset consists of over 90 h of oxygen production by potassium permanganate videos annotated with 32 actions. Carbon Dioxide Experiment dataset has 222 sets of Carbon Dioxide production by limestone videos with 11 actions. In comparison, the former is more complex and the latter has a shorter action duration. Details about the datasets can be seen in Fig. 1.

Evaluation Metrics. We evaluate the effectiveness of online action detection using per-frame mean Average Precision (mAP) on the two datasets. The mAP, a commonly used metric, requires averaging the Average Precision (AP) across each action class.

Implementation Details. Following prior works [28–31], we conduct our experiments on pre-extracted features. Unlike prior work, we adopt Videomae [25] to extract 1024-dimensions RGB feature with 1fps due to better efficiency.

Regarding training, we implement our proposed ExpT in PyTorch and conduct all experiments using Nvidia Geforce RTX 3090 graphics cards. Simplifying the setup, we employ the Adam optimizer [16] without unnecessary complexities. The batch size is configured as 128, the learning rate is set to 0.0001, and weight decay is set at 0.0005. For the model configuration, we choose $\ell_e = 1$ and $\ell_d = 2$, with the temporal stride T set to 63.

Table 1. Online action detection performances on Oxygen Experiment and Carbon Dioxide Experiment. All methods use pre-extracted RGB features by Videomae [25]. The mAP performance is reported for the two datasets and we use FPS of inference to measure the efficiency of the model.

Method	Oxygen Experiment	Carbon Dioxide Experiment	Speed(FPS)
TRN [29]	34.6	50.3	111.7
OadTR [28]	43.0	50.5	96.4
Colar [31]	42.5	50.7	119.5
LSTR [30]	44.4	51.8	83.4
ExpT(Ours)	**50.8**	**64.5**	**142.6**

4.2 Main Results

Comparison with State-of-the-Art Methods. We compare ExpT with prior methods on Oxygen Experiment and Carbon Dioxide Experiment for online action detection. The results, shown in Table 1, demonstrate that our ExpT achieves state-of-the-art performance. Specifically, it improves mAP by 6.4% and 12.7% on the Oxygen Experiment and Carbon Dioxide Experiment, respectively. The consistent improvements over current state-of-the-art methods verify the efficacy of our proposed exemplar-enhanced mechanism. We attribute this result to the fact that other methods focus excessively on long-range historical context modelling, which hinders their ability to react to transient changes. However, ExpT can escape the limitations of history via exemplars and capture the dynamic evolution of the video clip more accurately, particularly in the case of the Carbon Dioxide Experiment, which has shorter action duration.

In terms of inference speed, our model exceeds prior methods as well. In Table 1, ExpT is 1.7× faster than LSTR [30], the best performance of the other methods. In addition, Colar [31] and TRN [29] which contain simple attention are relatively faster, but ExpT is still 1.2× faster than them, regardless of the performance gap. This result demonstrates that with the complementary guidance of exemplars, our model eliminates considerable effort on temporal modelling, significantly reducing excessive use of attention and resulting in a leap in efficiency.

Table 2. Ablation studies about the efficacy of each component on Carbon Dioxide Experiment.

Aggregation Encoder	Temporal Fusion Encoder	Exemplar-enhanced Decoder	Carbon Dioxide Experiment
✓		✓	56.8
	✓	✓	56.9
✓	✓		62.4
✓	✓	✓	**64.5**

Ablation About the Efficacy of Each Component. The proposed ExpT method consists of Aggregation Encoder, Temporal Fusion Encoder and Exemplar-enhanced Decoder. Table 2 studies the efficacy of each component on Carbon Dioxide Experiment. Firstly, temporal modeling still plays a dominant role in online action detection task, directly reflected in the fact that there is a 7.7% drop when the Temporal Fusion Encoder is removed, and only a 2.1 % drop without the exemplars. Besides, the proper use of examplars can lead to remarkable results. In row 2, where we do not aggregate the video features and exemplar features beforehand, there is a drop of 7.6%, whereas when we properly utilize the exemplars, it is 2.1% higher than row 3, where only temporal modelling is used.

5 Conclusion

We present Exemplar-enhanced Transformer (ExpT), a novel mechanism that conducts exemplars as complementary guidance to capture long-term dependencies in video clips for online action detection. With the assistance of exemplars, ExpT is able to overcome the weakness of most existing methods that can only complete modeling temporal dependency within a limited historical context and free from undue attention, achieving dramatic improvements in both effectiveness and efficiency. The prominent efficacy of ExpT can help to analyze and evaluate students' experiments in real time, which is conducive to the establishment of a comprehensive evaluation system. This, in turn, enhances experimental skills of students, elevates the quality of experimental teaching, and ultimately improves the overall quality and outcomes of science education.

References

1. Arnab, A., Dehghani, M., Heigold, G., Sun, C., Lučić, M., Schmid, C.: Vivit: a video vision transformer. In: Proceedings of the IEEE/CVF International Conference on Computer Vision, pp. 6836–6846 (2021)
2. Ba, J.L., Kiros, J.R., Hinton, G.E.: Layer normalization. arXiv preprint arXiv:1607.06450 (2016)

3. Cao, S., Luo, W., Wang, B., Zhang, W., Ma, L.: E2e-load: end-to-end long-form online action detection. arXiv preprint arXiv:2306.07703 (2023)
4. Carion, N., Massa, F., Synnaeve, G., Usunier, N., Kirillov, A., Zagoruyko, S.: End-to-End object detection with transformers. In: Vedaldi, A., Bischof, H., Brox, T., Frahm, J.-M. (eds.) ECCV 2020. LNCS, vol. 12346, pp. 213–229. Springer, Cham (2020). https://doi.org/10.1007/978-3-030-58452-8_13
5. Chen, G., et al.: Videollm: modeling video sequence with large language models. arXiv preprint arXiv:2305.13292 (2023)
6. Chen, J., Mittal, G., Yu, Y., Kong, Y., Chen, M.: Gatehub: gated history unit with background suppression for online action detection. In: Proceedings of the IEEE/CVF Conference on Computer Vision and Pattern Recognition, pp. 19925–19934 (2022)
7. De Geest, R., Gavves, E., Ghodrati, A., Li, Z., Snoek, C., Tuytelaars, T.: Online action detection. In: Leibe, B., Matas, J., Sebe, N., Welling, M. (eds.) ECCV 2016. LNCS, vol. 9909, pp. 269–284. Springer, Cham (2016). https://doi.org/10.1007/978-3-319-46454-1_17
8. Devlin, J., Chang, M.W., Lee, K., Toutanova, K.: Bert: pre-training of deep bidirectional transformers for language understanding. arXiv preprint arXiv:1810.04805 (2018)
9. Dosovitskiy, A., et al.: An image is worth 16×16 words: transformers for image recognition at scale. arXiv preprint arXiv:2010.11929 (2020)
10. Eun, H., Moon, J., Park, J., Jung, C., Kim, C.: Learning to discriminate information for online action detection. In: Proceedings of the IEEE/CVF Conference on Computer Vision and Pattern Recognition, pp. 809–818 (2020)
11. Gao, M., Zhou, Y., Xu, R., Socher, R., Xiong, C.: Woad: weakly supervised online action detection in untrimmed videos. In: Proceedings of the IEEE/CVF Conference on Computer Vision and Pattern Recognition, pp. 1915–1923 (2021)
12. He, K., Zhang, X., Ren, S., Sun, J.: Deep residual learning for image recognition. In: Proceedings of the IEEE Conference on Computer Vision and Pattern Recognition, pp. 770–778 (2016)
13. Hochreiter, S., Schmidhuber, J.: Long short-term memory. Neural Comput. 9(8), 1735–1780 (1997)
14. Johnson, J., Douze, M., Jégou, H.: Billion-scale similarity search with gpus. IEEE Trans. Big Data 7(3), 535–547 (2019)
15. Kim, J., Misu, T., Chen, Y.T., Tawari, A., Canny, J.: Grounding human-to-vehicle advice for self-driving vehicles. In: Proceedings of the IEEE/CVF Conference on Computer Vision and Pattern Recognition, pp. 10591–10599 (2019)
16. Kingma, D.P., Ba, J.: Adam: a method for stochastic optimization. arXiv preprint arXiv:1412.6980 (2014)
17. Nawhal, M., Mori, G.: Activity graph transformer for temporal action localization. arXiv preprint arXiv:2101.08540 (2021)
18. Neimark, D., Bar, O., Zohar, M., Asselmann, D.: Video transformer network. In: Proceedings of the IEEE/CVF International Conference on Computer Vision, pp. 3163–3172 (2021)
19. Pang, G., Yan, C., Shen, C., Hengel, A.V.D., Bai, X.: Self-trained deep ordinal regression for end-to-end video anomaly detection. In: Proceedings of the IEEE/CVF Conference on Computer Vision and Pattern Recognition, pp. 12173–12182 (2020)
20. Park, H., Noh, J., Ham, B.: Learning memory-guided normality for anomaly detection. In: Proceedings of the IEEE/CVF Conference on Computer Vision and Pattern Recognition, pp. 14372–14381 (2020)

21. Radford, A., Narasimhan, K., Salimans, T., Sutskever, I., et al.: Improving language understanding by generative pre-training (2018)
22. Sharir, G., Noy, A., Zelnik-Manor, L.: An image is worth 16×16 words, what is a video worth? arXiv preprint arXiv:2103.13915 (2021)
23. Shu, T., Xie, D., Rothrock, B., Todorovic, S., Chun Zhu, S.: Joint inference of groups, events and human roles in aerial videos. In: Proceedings of the IEEE Conference on Computer Vision and Pattern Recognition, pp. 4576–4584 (2015)
24. Tan, J., Tang, J., Wang, L., Wu, G.: Relaxed transformer decoders for direct action proposal generation. In: Proceedings of the IEEE/CVF International Conference on Computer Vision, pp. 13526–13535 (2021)
25. Tong, Z., Song, Y., Wang, J., Wang, L.: Videomae: masked autoencoders are data-efficient learners for self-supervised video pre-training. Adv. Neural. Inf. Process. Syst. **35**, 10078–10093 (2022)
26. Touvron, H., Cord, M., Douze, M., Massa, F., Sablayrolles, A., Jégou, H.: Training data-efficient image transformers & distillation through attention. In: International Conference on Machine Learning, pp. 10347–10357. PMLR (2021)
27. Vaswani, A., et al.: Attention is all you need. Adv. Neural Inf. Process. Syst. **30** (2017)
28. Wang, X., et al.: OADTR: online action detection with transformers. In: Proceedings of the IEEE/CVF International Conference on Computer Vision, pp. 7565–7575 (2021)
29. Xu, M., Gao, M., Chen, Y.T., Davis, L.S., Crandall, D.J.: Temporal recurrent networks for online action detection. In: Proceedings of the IEEE/CVF International Conference on Computer Vision, pp. 5532–5541 (2019)
30. Xu, M., Xiong, Y., Chen, H., Li, X., Xia, W., Tu, Z., Soatto, S.: Long short-term transformer for online action detection. Adv. Neural. Inf. Process. Syst. **34**, 1086–1099 (2021)
31. Yang, L., Han, J., Zhang, D.: Colar: effective and efficient online action detection by consulting exemplars. In: Proceedings of the IEEE/CVF Conference on Computer Vision and Pattern Recognition, pp. 3160–3169 (2022)
32. Yu, C., Ma, X., Ren, J., Zhao, H., Yi, S.: Spatio-temporal graph transformer networks for pedestrian trajectory prediction. In: Vedaldi, A., Bischof, H., Brox, T., Frahm, J.-M. (eds.) ECCV 2020. LNCS, vol. 12357, pp. 507–523. Springer, Cham (2020). https://doi.org/10.1007/978-3-030-58610-2_30
33. Zhao, Y., Krähenbühl, P.: Real-time online video detection with temporal smoothing transformers. In: Avidan, S., Brostow, G., Cisse, M., Farinella, G.M., Hassner, T. (eds.) European Conference on Computer Vision, pp. 485–502. Springer, Heidelberg (2022). https://doi.org/10.1007/978-3-031-19830-4_28

Towards Performance Analysis for Online Data Science Learning Platform

Zijing Banyan, Xiaofeng Zou, Huarong Xu, Dan Ma, Chuan Lin, Bo Zhang, Mei Chen, and Hui Li[✉]

College of Computer Science and Technology, Guizhou University, Guiyang, China
cse.HuiLi@gzu.edu.cn

Abstract. The online data science learning platform offers students an adaptable educational experience and a versatile learning and experimental environment. However, with the escalation of system concurrency, performance concerns including resource limitations, protracted online experiment response, and platform breakdowns, all of which can have a detrimental effect on the advancement of data science experimental learning. This paper proposes a performance analysis system for online data science learning platforms. It uses the Application Performance Index (Apdex) to evaluate user satisfaction of system performance, and promptly detects real-time performance anomalies and forecasts performance trends by LightGBM and LSTM algorithm. Meanwhile, the performance bottlenecks are also identified and correlated based on the function invocation chains with various time series performance metrics data. Therefore, negative user experience is effectively prevented. Furthermore, we conducted a series of experiments based on 40 days of operational data from a real online data science learning platform, the effectiveness and superiority of the proposed method in this system are clearly verified.

Keywords: data science · online learning platform · performance analysis system · performance bottlenecks · performance anomalies detection

1 Introduction

In the era of big data, data science is an essential knowledge and skill for modern talents. With "big data" as its research object, data science draws extensively from theories and technologies in fields such as databases, data mining, big data analytics, and artificial intelligence machine learning [1]. It is an emerging interdisciplinary field that primarily focuses on activities related to data processing, management, computation, and analysis. In recent years, data science has been applied in various industries such as economics, management, advertising, and education. It emphasizes practical training and case-based teaching, making it a highly practical discipline that has become a major focus of curriculum design and teaching reform in higher education [2].

With the advent of the Internet 2.0 era, the load pressure on various web applications and online platforms has been rapidly increasing. This can lead to increased system latency and a decline in user experience. According to a report from Amazon, a 100-ms increase in system latency can result in a 1% decrease in sales [3]. Moreover, research data suggests that if Google's web page latency increases by 400 ms, user search volumes decrease by 0.59% [4]. If Bing's web page latency is 2 s, the company's related revenue declines by 4.3%; and if Yahoo's web page latency is 400 ms, traffic decreases by 5–9%. For data science online learning platforms, when a large number of students and teachers use the system simultaneously, performance issues such as resource scarcity, server congestion, and platform crashes may arise. These issues can significantly impact the user experience and the progress of experimental teaching. Therefore, promptly identifying system performance bottlenecks is beneficial for increasing system throughput and concurrency, enhancing user experience, and minimizing unnecessary losses.

The performance analysis system can help web platforms quickly identify performance bottlenecks. However, most existing performance analysis systems only visualize performance data such as resource metrics and business metrics [5], without truly exploring and analyzing the underlying value and insights in the data. This limits their ability to assist operations personnel in troubleshooting performance anomalies. Additionally, current monitoring systems often rely on setting fixed thresholds for performance data to trigger alerts. This post-processing approach has limitations and lags behind, making it difficult to address issues in a timely manner. Moreover, for operations personnel, manually analyzing the running status of a data science online learning platform and resolving performance problems requires a certain level of expertise and work experience, adding pressure to their workload. It is challenging to meet the requirements of intelligent monitoring, and the purchase cost of a comprehensive and professional monitoring system is also expensive [6]. Therefore, the low-cost and efficient monitoring and analysis of the running status of a data science online learning platform is an urgent problem that needs to be addressed.

This paper develops a performance analysis system that integrates performance evaluation management, automated performance metric data collection, real-time anomaly detection and analysis, performance data trend prediction, performance bottleneck identification and visualization. This system aims to reduce the workload of manually analyzing complex data, improve the efficiency of resolving platform performance issues, assist in performance testing and optimization, and reduce economic losses and operational costs resulting from performance problems. The rest of this paper is organized as follows: the related works are presented as Sect. 2, and the motivation is described in Sect. 3, then the developed system and its major technical work are illustrated in Sect. 4, and the evaluation and conclusion are drawn finally.

2   Related Work

The key technologies studied in this paper mainly include performance anomaly detection, performance trend prediction, and performance bottleneck identification. In recent years, both domestic and international scholars and industry practitioners have been devoted to studying these topics and achieved many significant results.

Anomaly Detection. Anomaly detection is identifying and detecting data points that deviate from the given dataset. There are different types of anomalies, including point anomalies, contextual anomalies, and collective anomalies. Research on anomaly detection primarily involves unsupervised and supervised anomaly detection algorithms. Popular methods for unsupervised anomaly detection include one-class SVM based on linear models [7], local outlier factor (LOF) based on density [8], isolation forest based on trees, K-Means clustering [9], and deep learning models based on autoencoders [10]. Unsupervised anomaly detection algorithms without labels often have strong assumption relationships, which can introduce biases in the detection results. Generally, supervised anomaly detection algorithms tend to be more accurate and can be categorized into statistical machine learning algorithms and deep learning algorithms. Common statistical machine learning algorithms include anomaly detection with minority sample augmentation (SMOTE) [11] and anomaly detection with gradient boosting decision trees (GBDT) [12]. XGBoost, an improved version of GBDT, is widely used in various industries such as high-tech, data science, and engineering fields and is considered a highly effective algorithm. The deep-learning based anomaly detection models involve feature extraction networks and classification networks. For example, Ruff [13] et al. proposed the Deep SVDD (Support Vector Data Description) model, which uses neural networks to minimize the hyper-sphere that encloses the feature space of the data samples, and uses the distance between the center of the sphere and the testing sample to determine if it is an anomaly. Su [14] et al. proposed a method called Random Recursive Neural Network for detecting anomalies in multivariate time series data. They demonstrated its effectiveness on a server dataset that included metrics such as CPU load, network utilization, and memory usage. The results showed that this approach achieved good detection performance on these metrics.

Trend Prediction. Trend prediction for performance metric data involves using the past performance of an application platform to forecast potential future trends. Common trend prediction algorithms include Bayesian models, Autoregressive Integrated Moving Average (ARIMA) models [15], and neural network algorithms. CPU utilization is a critical metric that significantly affects the overall performance of a service platform. By forecasting its future trends based on historical data, it is easier to prepare and implement preventive measures. Wang [16] used the Random Forest regression algorithm to estimate the CPU and memory resource consumption in a cloud computing environment, and achieved satisfactory results. Recurrent Neural Networks (RNN) are specialized neural networks for sequence data processing. Duggan et al. [17]. Used RNN to predict CPU utilization in virtual machines, demonstrating its relatively high accuracy. However, it is worth noting that the accuracy of RNN decreases linearly as the prediction time increases. Long Short-Term Memory (LSTM) is an extension of RNN that incorporates memory units to control the extent of historical information retention. It performs better than regular RNN in longer sequences. Rao [18] et al. compared three popular time series prediction methods, including Holt-Winters, ARIMA, and LSTM, for forecasting unstable CPU utilization data without clear seasonality. The results indicated that LSTM outperformed the other methods.

Performance Bottleneck Identification. When it comes to performance bottleneck identification, issues may be related to program code errors in the application platform. Poor-quality code often serves as the trigger for hardware resource problems. By accurately identifying the code execution logic through the paths of requests, it becomes possible to analyze and locate performance bottlenecks. Wang [19] implemented a full-stack tracing system that monitors the internal service interactions in a microservices architecture. This system intercepts and modifies the monitored network traffic using network proxy methods, enabling local chain tracing logic. It provides the duration of each code invocation and the overall topology of the call chain. Addressing difficulties in locating faults and mapping service dependencies in cloud platform requests, Wang [20] developed a monitoring system that employs point-to-point interceptors for tracking requests. This system offers comprehensive monitoring and fault detection, service analysis, and other capabilities, significantly improving the ability of operations personnel to locate faults in microservices.

3 Motivation

Intelligent operation and maintenance is an approach that combines operation and maintenance data (such as logs, monitoring data, and application information) with machine learning techniques [21]. It aims to automatically learn patterns from the data to provide decision support for solving operation and maintenance problems. In the context of data science online learning platforms, applying intelligent operation and maintenance techniques for performance analysis can improve efficiency to some extent and enable intelligent management.

In this section, we will review traditional performance monitoring tools to demonstrate the motivation for designing a new performance analysis system. Nagios [22] is an open-source tool for monitoring system status and network information. Its prominent feature is anomaly detection and alert notifications. It can monitor network services and server resources, but Nagios is difficult to scale and cannot identify the causes of anomalies through historical data analysis. Zabbix [23] is an enterprise-level open-source management system that provides distributed system monitoring and network monitoring capabilities. It offers both active and passive data collection methods with customizable time intervals and supports multiple databases such as MySQL and PostgreSQL for data storage. However, Zabbix has a steep learning curve for customization and complex threshold configuration, and lacks the ability to integrate multi-condition advanced alerting. Prometheus [24] is an open-source monitoring and alerting component based on a time-series database developed by SoundCloud. It uses an HTTP pull method for real-time metric collection and allows the definition of alerting rules. Its drawbacks include slow page rendering speed and incomplete documentation, requiring a deep understanding of code to explore additional features. It is more suitable for medium to large enterprises. ARMS [25] is Alibaba Cloud's application real-time monitoring and management product. It provides comprehensive performance monitoring and end-to-end full-chain tracing diagnosis, thereby making application operations and maintenance more efficient. However, it may be cost-prohibitive for small-scale application platforms, and performance testing may require additional paid products.

Traditional performance monitoring tools are not customized, and most of them are heavyweight solutions with specific focuses. Therefore, operations personnel need to select several suitable products based on their actual needs to monitor different metrics. Additionally, when performance optimization is required, separate performance testing tools need to be set up. Therefore, there is a need to design and implement a performance monitoring and analysis system tailored to the requirements and business of online learning platforms in order to provide a comprehensive solution.

4 System and Techniques

The creation of a performance analysis system for an online learning platform for data science is the main topic of this essay. Performance test management, automatic data collecting for performance metrics, real-time anomaly analysis and detection, core data trend prediction, performance bottleneck diagnosis, and visual display are all integrated into the system. The system's architecture is shown in Fig. 1.

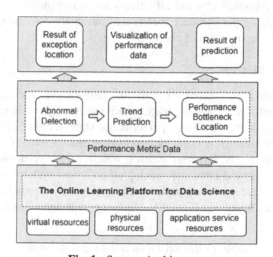

Fig. 1. System Architecture

The framework of this system mainly includes:

- **Building a performance evaluation system and gathering performance metric data using monitoring technologies.** Resource allocation and monitoring, which improve resource usage, depend on data on resource metrics. In order to enhance the user experience, business metric data measures variables such as mistake rate, throughput, and reaction time from the user's perspective. This article combines the two types of metric data to offer a way to assess performance.
- **Performing anomaly detection on the application based on the performance metric data.** Operation and maintenance staff can more quickly identify performance bottlenecks thanks to real-time performance anomaly detection that uses artificial intelligence algorithms. An improvement over the GBDT and XGBoost algorithms, the LightGBM algorithm provides support for distributed parallel computing, faster training speed, lower memory consumption, and higher prediction accuracy. It also handles massive amounts of data efficiently. LightGBM is appropriate for real-time anomaly detection in systems because it strikes a balance between prediction accuracy

and training speed. In order to detect performance anomalies based on performance metrics, this article uses LightGBM.

- **Making trend predictions using data from performance metrics.** In monitoring systems, time series data with time-dependent features are frequently encountered. The process of time series trend prediction entails examining the available historical time series, spotting patterns in the time trend that are based on the direction and method of development, and applying these patterns to project future circumstances. For instance, forecasting a website system's CPU usage and user growth trend. In order to precisely forecast trends in monitoring data with time-dependent features, this article uses an LSTM model.
- **Data visualization.** Compared to reading text, humans can process information more quickly through graphics. Operation and maintenance staff can more quickly identify performance bottlenecks and effectively assist in troubleshooting performance issues by visualizing performance metric data, anomaly detection results, and trend prediction results in the form of charts and graphs.

4.1 Performance Metrics

Monitoring tools are a useful tool for gathering performance metrics for data science online learning platforms. These metrics, which are mostly made up of resource and business metrics, show the platform's performance state. Resource metrics encompass, on the one hand, the following: network bandwidth, disk capacity, CPU utilization, and memory usage. Conversely, business metrics, which include response time, concurrent user count, throughput, and error rate, among others, show system performance as seen by users. These two categories of performance metrics are combined in this article to create a performance score that is used for further performance tracking.

Table 1. Resource indicator status distribution

Resource Status	CPU Utilization	Memory Usage	Disk Utilization
Optimal	<60%	<70%	<60%
Satisfactory	60–80%	70–90%	60–80%
Poor	>80%	>90%	>80%

The application's response time is measured by Apdex, a system health indicator, and converted into a user satisfaction score on a scale of 0 to 1. Equation (1) provides the formula for calculating the Apdex index. The number of times during the sampling period that the response time satisfies the user's requirements for satisfaction is represented by the SatisfiedCount. The number of times the response time meets the acceptable tolerance standards during the sampling period is indicated by the ToleratingCount. The total number of samples gathered is expressed as TotalSamples. Additionally, the operational efficiency of the system is impacted by the various resource metrics values. As a result, as Table 1 illustrates, resource metrics can be categorized into three states: optimal, satisfactory, and poor. The resource status can be used to evaluate the resource utilization score. Lastly, these two indicators are used to aggregate the performance metrics.

$$Apdex_t = (SatisfiedCount + ToleratingCount/2)/TotalSamples \qquad (1)$$

$$ResourceScore = (GoodCount + FairCount/2)/TotalSamples \qquad (2)$$

$$PerformanceScore = ResourceScore * 0.3 + ErrorRate * 0.4 + Apdex_t * 0.3 \qquad (3)$$

4.2 Anomaly Detection

This research suggests using the LightGBM algorithm for real-time anomaly detection and abnormal feature analysis of performance data in order to overcome the drawbacks of conventional fixed-threshold alarm methods as well as the timeliness problems associated with manual troubleshooting. Intelligent operations and maintenance can be accomplished by choosing the right model parameters, which will increase O&M productivity and lower the number of missed and false alarms.

The industry has utilized the XGBoost algorithm, a popular pre-sorting decision tree algorithm, as an anomaly detection method. It does, however, come at a significant time and space cost to compute. To increase operational efficiency, LightGBM, an enhanced version of XGBoost, uses histogram-based algorithms, gradient-based One-Side Sampling (GOSS), and Exclusive Feature Building (EFB) [26]. The decision tree's sub-models in LightGBM use a depth-limited leaf growth strategy (leaf-wise). Rather than splitting all nodes, it chooses the node with the highest gain among all of the leaf nodes that are currently in use for iterative splitting. In order to maintain efficiency and avoid overfitting, the maximum depth of the tree is also restricted, which shortens the time needed to determine the ideal depth [27]. With the same number of splits, this strategy reduces errors and achieves higher prediction accuracy. LightGBM is better suited for scenarios involving large feature sizes and multiple samples due to its advantages in speed and memory usage. As a result, the model construction and anomaly detection function implementation in this paper for performance analysis make use of LightGBM. The model is then encapsulated for convenience of system invocation after its parameters have been established and set. Figure 2 depicts the LightGBM model's training framework.

The parameter settings used in the experimentation phase have an impact on how well the model trains. Therefore, it is necessary to gradually change the default values in a methodical way to determine which ones are best. In order to find the ideal parameters, this study will experiment using Bayesian global optimization techniques. Initially, the number of iterations, initial leaf point count, and parameter search range are set. The validation set's Area Under the Curve (AUC) metric is then maximized through the application of the Bayesian optimization framework. Then, the obtained parameters are utilized to evaluate the training set's performance inside the model.

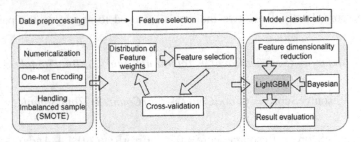

Fig. 2. The training process of LightGBM model

4.3 Trend Prediction

The utilization of historical data with temporal characteristics enables operations people to make accurate predictions regarding future performance metrics. By doing so, they may proactively implement corrective measures, thereby minimizing the occurrence of network platform delay and potential crashes. This approach ultimately ensures the stability of the system.

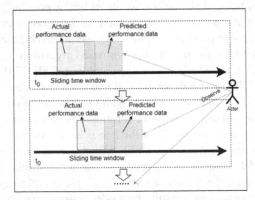

Fig. 3. The time series prediction of performance data

The main goal of creating Long Short-Term Memory (LSTM) networks is to find efficient solutions for long-range dependencies and related issues with vanishing and exploding gradients that occur when training long sequences. Compared to a regular recurrent neural network (RNN), LSTM is thought to be more appropriate for accurately forecasting trends by exploiting the relationships among long-term sequences. The LSTM model combines the basic architecture of an RNN with a gating mechanism, also known as gating. This procedure makes it easier to control how much of the past is remembered, which makes it easier to manage long-term temporal relationships. A cell state component of the LSTM architecture is used to maintain and preserve the hidden state data that is currently in place. The hidden state data is controlled by three gates: the forget gate, input gate, and output gate. It includes the previous hidden state as well as the current temporary hidden state. By using nonlinear computations, LSTM models can learn about long-term dependencies and efficiently extract important information from performance measurements. It can also deal with the non-uniform characteristics of metric data. As a result, the LSTM neural network is used in this study to forecast trends in performance measure data. Figure 3 shows the LSTM process in action.

The following is how the model is primarily established: Make a sequence model first. The model consists of three main layers: input, LSTM memory network, and output. The first learning rate is set to 0.01; mean square error is chosen as the loss function; there are 1000 iterations; the batch size is 128; time steps are 100; and future_predict_num is 60, which denotes the prediction of sixty consecutive future data points. Next, create an LSTM neural network model, set the Adam optimizer, and train the model. Lastly, create a prediction model for the performance analysis system by saving the model file. Place the model file for model invocation in the performance analysis system's deployment project after the model has been successfully defined.

4.4   Performance Bottleneck Identification

Generally speaking, the bottleneck analysis works layer by layer, starting with the hardware and moving on to the system, application, and software. The online data science experiment platform is a web application built on the B/S architecture that is deployed on the server. Most of the time, server-side bottlenecks are likely to appear. Since the test platform can only be accessed through a browser, the likelihood of client-side problems is greatly decreased. Therefore, the first step in locating anomaly bottlenecks is to examine the experimental online data science platform's server-side performance bottleneck. The hardware analysis is mainly concerned with how resources, such as CPU, memory, disk, and so on, are used. From the software's point of view, it is mainly composed of program codes, middleware indicators, and database indicators.

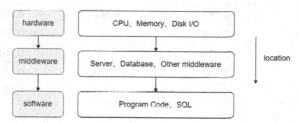

Fig. 4. The process for Layered Localization of Performance Bottlenecks

When a bottleneck resulting from program codes occurs, the server will become increasingly abnormal and use excessive resources, which will lead to a hardware bottleneck. The components of the upper layer will unavoidably be impacted by the occurrence of anomalous indicators or bottlenecks at the lower location because the upper layer places constraints on the lower layer. Therefore, using bottleneck stratification to analyze anomalous features independently and applying the bottleneck stratification positioning procedure shown in Fig. 4, this paper explores performance bottleneck stratification in accordance with the bottleneck analysis procedure. After the characteristics of every layer displaying the abnormal bottleneck are obtained, it is necessary to determine the experimental platform's running code by timing it in order to obtain the call chain information. By conducting a comprehensive analysis, the actual cause of the obstacle can be found, which will help the operation and maintenance team troubleshoot performance issues more successfully.

5   Evaluation

In this evaluation, a real online data science learning platform is used as the testbed. This platform supports various data science tasks, including data integration, visualization analysis, and data mining. To evaluate its performance, a stress testing tool, JMeter, is used to simulate a workload generated by 500 users on the platform. The performance metrics of the platform in a 40 days period are collected using the data collection tool, Telegraf, and stored in the InfluxDB time series database.

5.1   Effectiveness of Anomaly Detection

In order to evaluate the effectiveness of anomaly detection of the developed system, commonly used models such as logistic regression, support vector machine (SVM), random forest, and gradient boosting decision tree (XGBoost) were chosen to estimate over the dataset. Evaluation metrics including accuracy, recall, F1-Score, and ROC curve were used. The evaluation results are shown in Table 2.

Table 2. Evaluation results of five methods

Method	Accuracy	Recall	F1-Score
LightGBM	**0.909**	**0.807**	**0.873**
Lgistic Rgression	0.853	0.734	0.785
SVM	0.876	0.745	0.801
Rndom Frest	0.882	0.771	0.829
XGBoost	0.891	0.785	0.857

The experimental study revealed that the LightGBM model exhibits favorable classification accuracy and demonstrates a reduced processing time. Additionally, this method is well-suited for identifying irregularities in the performance metrics data gathered inside this study.

5.2   Effectiveness of Performance Trend Prediction

In order to further evaluate the effectiveness of the chosen prediction models, several widely employed algorithms including ARIMA, random forest, and RNN were chosen to conduct experiments on the identical dataset. The effectiveness of the model is

Table 3. Four forecasting methods evaluate results

Method	RMSE	MAE	R^2
LSTM	**0.187**	**0.124**	**0.901**
ARIMA	1.135	0.483	0.732
Random Frest	0.616	0.322	0.790
RNN	0.211	0.138	0.884

assessed using the following evaluation metrics: mean absolute error (MAE), root mean square error (RMSE), and coefficient of determination (R-Square). Table 3 displays the outcomes of the evaluations conducted on the four methods.

The results of the experimental comparison indicate that the LSTM neural network exhibits lower values of RMSE and MAE in comparison to the other three approaches. Moreover, it has a bigger R-Square coefficient. This suggests that the trend prediction model developed for the user's CPU usage percentage demonstrates a commendable level of accuracy and a degree of consistency.

5.3 System Evaluation

System evaluation is mainly used to verify the integrity of system functions and analyze accuracy. The intelligent performance monitoring system visualizes the collected key performance indicators, including experiment platform startup time, CPU cores, system load, total memory, CPU utilization rate, memory utilization rate, disk I/O, and total network packets sent and received, as shown in Fig. 5 below.

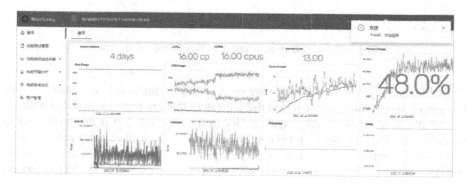

Fig. 5. Performance indicator visualization

The system regularly calls the HTTP interface of the encapsulated LightGBM anomaly detection model to realize the function of real-time detection of anomalies, and at the same time, the detection tag results are stored in the database and displayed to the interface, and the system administrator can modify the standard according to the

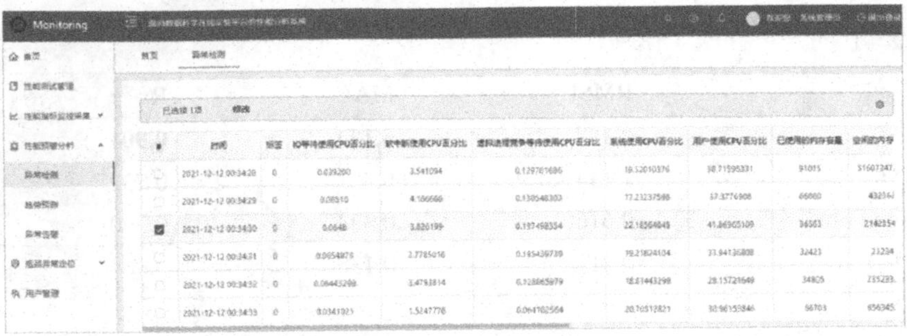

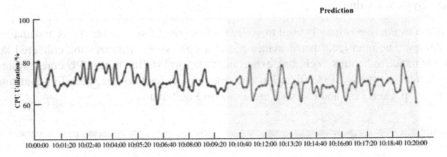

Fig. 6. The annotation list of system Anomaly Detection

actual anomalies through the page to ensure its authenticity and improve the accuracy in subsequent training. The annotation list of system anomaly detection is shown in Fig. 6.

For performance metrics that require trend prediction, the intelligent monitoring system will use the LSTM model to predict the selected performance metric based on the latest 60 time points to forecast the value trend for the next 60 time points. The predicted performance metric data trend is shown in Fig. 7.

Fig. 7. Performance indicator data Trend Prediction results

Additionally, the system can display the LightGBM model in accordance with the bottleneck layer, thoroughly analyze the indicators that are highly correlated with the abnormal characteristics of each layer, and locate the request call by using the timestamp to retrieve the link number from the database. Additionally, it can display more detailed call link information for each level in the link, giving O&M personnel strong support as they investigate the true causes of bottlenecks and exceptions. Figure 8: The page where the issue is located.

To analyze the superiority of the intelligent anomaly detection module of the performance analysis system, this paper compared the accuracy of ordinary fixed threshold anomaly alarms with intelligent anomaly alarms within 40 days of normal operation of the experimental platform and monitoring system. The experimental results are shown in Table 4 below.

Fig. 8. The Localization of System Problems

Table 4. Comparison of Fixed Threshold Anomaly Alarms and System Anomaly Alarms

Alarm Source	Total	Exception	Normal	Missing	Accuracy
Fixed threshold	84	50	34	24	59.52%
The system	61	52	9	16	85.24%

By conducting system functional testing and evaluation, the performance analysis system can enhance its ability to identify performance issues. This is achieved through the implementation of trend prediction and anomaly detection alarm methods, which decrease the probability of false and missed alarms. These enhancements increase the operational stability to a certain degree for the online data science learning platform.

6 Conclusion

This work introduces a comprehensive system for evaluating the performance of online data science learning platforms. The system encompasses various modules, including performance testing management, anomaly detection and trend prediction of performance data, identification of performance bottlenecks, and data visualization. The technology explores latent information within the data and aids operators in their efforts to enhance efficiency in addressing platform performance concerns. To assess the effectiveness of the proposed study, a series of experiments were conducted using a 40-day operational dataset obtained from a real online platform for data science education. The results yielded an accuracy rate of 85.24% for anomaly detection, surpassing the fixed threshold detection method by 25.72%. The proposed method in this system has been clearly proved to be successful and superior, as evidenced by a 33.33% decrease in the false positive rate.

References

1. Birkenkrahe, M.: Teaching data science in a synchronous online introductory course at a business school – a case study. In: Guralnick, D., Auer, M.E., Poce, A. (eds.) TLIC 2021. LNNS, vol. 349, pp. 28–39. Springer, Cham (2022). https://doi.org/10.1007/978-3-030-906 77-1_3
2. Atkeson, L.R.: Data assignments in substantive courses: getting undergraduates excited and interested in data science. PS Polit. Sci. Politics **55**(1), 206–209 (2022)
3. Lai, C.A., Kimball, J., Zhu, T., et al.: milliscope: a fine-grained monitoring framework for performance debugging of n-tier web services. In: 2017 IEEE 37th International Conference on Distributed Computing Systems (ICDCS), pp. 92–102. IEEE (2017)
4. Chen, Z., et al.: Design and implementation of real-time security monitoring platform for EAST based on microservice architecture. In: Sixth International Conference on Advanced Electronic Materials, Computers, and Software Engineering (AEMCSE 2023), vol. 12787. SPIE (2023)
5. Khan, W., et al.: SQL and NoSQL database software architecture performance analysis and assessments—a systematic literature review. Big Data Cogn. Comput. **7**(2), 97 (2023)
6. Miao, X., Liu, Y., Zhao, H., et al.: Distributed online one-class support vector machine for anomaly detection over networks. IEEE Trans. Cybern. **49**(4), 1475–1488 (2018)
7. Cheng, Z., Zou, C., Dong, J.: Outlier detection using isolation forest and local outlier factor. In: Proceedings of the Conference on Research in Adaptive and Convergent Systems, pp. 161–168 (2019)
8. Shorewala, V.: Anomaly detection and improvement of clusters using enhanced k-means algorithm. In: 2021 5th International Conference on Computer, Communication and Signal Processing (ICCCSP), pp. 115–121. IEEE (2021)
9. Sukumar, J.V.A., Pranav, I., Neetish, M.M., et al.: Network intrusion detection using improved genetic k-means algorithm. In: 2018 International Conference on Advances in Computing, Communications and Informatics (ICACCI), pp. 2441–2446. IEEE (2018)
10. Chen, J., Sathe, S., Aggarwal, C., et al.: Outlier detection with autoencoder ensembles. In: Proceedings of the 2017 SIAM International Conference on Data Mining, pp. 90–98. Society for Industrial and Applied Mathematics (2017)
11. Tan, X., Su, S., Huang, Z., et al.: Wireless sensor networks intrusion detection based on SMOTE and the random forest algorithm. Sensors **19**(1), 203 (2019)
12. Li, L., Yu, Y., Bai, S., et al.: Towards effective network intrusion detection: a hybrid model integrating gini index and GBDT with PSO. J. Sensors **2018**, 1–9 (2018)
13. Ruff, L., Vandermeulen, R., Goernitz, N., et al.: Deep one-class classification. In: International Conference on Machine Learning, pp. 4393–4402. PMLR (2018)
14. Su, Y., Zhao, Y., Niu, C., et al.: Robust anomaly detection for multivariate time series through stochastic recurrent neural network. In: Proceedings of the 25th ACM SIGKDD International Conference on Knowledge Discovery & Data Mining, pp. 2828–2837 (2019)
15. Calheiros, R.N., Masoumi, E., Ranjan, R., et al.: Workload prediction using ARIMA model and its impact on cloud applications' QoS. IEEE Trans. Cloud Comput. **3**(4), 449–458 (2014)
16. Wang, J., et al.: Research on virtual machine consolidation strategy based on combined prediction and energy-aware in cloud computing platform. J. Cloud Comput. **11**(1), 1–18 (2022)
17. Duggan, M., Mason, K., Duggan, J., et al.: Predicting host CPU utilization in cloud computing using recurrent neural networks. In: 2017 12th International Conference for Internet Technology and Secured Transactions (ICITST), pp. 67–72. IEEE (2017)
18. Rao, S.N., Shobha, G., Prabhu, S., et al.: Time series forecasting methods suitable for prediction of CPU usage. In: 2019 4th International Conference on Computational Systems and Information Technology for Sustainable Solution (CSITSS), vol. 4, pp. 1–5. IEEE (2019)

19. Wang, Y., et al.: Finite-time adaptive tracking control for a class of nonstrict feedback nonlinear systems with full state constraints. Int. J. Robust Nonlinear Control **32**(5), 2551–2569 (2022)
20. Wang, X., Chen, R.: Lightweight IT operation and maintenance integrated monitoring method for APP system. In: Journal of Physics: Conference Series, vol. 2209, no. 1. IOP Publishing (2022)
21. Soldani, J., Brogi, A.: Anomaly detection and failure root cause analysis in (micro) service-based cloud applications: a survey. ACM Comput. Surv. (CSUR) **55**(3), 1–39 (2022)
22. Nagios, B.W.: System and Network Monitoring. No Starch Press (2008)
23. Tader, P.: Server monitoring with zabbix. Linux J. **2010**(195), 72, 74–75, 77–78 (2010)
24. Moreau, Q., et al.: The performance monitoring system is attuned to others' actions during dyadic motor interactions. Cerebral Cortex **33**(1), 222–234 (2023)
25. Eitzinger, J., et al.: ClusterCockpit—a web application for job-specific performance monitoring. In: 2019 IEEE International Conference on Cluster Computing (CLUSTER). IEEE (2019)
26. Stanisic, L., Reuter, K.: MPCDF HPC performance monitoring system: enabling insight via job-specific analysis. In: Schwardmann, U., et al. (eds.) Euro-Par 2019. LNCS, vol. 11997, pp. 613–625. Springer, Cham (2020). https://doi.org/10.1007/978-3-030-48340-1_47
27. Casas, P., et al.: Mobile web and app QoE monitoring for ISPs-from encrypted traffic to speed index through machine learning. In: 2021 13th IFIP Wireless and Mobile Networking Conference (WMNC). IEEE (2021)

Author Index

W. Hong and G. Kanaparan (Eds.): ICCSE 2023, CCIS 2024, pp. 373–377, 2024.
https://doi.org/10.1007/978-981-97-0791-1

Printed in the United States
by Baker & Taylor Publisher Services